THE GOLDEN ENCYCLOPEDIA OF ART

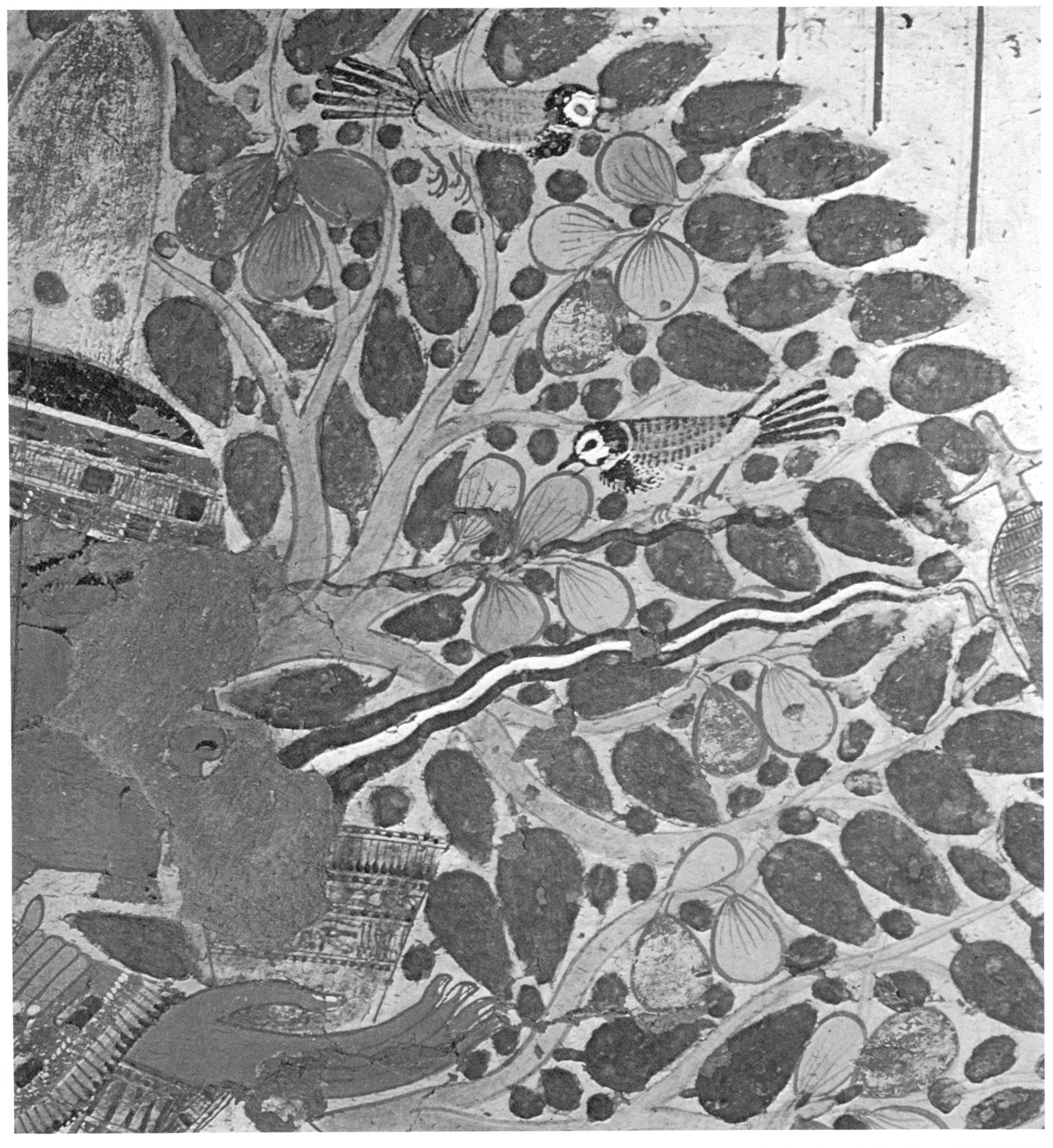

Egyptian painting: *Sycamore Tree*, detail. Tomb of Userhet, Thebes. About 1298–1235 B.C.

Paleolithic painting: "*Chinese Horse*." Lascaux. *l.* 56″.

THE GOLDEN ENCYCLOPEDIA OF ART

PAINTING, SCULPTURE, ARCHITECTURE, AND ORNAMENT, FROM PREHISTORIC TIMES TO THE TWENTIETH CENTURY

BY ELEANOR C. MUNRO

WITH A GLOSSARY OF ARTISTS AND ART TERMS

GOLDEN PRESS NEW YORK

1. *St. Matthew*, from Gospel manuscript of Ebbon. 830 A.D.

ACKNOWLEDGMENTS

We would like to express our deepest gratitude to the many persons and institutions who helped us to assemble the illustrations for this book. Without their patience and assistance, many of the pictures could not have been obtained. Our especial thanks are due to the following:

Dr. Alfred Frankfurter, of *Art News*

John Clark, of *Scala, Laboratorio Fotografico*, Florence

Mrs. A. K. Coomaraswamy, Cambridge, Massachusetts

Richard Okamoto, Tokyo

Hanna Gunther, of Frederick A. Praeger, Publishers

Earleen Field, of SKIRA Inc., Publishers

Milton Fox, of Harry N. Abrams Inc., Publishers

Mildred McGill, Photograph Sales Department, Metropolitan Museum of Art

Lnor West, Freer Gallery of Art, Washington, D.C.

G. W. Atkins, of the National Gallery, London

Pearl Moeller and Willard Tangen, Museum of Modern Art

Anselmo Carini, Art Institute of Chicago

COVER

Wadsworth Atheneum, Hartford. (*Francis G. Mayer, N. Y.*)

PAGE 1

(*SKIRA*)

PAGE 2

(*Alpha*)

PAGE 4

1. Municipal Library, Epernay, France

PAGE 7

1. Chiesa Or San Michele, Florence. (*Alinari*)
3. The Metropolitan Museum of Art, Gift of John Taylor Johnston, 1881
5. The Metropolitan Museum of Art

PAGE 8–9

1. Stedelijk Museum, Amsterdam
2. The National Gallery of Canada, Ottawa
3. Musee du Louvre, Jeu de Paume. (*Francis G. Mayer, N. Y.*)
4. Metropolitan Museum of Art, Rogers Fund, 1950

PAGE 10–11

1. (*Alpha*)
2. Naturhistorisches Museum, Vienna
3. The Cave of Altamira, *H. Breuil and H. Obermaier, plate 27* (*Louis H. Frohman*)
4. Ohio Historical Society, Columbus
5. Frobenius Institut, Frankfurt, Germany
6. Louvre, Paris. (*Robert Doisneau—R.G.*)

PAGE 12–13

1. Washington State Museum, University of Washington, Seattle
2. State Historical Society of Wisconsin, Madison
3. Owner: The Oni of Ife. (*British Museum*)
4. Coll. Eric A. Peters, N. Y. (*O. E. Nelson*)
5. Musée Royal du Congo Belge, Tervuren. (*Eliot Elisofon—Life*)
6. British Museum, London
7. British Museum, London

PAGE 14–15

1. (*Eliot Elisofon—Life*)
2. Brooklyn Museum, N. Y. (*Charles Uht*)
3. British Museum, London

PAGE 16–17

1. Metropolitan Museum of Art, Gift of Henry Walters, 1915
2. (*Eliot Elisofon—Life*)
4. Metropolitan Museum of Art, Rogers Fund, 1919
5. Metropolitan Museum of Art, Purchase 1958, Funds from Various Donors
6. Metropolitan Museum of Art, Rogers Fund, 1934
7. Metropolitan Museum of Art, Gift of Edward S. Harkness, 1913
8. Piero Tozzi Gallery, N. Y. (*John Schiff*)

PAGE 18–19

1. (*John G. Ross*)
2. (*Hampus Mörner*)
3. (*Philip Gendreau*)
4. (*Colorphoto—Trans World Airlines*)

PAGE 20–21

1. Museum of Fine Arts, Boston
2. National Gallery of Art, Washington, D. C. Gulbenkian Collection, Loan
3. Metropolitan Museum of Art, Rogers Fund, 1930
4. (*Eliot Elisofon—Life*)
5. Ehem. Staatl. Museen Berlin-Dahlem
6. Brooklyn Museum, N. Y.

PAGE 22–23

1. Cairo Museum. (*Colorphoto—Trans World Airlines*)
2. Cairo Museum. (*Eliot Elisofon—Life*)
3. Cairo Museum. (*Arab Information Center*)
4. Cairo Museum. (*Reproduced by the courtesy of the Oriental Institute of the University of Chicago from* Ancient Egyptian Paintings, *by Nina de Garis Davies. Plate 77.*)
5. (*Eliot Elisofon—Life*)

PAGE 24–25

1. Metropolitan Museum of Art. (*Francis G. Mayer, N. Y.*)
2. (*Reproduced by the courtesy of the Oriental Institute of the University of Chicago from* Ancient Egyptian Paintings, *by Nina de Garis Davies. Plate 48.*)
3. (*SKIRA*)

PAGE 26–27

1. (*Reproduced by the courtesy of the Oriental Institute of the University of Chicago from* Ancient Egyptian Paintings, *by Nina de Garis Davies. Plate 54.*) (*Louis H. Frohman*)
2. Metropolitan Museum of Art, Carnarvon Coll., Gift of Edward S. Harkness
3. British Museum, London
4. Metropolitan Museum of Art, Rogers Fund, 1915
5. Metropolitan Museum of Art, Rogers Fund, 1924
6. Metropolitan Museum of Art, Gift of Edward S. Harkness, 1926
7. British Museum, London

PAGE 28–29

1. Staatl. Museen, Berlin. (*Arab Information Center*)
2. British Museum, London
3. The University Museum, University of Pennsylvania, Philadelphia
4. Louvre, Paris. (*Giraudon*)
5. The Pierpont Morgan Library, N. Y.

PAGE 30–31

1. Museum of Fine Arts, Boston
2. British Museum, London
3. Metropolitan Museum of Art, Gift of John D. Rockefeller Jr., 1932
4. Nelson Gallery, Kansas City
5. Museum of Fine Arts, Boston
6. British Museum, London

PAGE 32–33

1. Oriental Institute, University of Chicago
2. Oriental Institute, University of Chicago
3. Oriental Institute, University of Chicago
4. Oriental Institute, University of Chicago
5. Oriental Institute, University of Chicago
6. Oriental Institute, University of Chicago
7. Aerial Survey, Oriental Institute, University of Chicago

PAGE 34–35

1. Denver Art Museum
2. Oriental Institute, University of Chicago
3. Metropolitan Museum of Art, Fletcher Fund, 1951
5. Metropolitan Museum of Art
6. (*Arab Information Center*)
7. Metropolitan Museum of Art, Fletcher Fund, 1937
8. Courtesy of Fahim Kouchakji, N. Y.
9. Dumbarton Oaks Collection, Washington, D. C.

PAGE 36–37

1. Acropolis Museum, Athens
2. National Museum, Rome. (*Alinari*)
3. Albright Art Gallery, Buffalo, N. Y.

PAGE 38–39

1. Museum of Fine Arts, Boston
2. (*Greek Information Service, N. Y.*)
3. Heraclion Museum, Crete. (*Nellys, N. Y.*)
4. Heraclion Museum, Crete. (*Pierre Martinot*)
5. Department of Antiquities, Ashmolean Museum, Oxford. (*Facsimile, original in Athens*).
6. Heraclion Museum, Crete
7. Heraclion Museum, Crete. (*Nellys, N. Y.*)
8. (*Greek Information Service, N. Y.*)

PAGE 40–41

1. Museum, Olympia. (*German Archeological Institute, Athens*)
2. Metropolitan Museum of Art, Rogers Fund
3. Louvre, Paris. (*Giraudon*)
4. Antikensammlungen, Munich. (*Meta Köhler, Munich*)
5. Metropolitan Museum of Art, Fletcher Fund, 1932
6. Staatl. Museen, Berlin
7. Glyptothek, Munich

PAGE 42–43

1. Delphi Museum. (*Pierre Martinot*)
2. National Museum, Rome
3. Staatl. Museen, Berlin
4. British Museum, London
5. British Museum, London
6. Museum, Olympia. (*Pierre Martinot*)
7. Uffizi, Florence. (*Alinari*)
8. National Museum, Athens. (*Pierre Martinot*)
9. Louvre, Paris. (*Giraudon*)

PAGE 44–45

1. (*Pierre Martinot*)
2. (*Pierre Martinot*)
3. (*Pierre Martinot*)
4. (*Greek Information Service*)

PAGE 46–47

1. British Museum, London
2. National Museum, Naples. (*Alinari*)
3. Koninklijk Kabinet van Munten en Penningen, The Hague
4. National Museum, Athens. (*Pierre Martinot*)
5. British Museum, London
6. Coll. Walter C. Baker, N. Y.
7. Metropolitan Museum of Art, Rogers Fund, 1909
8. National Museum, Athens. (*Pierre Martinot*)

PAGE 48–49

1. (*Scala*)
2. Museum, Rhodes. (*Pierre Martinot*)

PAGE 50–51

1. Metropolitan Museum of Art, Lee Fund, 1940
2. Kunsthistoriches, Vienna
3. (*French Cultural Services*)
4. (*Spanish Tourist Office*)
5. (*Arab Information Center*)

PAGE 52–53

1. Municipal Museum, Chiusi
2. Villa Giulia, Rome. (*Anderson*)
3. Metropolitan Museum of Art, Purchase, 1896
4. Walters Art Gallery, Baltimore
5. Palazzo dei Conservatori, Rome. (*Brogi*)
6. Museo Archeologico, Florence. (*Alinari*)
7. (*Alpha*)

PAGE 54–55

1. Museo Nazionale, Naples. (*Alinari*)
2. Nelson Gallery, Kansas City
3. Vatican Museum, Rome. (*Alinari*)
4. Kunsthistoriches, Vienna
5. (*Alinari*)
6. (*Italian Tourist Office*)
7. (*Reconstruction from* Restaurations des Monuments Antiques: Thermes de Dioclețien, *by Edmond Paulin, Paris,* 1890.)
8. National Gallery of Art, Washington, D. C. Samuel H. Kress Collection
9. (*TWA*)

PAGE 56–57

1. Uffizi, Florence. (*Alinari*)
2. (*Anderson*)
3. Vatican Library, Rome. (*Scala*)
4. Museo Nazionale, Naples. (*Scala*)
5. Museo Nazionale, Naples. (*Scala*)

PAGE 58–59

1. Museo Nazionale, Naples. (*Scala*)
2. Museo Nazionale, Naples. (*Scala*)

PAGE 60–61

1. Museo dei Conservatori, Rome. (*Anderson*)
2. (*Gabinetto Fotografico Nazionale, Rome*)
3. (*Scala*)
4. (*Religious News Service*)
5. British Museum, London
6. (*Arab Information Service*)
7. Lateran Museum, Rome. (*Alinari*)
8. Brooklyn Museum, N. Y.
9. (*Alinari*)

PAGE 62–63

1. Kunsthistoriches, Vienna
2. (*Scala*)
3. (*Monkmeyer*)
4. (*Philip Gendreau*)

PAGE 64–65

1. Bibliothèque Nationale, Paris
2. Metropolitan Museum of Art, Gift of J. Pierpont Morgan, 1917
3. Nelson Gallery, Kansas City
4. (*European Art Color*)
5. Metropolitan Museum of Art, Gift of J. Pierpont Morgan, 1917
6. (*Scala*)

PAGE 66–67

2. (*European Art Color*)

PAGE 68–69

1. National Gallery of Art, Washington, D. C. Mellon Collection
2. Guslitski Monastery Restoration Workshop, Moscow
3. Hermitage, Leningrad
4. Coll. S. Amberg, Koelliken, Switzerland
5. Tretyakov Gallery, Moscow

PAGE 70–71

1. (*Spanish Tourist Office*)
2. (*Spanish Tourist Office*)
3. (*TWA*)
4. (*Indian Government Tourist Office*)
5. (*Arab Information Center*)
6. (*Spanish Tourist Office*)

PAGE 72–73

1. Metropolitan Museum of Art, Rogers Fund, 1913
2. Metropolitan Museum of Art, Pulitzer Bequest, 1933
3. Courtesy, The Cleveland Museum of Art
4. Seattle Art Museum, Eugene Fuller Memorial Collection
5. Metropolitan Museum of Art, Rogers Fund, 1911
6. Metropolitan Museum of Art, Pulitzer Fund, 1936
7. Metropolitan Museum of Art, Gift of Alexander Smith Cochran, 1913
8. Metropolitan Museum of Art, Bequest of Benjamin Altman, 1913

Library of Congress Catalog Card Number 61-13297

Designed and produced by Artists and Writers Press, Inc. Printed in the U.S.A. by Western Printing and Lithographing Company. Published by Golden Press, Inc., New York. Published simultaneously in Canada by The Musson Book Company, Ltd., Toronto

9. Metropolitan Museum of Art, Pulitzer Bequest Fund

PAGE 74–75

1. Metropolitan Museum of Art, Hewitt Fund, 1911. (*Louis H. Frohman*)
2. Metropolitan Museum of Art, Gift of Alexander Smith Cochran, 1913

PAGE 76–77

1. (*Eliot Elisofon—Life*)
2. Sarnath Museum, India. (*Indian Government Tourist Office*)
3. National Museum, New Delhi
4. Victoria and Albert Museum, London

PAGE 78–79

2. National Museum, New Delhi
3. (*Eliot Elisofon—Life*)
4. (*Eliot Elisofon—Life*)
5. (*Eliot Elisofon—Life*)
6. (*Indian Government Tourist Office*)

PAGE 80–81

1. (*Eliot Elisofon—Life*)

PAGE 82–83

1. Indische Abteilung, Staatl. Museen, Berlin
2. (*Eliot Elisofon—Life*)
3. (*Indian Government Tourist Office*)
4. Courtesy, The Cleveland Museum of Art
5. (The Golden Age of Indian Art, *Pierre Rambach and Vitold de Golish, Thames and Hudson, London*, 1955).
6. Courtesy of the Smithsonian Institution, Freer Gallery of Art, Washington, D. C.

PAGE 84–85

1. Courtesy, The Cleveland Museum of Art
2. (*Free Lance Photographers Guild*)
3. Courtesy, The Cleveland Museum of Art
4. American Museum of Natural History, N. Y.
5. Musée Guimet, Paris
6. (*L. Green—Philip Gendreau, N. Y.*)
8. (*Embassy of Ceylon*)

PAGE 86–87

1. Museum of Fine Arts, Boston
2. Courtesy, The Cleveland Museum of Art
3. City Art Museum of St. Louis
4. Courtesy, The Cleveland Museum of Art. (*Braunmüller, Munich*)
5. Nelson Gallery, Kansas City

PAGE 88–89

1. Coll. Benjamin Sonnenberg, N. Y.
3. Courtesy of the Smithsonian Institution, Freer Gallery of Art, Washington, D. C.
4. Metropolitan Museum of Art, Rogers Fund, 1910
5. The Metropolitan Museum of Art, Rogers Fund, 1922
6. Nelson Gallery, Kansas City

PAGE 90–91

1. Metropolitan Museum of Art, Fletcher Fund, 1940
2. Nelson Gallery, Kansas City
3. Courtesy, The Cleveland Museum of Art. (*Braunmüller, Munich*)
4. Courtesy, The Cleveland Museum of Art
5. Courtesy, The Cleveland Museum of Art
6. Courtesy, The Cleveland Museum of Art

PAGE 92–93

1. Courtesy, The Cleveland Museum of Art
2. (*Wide World*)
3. Courtesy, The Cleveland Museum of Art
4. Bollingen Series XLIX, Bollingen Foundation, Inc.
5. Metropolitan Museum of Art, Gift of Heber R. Bishop, 1902
7. Courtesy, The Cleveland Museum of Art

PAGE 94–95

1. Hôryū-ji Museum, Nara. (*Manshichi Sakamoto*)
2. Courtesy, The Cleveland Museum of Art
3. Courtesy of the Smithsonian Institution, Freer Gallery of Art, Washington, D. C.
4. Courtesy, The Cleveland Museum of Art
5. (*Japan Tourist Association*)

PAGE 96–97

1. Hachisuga Collection, Shizuoka
2. Hôryū-ji Museum, Nara. (*Manshichi Sakamoto*)
3. Kozan-ji, Kyoto
4. Hokuen-dō, Kôfuku-ji, Nara
5. Tokyo National Museum
6. Kōzan-ji, Kyoto

PAGE 98–99

1. Museum of Fine Arts, Boston
2. Metropolitan Museum of Art, Fletcher Fund, 1928
3. Courtesy, The Cleveland Museum of Art
4. Tokyo National Museum. (*Manshichi Sakamoto*)
5. Shojiro Ishibashi's Collection, Tokyo
6. Courtesy, The Cleveland Museum of Art

PAGE 102–103

1. (*Nagoya City Foreign Trade Service*)
2. Atami Museum, Shizuoka-ken, Japan
3. Museum of Fine Arts, Boston
4. *From* The Hokusai Sketchbooks: Selections from the Manga, *by James A. Michener* (*Charles E. Tuttle Co., 1958*)
5. Museum of Fine Arts, Boston
6. (*Ezra Stoller*)
7. The Clarence Buckingham Collection, The Art Institute of Chicago
8. (*Consulate General of Japan, N. Y.*)

PAGE 104–105

1. Peabody Museum, Harvard University
2. American Museum of Natural History, N. Y.
3. Courtesy, The Cleveland Museum of Art
4. Instituto Nacional de Antropologia e Historia, Mexico City

PAGE 106–107

1. (*Fritz Henle—Monkmeyer*)
2. Instituto Nacional de Antropologia e Historia, Mexico City
3. British Museum, London
4. (*Marilu Pease—Monkmeyer*)
5. Louise and Walter Arensberg Collection, Philadelphia Museum of Art
6. Courtesy, The Cleveland Museum of Art
7. American Museum of Natural History, N. Y.
8. American Museum of Natural History
9. (*Pan American*)

PAGE 108–109

1. (*Réalitiés*)
2. Moravskě Museum, Brno
3. Louvre, Paris. (*Giraudon*)
4. Metropolitan Museum of Art, Gift of J. Pierpont Morgan, 1917
5. Kunsthistoriches, Vienna

PAGE 110–111

1. By permission of the Board of Trinity College, Dublin, Ireland
2. (*Norwegian Information Service, N. Y.*)
3. Universitetets Oldsaksamling, Oslo
4. Bibliotheek der Rijksuniversiteit, Utrecht
5. (*Wehmeyer—Roy Bernard*)
6. British Museum, London

PAGE 112–113

1. (*R. Doisneau—R.G.*)
2. (*R. Doisneau—R.G.*)
3. (*R. Doisneau—R.G.*)

PAGE 114–115

1. (*French Cultural Services*)
2. (*French Cultural Services*)
3. (*French Cultural Services*)
4. Musée de l'Oeuvre, Strasbourg. (*Giraudon*)
6. (*Herschel Levit, N. Y.*)

PAGE 116–117

1. (*Giraudon*)
2. (*Giraudon*)
4. (*Archives Photographiques—Paris*)
5. (*Giraudon*)
6. (*Jean Roubier, Paris*)
7. (*Giraudon*)

PAGE 118–119

1. (*Editions des Deux Mondes, Extrait du* Le Vitrail Francais, 1958.)
2. (*James Johnson—R. G.*)
3. (*Robert Doisneau—R.G.*)
4. (*Robert Doisneau—R. G.*)

PAGE 120–121

1. (*Giraudon*)
2. The Pierpont Morgan Library, N. Y.
3. The Pierpont Morgan Library, N. Y.
4. (*Archives Photographiques—Paris*)
5. (*Archives Photographiques—Paris*)
6. (*Internationes—Bonn*)

PAGE 122–123

1. Philadelphia Museum of Art
2. Musée d'Unterlinden, Colmar, France
3. Metropolitan Museum of Art, Dick Fund, 1926

PAGE 124–125

1. Prado, Madrid

PAGE 126–127

1. Musée Conde, Chantilly. (*Giraudon*)
2. Reproduced by permission of the Syndics of the Fitzwilliam Museum, Cambridge
3. Reproduced by courtesy of the Trustees, The National Gallery, London
4. Metropolitan Museum of Art, Gift of J. Pierpont Morgan, 1917
5. Kunsthistoriches, Vienna
6. Cluny Museum, Paris
7. Metropolitan Museum of Art, Dick Fund, 1940

PAGE 128–129

1. Louvre, Paris. (*Giraudon*)
2. Coll. Robert Lehman, N. Y.
3. Uffizi, Florence. (*Scala*)
4. (*Belgian Government Information Center*)
5. National Gallery of Art, Washington, D. C. Mellon Collection

PAGE 130–131

1. Metropolitan Museum of Art, Bequest of Maitland F. Griggs, 1943
2. Copyright: The Frick Collection, N. Y.
3. Coll. Robert Lehman, N. Y.

PAGE 132–133

1. (*Alinari*)
3. (*Italian State Tourist Office*)
4. Chiesa del S. Antonio, Padua. (*Anderson*)
5. Brancacci Chapel, Santa Maria del Carmine, Florence. (*Scala*)
6. (*Alinari*)

PAGE 134–135

1. (*Italian State Tourist Office*)
2. Bargello, Florence. (*Alinari*)
3. Bargello, Florence. (*Alinari*)
4. (*Alinari*)
5. (*Alinari*)

PAGE 136–137

1. Bargello, Florence. (*Alinari*)
2. National Gallery of Art, Washington, D. C.
3. (*Anderson*)
4. Bargello, Florence. (*Scala*)
5. Bargello, Florence. (*Alinari*)

PAGE 138–139

1. Brancacci Chapel, Santa Maria del Carmine, Florence. (*Scala*)
2. Isabella Stewart Gardner Museum, Boston
3. Reproduced by courtesy of the Trustees, The National Gallery, London
4. Chapel of San Brizio, Orvieto Cathedral. (*Scala*)

PAGE 140–141

1. By courtesy of the Ashmolean Museum, Oxford

PAGE 142–143

1. Uffizi, Florence. (*Scala*)
2. (*Brogi*)
3. Kupferstichkabinett, Berlin
4. (*Alinari*)
5. (*Alinari*)
6. Metropolitan Museum of Art, Rogers Fund, 1904
7. (*Jean Roubier, Paris*)

PAGE 144–145

1. Uffizi, Florence. (*Scala*)

PAGE 146–147

1. Brera, Milan. (*Scala*)
2. San Pietro in Montorio, Rome. (*Alinari*)
3. Brera, Milan. (*Scala*)

PAGE 148–149

1. Uffizi, Florence. (*Scala*)

2-3. Uffizi, Florence. (*Scala*)

4. Uffizi, Florence. (*Scala*)

PAGE 150–151

1. (*Scala*)

PAGE 152–153

1. Royal Library, Turin. (*Anderson*)
2. National Museum, Cracow
3. Royal Library, Windsor Castle, England
4. British Museum, London
5. Uffizi, Florence. (*Scala*)
6. Royal Library, Windsor Castle, England
7. Royal Library, Windsor Castle, England

PAGE 154–155

1. Uffizi, Florence. (*Scala*)
2. (*From* A Treasury of Art Masterpieces, *Simon and Schuster, Publishers*)
4. (*Anderson*)
5. (*Alinari*)

PAGE 156–157

1. (*Alinari*)

PAGE 158–159

1. Metropolitan Museum of Art, Bequest of Mrs. H. O. Havemeyer, 1929. H. O. Havemeyer Collection
2. (*Anderson*)
3. Bargello, Florence. (*Brogi*)
4. Metropolitan Museum of Art, Gift of J. Pierpont Morgan, 1917
5. Burndy Library, Norwalk, Connecticut
6. Metropolitan Museum of Art, Bequest of Benjamin Altman, 1913

PAGE 160–161

1. Reproduced by courtesy of the Trustees, The National Gallery, London
2. The Corning Museum of Glass, Corning, N. Y.
3. Accademia, Venice

PAGE 162–163

1. Galleria Nazionale, Palermo, Sicily. (*Scala*)
2. Copyright: The Frick Collection, N. Y.
3. Louvre, Paris. (*Giraudon*)
4. Kunsthistoriches, Vienna

PAGE 164–165

1. National Gallery of Art, Washington, D. C. Mellon Collection
2. Pinakothek, Munich
3. Pinakothek, Munich
4. San Giorgio Maggiore, Venice. (*Scala*)
5. Ducal Palace, Venice

PAGE 166–167

1. National Gallery of Scotland, Collection of the Earl of Ellesmere

PAGE 168–169

1. Metropolitan Museum of Art, The Jules S. Bache Collection, 1949
2. Accademia, Venice
3. Scoula Dalmata, Venice
4. (*Alinari*)

PAGE 170–171

1. Pinakothek, Munich
2. Ehem. Staatl. Museen Berlin, Kupferstichkabinett, Berlin-Dahlem
3. Kunstmuseum, Basel
4. Reproduced by courtesy of the Trustees, The National Gallery, London

PAGE 172–173

1. Louvre, Paris. (*Giraudon*)
2. (*French Cultural Services*)
3. The Metropolitan Museum of Art, Gift of William H. Riggs, 1941
4. The Metropolitan Museum of Art, Rogers Fund, 1941
5. National Portrait Gallery, London
6. Louvre, Paris. (*Giraudon*)
7. Metropolitan Museum of Art, Michael Friedsam Collection, 1931

PAGE 174–175

1. Kunsthistoriches, Vienna
2. The Bowdoin College Museum of Fine Arts, Brunswick, Maine

PAGE 176–177

1. (*Anderson*)
2. (*Alinari*)
4. (*Anderson*)

PAGE 178–179

1. Santa Maria del Popolo, Rome. (*Scala*)
2. Coll. Prof. Longhi, Rome
3. Santa Maria della Vittoria, Rome. (*Brogi*)
4. Villa Borghese, Rome. (*Alinari*)

PAGE 180–181

1. Church of St. Ignatius, Rome. (*Scala*)
2. Metropolitan Museum of Art, The Crosby Brown Collection of Musical Instruments, 1889
3. (*TWA*)

PAGE 182–183

1. Santo Tomé, Toledo. (*H. Hinz*)
2. (*Spanish Tourist Office*)

PAGE 184–185

1. Metropolitan Museum of Art, Rogers Fund, 1905
2. Gemäldegalerie, Dresden

PAGE 186–187

1. Prado, Madrid
2. Vaduz, Liechtenstein. (*Francis G. Mayer, N. Y.*)

PAGE 188–189

1. Prado, Madrid
2. Pinakothek, Munich
3. (*Spanish Tourist Office*)

PAGE 190–191

1. Collection of The Earl of Derby, Knowsley, Lancashire
3. The Pierpont Morgan Library, N. Y.
5. Reproduced by courtesy of the Trustees, The National Gallery, London
6. Allen Art Museum, Oberlin College

PAGE 192–193
1. Metropolitan Museum of Art, Dick Fund, 1946

PAGE 194–195
1. (*Giraudon*)
2. Metropolitan Museum of Art, Rogers Fund, 1904
3. *From* Album Charles Lebrun, Vol. I. Louvre, Paris. (*Pierre Belzeaux—R. G.*)
4. (*French Cultural Services*)
5. (*French Cultural Services*)

PAGE 196–197
1. Rijksmuseum, Amsterdam
2. Hermitage, Leningrad
3. Fogg Art Museum, Harvard University, Charles A. Loeser Bequest

PAGE 198–199
1. Royal Academy of Fine Arts, Stockholm. On loan to Nationalmuseum, Stockholm

PAGE 200–201
1. Coll. Baron Alain de Rothschild (*Robert Doisneau—R. G.*)
2. Metropolitan Museum of Art, Bequest of Benjamin Altman, 1913
3. Kunsthistoriches, Vienna

PAGE 202–203
1. Metropolitan Museum of Art, Bequest of Collis P. Huntington, 1925
2. (*British Information Service*)
3. (*British Information Service*)
4. (*British Information Service*)
5. Burndy Library, Norwalk, Connecticut
6. (*Zaharis*)
7. (*F. S. Lincoln*)
8. Coll. Nathaniel Hamlen, Wayland, Massachusetts

PAGE 204–205
1. Ehem. Staatl. Museen Berlin—Dahlem. (*Camera Clix*)
3. Metropolitan Museum of Art, Rogers Fund, 1920
4. (*French Cultural Services*)
5. Coll. Irwin Untermeyer, N. Y.
6. Kunsthistoriches, Vienna

PAGE 206–207
1. National Gallery of Art, Washington, D. C. Samuel H. Kress Collection

PAGE 208–209
1. (*Roy Bernard—Internationes*)
2. Museum of Fine Arts, Springfield, Massachusetts
4. (*O. Weiniger, Vienna*)
5. Würmgau Museum, Starnberg
6. The Museum of Fine Arts of Houston, Texas
7. Metropolitan Museum of Art, Rogers Fund, 1937

PAGE 210–211
1. Reproduced by courtesy of the Trustees of the Tate Gallery, London
2. Metropolitan Museum of Art, Dick Fund, 1917
3. Metropolitan Museum of Art, Rogers Fund, 1920
4. Metropolitan Museum of Art, Catherine D. Wentworth Fund, 1949
5. Louvre, Paris. (*Giraudon*)

PAGE 212–213
1. Metropolitan Museum of Art, Gwynne M. Andrews Fund, 1952
2. Metropolitan Museum of Art, Bequest of William K. Vanderbilt, 1920
3. Fogg Art Museum, Harvard University; Grenville Lindall Winthrop Collection
4. Brooklyn Museum, N. Y. (*C. Uht*)
5. Metropolitan Museum of Art, Gift of Bayard Verplanck, 1949
6. The Smithsonian Institution, Washington, D. C.
7. (*TWA*)
8. (*Joseph Scaylea from A. Devaney, N. Y.*)

PAGE 214–215
1. (*French Cultural Services*)
2. National Gallery of Art, Washington, D. C. Gulbenkian Collection, Loan
3. (*French Cultural Services*)
4. Comedie-Francaise, Paris. (*Giraudon*)
5. Louvre, Paris. (*Robert Doisneau—R. G.*)
6. (*French Cultural Services*)

PAGE 216–217
1. Prado, Madrid
2. Courtesy, Museum of Fine Arts, Boston
3. Prado, Madrid
4. The Collis P. Huntington Memorial Collection, California Palace of the Legion of Honor, San Francisco, California

PAGE 218–219
1. Louvre, Paris. (*Giraudon*)
2. The Walters Art Gallery, Baltimore
3. Louvre, Paris. (*Giraudon*)
4. Louvre, Paris. (*Giraudon*)
5. (*Giraudon*)
6. Louvre, Paris. (*Giraudon*)

PAGE 220–221
1. Metropolitan Museum of Art, Bequest of Catharine Lorillard Wolfe, 1887
2. Louvre, Paris. (*Giraudon*)
3. Louvre, Paris. (*Giraudon*)
4. Coll. Mr. and Mrs. William Goetz, Los Angeles
5. Metropolitan Museum of Art, Bequest of Mrs. H. O. Havemeyer, 1926, Mrs. H. O. Havemeyer Collection
6. Metropolitan Museum of Art, Bequest of Mrs. H. O. Havemeyer, 1926, The H. O. Havemeyer Collection

PAGE 222–223
1. Reproduced by courtesy of the Trustees, The National Gallery, London
2. Victoria and Albert Museum, London
3. Musée Marmottan, Paris. (*Pierre Belzeaux—R. G.*)
4. The Collis P. Huntington Memorial Collection, California Palace of the Legion of Honor, San Francisco, California
5. Anonymous Loan to the Museum of Fine Arts, Boston. (*Barney Burstein, Boston*)
6. Fogg Art Museum, Harvard University, Maurice Wertheim Collection
7. Mr. and Mrs. Martin A. Ryerson Collection, The Art Institute of Chicago

PAGE 224–225
1. Collection of The Rev. T. Pitcairn, Bryn Athyn, Pennsylvania

PAGE 226–227
1. Metropolitan Museum of Art, Gift of Thomas F. Ryan, 1910
2. Louvre, Paris. (*Giraudon*)
3. Rodin Museum, Paris. (*French Cultural Services*)
4. Coll. Richard L. Davisson, Jr., Westwood, Massachusetts
5. Metropolitan Museum of Art, Abrams Collection
6. The Art Institute of Chicago, Arthur Heun Fund

PAGE 228–229
1. Phillips Collection, Washington, D. C.

PAGE 230–231
1. Coll. Dr. and Mrs. Harry Bakwin, N. Y. (*Francis G. Mayer, N. Y.*)
2. Musée du Louvre, Galerie du Jeu de Paume, Paris. (*Giraudon*)
3. Hermitage, Leningrad

PAGE 232–233
1. National Gallery of Art, Washington, D. C., Chester Dale Collection
2. The Minneapolis Institute of Arts, Dunwoody Fund

PAGE 234–235
1. Helen Birch Bartlett Memorial Collection, The Art Institute of Chicago

PAGE 236–237
1. Coll. of Mrs. Albert D. Lasker, N. Y.
2. Stedelijk Museum, Amsterdam
3. Museum of Modern Art, N. Y., Lillie P. Bliss Bequest
4. Coll. of Mrs. Albert D. Lasker, N. Y.

PAGE 238–239
1. Courtauld Institute of Art, London

PAGE 240–241
1. Metropolitan Museum of Art, Abrams Collection
2. Courtesy of The Smithsonian Institution, Freer Gallery of Art, Washington, D. C.
3. Musée Toulouse-Lautrec, Albi, France
4. Art Institute of Chicago, Helen Birch Bartlett Memorial Collection

PAGE 242–243
1. Coll. Stephen C. Clark, Sr., N. Y.
2. The Pennsylvania Academy of the Fine Arts, Philadelphia
3. The Smithsonian Institution, Washington, D. C.
4. Jefferson Medical College, Philadelphia
5. Worcester Art Museum, Worcester, Massachusetts
6. American Museum of Natural History, N. Y.
7. Courtesy, The Cleveland Museum of Art

PAGE 244–245
1. Private Collection, N. Y.
2. National Gallery of Art, Washington, D. C. Gift of Stephen C. Clark
3. Museum of Modern Art, N. Y., Mrs. Simon Guggenheim Fund
4. Metropolitan Museum of Art, Morris K. Jessup Fund, 1933
6. Coll. A. Conger Goodyear, N. Y.

PAGE 246–247
1. Coll. Mr. and Mrs. Donald S. Stralem, N. Y.
2. The Baltimore Museum of Art, Cone Collection
3. *From* Le Chef-d'oeuvre Inconnu, *by Balzac. Albert Skira, Publishers.*

PAGE 248–249
1. Museum of Modern Art, N. Y., Mrs. Simon Guggenheim Fund

PAGE 250–251
1. National Gallery of Art, Washington, D. C. Rosenwald Collection
2. Smith College Museum of Art, Northampton, Massachusetts
3. Busch-Reisinger Museum, Harvard University, Cambridge, Massachusetts
4. Coll. Mr. and Mrs. John Hay Whitney,
5. Coll. Alex L. Hillman, N. Y.
6. (*Helene Adant*)

PAGE 252–253
1. Museum of Modern Art, N. Y. Lillie P. Bliss Bequest
2. Museum of Modern Art, N. Y. Lillie P. Bliss Bequest
3. Museum of Modern Art, N. Y. Lillie P. Bliss Bequest
4. Museum of Modern Art, N. Y. Benjamin Scharps and David Scharps Fund
5. National Museum of Modern Art, Paris. (*Robert Doisneau—R. G.*)
6. (*Eliot Elisofon—Life*)
7. Roland P. Murdock Collection, Wichita Art Museum, Wichita, Kansas
8. Galleries of Cranbrook Academy of Art, Bloomfield Hills, Michigan
9. Reproduced by courtesy of the Trustees of the Tate Gallery, London

PAGE 254–255
1. Musée des Beaux-Arts, Anvers
2. Museum of Modern Art, N. Y.
3. Coll. Joseph Slifka, N. Y.
4. Room of Contemporary Art, Albright Art Gallery, Buffalo, N. Y.
5. Coll. Joseph Hirshhorn, N. Y.
6. Coll. Mr. R. Sturgis Ingersoll
7. Galerie Maeght, Paris
8. Museum of Modern Art, N. Y. Mrs. Simon Guggenheim Fund (*Eliot Elisofon—Life*)

PAGE 256–257
1. The Solomon R. Guggenheim Museum, N. Y. (*Francis G. Mayer, N. Y.*)
2. Museum of Modern Art, N. Y.

PAGE 258–259
1. Private Collection, N. Y.
2. Paul Kantor Gallery, Beverly Hills, California
3. (*François Bucher*)
4. Coll. of Whitney Museum of American Art, N. Y. (*O. Baker*)
6. Coll. Mrs. Jack Stewart, N. Y.

PAGE 260–261
3. (*Roy Bernard—Internationes*)
5. Louise and Walter Arensberg Collection, Philadelphia Museum of Art
6. (*Hedrich-Blessing*)
7. Coll. Mrs. George Heard Hamilton, New Haven, Connecticut
9. (c *Ezra Stoller*)
10. Courtesy: Sidney Janis Gallery, N. Y. (*O. Baker*)
11. (*Halley Erskine*)

PAGE 262–263
1. Life Magazine (© Time Inc.)
2. Coll. Richard Brown Baker, N. Y. (*Francis G. Mayer, N. Y.*)
3. (*TWA*)

1. *Stonemasons and sculptors at work on bricklaying, drilling, measuring and sculpting.* Nanni di Banco. About 1408.

2. *Fresco painting and color grinding.* Florentine print. About 1465.

3. *Sculptor seated on a stool, working.* Italic gem, 3rd-1st centuries B.C.

4. *The painter studying the laws of foreshortening by means of threads and a frame.* Dürer. Woodcut.

5. *Sculptor and metalworker with vase.* Egyptian wall painting from the Tomb of the Two Sculptors, Thebes. 18th dynasty. (About 1400 B.C.)

TABLE OF CONTENTS

1. Paul Gauguin: *Van Gogh Painting Sunflowers*. 1888.

2. Marc Chagall: *The Artist and His Model*.

INTRODUCTION

Art, the creation of things that have form and beauty, is discussed in this book in terms of the painting, sculpture, the architecture and the ornaments made by man from prehistoric times to the present century. The author has attempted to show the development and growth of various art forms, from their earliest conception in the mind of primitive man up to the technical virtuosity and esoteric creations of twentieth century works.

Art, perhaps man's highest achievement, has mirrored the images of his time far beyond the individual excellence of the sculptor's model or the painter's canvas. In the monumental rock sculptures of Rameses II at Abu Simbal, the magnificent despotism of the Egyptian pharaohs is reflected as well as the taut, supremely disciplined character of this absolute monarch. The classic beauty of the Greek discus thrower or the figures on the caryatid porch of the Erectheum show us not only a sublime artistic achievement, but tell also what was known of anatomy, theology, and the condition of man in this golden civilization.

The vast military might of the Roman Empire is exemplified in the equestrian statue of the Emperor Marcus Aurelius. Just as the aqueducts and fora record the engineering and architectural knowledge achieved by the Romans, so also do the triumphal arches and the Roman eagle standards show us the importance of military conquest. The baths of Diocletian indicate a material and spiritual luxury unequalled ever since, while Pompeiian wall frescoes show us the sports and amusements of that age. The cultural heritage of the early Eastern Empires, the spread of the great religions of the world throughout Asia and Europe, the development of spiritual discipline are reflected in the early Christian mosaics, Coptic tapestries, and demon masks from Thailand.

Centuries of Oriental art have preserved for future generations not only scrolls and paintings of exquisite beauty, but also the graphic history of one of the world's oldest civilizations. Not only are the scenes, the activities, the manner of dress and decoration

3. Jean-Frédéric Bazille: *Studio in the rue de la Condamine*.

4. *Artist painting a statue of Hercules*, detail of vase painting. South Italian. 4th century B.C. Terra cotta. h. 20¼″.

5. Antonio Grassi: *The Portrait-painter*. Viennese porcelain. h. 11¾″.

depicted, but also the deeply introspective philosophy of Buddhism is recorded in delicate brushwork; the discipline of spirit is reflected in the discipline of artistic technique.

The spread of Christianity throughout the West is preserved in minute detail in church architecture and manuscript illustration. The terrible conflict between Christian and pagan, the struggle of man against man and nation againt nation is unfolded, as are also the worldly and lighthearted dramas, and the absurdity of mankind.

The resurgent desire of men to know and understand their world and themselves, culminating in the glorious blaze of the Renaissance, can only be fully understood—indeed, lived again—through the magnificent works of art produced in these centuries.

As the Renaissance spread and gave way to Baroque, and in turn, to Rococo, Neo-Classicism and Romanticism, so also were man's condition, his achievements and his depths recorded by the brush of the artist, the walls of the architect, and the clay of the sculptor. Man's curiosity, his increasing understanding of the complexities of his world, are never so acutely preserved as in his art. In the twentieth century, man has finally broken the bounds of his earth, and is profoundly concerned with the unseen and unknown worlds—of himself, and of space. The abstract art of this century as surely and inevitably records the continuing search.

The first part of this book is a visual survey of the historical development of style, as new knowledge and techniques brought about new ways of handling the materials of art. In the latter part of the book, the author discusses the emergence of individuals who crystallized the spirit of their times in the masterpieces of art presented here.

At the end of the book a chronological chart of periods of art, and of major artists of each period is shown. A glossary of artists and art terms, compiled by a team of experts in art history and architecture, is listed for easy reference in a separate section of the book.

THE EDITORS

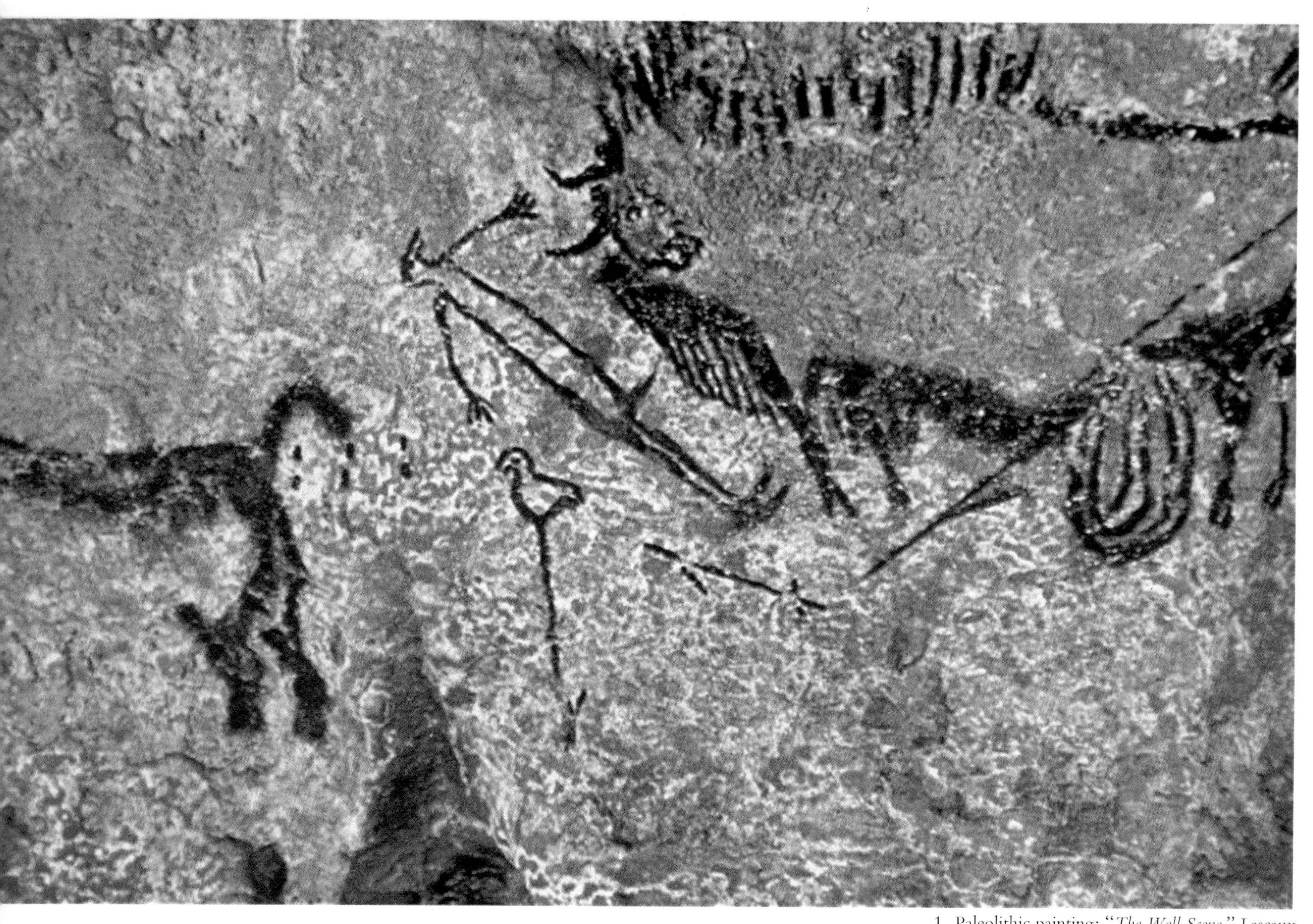

1. Paleolithic painting: "*The Well Scene.*" Lascaux.

PREHISTORIC AND PRIMITIVE ARTS

Men first began to make the objects which we call works of art some 25,000 years ago in the Paleolithic, or Old Stone Age. These early men were hunters, and the pictures they drew were of wild animals and hunting scenes. Such paintings were probably looked upon as a kind of magic, for by imitating the shape of an animal, or the rounded forms of a human body, the artist may have felt that he had power over the subject of his art.

Ten to fifteen thousand years later, in the Neolithic, or New Stone Age, tribes banded together to build villages, and hunting partly gave way to farming. Men were occupied with clearing the land, and with planting and harvesting their crops. The changing seasons and the powerful forces of the sun, wind, and rain became matters of deep concern. Now, instead of drawing pictures of leaping bison and deer, these early artists built the earth itself into monuments of stone and clay. Gradually, they began to use symbols and abstract patterns. Simplified animal and human stick figures were used now to decorate their tools and ornaments.

Some primitive peoples in the world today draw pictures and create sculptures much like those which were made in the Stone Age. And the symbols and god-figures created by primitive tribes of the modern world are intended to soothe the evil spirits and bring good fortune, just as they once were by Stone Age artists.

Prehistoric drawings of animals were usually correct in their proportions, for Paleolithic men, to whom animals were the source of all food and clothing, needed accurate knowledge of an animal's anatomy, if the hunt was to be successful. Paintings like these (*Figs. 1, 3*) were rubbed on the walls of caves with red and yellow earth mixed with animal fat. The artists usually drew single animals, although sometimes they portrayed a dramatic scene like the one at left, of a hunter gored by a mortally wounded beast. When the artist painted or carved the human body, however, he was less concerned with correct anatomy than with his own feelings about the body. So, often it was only sketched in, as is the stick-figure of the slain hunter, in Figure 1. Sometimes, parts of the body were exaggerated for magical reasons. The sculpture in Figure 2, with its heavy breasts and hips, was probably a charm to ensure fertility.

2. Paleolithic sculpture: *Venus of Willendorf.* Limestone. *h.* 4½″.

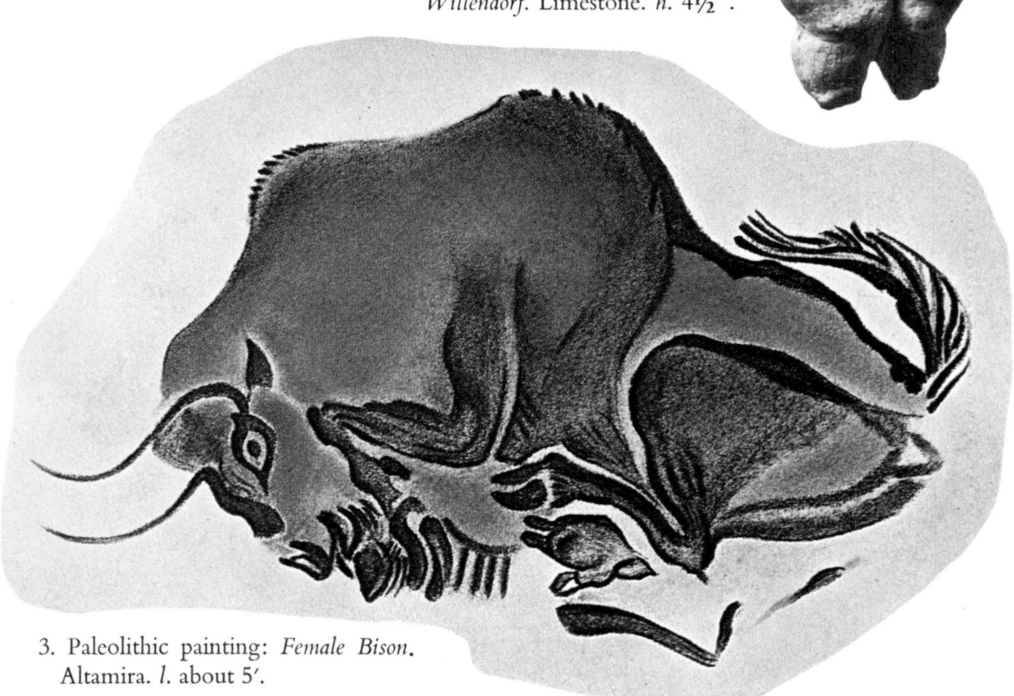

3. Paleolithic painting: *Female Bison.* Altamira. *l.* about 5′.

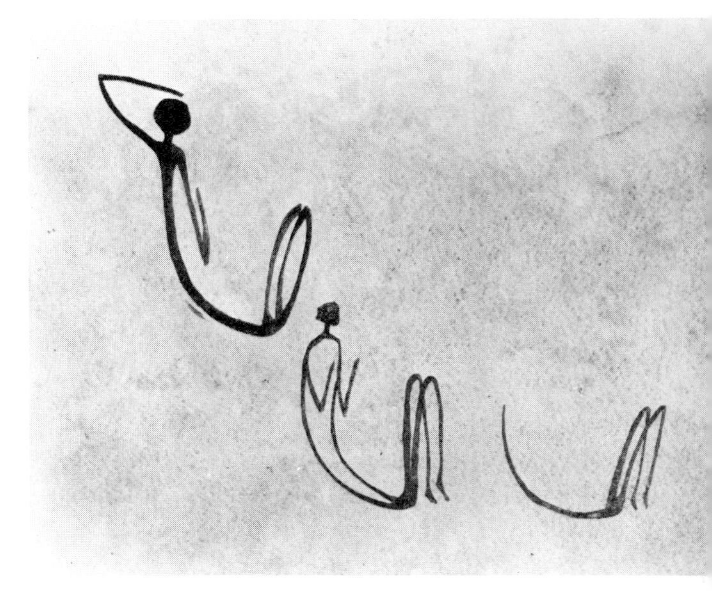

5. Neolithic painting: *Three Figures.* Southern Rhodesia. 4000–3000 B.C.

6. Neolithic pottery: *Painted Vase.* Susa, Persia. About 3000 B.C. *h.* 11½″.

4. Neolithic Structure: *Serpent Mound.* Adams County, Ohio. About 900 A.D.

In Neolithic times, artists no longer made such dramatic paintings and sculptures. Now, they decorated objects such as clay pots, painting them in stiff, geometric patterns. During the same centuries, representations of the human body were even sketchier than in some Paleolithic art (*Fig. 5*). These quick, repeated images were probably early steps toward the invention of picture-writing.

The people whom we call "primitive" today, have changed very little from the ways of their earliest ancestors. They use only the most elementary tools and materials: a loom, a knife, a pot of earth color, a block of wood, shredded palm leaves, and so forth. But their arts may be as accomplished in design and feeling as any in what we think of as the civilized world. The modern primitive, like his Paleolithic ancestor, takes a recognizable shape—animal or human—and then transforms the body into an extraordinary pattern of sharp angles or curves, or lines and circles.

3. African art: *Female Head.* Ife, Nigeria. 12th–15th centuries. Terra cotta. *h.* 9¼″.

1. Northwest Indian art: *Painted Ceremonial Shirt.* Tlingit Indian. Alaska.

4. African art: *Ancestor Figure.* Senufo tribe, Ivory Coast. 1840–1850. *h.* 21″.

Indian artists of the American northwest coast still decorate their houses, their clothing and utensils with carved and painted figures of animal spirits, called "totems." The original families of each tribe are thought to descend from such animal spirits, like the Bear, or the Lynx. A family today may have several such totems in its family tree. The huge tub below is like those still used during the Potlatch, an event of feasting and gift-giving.

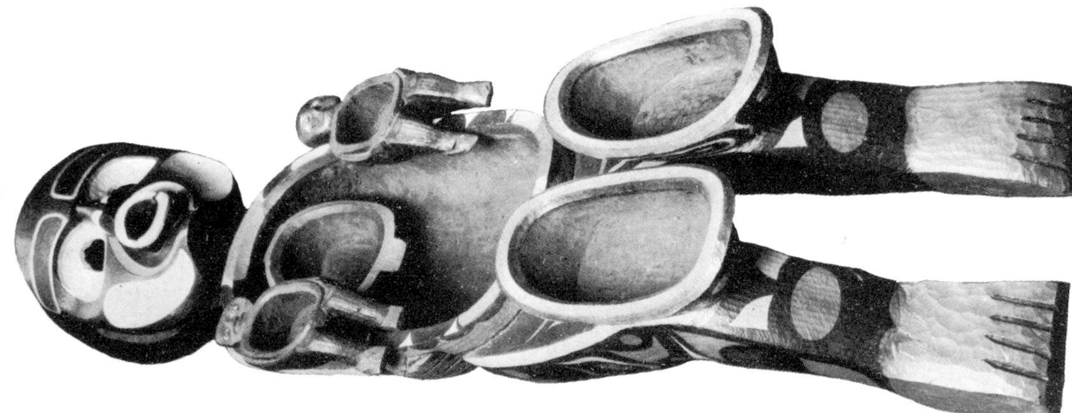

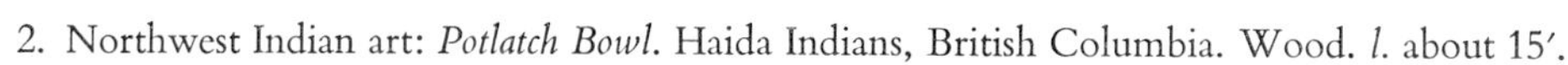

2. Northwest Indian art: *Potlatch Bowl.* Haida Indians, British Columbia. Wood. *l.* about 15′.

The sculptors of Africa were, until quite recently, among the most intense and imaginative artists of the world. The Ife head (*Fig. 3*), realistically moody, was made during one of the high periods of African culture, when great empires existed in what is now only jungle. Figures 4 and 5 are more typical primitive carvings made by tribal artists. These represent the spirits of ancestors, which were believed to hover about the huts and sacred places of the tribe. In each case, the artist has selected a particular visual idea—a springy posture or a slanting, crouched position—and made it the basis for a clear-cut pattern.

6. Pacific Ocean art: *Kukalimoku*, God of War. Hawaii. 18th century. Wood. *h.* 7′2″.

5. African art: *Female Figure*. Baluba Tribe, Belgian Congo. Wood. *h.* 20″.

The artists of the Polynesian and Melanesian island-chains, like those in Africa, were brilliant carvers in wood. Sometimes these sea-surrounded artists added cowrie shells, bits of coral, or fringes of palm leaves to enhance their wiry patterns.

7. Pacific Ocean art: *Ritual Mask*. New Guinea. Mid-19th century. *h.* 5′4″.

1. *Pyramid of King Djoser,* near Sakkara. III dynasty, about 2900 B.C.

In Egypt, architecture first became a noble art form, with the building of tombs and temples. In Neolithic times, the first kings of Egypt were buried in pits dug in the earth and lined with rocks. Later, rectangular tombs called "mastabas" were built above the ground. These had tunnels and rooms within, where religious rituals for the deceased took place. During the reign of the Pharaoh Djoser, around 2900 B.C., a famous architect named Imhotep conceived the idea of setting one mastaba on top of another to make a colossal pyramid shape. Later Pharaohs like Khufu and Khafre tried to outdo Djoser by building even larger pyramids with the sides smoothed off and faced with polished stone. The builders had neither dynamite nor pulleys or wheels, but they had thousands of slaves and abundant stone in the Nile quarries. Millions of blocks of stone, each weighing tons, were cut, floated across the river on flat barges, dragged over the sands, and finally tugged into place. The great pyramids were built during Egypt's first period of unified activity, known as the Old Kingdom, from about 4000 until 2260 B.C.

2. *Temple of Queen Hatshepsut* (1504–1483 B.C.). Deir el-Bahari, Thebes. XVIII dynasty, 1500 B.C.

Not until a thousand years after the end of the Old Kingdom did building again proceed vigorously. Then for a while, the Pharaohs built more delicate structures—temples and tunnel-tombs in the Nile cliffs. The most elegant of these was built for Queen Hatshepsut. It seems likely that Greek architects of a later period visited Egypt and carried home memories of these slender, horizontal rows of plain columns, the wide, gently sloping runways and statue-filled garden terraces.

4. *The Goddess Hathor.* XVIII dynasty, (1570–1465 B.C.). Diorite. *h.* 20″.

Hathor, the cow, bearing the full moon between her curved horns, watched over beautiful women. Her image often adorned the handles of their hand-mirrors.

6. *The God Horus and King Nectanebos.* Heliopolis. XXX dynasty, about 350 B.C. Basalt. *h.* 29″.

7. Relief sculpture: *The Goddess Nut* from a sarcophagus. Sakkara. XXX dynasty, about 350 B.C. Diorite. *l.* 2′5″.

Goddess of the sky was Nut. Each day the Sun-god's ship sailed through her bending body. Here, the ship is seen at three stages of its journey. Thoth, the beaked and beady-eyed ibis, was the god of writing.

On his coronation day, each Pharaoh of Egypt was believed to change mysteriously into a descendant of Horus, the hawk, who then protected him in life and in battle. Here, Horus shelters the Pharaoh Nectanebos, who reigned in 350 B.C.

8. *The God Thoth.* XXVI dynasty, 663–525 B.C. Bronze, *h.* 7¼″.

5. *Bastet,* statuette of Ptolemaic period, (332–30 B.C.). Bronze. *h.* 15″.

Egypt's favorite animal was the cat, sacred to the goddess Bastet. The sleek lines of the feline body, the silky motion of her prowl, the secretive stare of her yellow eyes, all appealed to the Egyptian's sense of form and mystery. Pet cats were embalmed and buried in gold and bronze coffins like this one (*Figs. 3, 5*), which is adorned with golden earrings and a lotus-blossom necklace.

These were some of the gods of Egypt that sculptors and painters portrayed in the same shapes for over three thousand years. Some had human forms, while others bore the heads or whole bodies of animals. These curious images took shape in the earliest days of Egypt's religion, around 3500 B.C., when the first kings, noble families, and professional groups believed that they could trace their ancestry to animals whose qualities seemed like their own. The lion's courage and power was said to have been passed down to the king, and the stiff-legged ibis' prying intelligence seemed suited to the scribe.

1. *The Goddess Sakhmet.* Karnak. XVIII dynasty, (1411–1375 B.C.). Diorite. *h.* 7′.

Sakhmet, the lioness, was the goddess of war. Here, in her hand she holds the Egyptian symbol of life.

2. *The God Osiris Seated, with Table of Offerings.* Tomb of Queen Nefertari, Thebes. XIX dynasty about 1350 B.C.

Favorite of the human-like gods was Osiris, ruler of the Underworld and god of the fields and harvests. Each autumn he was believed to be slain; each spring, his beloved sister Isis restored his broken body and brought life back to the dry fields.

3. Detail of 5.

EGYPT

2. *Ritual Figure.* Pre-dynastic, about 4000 B.C. Painted terra cotta.

By 3500 B.C. some Stone Age settlements around the Mediterranean Sea had advanced to a new state of civilization. Men began working with bronze and copper, building protected cities, and writing down their history and the legends of their gods. Art advanced from the stiff designs of the Late Stone Age, and now began to express men's growing ambitions. In Egypt, the first great art style of the world was born. It was conceived and designed by the priests and kings of the land, and was brought into being by the labor of thousands of slaves from Asia, Africa, Phoenicia, and every part of the ancient world.

There were three kinds of art in ancient Egypt. Art was used in the home—in furniture, jewelry, dishes, musical instruments, and many household furnishings. Art was made for the dead—on tombs, masks, mummy cases, and wrappings for the body. Models were made of all the things that the dead person had owned in his lifetime. These were buried with him, for the Egyptians believed he might need them on his journey to the Underworld. Finally, art was created for the gods and their priests and kings—in temples, paintings, and statues.

Each Egyptian artist worked according to strict "conventions" or rules, laid down in pre-history and said to have been taught by the gods. Some of these conventions are obvious to our eyes. For example, figures drawn by the Egyptian craftsman were shown in a rigid pose, gazing forward with expressionless faces. Other conventions are less obvious, but they, too, help to identify the style as Egyptian. The sculptors worked in hard stone, such as granite or diorite, or upon difficult surfaces like the great cliffs of the Nile, or they used fragile materials like glass and gold. Because these materials were hard to shape, the Egyptian artist learned to turn his surfaces simply. He learned to shape the outline of the body in long, taut, unbroken lines. Each work of art made in Egypt, from the towering pyramid to the tiniest glass vessel, has the same smooth surface.

Stone Age settlers in Egypt made this figurine of a woman with outstretched arms. Perhaps the tall figure represents a priestess performing a sacred dance. If so, these pre-Egyptians may already have been sun-worshipers like their descendants, whose greatest god, Amen-Ra, sailed across the sky in his sun-boat.

Egyptians, who became master craftsmen in every material, used glass for many delicate works of art. This head (below), was colored to make it appear to be made of the more precious lapis lazuli and turquoise. Glass was also made into striped beads, blown goblets, and other molded ornaments. Always, however brilliant their techniques became, Egyptian craftsmen repeated over and over the same images which had been handed down through the centuries.

3. Ornament for inlay: XIX–XX dynasties, about 1200 B.C. Glass. *h.* 4⅛″.

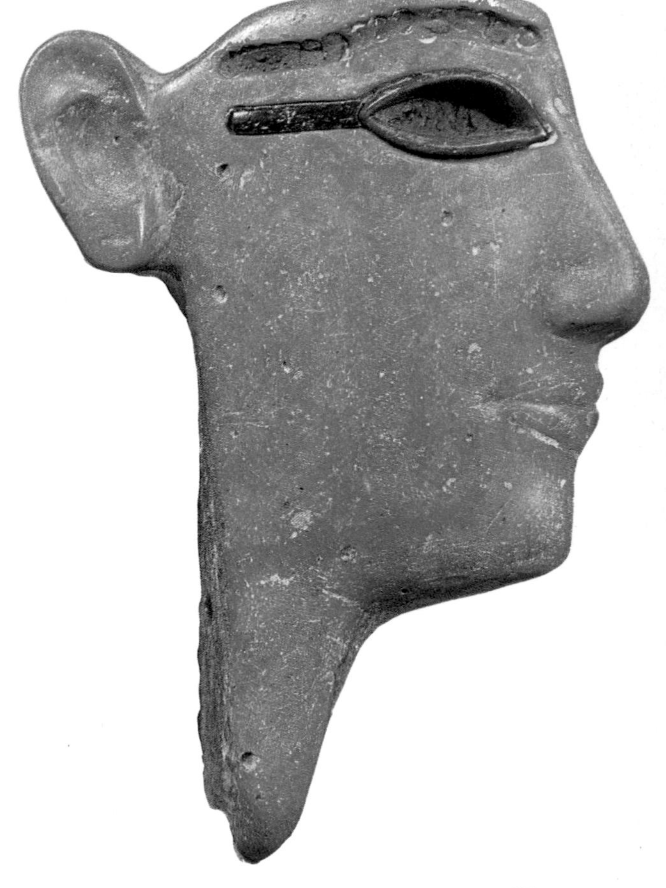

One of the greatest monuments of the Egyptian Empire is the colossal carving at left (*Fig. 1*). It is a row of portraits of Pharaoh Rameses II, cut out of a sheer cliff that towers 65 feet over the desert at Abû Simbel on the Nile. Rameses, the Egyptian Empire's most powerful ruler, erected huge monuments like these all along the Nile. They were to be the last great works of Egypt, for no one could continue to expend such vast amounts of manpower and money on personal luxury and still maintain the country's defenses against invaders. The simple outlines of Rameses II's giants show how little Egyptian style had changed from Neolithic times, for the taut Stone Age priestess (*Fig. 2*), is remarkably similar in simple profile to these Egyptian monuments made centuries later.

1. *Colossi of Rameses II* at Abû Simbel. XIX dynasty, 1257 B.C. *h.* 65′.

The Egyptian temple was built according to the same plan for over two thousand years: it was a walled and gloomy place with an exposed courtyard where the common people gathered. Inside were dark, protected sanctums for the nobles and priests. The heavy gateway is flanked by ponderous "pylons" or piers marking the entranceway—decorated with relief sculptures of the gods and kings. At the gate, tall obelisks with metal tips once flashed in the sunlight, and flags dyed red, blue, green, and yellow fluttered in the river breeze.

3. *Temple of the God Horus.* Edfu. About 257–237 B.C.

The colossal columns, below, stand in the "hypostyle" or inner columned hall of the great temple built by Rameses II at Karnak. Once gaudily painted, these 66-foot-high columns end in a swollen capital or head, the shape of which was copied from the lotus flower. Almost all the column designs in Persia, Greece, and Rome were patterned after natural forms such as leaves, shells, and plants. These designs are believed to be faint echoes of the earliest "post-and-lintel" architecture, when tree trunks, bundles of lotus, or papyrus stalks were set upright and roofed over with flat branches and thatch. When later architects began to use stone, they copied in their carvings the appearance of the older temples.

4. *Hypostyle Hall of Kings Sethos I and Rameses II.* Temple of Amon, Karnak. XIX dynasty (1349–1197 B.C.).

Portrait sculpture developed into a great art in Egypt, along with the belief that the spirit of a man could live forever if a recognizable portrait statue were kept in his tomb. Old Kingdom portraits were always presented in rigid postures, and were simple and powerful, with very little show of private emotion. Later, in the Middle Kingdom, from 2100 to 1700 B.C., somewhat more personal moods and characters were represented.

1. *King Menkawra and Wife.* IV dynasty, 2580 B.C. Slate. *h.* 4′7″.

King Menkawra and his wife, portrayed in this sculpture, reigned in the Old Kingdom at the end of the Fourth Dynasty (2680–2565 B.C.). Within the narrow conventions, the Egyptian sculptor managed to express the spirit of his subjects. On a block of hard stone, he marked off simple areas of rectangles and squares. These became the body, legs, and arms of a rigid figure, with jutting beard or crown, all in balance.

2. *Head of Pharaoh Amenemhat III.* XII dynasty (1850–1800 B.C.). Obsidian. *h.* 4″.

In the Middle Kingdom, the head of Amenemhat III, shown above, was carved on a small piece of obsidian, a kind of volcanic glass, which must have been extremely difficult to shape into these sorrowful, meditative, and proud features. A queen, Hatsheput, had a statue carved of herself as a sphinx, to express the moody power and dignity of her reign.

3. *Sphinx with Portrait of Queen Hatsheput.* XVIII dynasty, (1504–1483 B.C.). Red granite. *h.* 5′5½″, *l.* 11′5″.

4. *Colossi of Pharaoh Amenhotep III.* Thebes. XVIII dynasty (1411–1375 B.C.). *h.* 63′.

The traditional Egyptian style of portrait sculpture reached a climax in these colossi of Amenhotep III, which tower 63 feet over the bare desert. A later follower to the throne of Egypt obliterated the faces of these high statues, perhaps hoping thereby to wipe the memory of his rival from the earth.

6. *Pharaoh Ikhnaton.* Amarna period, about 1365. Limestone. *h.* 8⅜″.

It was Amenhotep III's immediate follower, Amenhotep IV, who instigated Egypt's first real revolution in art and ideas. Brilliant, poetic, and visionary, Amenhotep IV banished the thousands of animal gods which had always been worshiped in Egypt. For them he substituted a single god of heat, called Aton, and in the new god's honor, he changed his own name to Ikhnaton. Now, for the first time, artists were urged to show figures in natural positions, dancing, turning, and conversing. The King even permitted himself to be portrayed as wide-hipped and soft, unlike the stern, taut-skinned Pharaohs of the past. His beautiful queen Nefertiti was also shown realistically, with heavy-lidded eyes and a strong jaw.

5. *Queen Nefertiti.* XVIII dynasty (1375–1357 B.C.). Painted limestone. *h.* 19⅝″.

1. *Coffin of Pharaoh Tutankhamen.* XVIII dynasty (1362–1253 B.C.). *l.* 73″.

Inside a stone coffin resting on the bier lay the mummy of the King, beneath a golden mask inlaid with jewels and enamel (*Figs. 1, 2*). Paintings on the walls showed events in the life of the King on earth, and the scenes he expected to encounter in the Underworld, after death.

The royal viscera of the King lay in a great canopic chest, guarded by four goddesses (*Fig. 3*).

2. *Portrait Mask of Tutankhamen.* Gold. *h.* 20″.

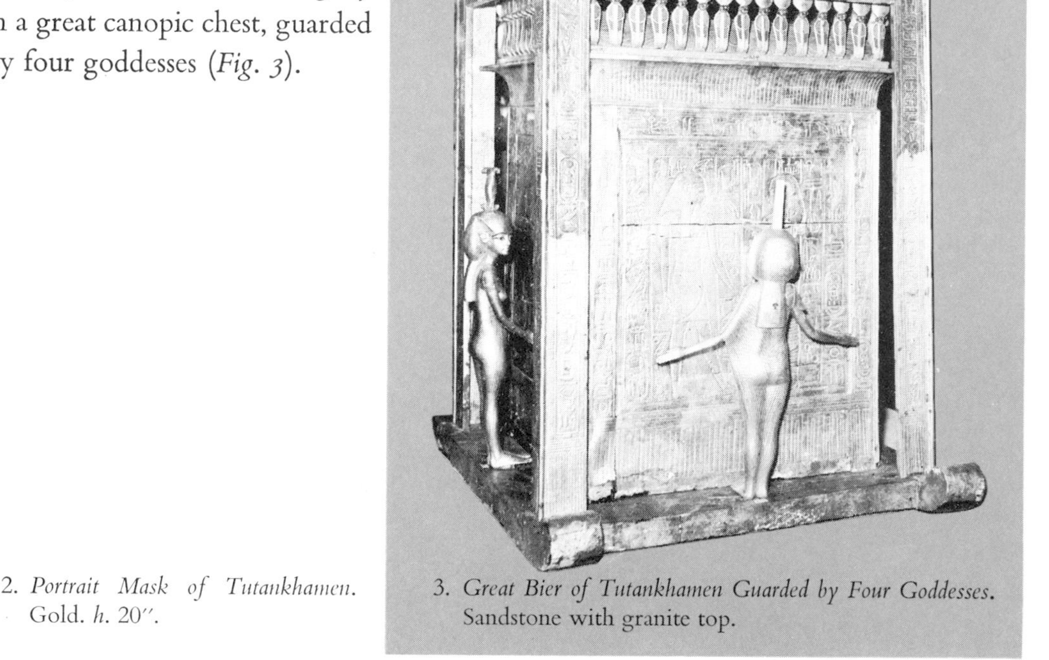

3. *Great Bier of Tutankhamen Guarded by Four Goddesses.* Sandstone with granite top.

4. Egyptian wall painting: *Tutankhamen Hunting Lions.* 1357–1349 B.C.

When, for economic reasons, the age of pyramid-building had ended, the kings of the Empire built smaller tunnel-tombs into the hills in the Valley of the Kings, a desolate ravine west of the Nile at Thebes. Unfortunately, by the time archaeologists discovered these well-hidden tombs, almost all had long since been rifled by robbers. The discovery of the untouched tomb of King Tutankhamen, in 1922, was therefore an extraordinary event. Here were found Tutankhamen's furniture, his throne, his tables and chairs, and provisions for the long, dangerous journey through the winding caverns of the Underworld.

Tutankhamen was the son-in-law of Ikhnaton, the artistic revolutionary. After Ikhnaton's death, the priests of Amen quickly put a stop to Aton-worship and the stylistic revolution, but some artists continued to work in the more lifelike style. The paintings of Tutankhamen (*Figs. 4, 5*), still appear to have been drawn with a lively, free hand.

5. *The Priest Ai Performing the Rite of Opening the Mouth of the King, Tutankhamen.* Tomb of Tutankhamen. XVIII dynasty, (1362–1353 B.C.).

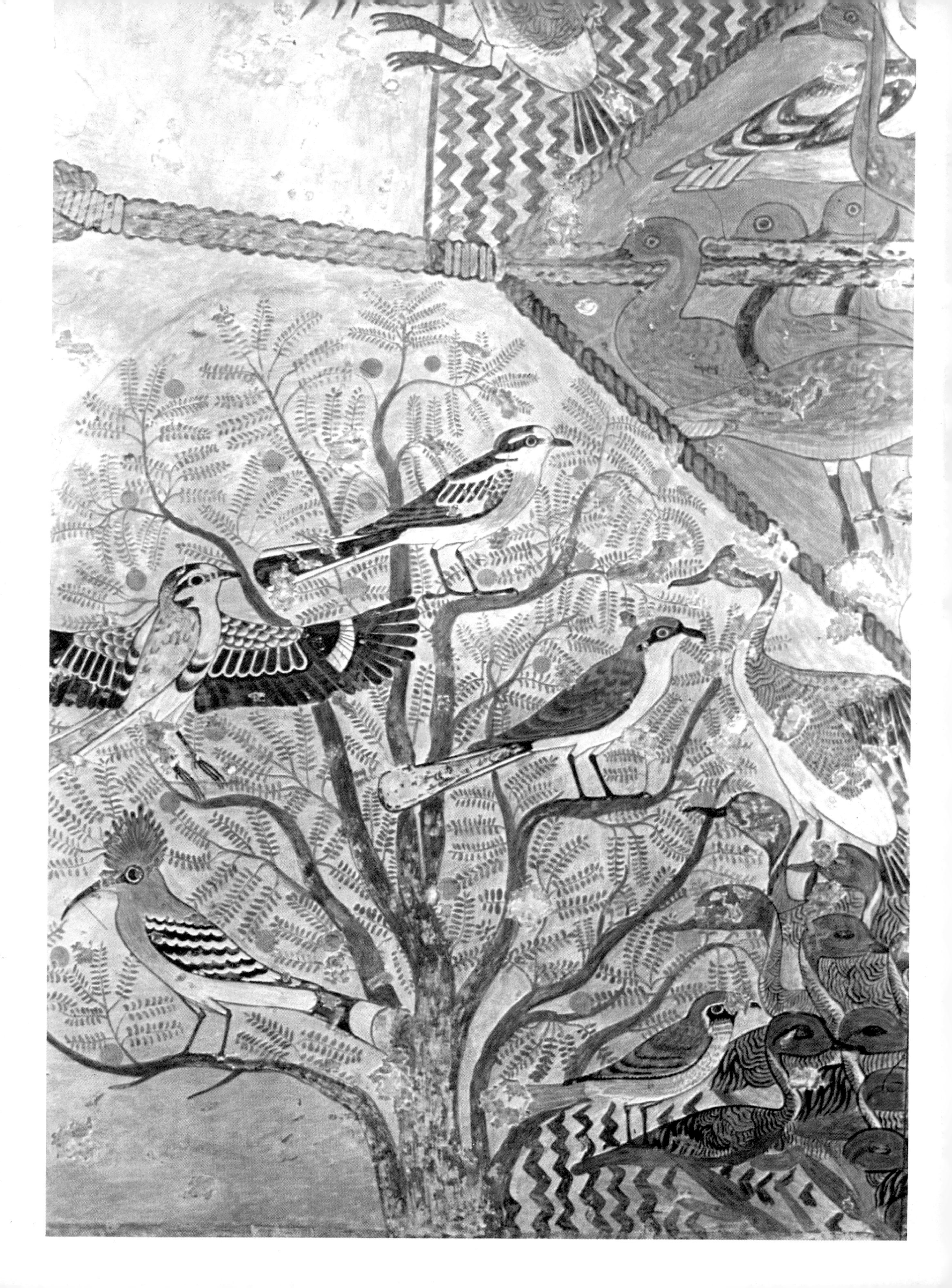

2. *Vintagers,* detail. Wall painting from Tomb of Nakht, Thebes. XVIII dynasty, (1420–1411 B.C.).

1. *Fowling Scene,* detail. Tomb of Khnum-Hotep at Beni Hasan. XII dynasty, about 1900 B.C. (Facsimile copy.)

3. *Girl Picking Flax.* Detail from Tomb of Nakht, Thebes. XVIII dynasty, (about 1420–1411 B.C.)

1. *Menena Accompanied by his Family on Two Outings in the Marshes.* At the left he hurls throwing sticks at waterfowl; at the right he spears fish. Tomb of Menena, an official on the estates of Thutmose IV, about 1415 B.C. Thebes.

The Egyptians were masters at capturing the fluid lines of an animal's body in the sleek material with which they worked. While the religious and royal art of Egypt conformed to strict conventions of style, art in the home and paintings depicting the pleasures and labors of men and women, were drawn with a freer hand.

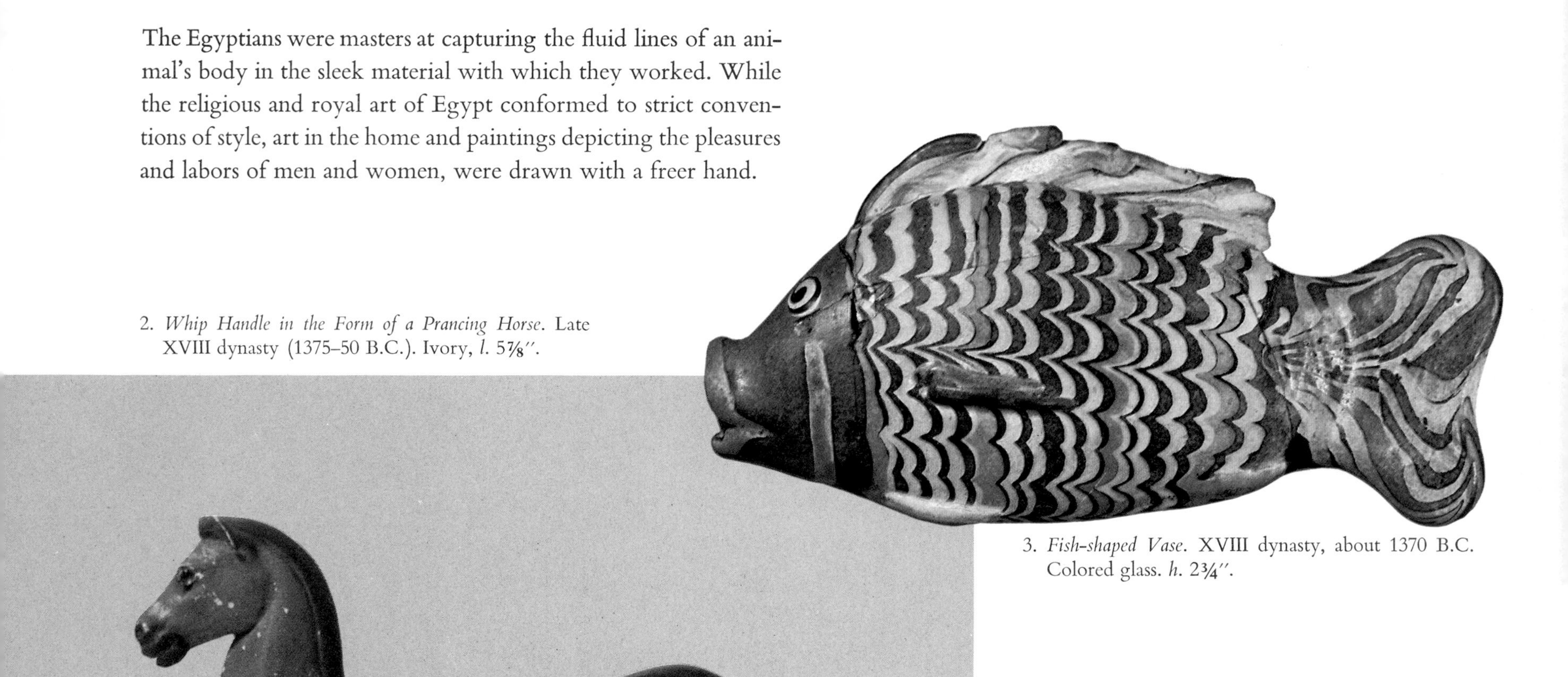

2. *Whip Handle in the Form of a Prancing Horse.* Late XVIII dynasty (1375–50 B.C.). Ivory, *l.* 5⅞″.

3. *Fish-shaped Vase.* XVIII dynasty, about 1370 B.C. Colored glass. *h.* 2¾″.

4. *Horse and Rider*. XVIII dynasty, about 1550 B.C.
Painted wood. *h*. 12″.

6. *Falcon*. From the decoration of a shrine.
Late Dynastic period (945–332 B.C.). Faience inlay. *h*. 6½″.

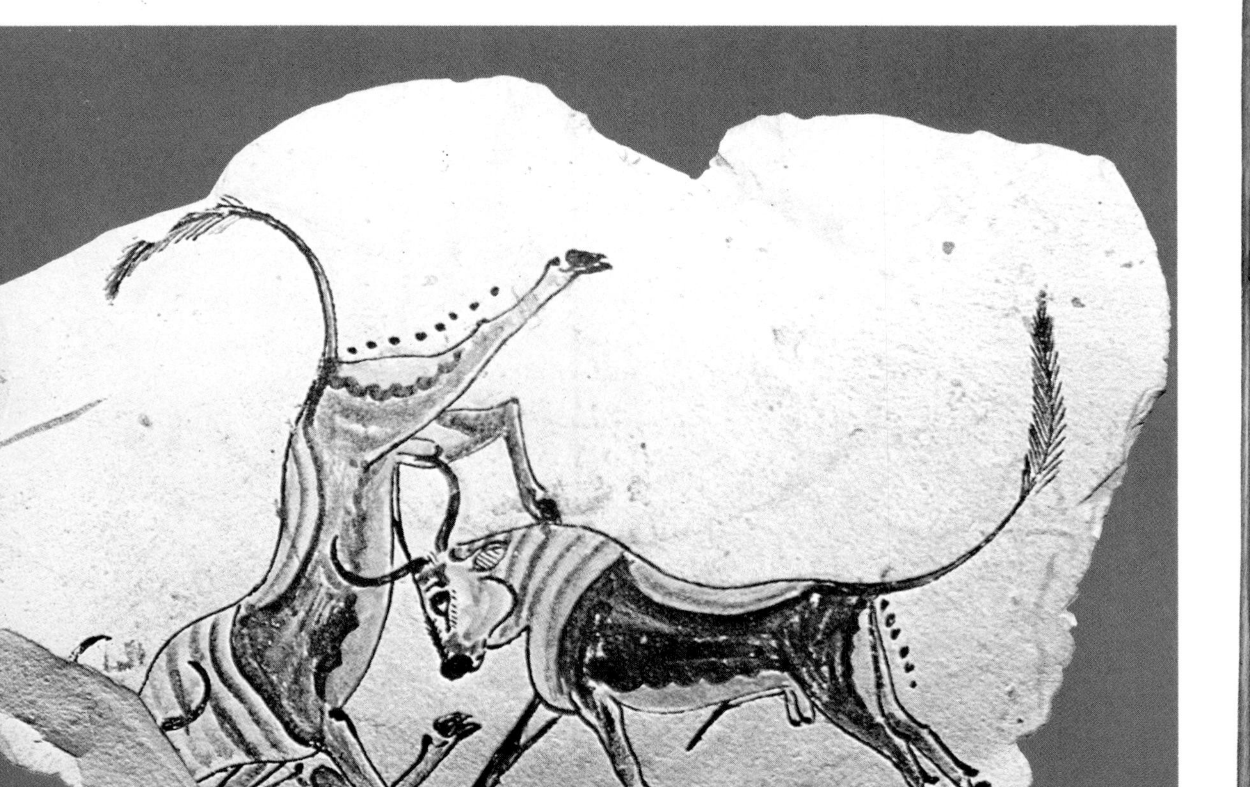

5. *Sketch of Two Bulls Fighting*. Thebes. New Kingdom (1567–1085 B.C.). *l*. 7¼″.

7. *Mummy with mask painted in Roman style*. 2nd century A.D. *h*. 5′6″.

So strong were the conventions of Egyptian art that they persisted on into the Roman and even the Christian eras. Under the rule of the Roman Empire, Egyptian embalmers continued to bury their dead in mummy cases decorated with scenes from the ancient past. Now, however, they often painted a portrait on wood, in a style half-Roman, half their own, and set it atop the mummy case, in place of the golden mask of antiquity. Figure 7 shows the deceased wearing a classical wreath of olive leaves.

1. Akkadian sculpture: *Head of a Mesopotamian Ruler*. From Nineveh. 2270–2233 B.C. Bronze.

2. Sumerian figurine: *Ram in a Thicket.* From Ur. About 2500 B.C. Shell, lapis-lazuli, and gold. *h.* 18″

The earliest Mesopotamian city to achieve a high degree of civilization was Ur, which flourished around 3000 B.C. under a pastoral people called the Sumerians. Economic life in Ur depended upon raising great herds of cattle, so the soft-eyed bull became a motif for the goldworkers and sculptors. Around 2500 B.C., the Sumerians were conquered by a northern Semitic people, the Akkadians, whose art was more vibrant and biting in pattern (*Fig. 1*). In time, however, the Sumerian culture absorbed these invaders, and a second great Sumerian age dawned, with gentle priest-kings like Gudea (*Fig. 4*), and the long-remembered lawmaker, Hammurabi. It was in this age that Abraham went forth from Ur to found the tribe of Israel. The Israelites always remembered the "brazen bulls" of Ur with distaste, and later tried to stamp out animal worship and animal art.

MESOPOTAMIA

After about 3500 B.C., many great civilizations succeeded each other upon the fertile plains of Mesopotamia. Each produced an art somewhat influenced by the style of nearby Egypt, although it was more varied and experimental. Unlike isolated, long-enduring Egypt, Mesopotamia had no strong religious faith in an afterlife, nor in the divine power of long dynasties of kings; rather, the people believed in various animal gods, human god-heroes, and in curious superstitions based on the stars and sorcery.

The Mesopotamians had little stone, so they built in sun-dried brick. They invented the arch and the dome, two architectural devices that influenced most later building throughout the world. Since they lacked granite or marble, they turned to bronze, gold, and silver, and excelled at small, brittle carvings in ivory and bone. In the Mesopotamian melting pot of many peoples, languages, religions, and art styles, much of Western civilization was born.

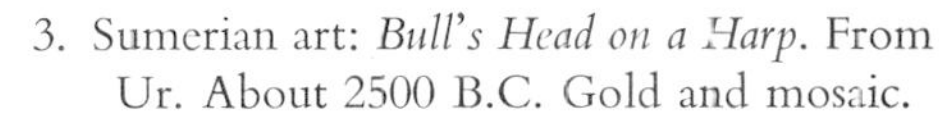

3. Sumerian art: *Bull's Head on a Harp.* From Ur. About 2500 B.C. Gold and mosaic.

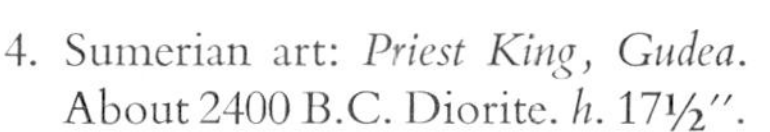

4. Sumerian art: *Priest King, Gudea.* About 2400 B.C. Diorite. *h.* 17½″.

The ancient Mesopotamians made tiny cylindrical seals of ivory or bone, carved with mythological figures like the horned bull-man conquering a lion (*Fig. 5 below*).

5. Akkadian sculpture: *Cylinder Seal.* About 2300 B.C. *diam.* 1.04″, *h.* 1.1″.

In the 10th century B.C., Sumeria fell to the Assyrians, a warlike people from the north. The Assyrians worshiped a fierce sun-god, Ashur. For sport, they hunted lions with bows and arrows. The Assyrians built great cities, like Nimrud and Nineveh, and lined the walls of their palaces with huge stone reliefs. These depicted their kings hunting and at war, and showed processions of grim, winged monsters, whose feathers, beards, robes, and muscles were fashioned into patterns somewhat like the less violent Akkadian sculptures. The Assyrians excelled all their neighbors in carving the free, wild action of animals. Perhaps their love of sport and the hunt sharpened their eyes, and made them as bold with a chisel as with a sword.

2. Assyrian sculpture: *Assurnasirpal II Storming a City*. Relief from Palace at Nimrud. 883–859 B.C. *h.* 3′2″, *w.* 7′1″.

3. Assyrian sculpture: *Guardian Bull*, gate of Palace of Assurnasirpal II. Nimrud. 883–859 B.C. Alabaster. *h.* 10′3½″.

4. Assyrian sculpture: *Winged Diety from Nimrud*. 883–859 B.C.

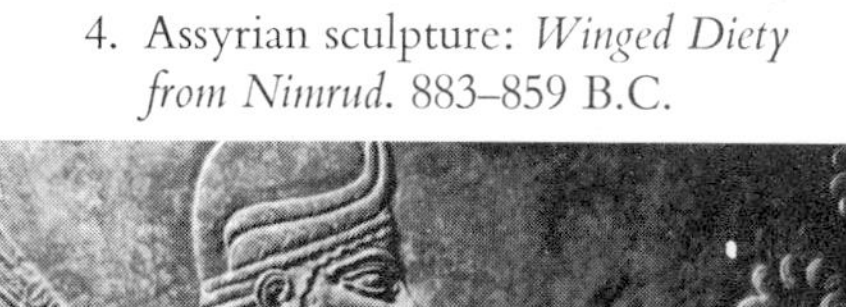

1. Assyrian sculpture: *Assurnasirpal II*. 883–859 B.C. Amber. *h.* 9½″.

6. Assyrian sculpture: *King Assurbanipal Hunting Lions.* Relief from Palace at Nineveh. 668–630 B.C. Alabaster. *h.* 21″.

In the 8th century B.C., the Assyrian civilization began to decline, and a new empire arose. The new capital became Babylon, rebuilt in the 6th century B.C. by Nebuchadnezzar. The chief religious deity of the Babylonians was Ishtar, the goddess of love. The city gate, dedicated to her, is shown at right, with a detail, below. It is covered with turquoise blue tile and adorned with golden lions and griffins. Far behind the gate rose a great temple-tower, the "Tower of Babel" of the Old Testament. Like all the temples in flood-prone Mesopotamia, it was built high upon a stepped-up brick platform called a "ziggurat."

Babylon was a very luxurious and cosmopolitan city. From its arched balconies tumbled the vines and flowers of the famous Hanging Gardens, fed from the River Euphrates by an extraordinary system of water wheels.

It was in this setting that the Hebrew prophets, imprisoned in exile, composed their lamentations. Into their writings crept descriptions of the animal carvings they saw all about them. From these writings, now found in the Book of Isaiah, later Christian artists took motifs for the animal signs of the Evangelists.

7. Babylonian construction: *Ishtar Gate.* 6th century B.C. (Reconstruction).

5. Babylonian sculpture: *Lion* from the Gate of the goddess Ishtar. 6th century B.C. 3′6″ by 7′6″.

1. Persian architecture and sculpture: *Audience Hall, the Great Stairs and Temple Platform*. Persepolis.

3. *Persepolis:* Detail of 1.

2. *Persepolis:* Detail of 1.

4. *Persepolis:* Detail of 1.

In 539 B.C., Babylon in turn fell to the Persian King Cyrus. Cyrus' successors, the Kings Darius and Xerxes, built the great city of Persepolis, the ruins of which are among the best preserved in Iran today. These are some of the carved scenes and details which surrounded the great hall: sacred processions, robed shepherds and kings, merchants and farmers, bearing gifts of grain, deer, gold, and other riches. The sculptors and architects of Persepolis had surely seen the art of Greece, which was now entering its greatest period, for the figures of these reliefs are Greek in both spirit and style, carved with an easy grace seldom achieved by other Mesopotamian artists. The columns which once rose from this platform are Greek in their slender proportion, although their capitals were not patterned after plants or trees, but were instead the figures of rams set back to back. Greek culture was soon to sweep over all of Mesopotamia. In 480 B.C., the Greeks conquered King Xerxes; a century and a half later, the Greece-loving Alexander the Great bore Hellenic culture all the way East, even as far as the borders of India.

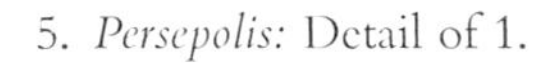

5. *Persepolis:* Detail of 1.

6. *Persepolis:* Detail of 1.

7. *The Ruins of Persepolis today.*

In the 3rd century A.D., another Persian civilization arose, and throwing off the influence of Greece and Rome, it revived the old Persian religion and arts. The Sassanian Persians, like their ancestors in Persepolis, were brilliant artists, and their inventions and styles spread throughout the Western world. In their capital city, Ctesiphon, the Sassanians built the soaring, arched palace (*Fig. 6*), from which the architects of the later empire of Byzantium took inspiration for their own domed buildings.

It was through their silverwork and textiles that the Sassanians exerted their strongest artistic influence over later civilizations. The Byzantine and Islamic empires were affected most directly, but, eventually—through the Renaissance and Baroque craftsmen of Italy—all Europe was influenced by Sassanian techniques and designs. One pattern which Sassanian textile designers used, a double figure inside a round medallion (*Fig. 7*), is still employed today on many satins and brocades of great elegance.

1. Luristan style: *Luristan Horse-bit Plates.* One of a pair in the form of a human-headed winged bull. About 1200 B.C. Bronze.

3. Achaemenid Persian style: *Gold Plaque.* 8th century B.C. *h.* 4″, *w.* 6⅛″.

4. Modern Persian style: *Flag of Iran Showing Lion Motif.*

2. Achaemenid Persian style: *Lion Roundel.* 6th–5th centuries B.C. Gold.

5. Achaemenid Persian style: *Ibex Head.* 6th–5th centuries B.C. Bronze. *h.* 13⅜″, *w. at horns* 9″.

6. Sassanian Persian style: *Palace at Ctesiphon*. 3rd century A.D.

7. Sassanian Persian style: *Silk textile*. Early 7th century A.D.

While the architecture and sculpture of Persepolis was inspired by Greece, the metalwork of Persia traced its style to a different source: the workmanship of the free-roaming steppe peoples of Russia, and Luristan, in Persia. These nomadic people made their battle costumes and trappings for their horses in the shape of elegant, prancing animals or imaginary, winged beasts (*Fig. 1*). Persian artists perfected the techniques of metal casting, and turned out marvelous objects in silver, gold, and bronze (*Figs. 2, 3, 5, 8*). But however sophisticated their techniques, they always preferred the ancient images of the steppes: flying and winged beasts and prancing horses. The style spread through the Near East and even in late Roman times produced such masterpieces as the rearing horse below (*Fig. 9*). Such images are alive even today: the modern flag of Iran bears a winged lion (*Fig. 4*).

8. Sassanian Persian style: *Silver Plate with a Hunting Scene*. 488–532 A.D. Repoussé in parcel gilt.

9. Roman Persian style: *Bronze Horse*. Yemen, Saudi Arabia. 5th–6th centuries A.D.

THE CLASSICAL WORLD

GREECE

In Greece, the Western taste for realism or "naturalism" in art was born. Beginning close in feeling and form to the rigid styles of Egypt and Mesopotamia, Greek statues and paintings gradually became more natural and active as the artists, no longer employed only by the priests, began to share in the great intellectual exploration then beginning in Athens. The Greek artists must have studied anatomy, physics, and optics, as well as the techniques of carving, painting, building, gold-working, and ceramics. They learned the Homeric myths and the more ancient, compelling nature myths of the Aegean world. When they began to make images of their gods, they gave them the most perfect human forms they could imagine and create, as lithe and controlled as an athlete, as grave and contained as an Athenian girl. This same spirit of gravity, control, and naturalness infused the Greek art of architecture as well.

In the 6th century B.C. Greece was ruled by a succession of dictators, and in later times by groups of citizens, so there was no call for splendid, monumental palaces or sumptuous temple enclosures for royalty. Instead, the Greeks built isolated temples and public buildings, according to the simplest of all architectural forms, the post and lintel, which had originated in Egypt but was refined to its greatest beauty in Greece. Flexible, but strictly controlled in ornament and proportions, Greek architecture, like its sculpture, became a touchstone for Western styles ever afterward.

The Cycladic idol, below, was made over a thousand years before the Classical flute player, below. Yet in the simple crossing of its arms, and slight tilting of its face, it seems to foreshadow the feeling of the Classic style.

3. *Idol of a Woman.* Cycladic period, about 3000 B.C. Marble. *h.* 13½″.

2. *Flute Player.* Side panel from Ludovisian Throne. Classic period, about 460 B.C. Marble.

Clear-browed and reflective, and once painted in lifelike colors, the figure at left is a masterpiece of Greek style. It stood on the Acropolis, in honor of Athena, goddess of wisdom.

1. *Standing Girl.* Archaic period, about 530 B.C. Found on the Acropolis. Painted marble. *h.* 3′.

The Minoan palace in Cnossos, chief city of ancient Crete, was constructed of heavy columns and gaily painted stone walls. There probably was a brisk sea trade between the Nile ports and the rock-ringed coves of Crete.

2. Cretan style: *Interior of Palace of Cnossos.* Crete. (Restored.)

Greek civilization rose out of the ruins of two great earlier civilizations in the Aegean world. One flourished around 2000 B.C. in Cnossos on the island of Crete, off the southern tip of the Greek mainland. About 1500 B.C., when the Egyptian Empire was also at its height, Cretan power passed to the mainland city of Mycenae. Four centuries later, both these civilizations fell before invaders from the north, the Dorians, who ushered in Greece's Dark Ages. All during these unsettled centuries, the story-loving Dorians embroidered and handed down myths and legends, based on half-remembered details of earlier civilizations. Written down by Homer, the great Greek poet of the 8th century B.C., these tales became the Greek myths which have been taught to children of every Western land. However, for centuries the West believed, as Classical Athens did, that the cities of King Minos and Agamemnon were only legendary. It was not until our own century that archaeologists uncovered these astonishing ruins, bringing to light the walls, statues, and paintings shown on these pages.

The Aegean peoples worshiped many fertility gods who watched over the fields and crops and the changing seasons. In Crete, the main deity was the Snake Goddess. During the Classical Greek age, this kind of nature worship gave way to the human-like gods of Olympus. Later, however, when Athenian rule collapsed, many people returned to the worship of the ancient and cruel fertility gods.

1. Cretan style: *Minoan Snake Goddess.* 1500 B.C. Ivory and gold. *h.* 9″.

The Cretans exported olive oil and wine to the entire Mediterranean world in gaily decorated pots like the octopus jar, below.

3. Cretan style: *Octopus Vase.*

4. *Young Prince*. Crete. Restored fresco.

6. Cretan toy: *Girl in Swing*. Found near Phaestos. 1550–1400 (?) B.C.

7. Cretan painting: *Bull Dancers*. Palace at Cnossos. About 1500 B.C. Fresco. *w*. 5′3″, *h*. 24″.

Judging from their arts, the Cretans were a gay and playful people. Swings and toys were made for their children (*Fig. 6*), and one of the central religious rituals was a kind of bull fight, in which nimble dancers teased the bull by leaping over its horns. The elegant, slim-waisted youths in these paintings (*Figs. 4, 7*) obviously belong to a different world from the Egyptians and Mesopotamians.

5. Mycenaean style: *Funerary Mask*. Gold. 1600–1500 B.C. *h*. 10½″.

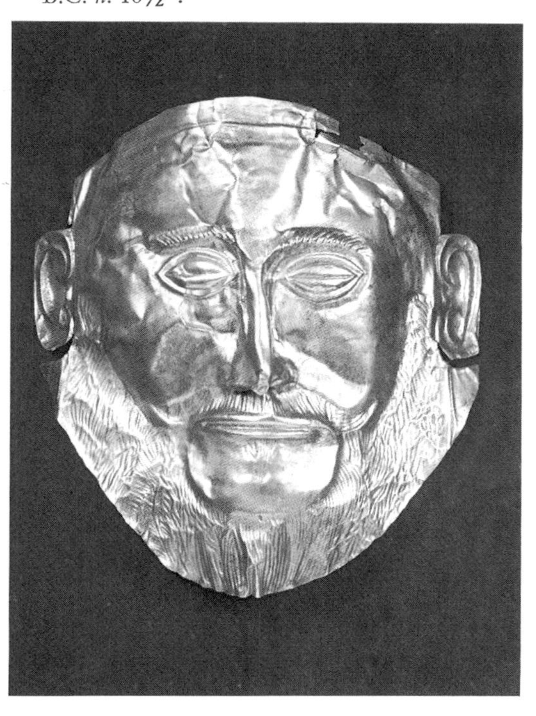

Mycenaean arts were less playful and more adapted to warfare or honoring the dead. Mycenaean cities were ringed with great stone walls: over this gateway (*Fig. 8*), two rearing lions were carved, symbolic of Mycenaean power. Kings and heroes were buried in underground tombs, built with domed crypts and arched passageways. The gold mask (*Fig. 5*) was laid over the dead face of one of Agamemnon's countrymen.

8. Mycenaean architecture: *Lion Gate*. 1350–1300 B.C.

1. Pre-Greek style: *Head of a Griffin*. Found at Olympia. About 650 B.C. Bronze. *h.* 11½″.

2. "Geometric Style": *Colossal Vase of Terra Cotta,* showing the lying-in-state of the dead and the funeral procession. 8th century B.C. *h.* 42⅝″.

4. Archaic style: *Drinking Cup with "Dionysus Sailing over the Sea."* By Exekias. 550–525 B.C. *diam.* 12″.

3. Archaic style: *Rider's Head* ("*Rampin Head*"). About 560 B.C. Marble. *h.* 11½″.

The Dark Ages wiped out all memory of Cretan and Mycenaean art, and when the new Greek world began to form in the late 9th century B.C., artists had to gradually rediscover the old artistic freedoms. On the huge, 4-foot-high vase shown above (*Fig. 2*), every detail of the funeral procession is clipped off to fit into a stiff pattern, as in the designs on Neolithic pottery. The great bronze griffin (*Fig. 1*), which adorned the handle of a ritual vessel, takes its extraordinary design from some Oriental model. Early in the 6th century B.C., artists evolved a style now called "Archaic," which was a step toward naturalism but was still based on stiff geometry. Geometric patterns still controlled the brush of the great Greek vase-painter, Exekias, and the chisel which shaped the marble head at left (*Fig. 3*). Tight curls, like those seen on Mesopotamian carvings, frame the triangular eyes, and the mouth is drawn up tensely into an expression called the "Archaic smile."

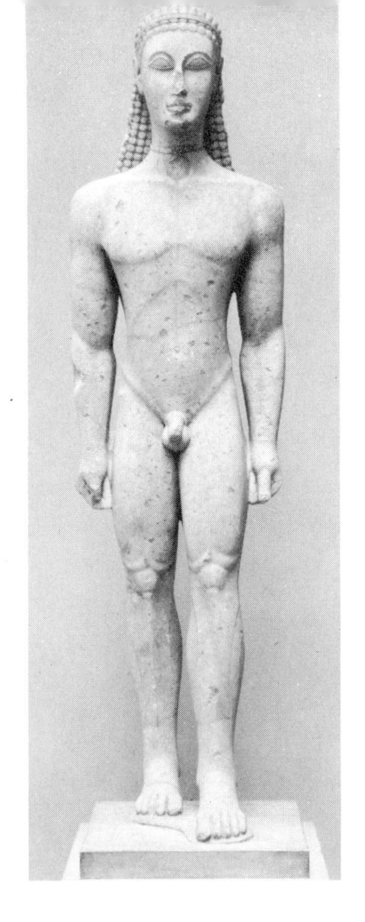

5. Archaic style: *Youth of Apollo "Type."* Found in Attica. 615–600 B.C. Marble. *h.* 6′1″.

6. Archaic style: *Goddess with Pomegranate.* Found in Keratea, Attica. Early 6th century B.C. Marble. *h.* 6′5¼″.

Geometry also ruled the representation of human bodies during the Archaic period. Perhaps the first standing statues in Greece were made from tree trunks, and had to be made straight and stiff; or perhaps these first figures were copied from Egyptian models. But bit by bit, the sculptor learned to divide the human body into geometric areas, to show how clothing falls in geometric patterns, and how even the bent body of an archer falls into an almost square pattern. Coincidently, during these very years, the mathematician Pythagoras was drawing figures in the sand, proving that the harmony of the whole universe is based upon geometry.

The sculpture on the Archaic temple below is fitted stiffly into place in the pediment and along the frieze. The same sculptured plan was used on later temples, but the figures were placed with greater freedom.

7. Archaic style: *Treasury of the Athenians.* Delphi. About 515 B.C. (Reconstruction.)

8. Early Classic style: *Hercules as an Archer* from the temple of Aphaia on Aegina. About 480 B.C. Marble. *h.* 2′6″.

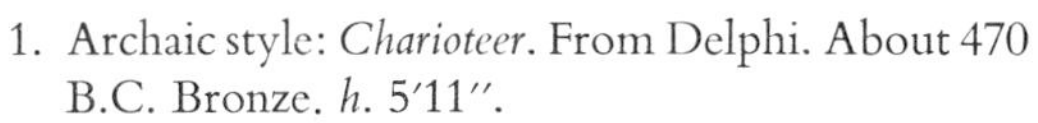
1. Archaic style: *Charioteer*. From Delphi. About 470 B.C. Bronze. *h.* 5′11″.

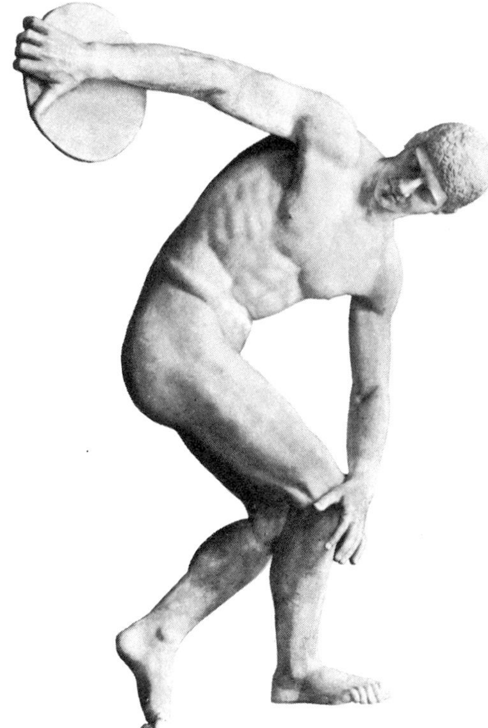

2. Early Classic style: Myron: *Discus Thrower*. About 450 B.C. A copy of the bronze original.

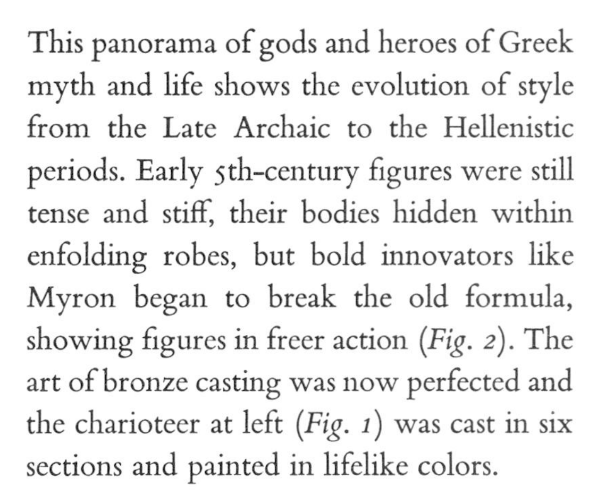
This panorama of gods and heroes of Greek myth and life shows the evolution of style from the Late Archaic to the Hellenistic periods. Early 5th-century figures were still tense and stiff, their bodies hidden within enfolding robes, but bold innovators like Myron began to break the old formula, showing figures in freer action (*Fig. 2*). The art of bronze casting was now perfected and the charioteer at left (*Fig. 1*) was cast in six sections and painted in lifelike colors.

4. Classic: *Dionysus*. East Pediment of the Parthenon, Athens. About 435 B.C. Marble. *h.* 4′2½″.

3. Archaic: *Enthroned Goddess*. From Taranto. About 480 B.C. Marble. *h.* 5′.

"Classical" Greek style is represented at its height in the sculptures of the Parthenon (*Figs. 4, 5*). In 483 B.C., Greece had defeated the invading armies of Persia; soon after, the brilliant Athenian leader Pericles commissioned his sculptor-friend Phidias to carve a series of figures of the gods in their most heroic and splendid postures. After three centuries of experiment, Greek sculptors had mastered all points of human anatomy and proportion. Now they set out to create perfect forms.

6. Post-Classic: Praxiteles: *Hermes with the Infant Dionysus*. About 340 B.C. Marble. *h.* 7′.

The Age of Pericles, however, was short-lived. Within sixty years, Pericles was dead, and Athens was defeated by Sparta. Now, philosophers, poets, and artists turned inward, to a mood of meditation. Praxiteles was a master of the new style of sculpture which reflected the changing spirit: a mist seemed to surround his sculptures, and others of the time (*Figs. 6, 7*). Their bodies appear soft-skinned and pliable; their contours undulate like sea currents. They stand slightly off-balance, perhaps leaning against a tree stump for support. Hermes and Venus are not the energetic young heroes and heroines of Olympus, but are dreamy and mysterious. They are revived forms of the ancient nature gods of the Aegean civilization.

5. Classic: *Three Fates (Demeter, Persephone and Artemis?)*. East Pediment of Parthenon. 447–432 B.C. Marble.

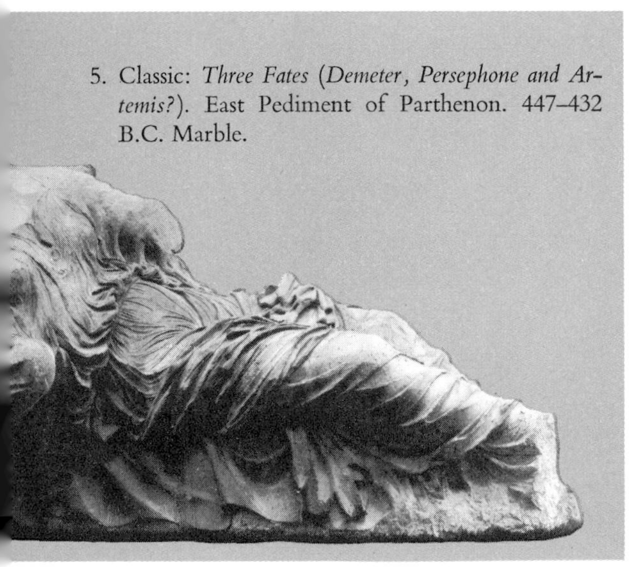

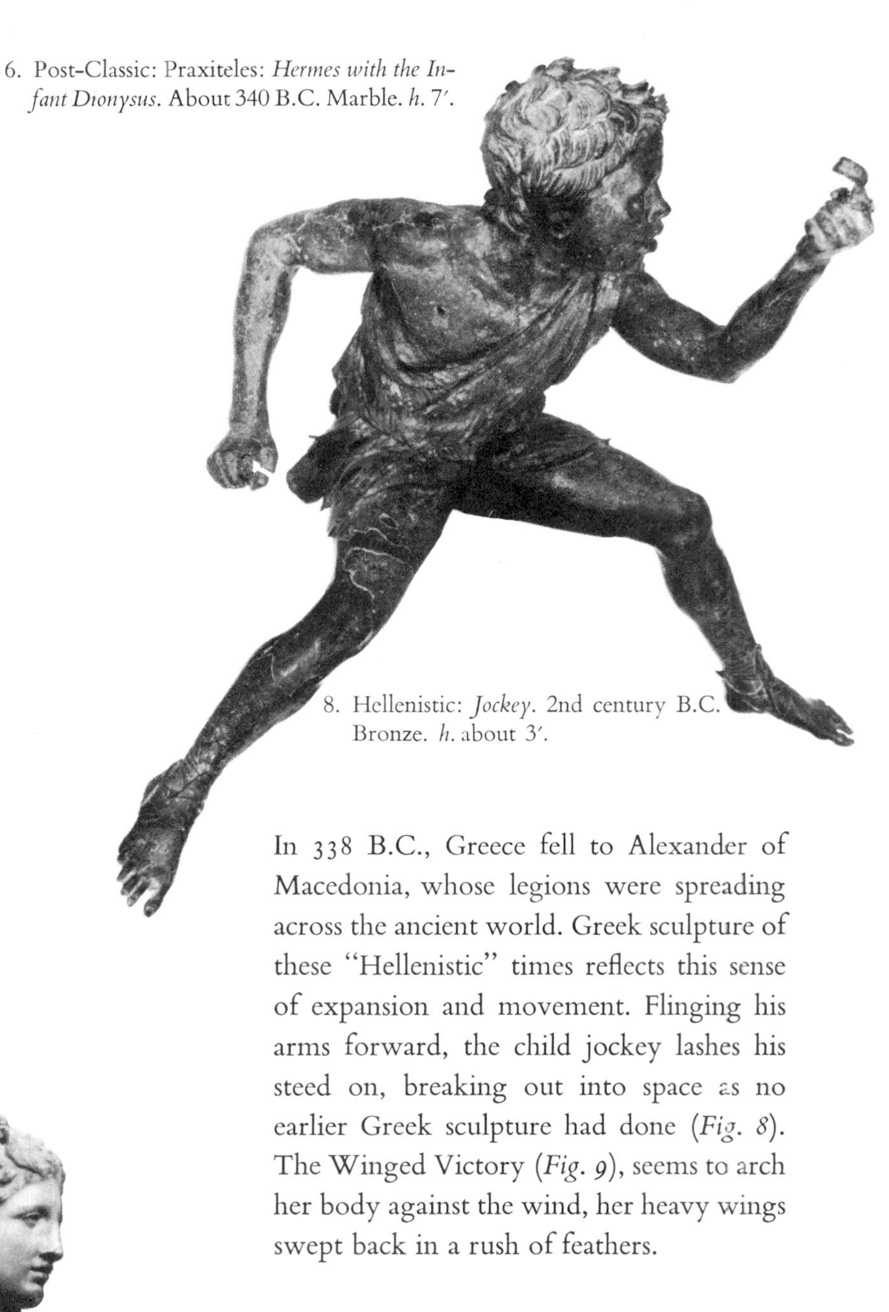

8. Hellenistic: *Jockey*. 2nd century B.C. Bronze. *h.* about 3′.

In 338 B.C., Greece fell to Alexander of Macedonia, whose legions were spreading across the ancient world. Greek sculpture of these "Hellenistic" times reflects this sense of expansion and movement. Flinging his arms forward, the child jockey lashes his steed on, breaking out into space as no earlier Greek sculpture had done (*Fig. 8*). The Winged Victory (*Fig. 9*), seems to arch her body against the wind, her heavy wings swept back in a rush of feathers.

7. Post-Classic: *The "Medici" Venus*, by a follower of Praxiteles. About 300 B.C. Marble.

9. *Winged Victory*. Samothrace. Early 2nd century B.C. Marble.

1. Classic architecture styles: *The Parthenon*. Acropolis, Athens. 447–432 B.C.

The Acropolis, the upper, fortified part of Athens, was built on a flat-topped hill rising steeply within the city. Covered with temples, it was the city sanctuary and the scene of religious festivals and processions. There, the Archaic figures of Athenian maidens and youths stood until the Persians, under Xerxes, ground them into the earth. There, Pericles ordered the building of the Parthenon after the enemy had been vanquished. The Greek temple was, in a sense, the Egyptian temple turned inside out. Instead of ponderous, gloomy stone walls and pylons enclosing an inner court, Greek builders aligned their columns along the outside of the enclosed sanctuary, making a fringe through which the sunlight splashed.

The relationship of the column to the structure it bears was of first importance to Classic builders. The Parthenon, the greatest Classic temple, was ingeniously engineered to correct an optical illusion. Its columns were slightly distorted, swollen at the center and leaning inward, to correct what would have otherwise been an impression of deadness and topheavy imbalance.

Since the form of the human figure stood erect like a column, it was not surprising that an architect thought of making human bodies bear the lintel. The slightly bent bodies of these *caryatids,* or priestesses of Diana's temple, bear their burden with the same vitality found in the Parthenon columns (*Fig. 2*).

2. *Erechtheum, Caryatid Porch*. Acropolis, Athens. About 421–405 B.C.

Each Greek temple was designed in one of three architectural plans: the Doric, the Ionic, or, later, the Corinthian. These plans were called the "Orders." An Order consisted of the base, its column, and its capital, and the roof which it supported. In the Order, as in all Greek sculpture, the proportion of the parts determined the design. A thick Doric column, like those of the Parthenon, must bear a sturdy crossbeam divided up into simple alternating blocks of sculpture and blank stone. The taller, slimmer Ionic column carried a more delicate beam, carved with a molding, or strip of darts and ovals or leaves. The Doric capital ended in a sturdy, flat slab. The Ionic capital was a graceful double spiral, perhaps derived from the Egyptian lotus, the curl of the nautilus shell, or the horns of a ram. Most elegant of all was the Corinthian Order, invented around 420 B.C. in the rich merchant city of Corinth. Legends say that the inventor was a young bronzeworker who saw a wicker basket, overgrown with acanthus leaves, decorating the grave of a young girl. But this design, too, may actually have originated in Egypt, becoming more naturalistic as it passed into Greece. The Greek Orders were perfectly proportioned and so well suited to their purpose that they have inspired Western architects ever since.

3. *Temple of Athena Nike*, Acropolis, Athens. About 426 B.C.

4. *Olympieum*. Athens. 131 A.D.

1. Realism in Classic art: *Parthenon Frieze*. Detail of mounted procession. Acropolis, Athens. 447–432 B.C. Marble. *h.* 40″.

3. Realism in Classic art: *Silver Coin* from Syracuse, chariot on obverse, head on reverse. About 400 B.C. *diam.* 1½″.

The predominant direction of Western art has been toward a greater illusion of life within the static materials of art. In this respect, Western art differs from primitive and Oriental arts, which aim less for the illusion of reality, and more for a brilliant design or a poetic mood. Of course, the Western school of realism could develop only when artists had mastered their techniques and increased their knowledge of the physical world. They had to study anatomy and proportion, the laws of motion and perspective, optics, and other sciences. The works on these pages trace the progress of Greek artists from the height of the Classical style to the Hellenistic period. Sculptors gradually learned to suggest realistic space and anatomy, and a sense of individual personality.

4. Realism in Classic art: *Abduction of the Goddess Basile from the Underworld*. About 400 B.C. Marble relief.

2. *Battle Between Alexander and Darius*. Floor mosaic from the House of the Fawn, Pompeii. 4th century B.C. *l.* 17′.

5. Realism in Hellenistic art: *Battle of the Greeks and Amazons.* From the Mausoleum at Halicarnassus. About 350 B.C. Marble.

6. Realism in Hellenistic art: *Veiled and Masked Dancer.* About 200 B.C. *h.* 8¼″

7. Realism in Hellenistic art: *Old Market Woman.* 2nd century B.C. *h.* 4′5⅛″.

8. Realism in Hellenistic art: *Portrait Head of a Philosopher.* 3rd century B.C. Bronze. *h.* 11½″.

At other times, sculptors labored to copy every detail of the human body, unlovely, wrinkled, or staring with intensity. Such faces and figures as these, which were made in abundance in the late Hellenistic world, would not have appealed to the artists of Archaic or Classical Greece, who chose instead to represent the serene and beautiful forms of heroes and goddesses. Greek painters in the Hellenistic city of Alexandria carried their art to its climax. They learned to splash on colors with a loose wrist, with a quick stroke for the head, a speck of white for a glancing eye. This manner of painting gave an impression of swift, flickering action: we might call it "impressionistic." This style was carried to Rome, where it became the basis for a great school of copyists and original painters and workers in mosaic. The mosaic battle scene at left (*Fig. 2*) is a copy, made near Rome, of a lost Greek painting.

2. *Head of Helios.* Mid-2nd century B.C. Marble. *h.* 22″.

The creator of the Alexander mosaic (*p. 46, Fig. 2*), of which the work at left is a detail, used many of the same devices that sculptors did to suggest an illusion of deep space and vibrant personality. The young Alexander the Great is shown at left; at right is a masterpiece of late Greek sculpture. In each medium, the artist has brilliantly brought to life a figure with luminous eyes, tossed head, and streaming hair: a perfect image of youthful exultation.

1. *Head of Alexander.* Detail of page 46, fig. 2.

1. *Portrait Head of the Emperor Caracalla.* 3rd century A.D. Marble. *h.* 14¼″.

THE CLASSICAL WORLD

ROME

Roman artists were realists. In their statues and paintings they strived to reproduce the world around them as realistically as they could, and to give an illusion of life itself flickering in the stone wrinkles of a portrait bust or in the painted glint of an eye. On the other hand, Roman architecture was often consciously designed to reflect the power of the Empire, and to create in people an awe of this power. So, while Roman painting and sculpture traced its roots to Greece and the advanced technical inventions of the Hellenistic artists, her architecture went back beyond Athens to the towering brickwork arches, domes, and ramparts of Mesopotamia. This double heritage gave to all Roman art its curious mixture of the prosaic and the supernatural. Eventually, as the Empire collapsed, the awesome, supernatural kind of art prevailed, and ideals of naturalistic Classical art shriveled before the burning, otherworldly visions of the first Christians.

Romans built monuments like those shown at right wherever they went, so that distant peoples of the world could enjoy the same pleasures and bow before the same Imperial standards as men at home.

3. Roman architecture in France: *Pont du Gard.* Nimes. 27 B.C.–14 A.D. Total height, about 160′.

4. Roman architecture in Spain: *Arch of Bara.* Tarragona, Spain. Early 2nd century B.C.

2. *Roman Eagle.* End 1st century B.C. Onyx cameo.

Above every Roman citizen or slave loomed the idea of the Empire, symbolized by this arrogant eagle (*Fig. 2*), carved during the very years the early Republic was being reshaped by Augustus Caesar. One of his successors, the scowling Emperor Caracalla (*Fig. 1*), murdered hundreds of Romans, then built stupendous public baths to placate the angry mobs.

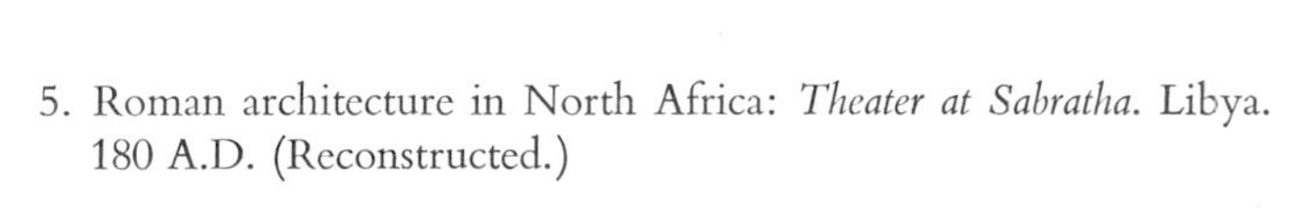

5. Roman architecture in North Africa: *Theater at Sabratha.* Libya. 180 A.D. (Reconstructed.)

Before the Romans conquered it, West Central Italy was occupied by the Etruscans. No one knows exactly where these people originally came from, but their arts seem to link them with a Mediterranean homeland. Like the Minoan and Mycenaean peoples, they became builders in stone, piling huge boulders together into walls and palaces, and constructing underground tombs. These tombs were painted with brightly colored birds and flowers and dancing youths, in freer postures and more realistic anatomical details than in Egyptian or Cretan paintings. The Etruscans excelled in bronze casting as well as in stone carving. The figures they made varied from the realistic to the ghostly. Traveling Greek artists certainly influenced Etruscan art, but more influential was a gloomy religious point of view, which appeared in monsters and death-goddesses more like those of Mesopotamia than of Athens.

1. Etruscan pottery: *Burial Urn.* About 600 B.C. Terra cotta. *h.* 32″.

As in Egypt, funeral arts were important in Etruria. Sometimes Etruscans put ashes of their dead in an urn like the one above (*Fig. 1*), surmounted by the Death Goddess. At other times the Etruscans used coffins decorated with life-size figures of the deceased, smiling like the Apollos and maids of the Archaic Greeks, and holding out a coin for the fare into the Underworld (*Fig. 2*).

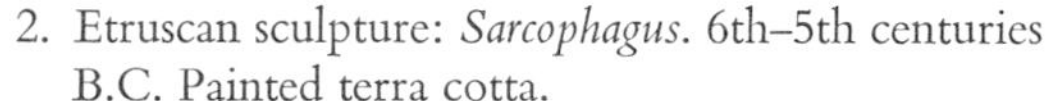

2. Etruscan sculpture: *Sarcophagus.* 6th–5th centuries B.C. Painted terra cotta.

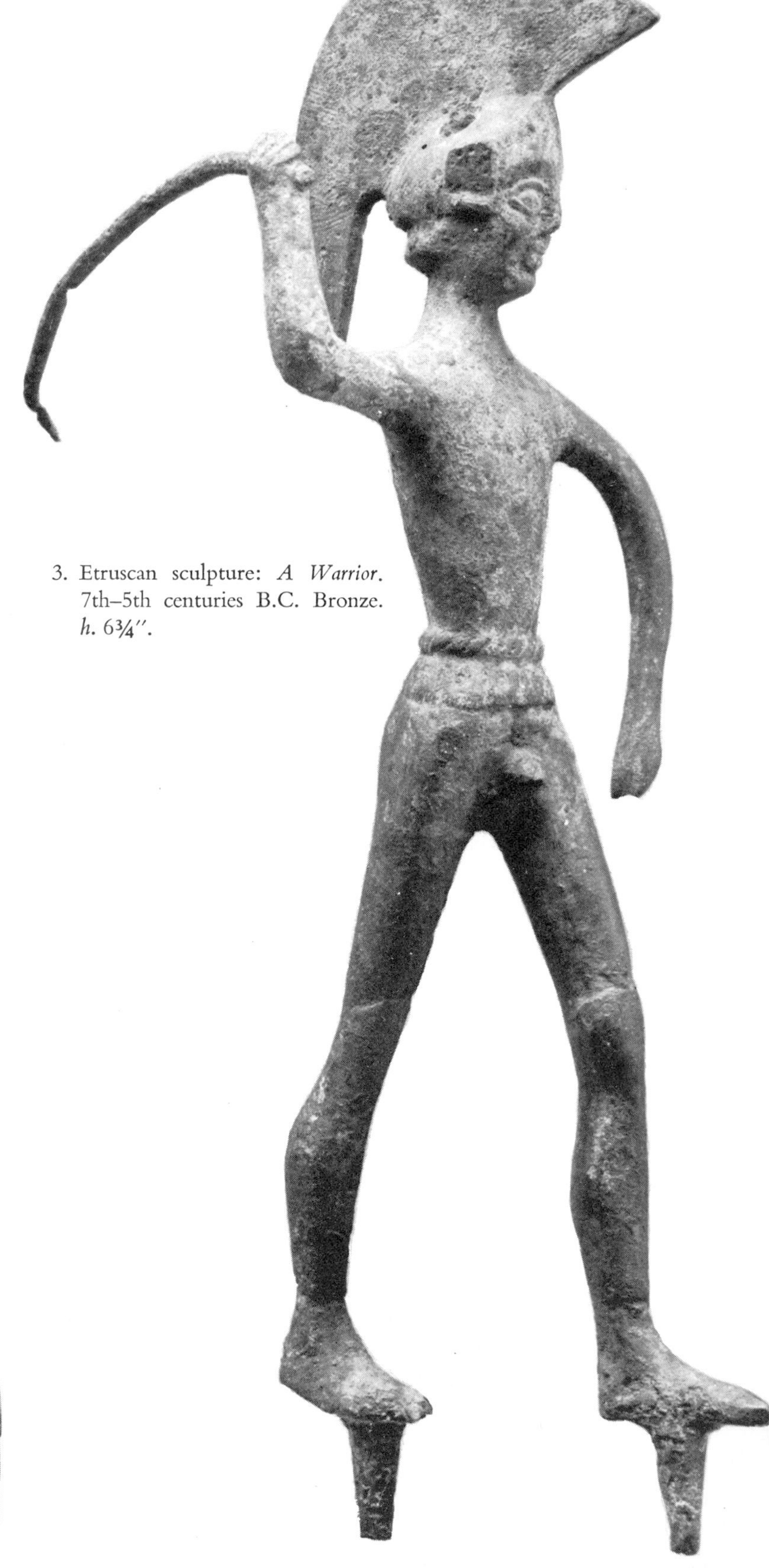

3. Etruscan sculpture: *A Warrior.* 7th–5th centuries B.C. Bronze. *h.* 6¾″.

4. Etruscan sculpture: *Two Wrestlers*. From the handle of a vessel cover. 4th–3rd centuries B.C. Bronze.

6. Etruscan sculpture: *Mother Goddess*. 5th century B.C. Stone.

Cast in bronze like the Hellenistic man on page 47, the Etruscan portrait below is even more realistic in its details and expression. Later, this kind of fascination with personality led Roman sculptors to found the world's first great style of portrait art. The Etruscan mother and child (*Fig. 6*), perhaps a goddess with her offspring, curiously foreshadows the Christian image of the Madonna, and in the very country which five centuries later would give birth to the great arts of Christianity.

5. Etruscan portraiture: *Capitoline Brutus*. 3rd century B.C. Bronze.

7. Etruscan painting: *Pipe-player and Birds*. From a tomb in Tarquini. About 475 B.C.

1. Roman portrait sculpture: *Julius Caesar*. 48–44 B.C. Marble.

2. *Emperors Claudius and Germanicus with their Wives*. Mid-1st century A.D. Onyx cameo.

The Republican Romans who drove back the Etruscans and laid the foundations for the Empire, portrayed themselves with no attempt to glamorize or idealize their faces. One of the most powerful of such sculptures was of Julius Caesar (*Fig. 1*), who explored and opened the northern lands of Gaul. Through this gateway, art and ideas were to flow freely in later centuries, linking the whole Western world to Italy.

3. *Portrait of Emperor Augustus*. Rome. About 10 B.C. Marble. *h.* 6′8″.

Julius Caesar's nephew brought to an end the civil wars which had wracked Rome since Caesar's assassination. The younger Caesar crowned himself with oak leaves, and called himself "Augustus," or "most high." Augustus loved Greece, and had carvings of himself made in the serene "Classical" fashion (*Fig. 3*), although Greek sculptors would not have shown him in armor. During his reign, some of Rome's greatest poetry, philosophy, and art was created. The luxury-loving emperors who followed Augustus commissioned many extravagant works of art. On the cameo above (*Fig. 2*), the two emperors and their wives are surrounded by cornucopias and a Roman eagle, symbols of the magnificent wealth and power of their reigns.

4. *Pendant with Portrait of a Consul*. 238–243 A.D. Gold.

5. *Equestrian Statue of Emperor Marcus Aurelius*. Rome. 161–180 A.D. Bronze.

The Greeks had made "equestrian" portraits, showing a figure astride a horse, but none of these have survived. This Roman one of the Emperor Marcus Aurelius stood untouched by Christians and barbarians throughout the Dark Ages, spared only because people thought it portrayed the first Christian Emperor, Constantine. Later, it came to be an inspiration to artists of the Italian Renaissance, and the equestrian statue became one of the most popular subjects of Western art. The portrait-pendant above, found in Egypt, near Alexandria, probably belonged to a consul or official.

6. *Colosseum.* Rome. 70–82 A.D.

8. *The Pantheon,* painted by Giovanni Paolo Panini about 1740.

7. Roman architectural styles: *Baths of Diocletian.* Rome.

9. *Arch of Constantine.* Rome. 312 A.D.

Imperial Rome had changed greatly from the early Republican days when Greek-style temples filled her forums. In order to dispel the rising discontent of the populace, the emperors erected huge buildings for public games, baths, and processions. They built these of gigantic arches of stone and cement, held in place by wooden scaffolds until the cement dried. Sometimes plain "barrel vaults" were built out of rows of arches set back to back to form a great tunnel; other times, the arch was closed over into a dome (*Fig. 8*), or two barrel vaults were set at right angles making a "groined vault" (*Fig. 7*) which could rise even higher. The rough building surfaces were covered with sheets of marble or bronze, and elaborate mosaic floors were laid. The old Greek Orders were still used, now sometimes laid flat against a wall as decoration instead of being used to hold up the structure, (*Fig. 9*).

1. Evolution of realism in Roman art: *Ara Pacis*. Rome. Frieze showing priest and the imperial family. 13–9 B.C.

2. *Arch of Titus*. Rome. Relief showing sack of Jerusalem. 81 A.D. Marble. *h.* 7′10″.

The artists of Rome, like those of Hellenistic Greece, continued to try to create an illusion of reality. In the days of Augustus, artists still worked in the Classical fashion; figures carved upon the great Peace altar which Augustus erected (*Fig. 1*) stand gracefully and serenely, gently shouldering each other. But a century later, the sculptor who carved the exploits of the Emperor Titus (*Fig. 2*) turned the stone into a flickering scene in which spears, trophies, and the great seven-branched candlestick stolen from the Temple in Jerusalem are carried on the shoulders of the rioting troops.

3. *Ulysses in the Land of the Lestrygonians*. 1st century B.C.

Romans continued the splendid style of painting invented in late Classical and Hellenistic Greece. Sometimes the artists let their imaginations run to games in paint. They covered entire walls with mazes and webs of slender columns and painted architecture as though, like modern interior decorators, they were trying to expand the room with these false arches (*Fig. 5*). Elsewhere, they used a solid, sculptural style to portray scenes of gods and heroes from their own and the Greek myths and legends (*Fig. 4*). Although they sometimes copied Greek originals of earlier date, the Romans too had mastered the technique of creating with flecks and daring streaks of paint, an illusion of deep, light-filled space and swift motion. Among the masterpieces left to us of this style of Roman painting are these fragments of a long series of scenes from "The Odyssey" (*Fig. 3 and pages 58–59*).

4. *Hercules Finding His Son Telephos.* From Herculaneum. 1st century A.D.

5. *Decorative Architecture with Dionysian Figure.* From Pompeii. Fresco.

1. *The Lost Rams.* Pompeii. Fresco.

2. *Idyllic Sacred Landscape,* from the "Odyssey" series of paintings. Pompeii. Fresco.

1. *Bust of Constantine*. 306–327 A.D. Marble.

3. Early Christian architecture: *The Original Basilica of St. Peter, Rome*. Grotto, Vatican. Fresco.

The dissolution of the Empire and the coming of Christianity radically changed Roman art. As the Empire had expanded, incorporating many Eastern Mediterranean peoples, various religious cults spread throughout the Classical world. Christianity gradually became the most popular of these, although for three centuries, official Rome held fast to her old Classical gods, and persecuted the Christians. Down in the catacombs—underground chambers beneath the city of Rome—the Christian survivors met to pray. There, they painted sketchy scenes upon the walls to illustrate their Gospel stories (*Fig. 4*). Finally, in the year 313, the Emperor Constantine made Christianity official, and the early Christians were allowed to build public places of worship. The plans of the first churches were based on the old Roman marketplace, a straight hall with side aisles and a wooden roof (*Fig. 3*). Often, Classical columns taken from ruined temples were used to hold up the side arches. The first great "basilica" was St. Peter's in Rome, torn down during the Renaissance to make room for the present building by Michelangelo. Until the barbarians destroyed their communities, similar basilicas were built throughout the whole Christian world and decorated with teaching-pictures in fresco, mosaic, and sculpture. The mosaic at left (*Fig. 2*) is from a church in Aquileia, on the northern coast of the Adriatic.

2. Early Christian mosaic style: *"Fishing for Marine Monsters,"* detail of mosaic pavement in the Basilica at Aquileia, Italy. 4th century A.D.

4. Early Christian painting: *Meeting of Christ and the Samaritan Woman at the Well*, from a catacomb, Rome. 4th century A.D.

5. Early Christian style in Egypt: *Coptic Tombstone*. 7th century A.D. Limestone. *h.* 2′8″.

8. Early Christian style in Egypt: *Coptic Textile*. 6th century A.D.

The art of early Christian Egypt, called "Coptic," greatly influenced later Christian art. These Egyptians inherited a love of flat patterns, of staring figures with large, dark-rimmed eyes (*Fig. 8*), and the ancient Egyptian taste for intertwined plant and animal decorations.

7. Early Christian sculpture: *Good Shepherd*. Marble.

With Christianity, a new attitude toward art spread westward. Even at the height of the Empire, throughout Egypt, Syria, and Asia Minor, sculpture had been made in crude, stumpy shapes which copied the details, but not the careful proportions of Classical art (*Fig. 6*). Eventually, this ungraceful, chunky style spread to Rome itself. The figures on the Arch of Constantine (*Fig. 9*) are almost as squat and rigid as the old Sumerian sculptures. Converts to Christianity, afire to express their new love of Christ, cared less for graceful form than they did for a clear, easily understood message. The *Good Shepherd* is one of the last Christian works of art made in the West, whose forms are correctly modeled (*Fig. 7*). At first, Christ was seen as a Classic youth. Later, in the 5th century, as more Near-Eastern disciples came west, Christ was pictured as a dark-bearded man with haunting eyes, like a shepherd of Syria.

6. "Debased" Roman style: Part of the *Gate of the Roman Forum*, Sabratha, Libya. 2nd century A.D.

9. "Debased" Roman style: *Arch of Constantine*, relief detail. Rome. 315 A.D.

This Empress is carved in Byzantine style: part Greek-Roman, part Oriental. Roman eagles and degenerated Corinthian columns flank her. Even though she holds an orb surmounted with the Christian cross to show that she ruled the Eastern Roman Empire, her jewels and her stiff, staring pose are Oriental.

1. *Byzantine Empress.* About 800 A.D. Ivory.

2. *Mausoleum of Galla Placidia.* Ravenna. 5th century A.D.

One of the last centers of Classical art in the crumbling West was Ravenna, an outpost of the Byzantine Empire. Many works of art were created there which bridge East and West. One such is a tomb decorated with mosaics (*Fig. 2*) showing Christ as a Greek shepherd among his flock.

THE EASTERN EMPIRE

BYZANTIUM

In Byzantium, two rivers of style, the Greek and the Oriental, flowed together. Constantinople, capital of the Byzantine Empire, was established in 330 by Emperor Constantine, and stood at the junction of East-West trade and pilgrimage routes. Byzantine art served the Eastern Christian church, always more resplendent than its Western counterpart. It also served the tastes of its Oriental emperors for brocades, silks, ivories, and painted manuscripts. Yet, in Constantinople, during the western Dark Ages, Greek standards of craftsmanship persisted, and many treasures of Classical art survived, and from time to time, filtered into the West. At other times, Byzantine art was overwhelmed by the Oriental taste for mystical impressions and bold, splendid pattern-art. In the 15th century, Byzantium fell to the Ottoman Turks, and her arts and artists were scattered to the West.

The Byzantine Empire reached its first peak of power in the 6th-century reign of Justinian. The great church in Constantinople, called Hagia Sophia, was his most splendid undertaking (*Fig. 3, 4*). The dome is lifted upon four "pendentives," or triangle-shaped corner pieces, visible in the photograph of the interior. These devices allowed the architects to lift the vast dome upon a square base of columns and arches, like the groined vault of the Romans. At one time the whole interior shimmered with mosaics. Captured by Moslem Turks in the 15th century, the church was turned into a mosque, and its splendid mosaics were painted out.

3. *Interior of Hagia Sophia.* Istanbul. 532–537 A.D.

4. *Hagia Sophia.* Istanbul. 532–537 A.D.

1. Classical influence in Byzantine art: *David the Musician.* Byzantine manuscript page by an Alexandrian artist working in Constantinople. Late 7th century A.D.

The works on these pages illustrate the two differing tendencies of Byzantine style: on page 64, the Greek-Roman, or Classical; on page 65, the Oriental. The brilliant style of painting which had been invented by Hellenistic artists and later transmitted to Rome, lived on in Byzantium, although it was now used for Christian subjects. The illustration at left for a Christian book of psalms might be a Classical scene of any shepherd boy among his animals. Objects of silver and ivory were made in the same style with gracefully proportioned figures in free action.

Works of art like these were carried into Western Europe from time to time and kept the Classical tradition alive there during the Dark Ages.

2. Classical influence in Byzantine art: *David Slaying the Lion.* Byzantine silver plate found in Cyprus. Early 7th century A.D. *diam.* 5½″.

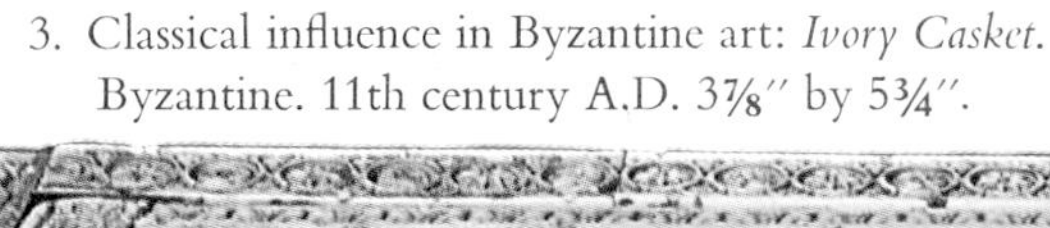

3. Classical influence in Byzantine art: *Ivory Casket.* Byzantine. 11th century A.D. 3⅞″ by 5¾″.

4. Oriental influence in Byzantine art: *Empress Theodora and her Suite.* Mosaic from San Vitale, Ravenna. 6th century A.D.

5. Oriental influence in Byzantine art: *Byzantine Christ.* From Djumati, Georgia. 11th century A.D. Cloisonné enamel on gold. *diam.* 3¼″.

During these same centuries, the Oriental tradition slowly began to infiltrate Byzantium. Craftsmen and artists who had learned their trade in the Near East brought their own style into the country. Only one century after Galla Placidia's tomb was decorated in Ravenna (page 63), the Emperor Justinian commissioned these mosaics showing his wife, himself, and their servants, for another church in the city (*Fig. 4*), *and pages 66–67*). Theodora was an Asian queen, with dark eyes and hair, and a haunted expression. She wears jewels like the ivory empress on page 62, and her servants are clothed in sumptuous brocades and silks. By the 11th century, Greek and Oriental styles seem to blend together in magnificent, towering images like this, which adorned the small and large churches of many lands, from Armenia to Italy.

6. Oriental influence in Byzantine art: *Virgin with Apostles.* Apse mosaic, Torcello Cathedral. Torcello, Italy. 11th century A.D.

1. *Empress Theodora* (detail of p. 65, fig. 4). San Vitale, Ravenna.

2. *Emperor Justinian.* Detail from mosaic in San Vitale, Ravenna. 6th century A.D.

Two centuries after Justinian, a controversy began among the Byzantine priests as to whether artists should be allowed to make any pictures of the Holy Family at all. One result of the argument was that a new importance came to be attached to such holy pictures. A painting of Christ or His family, or of angels and saints, done on a wood panel, was called an icon; it was intended to be revered, just as the cross on the altar was. Soon, artists began to decorate the icons with pure gold leaf or gold paint to indicate their preciousness. This style of painting spread east and west, to Russia, and into parts of Italy like Siena, where many artists of a particularly devout nature lived. In the painting below, made in an outpost of Byzantium, the artist was obviously more interested in making a precious object of gold paint and bright colors, almost like a jewel, than in showing realistic details and shapes. Since icons were often worshiped in dark, incense-filled churches, they were painted in bold, stark shapes and colors which could easily be seen.

2. Byzantine art in Russia: *St. George and the Dragon*. Icon. 16th century.

1. Byzantine art in Italy: *Enthroned Madonna and Child*. 13th century.

3. Native Russian tradition: *A Horse being Attacked by a Lion*. Scythian belt buckle. Gold.

4. Byzantine art in Russia: (Novgorod School): *St. George*. Icon. About 1400.

5. Byzantine art in Russia: *Old Testament Trinity*, by Andrei Rublev. About 1410.

Before Byzantine missionaries penetrated the North, the only art in Russia was made by nomadic tribes called the Scythians and Sarmatians. These brilliant metalworkers roamed the steppes between about 700 B.C. and 400 A.D. The influence of their art was felt by many great civilizations: China to the east; Greece and Persia to the south, and the barbarian Goths and Franks to the west.

In deep forests far from the Russian cities, there was little or no communication with the great art centers of the Mediterranean. In these rural communities, church builders made curious buildings like the one below (*Fig. 6*), of great timbers, rising to a cluster of fanciful, onion-shaped domes. Art in Russia remained practically unchanged until the 18th century, when Peter the Great urged his nobles to imitate the French culture that he loved.

This particular phase of Byzantine art influenced the arts of Russia. In the 10th century, King Vladimir I of Russia was baptized in the Christian faith by missionaries from Byzantium. Soon, churches were being built throughout Russia and filled with icons in the Byzantine style. The greatest master of this art was Rublev (*Fig. 5*); other icon painters seem to have been more influenced by an ancient, native style: the curling shapes achieved by Scythian metalworkers. Such figures are bent and twisted as though formed with tongs over hot flames (*Fig. 3*).

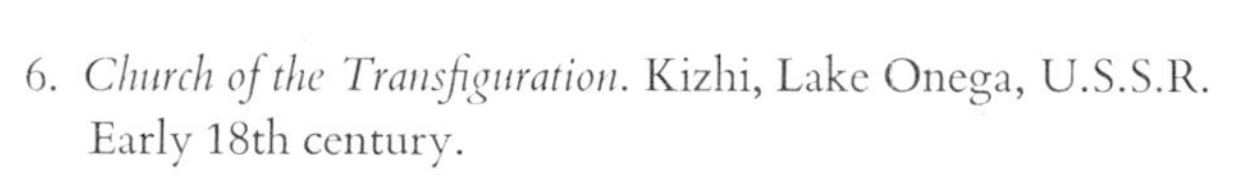

6. *Church of the Transfiguration.* Kizhi, Lake Onega, U.S.S.R. Early 18th century.

1. Islamic influence in Spain: *A Wall of the Alcazar*. Seville, Spain. 14th century. Tile and ceramic.

2. Islamic influence in Spain: *Interior of the Mosque*. Cordova, Spain. 8th–9th centuries.

THE ISLAMIC EMPIRE

The Islamic Empire, which at its height extended from Persia and Mesopotamia to North Africa and Spain, was established in the 7th century by the Arabian prophet Mohammed. This vast empire was, with Byzantium, a treasure house of artistic knowledge and craftsmanship during the western Dark Ages. The Arabs loved both the bright designs of ancient Sumeria and the flowing, twining lines of Greek and Coptic Egyptian art, and they combined these elegant "arabesques" or lacelike ornamentations with sharp contrasts of color and shadow. But Mohammed, like the Hebrew prophet Moses some 1,500 years earlier, had forbidden the making of images, so early Islamic religion gave rise to no figurative art. Instead, the Islamic artists became great builders and decorators. European Crusaders took home many Islamic architectural ideas—the horseshoe and pointed arches, pierced battlements and ornate brickwork—which later found their way into Gothic and Renaissance structures. By the 15th century Mohammed's taboo against portraying human images was finally overcome, and a great school of manuscript painting was born. Eventually, brought West by travelers from the Dutch East Indies to Holland, these miniature Islamic paintings caught the eye of artists like Vermeer and Rembrandt, and thus added another facet to modern Western art. Although the Islamic Empire is alive today, its once high standards of craftsmanship have been lost.

3. Islamic influence in India: *Taj Mahal*. Agra, India. 1630–1650.

4. Islamic influence in India: *Kutub Minaret*. Delhi. 1200 A.D.

5. Islamic influence in the Near East: *The Minaret of Samarra Mosque*. Baghdad. 9th century.

The major Islamic buildings were mosques and minaret towers for worship, palaces for the sultans, and battlements. The dome and the arch were favorite architectural devices, and ornament was used lavishly, according to the spirit of the different countries. For instance, the Spanish Moslems built the somber mosque in Cordova (*Fig. 2*), while the Mogul, or Indian Moslems preferred the lacy bubble-forms of the Taj Mahal (*Fig. 3*).

In Spain, the Islamic invaders were called Moors. The battlement below (*Fig. 6*) is in typical Moorish style, with horseshoe arches and brickwork which often were copied by Christian Spaniards, and later adapted in some buildings in France.

6. Islamic influence in Spain: *The Puerta del Sol*. Toledo, Spain. 1200 A.D.

Islamic art flowered in Persia under the patronage of the sultans of Baghdad, who were among the greatest connoisseurs of art and learning in the world. At first, art styles were borrowed from the Sassanian Persians, whose brilliant culture the Islamic artists had absorbed. Later, they made illustrations for scientific treatises and books of legends (*Figs. 1, 5*). By the 16th century, the Islamic style of book illustration reached its height and was carried into India when Islamic forces captured part of that country. Such manuscript pages showed patterns as bold and brilliant as those of a Persian carpet. These artists did not care to imitate reality. When they drew a group of figures, they did not set them one behind another in receding perspective. Instead, they set elegantly drawn images just as a mosaicist might set his stones into a pattern. Still, these pictures give a fascinating view of life in the sumptuous Persian and Indian courts, hung with rugs, filled with tulips and lilacs, peopled with deer-eyed dancers and polo-playing princes. In these courts, the Arabian Nights were lived and Omar Khayyam wrote his melancholy poems. Baghdad was captured in the 13th century by the brother of Kublai Khan, ruler of China; it grew more and more Oriental in spirit and finally was replaced, in the 15th century, by Samarkand, another capital city even nearer China.

1. Islamic influence in the Near East (Persia): *A Physician Preparing Medicine*. Baghdad School, about 1520.

2. Islamic influence in the Near East (Persia): *Jonah and the Whale*. Mongol Period, Tabriz School. End 14th century.

3. Islamic influence in the Near East (Persia): *Persian Textile*. Buyid Period. 998 A.D.

4. Islamic influence in the Near East (Persia): *Tile Medallion*. Damghan. 1263 A.D.

5. Islamic influence in the Near East (Persia): *Garden Scene*. Period of Shah Tahmasp, School of Sultan Muhammed. 16th century.

6. Islamic influence in India: *Portrait of Shah Jahan on Horseback*. Indian album leaf. Mughal, 17th century.

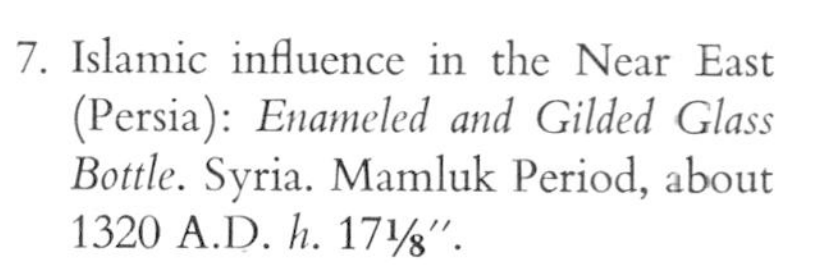

7. Islamic influence in the Near East (Persia): *Enameled and Gilded Glass Bottle*. Syria. Mamluk Period, about 1320 A.D. *h.* 17⅛″.

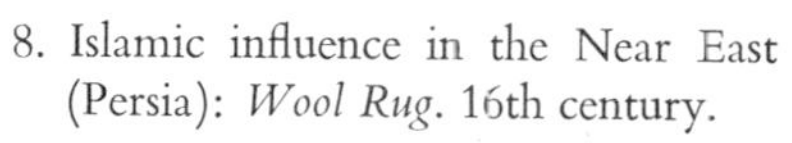

8. Islamic influence in the Near East (Persia): *Wool Rug*. 16th century.

9. Islamic influence in the Near East (Persia): *Horseman Leading a Mongolian Captive*. Detail from silk brocade. Safavid Period, second half of 16th century.

2. Islamic influence in the Near East (Persia): *Gushtasp Slays a Wolf.* 1605–1608.

1. Islamic influence in the Near East (Persia): *A Polo Game.* School of Bokhara. From manuscript of the Bustan by Sa'di, 1522–3(?).

INDIA AND INDONESIA

As Greece was the wellspring of naturalistic Western art, so India was the birthplace of many Oriental art styles. Like the devout Christian painters of the Middle Ages, Oriental artists were mainly concerned with representing the unseen world of gods and supernatural forces. Often they cared less for realistic representations of anatomy and proportion than they did for the feelings of awe, terror, or reverence that their art could produce. Indian art tells the stories of two religious systems: the Hindu religion, which developed first, and to which India later returned, and the Buddhist religion, born in the 6th century B.C. in the preachings of Gautama Buddha, a simple prince from a small Himalayan village. Buddhist thought, sculpture, and painting spread eastward across the caravan trails of the Gobi Desert into China, and from there into Japan. India itself, however, slowly returned to the more complicated Hindu religion, which was based on a vision of the world as a vast dream called "Maya." In this dream all created things appeared to pour forth like swift rivers, to swirl across the earth, and then vanish into eternal darkness. It was this endless motion and change in the Maya world, set against the eternal natural forces, that Hindu art sought to portray.

The three main Hindu gods were Brahma the father, Vishnu, and Shiva. Each of these gods appeared in many shapes, both animal and human. Vishnu, for instance, sometimes was carved and painted as a boar or a lion, or as a human hero called Krishna. Sometimes he was the river Ganges, sometimes the glorious Sun God on a jewel-decked horse (opposite). In Hindu art, also, spirits of the air and the waters abounded, left over from prehistoric nature worship.

These are three of the steps which were taken in developing the image of Buddha, which spread gradually throughout the Orient. In the beginning, Buddha was considered too holy to be carved as a man. So the first Buddhist sculptors chose simple animal forms such as the lion or the bull, which suggested Buddha's strength and majesty.

3. *Asokan Bull Capital.* From Rampurna (Bihar). 3rd century B.C.

In the 2nd century, Buddhist sculptors began to make images of Buddha in a style similar to Roman sculptures. Buddha was thought to have had certain curious physical characteristics: he had a third eye, of wisdom, between his brows; his head rose up in a lump of knowledge on top, and his earlobes were very long (*Fig. 4*).

4. *Head of Buddha.* From Gandhara. 4th–5th centuries.

In the 5th century, the Gupta dynasty of kings began to rule India. They were proud of India's native art style, and under their rule, Indian sculptors began to carve figures of a more Oriental nature, with surfaces taut and glistening. But at the same time, the old Hindu religion was regaining popularity in India. The gentle Gupta Buddha (*Fig. 2*) is accompanied by air spirits flying above, and winged horses prancing to each side. The majestic Sun God (*Fig. 1*) is carved in the Gupta tradition, too: his chest seems filled with air, like the body of a yogi.

1. *Surya, the Sun God.* Konarak. 13th century A.D.

2. *The Teaching Buddha.* Sarnath. Gupta Period, 5th century A.D. *Total h.* 5′3″.

1. *A Yakshi.* At Bhārhut. Early 1st century B.C.

2. *Dancing Girl.* From Mohenjo-daro. 3000–1500 B.C. Bronze.

3. *The Great Stupa of Sānchi.* Early 1st century A.D.

Unlike Western churches, Indian places of worship usually were not places of group congregation. Instead, solitary shrines were set up, which the pilgrim visited alone. Buddhist shrines were called "stupas." A stupa is a large mound of earth surrounded by a stone wall and four carved gates. Buried inside the mound was a relic of Buddha—a bone or a bit of his hair. The picture above shows one of the earliest stupas still standing. It was built during the time when Buddha was still considered too holy to portray in sculpture. So there is no picture of Buddha in all the sculpture of Sanchi. Instead, the gates are covered with animals which suggest his power and majesty, and with Hindu nature spirits (*Fig. 4*).

4. *North Gate at Sānchi.* Early 1st century A.D.

So strong was the Hindu tradition in India, that even when Buddhism was made the official religion, Indian sculptors could not resist adding hosts of their beloved nature gods to the Buddhist shrines. One of the favorite nature gods was the "yakshi," or tree sprite. The yakshi was always shown grasping a branch of a tree, and giving it a gentle kick with her heel. It was believed that when she kicked it, the tree would burst into bloom.

5. *A Yakshi from East Gate at Sānchi.* 1st century A.D.

After Buddhism was replaced by a revival of Hinduism, the shrine became an even more complicated sculpture. On a lonely seacoast stand seven enormous granite boulders, carved into this fantastic scene (*Fig. 6*). Thousands of elephants, deer, rabbits, men, and gods are carved, life-size, proceeding toward the sea. The shrine is dedicated to Vishnu, as the river Ganges, flowing down from heaven to water the earth, then swirling away into the dark ocean. Tangled and confused like the Hindu gods themselves, there is no plan to the way these figures are arranged. They do not fall into a pattern like Greek temple sculpture, nor align into rows and sequences like Assyrian or Egyptian works.

There were some thirty million gods to which Hindu priests prayed, and many of their rock-cut shrines stand throughout India, each representing a particular Hindu belief. The shrine at Konarak (see page 77) is carved into the shape of a colossal chariot, with wheels ten feet high. The whole rock is intended to be seen as if moving forward majestically, drawn across the sky by Vishnu's steeds. Other rock temples had hollow chambers with awesome sculptures of Hindu monsters and gods (pages 80–81).

Sculptures of Buddha in India were usually solemn and straightforward, like the Roman sculptures which influenced them. But whenever Indian sculptors carved the nature spirits and gods of the Hindu religion, they used a very different style. Then, they showed figures swaying and dancing, floating as though borne along on the seething waters of Maya. This love of dancing figures was already apparent in the very first art of India, for one of the earliest works, made two to three thousand years before Christ, shows a lithe and graceful dancer, hand on her hip (*Fig. 2*). The yakshini at Sanchi cling to mango trees like acrobats (*Fig. 5*), their rounded bodies seeming swollen with the riches of the earth.

6. *The Descent of the Ganges.* Relief carved on cliff at Māmallapuram. Early 7th century A.D. *l.* 88½″, *h.* 30′.

Pages 80–81

1. *Indra, King of the Gods.* From Elūrā. Gupta period, 750–850 A.D.
2. *Vishnu in the Guise of a Cosmic Boar Rescuing Bhūdēvi, Goddess of the Earth.* From Udayagiri. About 400 A.D.

1. *Female Donors.* Fragment of fresco from Sorcuq, Kirin Caves, Chinese Turkestan. 8th–9th centuries A.D.

Buddhist monks decorated the rock temples with paintings like those of their Gupta homeland. From such paintings (*Fig. 1*), drawn with a simple, clear brushstroke called the "iron wire line," a great style of Chinese painting grew up during the T'ang Dynasty.

3. *Interior of Chaitya Hall.* Ajanta. 1st century B.C.

Although almost all the paintings made during the Gupta period have rotted away in the damp climate, a few tatters remain in the cave temples of Central India, particularly in Ajanta. Cut into sheer rock, these temples gave shelter to the wandering monks during the rainy season, and also made more permanent shrines than the outdoor stupas. A typical rock cave had a long hall ending in a small rock stupa surrounded by a narrow path for the pilgrims (*Fig. 3*). The walls at Ajanta were first coated with plaster, then with white clay. Afterwards, watercolor paints were quickly stroked on. Drawn in graceful, flowing lines, the figures undulate like snakes with sleepy, half-closed eyes.

2. *Air Sprite or "Asparas."* Ajanta. 470–480 A.D. Fresco.

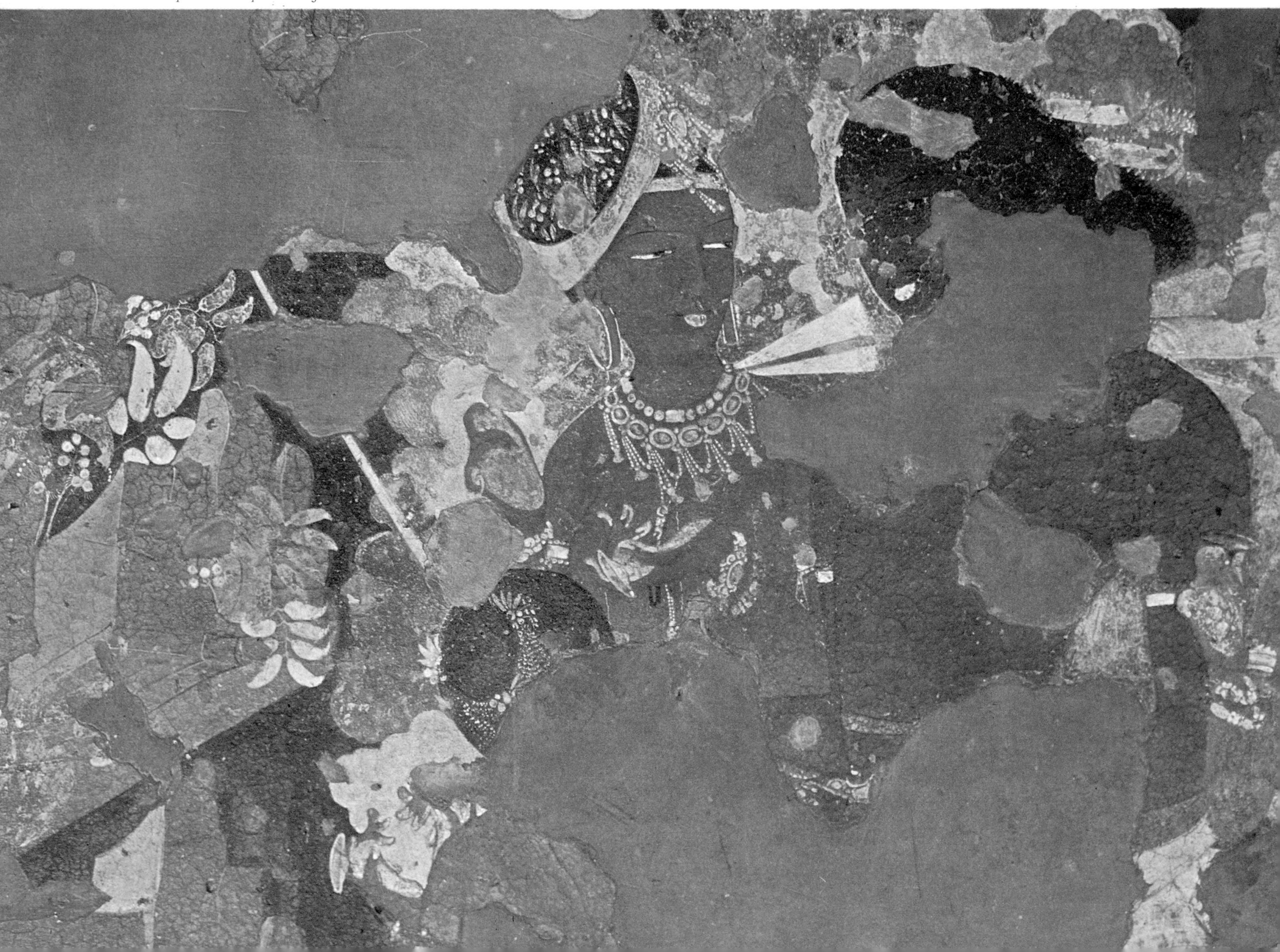

4. *Palace Ladies Hunting from a Pavilion.* Indian, Rajasthani, Kotab School. 1760–1770 A.D.

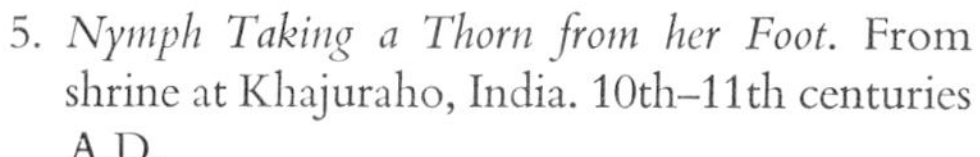

5. *Nymph Taking a Thorn from her Foot.* From shrine at Khajuraho, India. 10th–11th centuries A.D.

6. *Srī Krishna with the Flute.* Indian, Rajput, Pahārī (Kāngrā). Early 19th century.

The Gupta style of painting probably continued unchanged very much as Gupta style sculpture did (*Fig.* 5), for many centuries, but no traces of paintings made before the 16th and 17th centuries remain. Then a number of rich Rajput princes in the northeastern hills began to commission court painters. Rajput paintings still retain the same grace and flowing lines of the Ajanta murals. They are painted in flat, strong colors, outlined with a curving, clear stroke. While Mogul paintings (pages 72–75) only described life in the courts, Rajput pictures dealt with the adventures of the Hindu gods, usually in their human incarnations, beloved by beautiful shepherdesses and princesses. Sometimes, Rajput paintings illustrated various kinds of Indian music. Each piece of music, played on shrill, melodious strings and flutes, was intended to create a different mood—such as longing, or joy, or anticipation. Each mood was called a "raga," and could be described in a brisk little scene of lovers and their trials.

1. *Nataraja, Lord of the Dance*. South Indian. Chola period, 9th century A.D. Copper. *h*. 43⅞″.

2. *Temple of Tirukalikunram*. South India.

South Indian artists, who excelled in bronze casting, invented the image of Shiva in his incarnation as Nataraja, "The Dancer." The Hindus believed that when Shiva danced, the universe would fall into ruin and the stars wheel dizzily through the skies. At such a moment, Shiva was dancing his magical dance, destroying the universe and creating it over again. In this incarnation, he has four arms, one for each of the different actions he performs. With a flame, he destroys; with a tiny drum, he taps the rhythm of things being born again. With an uplifted hand, he stills the wild night; with another, he points to his big toe, where believers can hide for safety. A screaming demon sprawls beneath him; this is the evil world. Shiva's arms flail, his hair and scarves fly; all around him flames dance, but at the center his face is calm, for he is in "Nirvana": he has escaped from the world into eternal peace. The rhythm and tension make this figure one of the greatest achievements of Indian art.

3. *Vasudhara, Goddess of Abundance.* Nepalese. 14th–15th centuries A.D. Gilt copper. *h.* 6⅜″.

5. *Dancing Asparas.* Cambodian. About 1200.

The Khmer, a dynasty of rich kings in Cambodia, built two huge temple-cities adorned with gigantic but delicate sculptures. These ancient temple-cities, and the one in Borobudur, were discovered only in this century, almost ruined by jungle undergrowth.

7. *Stupa at Borobudur.* Java. Late 8th century A.D. Aerial view.

Hindu and Buddhist art spread eastward to Cambodia and the islands of Indonesia. Two main outposts of Indian civilization were in Borobudur, Java, and in Angkor Wat and Angkor Thom in Cambodia. The pilgrim to Borobudur trod a long, spiral path around a huge stupa (*Fig. 7*). As he ascended, he passed pictures of Hell, then scenes of Buddha among elephants, deer, and birds. At last, he stepped out on top where seventy-two Buddhas sat within stone alcoves.

6. *Faces of Shiva.* Angkor Thom. Tower of Bayon. Early 8th century A.D.

Today, Buddhist and Hindu beliefs linger on in the kingdoms of Nepal, Thailand, and neighboring countries. In Thailand and Bali, dancers wear grotesque, brilliantly colored masks, like the one below, in their religious festivals.

4. *Demon Mask.* Thailand. Recent period, 1900's. *h.* 24″.

In a lonely sanctuary the 46-foot-long Buddha at right lies dreaming. He is supposed to be in Nirvana, and is an example to all who pass by to escape, as he has, from the evils and sorrows of this world.

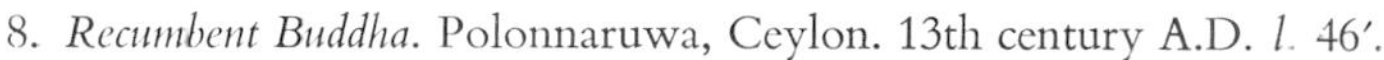

8. *Recumbent Buddha.* Polonnaruwa, Ceylon. 13th century A.D. *l.* 46′.

1. *Lady Wen-chi's Return*. Sung dynasty, 12th century. Detail.

CHINA

China has had a more continuous and uninterrupted development in its civilization than any Western nation, and this continuity is reflected in its art. Partly because of the immense size of the country, and because it has always been able to absorb repeated influxes of foreign invaders, and partly because of the influence of Confucianism and Taoism, Chinese art showed a development of style unbroken throughout the centuries. Very few motifs, once developed, were ever lost; certain ideas and styles were repeated over and over again. Copyists in each age repeated the great paintings of the past; the most precious ceramics were those which were artificially crackled to look ancient. For with few exceptions, art in China was made to assist the rich and intelligent scholars, emperors, and priests in their meditations upon religious and poetic subjects. Most important and profound of the Chinese arts were the quiet, meditative sculptures of Buddha and his saints, and the Taoist landscape painting that had a form and technique unknown in the West and unmatched in the world.

In China, the complicated, confused aspect of Indian art did not take root. However, another lively style, borrowed from the nomads of the northern steppes, influenced the design of the graceful tendrils and animal forms of Chinese decorative arts—the gorgeous silks, jades, ceramics, and ivories for which the country later was to become famous.

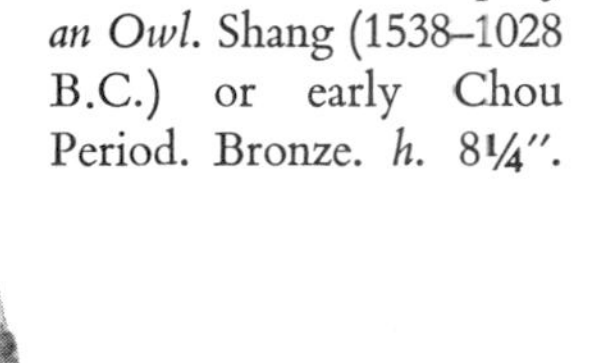

2. *Ritual Vessel in the Shape of an Owl.* Shang (1538–1028 B.C.) or early Chou Period. Bronze. *h.* 8¼″.

The earliest works of Chinese art were bronze vessels used in religious rites. Made in bird or animal shapes, magical masks (*Fig. 3*) sometimes were attached to their sides to invoke the protection of animal spirits.

The makers of these bronzes were conquered by a barbaric people, the Chou, from the northwest, whose lively art used dashing animal shapes and leaping figures, like those of the Scythians (see page 69). The jade disk at right (*Fig. 5*) was a symbol of the revolving universe, and of the king, believed to be heaven's ambassador on earth.

3. *T'ao T'ieh Monster Mask.* Shang dynasty (1538–1028 B.C.). Bronze.

5. *Jade Disk.* Late Chou dynasty, 5th–3rd centuries B.C.

In every part of the ancient Orient, scholars had written their sacred texts upon scrolls which could be rolled up and taken from place to place. But in China, the painting of scrolls became a great art (see page 90). Figure 1 is a part of a long scroll telling the story of the beautiful Lady Wen-Chi, who was kidnaped by barbarians in the north of China. She fell in love with the Mongol chief who had captured her and lived happily in her new home, but after some years, her father arranged for her return. Her heartbroken leave-taking from her husband, and her lonely return by horseback to her father's palace, are described in delicate touches of ink and color upon the fragile silk.

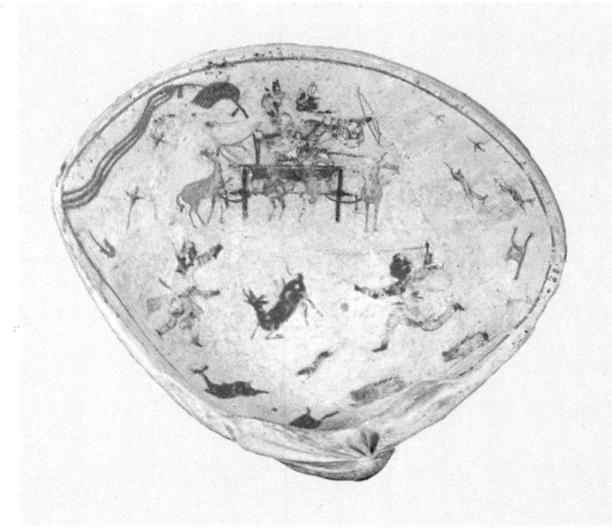

4. *Hunting Scene.* Late Chou, 4th–3rd centuries B.C. Painted shell. *w.* 3⅛″.

During the first great Chinese Empire, under the Han emperors, artists drew with a sweeping line and with the same explosive energy as the Chou designs. The tiny clam shell at left holds one of the earliest examples of painting found in the Orient.

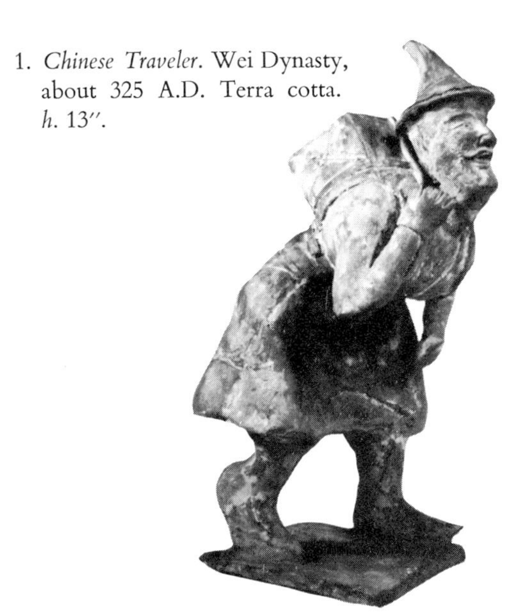

1. *Chinese Traveler*. Wei Dynasty, about 325 A.D. Terra cotta. *h*. 13″.

Buddhism in China reached the height of its popularity in the T'ang Dynasty, a period of peace and prosperity in the huge empire. T'ang artists expanded on styles which had originated in northwestern India. The sculptors carved figures which moved gracefully and serenely, like the musicians at right. The first one taps a small drum. Perhaps the second figure once played a flute. They are clothed in gracefully draped scarves, and their quiet faces are carved in flat, simple forms. T'ang artists also made droll animal and human figures which were meant to be placed in tombs (*Figs. 1, 4*).

2. *Guardian*. Lung-men Caves, Honan, North China. 672–676 A.D. *h*. 50′.

3. *Detail from Frieze of a Buddhist Procession of Three Musicians and One Dancer*. Sung Dynasty, 10th–11th centuries A.D.

During the 3rd century A.D., missionaries from Buddhist India began drifting into China. They traveled the long, perilous caravan trails on foot or on camelback, stopping at oases for water and rest, and for sanctuary from bandits who preyed on lonely travelers. In some of the desolate hills and rocks, the Buddhists carved great temples and shrines, like those they had left behind in India. The temples were adorned with paintings and sculptures—some in the Roman-influenced style born in Gandhara, and some like the colossal demon-guardian shown at left, in a style closer to that of the earlier Chou and Han artists, more electric and full of action and explosive energy.

As time went on, Buddhist sculpture gradually became more elaborate. First, the rather simple faces of early T'ang figures grew plump, with rosebud lips, sly, fish-like eyes, and rolls of fat under their chins. As the T'ang Dynasty declined, China was beset by a period of civil wars. Now, from India, a new saint appeared: the goddess of mercy, Kuan Yin, who was believed to hear every cry of sorrow, and bring forgiveness (*Fig. 6*). She was shown seated on a rocky island in the Indian Ocean. She wears the scarves and necklaces of an Indian princess, and her hands and feet seem as fastidiously posed as those of a court dancer..

5. *Mirror.* T'ang Dynasty (618–906 A.D.). Silver and lacquer inlay. *diam.* 11″.

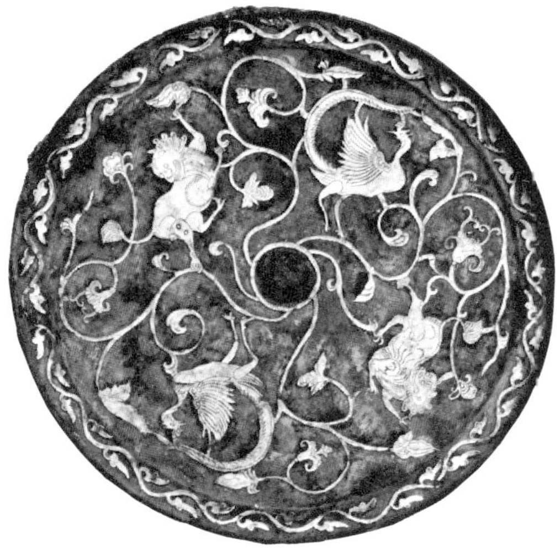

Luxurious articles like this mirror (*Fig. 5*) were made for the elegant ladies of the court. Some of these precious baubles were transported thousands of miles on the backs of peddlers, and found their way to Islamic and European artists, who sometimes copied their intricate designs.

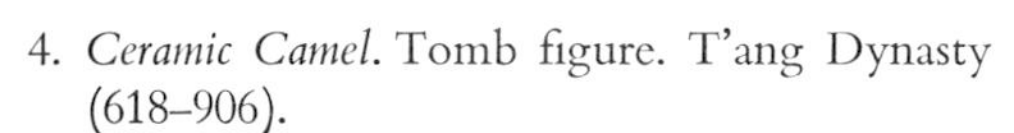

4. *Ceramic Camel.* Tomb figure. T'ang Dynasty (618–906).

6. *Kuan Yin Bodhisattva.* Yuan Dynasty, 12th–13th centuries A.D. Wood with gold leaf. *h.* 7′11″.

1. Scroll painting: "*Play with Infants,*" detail. Sung Dynasty (960–1279 A.D.). Painted silk.

During the T'ang period, the art of representing human personalities instead of saints gradually became more popular. T'ang women were shown tending their children, making silk, and learning rules of etiquette (*Fig. 1*). One emperor had portraits made of all his favorite horses. Many personalities and races are represented in the crowd of kings and ambassadors paying homage to the Buddha, seated like a neighborly priest upon a lotus blossom (*Fig. 3*). The sturdy "iron wire" brushstroke which outlines all these figures seems to express the stability of the times.

In the 10th century, the Sung Dynasty replaced the sturdy T'ang, and a new kind of art appeared. This new art was landscape painting, and it became China's greatest achievement. Behind the new art form lay the Taoist religion, established in the 6th century B.C. and followed particularly by the mountain and forest people of South China. These were lonely people whose huts were blanketed by mists or drenched by soaking gray rains much of the time. These people believed that behind all the mist and space and vegetation lay a force called "Tao." The Taoist painters turned their backs on politics and personal comfort, and meditated in the hills and

forests. The scroll paintings they made are organized in a completely new way. All the details are drawn into a wide vista which stretches out like a scene one sees from a passing car. Bit by bit, one could turn the scroll, uncovering only a part at a time. Then he would see a kind of moving picture. Look at the scroll below slowly, from right to left. First one sees a misty mountain top. Then from the low, piny shore, tiny boats put out into the river.

2. Scroll painting: "*Twelve Views from a Thatched Cottage,*" by Hsai Kuei (active about 1180–1230 A.D.). Sung Dynasty (960–1279 A.D.).

5. *Incense Burner.* Sung Dynasty (960–1279 A.D.). Dark-bodied porcelain. *w.* 6⅛″.

4. *Ewer in the Shape of a Court Lady.* T'ang Dynasty (618–906 A.D.). *h.* 8⅜″.

3. Scroll painting: "*Barbarian Royalty Worshipping Buddha.*" 10th–11th centuries A.D.

They cross, and touch the opposite bank. The eye rests for a moment on the dark clumps of trees, then discovers fishing boats behind them, moored in a peaceful cove at twilight. A rising cliff with bushes and lonely trees lifts up our eyes and ends the story of this scroll. Sung pottery (*Figs. 5, 6*) has the same gentle, simple lines; sometimes its glaze was crackled to make it look more ancient and so, more poetic. Sung emperors treasured these scrolls and bowls. They kept them in silken boxes, now and then lifting them out to stroke their cool surfaces and turn them gently in their hands.

6. *Vase with Peony Decoration.* Sung Dynasty (960–1279 A.D.). *h.* 13½″.

1. *Landscape Album in Various Styles,* a detail, by Ch'a Shih-piao (1615–1698). Ch'ing Dynasty. Ink and slight color on rice paper.

Chinese landscape painters worked with ink upon silk or paper, and could never erase a line. They learned to look very carefully at trees, rocks, and clouds, to remember every detail of the way they grew or were formed, and then to paint swiftly without making an error. So they worked, even after the Sung Dynasty fell to the Mongols of the Yuan Dynasty, until the Yuan was replaced by the powerful Ming and Ch'ing dynasties of the modern era. In time, the painters set down certain rules for their art, listing the various ways that leaves might be painted, or explaining the several methods that could be employed to reproduce a hill or tree. Sometimes artists splashed ink on their paper, or smeared it with their hands. Sometimes their paintings became ghostly, with only one or two lines in one corner. In the three paintings (*Figs. 1, 3, and 6*), a great variety in subject, mood, and style was achieved with the simplest materials and forms that any artists in the world have ever used.

2. *Temple of Heaven.* Peking, China. 15th century.

3. *Album of Seasonal Landscapes,* a detail, by Hsaio Yun-Ts'ung (1596–1673). Dated 1668. Ink and color on paper.

1. *Short strokes to represent clumps of leaves*
2. *Brushstrokes to represent pine needles*
3. *Another type of leaf*
4. *Flower-like form*
5. *Autumn willow, in the Sung style*
6. *Autumn willow, in the T'ang style*
7. *Rocks, made with brushstrokes like the veins of a lotus leaf*
8. *Simple brushstrokes to indicate figure*
9. *Simple brushstrokes, beginning with the beak, show method of drawing a bird*

4. Brush stroke drawings: from *The Tao of Painting*, by Mai-mai Sze.

Shown above are some diagrams from a book of instructions for painters, called "The Mustard Seed Garden." They describe how to apply ink to achieve various effects.

6. Scroll painting. By Chu- chuang of Lao-jen. 18th century.

These are two Taoist painters. Behind them, in wood boxes, are their fresh scrolls; their bamboo brushes are in a simple jar. One painter studies the slender, drooping branches of the willow, while the other meditates.

5. *Horse*. Ch'ing Dynasty, K'ang-hsi reign (1662–1722). Nephrite. *h.* 8″.

7. *Bottle Vase*. Ch'ing Dynasty, K'ang Hsi reign (1662–1722). Porcelain with green and black enamel. *h.* 10¾″.

Later Chinese artists excelled in fashioning precious small objects. By camelback and on ships from Portugal and Italy, many of these riches were transported to Europe, where they inspired various "Chinoiserie" styles of the 18th and 19th centuries.

1. Japanese painting: *Shashin Shiko*. Detail from the Tamamushi Shrine. Artist unknown. Asuka period, about 600 A.D.

2. *Horse*. Haniwa period, 2nd–4th centuries A.D. Terra cotta. *h*. 23½″.

Among the earliest works of art found in Japan are clay figures like the one at the left (*Fig. 2*) with alert stance and stubby limbs. Some are animals, some are soldiers or dancers, and some are complete little houses with cut-out doors and windows. These figures were buried upright like fence posts around graves. Probably they represented spirits which were supposed to guard the body.

4. *Heavenly Musician*. Haluho period, 646–709 A.D. Camphor wood. *h*. 6⅜″.

JAPAN

Japanese art, like Chinese, grew up indirectly from Indian Buddhism, and many of the greatest paintings and sculptures in Japan represent the gods of Buddhist heaven and hell, although these had grown considerably more complicated over the centuries. In the 8th century, and again in the 15th, religious teachers, artists, and craftsmen from many parts of China traveled down the peninsula of Korea and into the Japanese islands. From these travelers, Japan learned the styles of Chinese Buddhist sculpture and painting, and the techniques of ink painting upon silk, which had produced the landscape schools of the Sung Period. Each of these styles was adapted in a way that was purely Japanese, but it was not until the 17th century that a series of original Japanese styles and techniques appeared.

Shinto, the ancient native religion in Japan, taught that the world, ruled by the Sun-god, was infested with hosts of evil spirits, ready to snap at the carpenter's hand if he handled his wood carelessly, or to break the potter's bowl if he treated his clay rudely. Cleanliness, great care, and simplicity in the handling of tools and materials were of first importance.

3. *Guardian Figure*. Kamakura period, 1185–1392 A.D. Wood. *h*. 92″.

5. *Horyu-ji Temple*. Nara, Japan. Asuka period, 7th century A.D.

Buddhist missionaries began entering Japan in the 6th century. Soon, a great Buddhist sanctuary arose in the capital city, Nara. Its temples, walls, shrines, and monastery buildings, although patterned after South Indian models, were constructed in a much more delicate way, of slender wood poles and with roofs of curled cedar shavings. Color was everywhere: walls were painted red, blue, green, and gold. Silk streamers floated, and bronze bells tinkled. Bright tiles, set beside carved and painted panels, were decorated with flowers and vines and trailing clouds, like the scenes of Asparas in India (page 82, *Fig. 2*). The influence of Chinese T'ang Dynasty sculpture was strong upon figures like the pensive lute player (*Fig. 4*), and the snarling demon (*Fig. 3*). But already, the typical Japanese love of elegant, flat designs began to make itself felt, particularly in the trellised background and pointed halo of the musician.

1. *Scroll painting: Lady Murasaki's Diary*, a detail. Heian period, 12th–13th centuries.

The painting style of China's T'ang Dynasty was borne into Japan with the Buddhist missionaries. At Nara, plump Buddhist saints were drawn in the same strong "iron wire" line which had originated long before in Northwest China (*Fig. 2*). The flat sunlike halo behind this saint is typically Japanese, but the flowing garments and graceful gesture might have been drawn in India or China.

2. *Wall painting: Amida Triad,* a detail. Artist unknown. Early Nara period, about mid-7th century A.D.

As the Chinese T'ang Dynasty began to crumble at the end of the 9th century, Japan cast off foreign influences. At first, the ruling power came into the hands of a single family, the Fujiwara, who gave their name to the art of their time. Fujiwara paintings reflect the precious, pleasure-loving spirit of courtiers and ladies who played on bamboo flutes, sent love letters on silk and colored paper, and wrote poems. One of the few scrolls still in existence tells the story of Prince Genji, beloved by all the ladies of the court. Here they sit, like butterflies upon silken cushions. Already, Japanese taste for astonishing, off-balance designs had begun to make itself felt.

Toward the end of the Fujiwara period, Japanese artists began to explore a new kind of art, that of caricature. In it, they were able to portray all the witty details of personality that they found so fascinating. The scroll below showed all kinds of animals, behaving like the pompous and decadent upper classes of the late Fujiwara period. Later, many Japanese artists turned their attention to the lively and humorous events in the lives of ordinary men and women, a subject which the Chinese landscape artists tried to avoid.

3. *Animal Scroll: Chōjū Giga.* Artist unknown. Late Heian period, 12th century A.D. *h.* 12″.

4. Unkei: *Muchaku*. Detail. About 1208. Wood. *h.* 75″.

Later, this fascination with men's lives and personalities produced a great theatrical art theater, called "Noh drama," which became the main form of entertainment for the aristocrats and military leaders of feudal Japan. Noh actors always wore masks, which announced to the audience just what kind of character they were playing. These masks, made into bold patterns which could be seen beyond the proscenium of the stage, had strong expressions, like that of a beautiful girl, a cruel lord, or the gods of hell, or any other typical character.

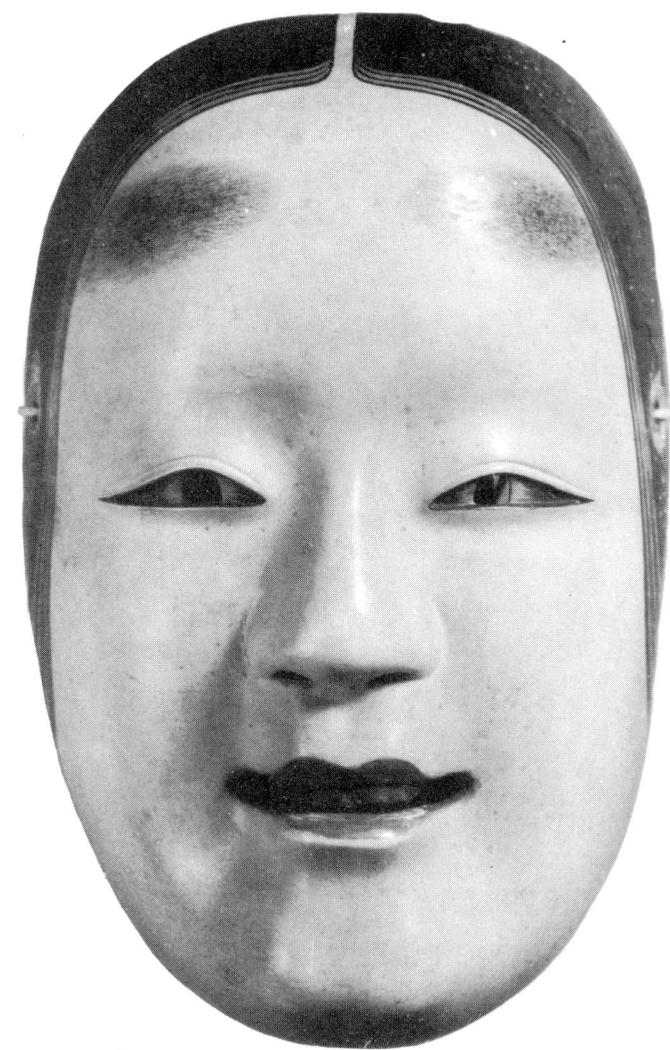

5. Noh mask: "*Hōrai Onna,*" attrib. to Taikōbō. Edo period (1615–1867).

About 1185, the Fujiwara gave way to the aggressive soldiers of the Kamakura, who preferred the swashbuckling arts of war to the elegant and intellectual refinements of court life. With this more outgoing and vigorous rule of feudal nobles, a new art style was born, which emphasized strength and realism, but also probed the human personality more acutely than previous oriental styles had done. One of the greatest Kamakura artists was a sculptor, Unkei. His carved portraits of human faces and figures were almost the first examples in the Orient of a careful, close study of a man's personality. Unkei's figures were carved of thin pieces of wood, joined and painted.

6. *Animal Scroll: Chōjū Giga*. Artist unknown. Late Heian period, 12th century A.D. *h.* 12″.

1. Scroll painting: *Burning of the Sanjo Palace,* a detail. Kamakura period, mid-13th century A.D.

These scrolls of the Kamakura period are designed, like Chinese landscape scrolls, to be read from right to left. But a vastly different world is reproduced here (*Fig. 1* and pages 100–101)—a world of battles and rearing horses, of grumbling or sleepy men and women. Perhaps even more distinctly Japanese is the new manner of composing these scrolls: the artist often seems to have taken a position in some small corner, from which he saw his scene at an odd, oblique angle. Obviously, the artist was not trying to present a perfectly harmonious scene, but rather one full of the accidents and mischances of life itself. His eye was a camera which clicked abruptly and caught the world off guard. This kind of artistic vision was later exploited even further.

3. Scroll painting: *Fukutomi Zoshi,* a detail. Late Kamakura period, 14th century A.D.

2. *Suit of Armor.* Late Kamakura period, 14th century A.D.

4. *Buddhist Monks, Han-shan and Shihte.* Attrib. to Shubun. Ashikaga period, 15th century.

5. *Landscape.* By Sesshu. Ashikaga period (1420–1506).

In the 14th and 15th centuries, new waves of Chinese scholars and artists entered Japan from the great Sung and Ming courts. Now, the Japanese, too, turned to landscape painting, trying to recreate in their own spiny countryside the poetic mood of the Chinese. But their hands seemed trained to make more brittle, choppy lines. Their brushstrokes often lie like ax marks on the silk. Most Japanese landscape painters were members of the "Zen" Buddhist sect, which had spread into Japan from China during the 12th century. Zen artists behaved in odd ways, riding backwards on donkeys, drinking beer, making jokes, and slapping one another on the head. In all these ways, they tried to shock both themselves and one another into suddenly reaching the kind of "Enlightenment" which Buddha had found, and which many Buddhist philosophers felt they reached as they meditated. Zen artists tried to see, in every detail of nature, animals, and men, a clue to the meaning of the universe. Every act of the day—pouring tea, fencing, writing poems, even going to market—might set off a chain of ideas and feelings which would lead to "Enlightenment." Zen artists trained themselves by long years of practice at the simplest steps. "Draw bamboos for ten years," said one Zen artist. "Become a bamboo Then forget all about bamboos when you draw." Partly a philosophy, partly a wonderfully buoyant art style, Zen has become an important influence on Western art today. In the upright scroll (*Fig. 4*), called a "Kakemono," two Zen priests struggle over their broom as they do their daily chores.

6. *Landscape*, a detail. By Sesshu. Middle 15th century.

1. *Burning of the Sanjo Palace* (p. 98, fig. 1)

1. *Nagoya Castle*. Nagoya, Japan. 1610–1612.

In the 17th century, Japanese artists were faced with a new challenge. A powerful military rule had once more imposed itself upon the country, and the nobles of the new Momoyama period demonstrated their power and wealth by building huge, fortified castles (*Fig. 1*). Within these fortresses were great banquet halls, where courtiers gathered for conversation and festivals. There was no place for diminutive, black-and-white Zen drawings here, nor even for the jovial comedies of the Kamakura scrolls. Flashing and imposing decorations were needed which could be moved about as the Shogun, or ruler, commanded. Therefore, a group of painters set to work making handsome screens, painted with bold, bright designs that would be visible across a long hall. Each screen had six panels and was painted with islands or frothy waves, irises, or bright-kimonoed girls—subjects which did not call for close study. The colors were intense and flat, and the compositions even more startling than the Kamakura scrolls. They literally held the eye transfixed by their daring form. The greatest of these Momoyama artists was Korin (*Fig. 3*).

2. *Women of the Gay Quarters*. Artist unknown. Early Edo period, about 1650.

4. Hokusai: *Sumo Wrestlers Bathing*. 1817. Woodblock print.

While the nobles called for extravagant palace decorations, the rising middle classes of 17th- and 18th-century Japan wanted art that they, too, could afford and enjoy. So some artists began making hundreds of little wood-block prints which could be sold cheaply. At first, these prints were made in black and white, but by the 18th century they were usually colored by hand.

3. Korin. *Folding screen: "Waves at Matsushima."* Early 18th century.

5. Andō Hiroshige: *One of "Fifty-three Stages of the Tōkaidō Shōno."* About 1834. Woodblock print.

Like the screens, these prints had a chopped-off look, as though the artist meant to tease, saying, "so much more goes on in the world besides this little scene, which is only a fragment of what I know!" These prints were all called bits of "Ukiyo-e," or the "floating world." They poured forth by the thousands, showing babies, soldiers and dancers, and events both serious and funny. There were many great Ukiyo-e artists, and among them the most famous were Hokusai, Hiroshige, and Utamaro (*Figs. 4, 5, 7*). These little prints found their way to Paris in the 19th century and stirred up much excitement among the French painters, who copied their off-balance compositions and muted, flat colors.

6. *Japanese House Interior.* Now in Garden Park, Philadelphia.

7. Utamaro: *Three Geisha.* About 1793. Woodblock print.

8. *Japanese Garden of the Prefecture.* Osaka.

Modern artists in the West have been influenced by many Japanese ideas and styles, for it is not only in the arts of painting and sculpture that Japan expresses its taste and high standards of craftsmanship. Almost everything made and used in Japan can be considered a work of art—a sword, a teapot, a garden, or an arrangement of three blue irises in a bowl. Japanese houses, built of wood, can be made to change shape. The rooms flow into one another as paper screens are slipped silently back and forth in their grooves. Japanese gardens are planted with the same taste for quiet, empty spaces broken into oblique, startling patterns (*Fig. 8*). Japanese gardens are planted not only with flowers; they also have beds of sand, carefully raked into designs punctuated by small rocks, trees, and ponds which are meant to remind the owner of the mountains and rivers of the world.

1. *Corn God*. Maya. 600–900 A.D.

PRE-COLUMBIAN ART

After about 25,000 B.C. the Americas began to be populated by migrations of Old Stone Age peoples who came across the Alaskan peninsula from Asia. Slowly, these people fanned out over the two continents, building a series of complex civilizations in Mexico, Central America, and South America. Although they were cut off from all intercourse with the high civilizations rising in the rest of the world, they built cities curiously similar to those in the Old World. Pyramid-temples, game courts, and astronomical observatories, all covered with sculpture and painted decorations, were constructed in most of these ancient cities.

The arts which embellished these structures evolved in rather rigid and limited ways. Although some extraordinarily expressive images were created in the Maya, the Aztec, and the Inca cultures, for the most part Pre-Columbian art remained a rigid and formal language of signs, like the Neolithic arts of Europe and the Orient. In some provocative cases, the works of art seem to be related to the earliest art of China—that of the Shang and Chou peoples. However, our knowledge of Pre-Columbian art is still scanty, for much has been overgrown and engulfed by jungles. Moreover, many treasures of the civilization were destroyed by the Spaniards in the 16th century.

2. *Ax Carved with a Tiger God.* Olmec, from Mexico. 1st century B.C. Jade. *h.* 11″.

4. *Warrior Holding a Club.* Tarascan. Western Mexico. End of 7th century A.D. Clay. *h.* 20″.

As other early civilizations sprang up in the valleys of Mexico and South America, each one created arts quite distinct from the others. The Tarascans modeled clay into all sorts of lively figures going about their daily tasks; the Olmec worked in polished jade, which they carved into blunt-nosed, scowling faces; and the early Chimu created in pottery and gold-work, later to be one of the great arts of South America.

3. *Gold Mask.* Mochica or Chimu. Peru. 400–1000 A.D. *h.* 10¾″.

Grave and brooding, crowned with a curving plume, the Corn god was one of the most important deities of the Maya. The most brilliant and artistic of the ancient Americans (*Fig. 1*), the Maya built great pyramid-cities, and followed a bloodthirsty religion, which demanded the sacrifice of thousands of human beings to the gods of rain, of the fields, of the wind, and of death.

1. *Serpent's Heads on the Temple of Quetzalcoatl.* Teotihuacan. Mexico. 770–829 A.D.

4. *Figures at Tula.* Toltec. Near Mexico City. 12th–13th centuries.

3. *Aztec Snake.* Late 15th or early 16th century. Turquoise mosaic. *l.* 16½″.

2. *Coatlicue ("Lady of the Serpent Skirt"), Goddess of Earth.* Aztec. End of 15th century. *h.* about 8½″.

Three major cultures flourished in Mexico: the Toltec, builders of Teotihuacan, a great city of pyramids, avenues, and monster sculptures (*Figs. 1, 4*); the Maya, who built great cities and developed a calendar and a complex system of writing; and, finally, the Aztec, who appeared in the Valley of Mexico around 1300. Savage and bloodthirsty, the Aztecs believed that their gods must be fed fresh human blood each day. Among their gods were the "Plumed Serpent," a grotesque monster made of tusks, skulls, claws, and snakes (*Fig. 2*), and Xipe, God of Fertility. The priest who sacrificed a victim to Xipe had to skin the body and dress himself in the hide, like the god, who put on a new garment of vegetation each spring. The carved head in Figure 5 represents the priest dressed in the victim's flayed skin.

5. *Xipe Totec, God of Fertility.* Aztec. Central Mexico. 15th century. *h.* 8¾″.

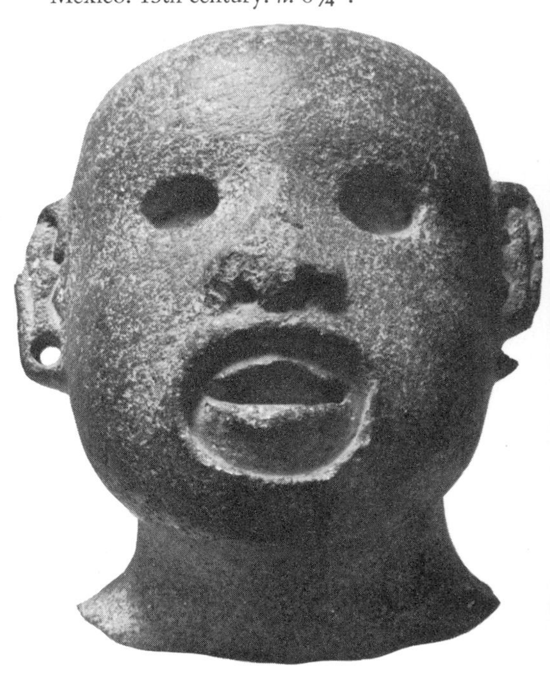

In the 5th century A.D., when the Roman Empire finally fell and the Byzantine Empire set upon an independent course, Western art was strongly influenced by two forces, neither of which cared for craftsmanship or beauty in the Classical sense. These forces were the Early Christian Church, which employed art as a language of propaganda to teach the Gospels to illiterate barbarians; and those barbarians themselves, for whom art was only decoration for their swords, chariots, and shields, and for the burials of their warrior chieftains.

The development of medieval art in the West involved a blending of these unlike ideas and styles, and later, a re-learning of the arts and techniques of the Classical past. Christian monasteries were the first strongholds of learning and art. Later, kings creating small empires for themselves called for arts to express their achievements. It had long been prophesied that the world would come to an end in the year 1000. But after the century passed and the superstitious population of Europe no longer feared this catastrophe, art again flourished on a new wave of enterprise. Church construction flourished, and travel became popular once more, bringing the art forms and techniques of distant lands. Gradually the stonecutters and builders, the painters of manuscript pages, and the enamelists and bronze workers rediscovered the ancient secrets of their arts or learned new techniques from imported Byzantine and Islamic examples. Finally, artists once again discovered the individual personality and the world of man. This resurgent interest touched sculpture, painting, and all the decorative arts—like gold-work, tapestry weaving, stained glass, and enamel work—while the art of architecture itself reached new heights in the soaring Gothic cathedrals with their rose and blue windows.

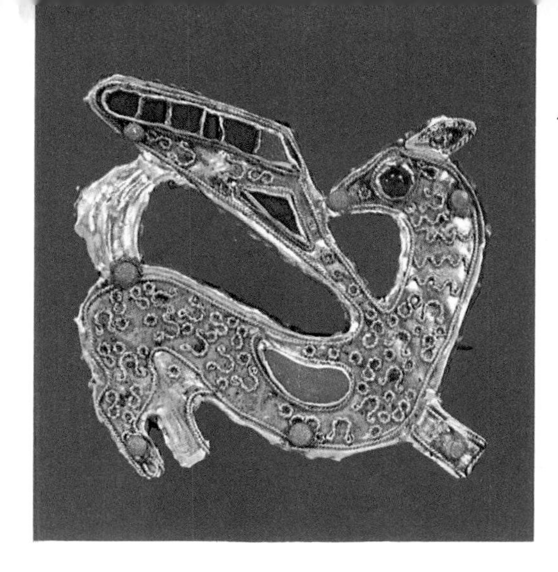

4. Frankish: *Gold Fibula,* set with red and blue paste, eyes studded with garnets. 7th century.

The Franks, who appeared in mid-Europe in the 4th century A.D., apparently learned their arts from nomadic Eastern tribes, and they continued to make jeweled bronze swords, helmets, and animal pins as their ancestors had done (*Fig. 4*). As the barbarian chieftains were replaced by the kings of later empires, more richly encrusted ornaments were created for the royal personages. This crown (*Fig. 5*) was used by emperors of the Holy Roman Empire up until the time of Napoleon, in the early 19th century.

5. *Crown of the Holy Roman Empire.* Gold. About 962 A.D.

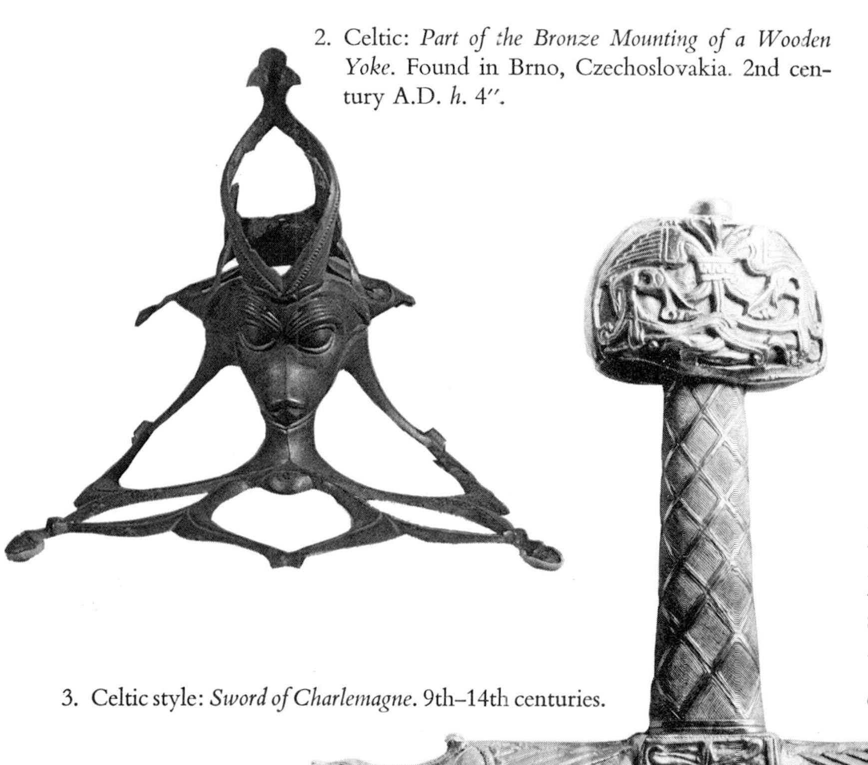

2. Celtic: *Part of the Bronze Mounting of a Wooden Yoke.* Found in Brno, Czechoslovakia. 2nd century A.D. *h.* 4″.

3. Celtic style: *Sword of Charlemagne.* 9th–14th centuries.

The art styles of two "barbarian" peoples, the Celts and the Franks, infiltrated medieval Europe. The Celts, whose camps were scattered from Spain to Scandinavia as early as 1000 B.C., made bronze and iron tools, weapons and ornaments, often in the shapes of animals (*Fig. 2*). Like many wandering peoples, particularly the Russian Scyths (see page 69), Celtic artists wove complex, twining patterns around these animal shapes, as shown in the design of the splendid sword (*Fig. 3*), which was handed down to posterity by the kings of France. This intense and energetic style later influenced a brilliant school of painting (see page 111).

1. Celtic book illumination: Initial from *Book of Kells.* 8th century. Parchment.

By the 8th century, the Celts had been driven from the European mainland into England and Ireland. There, converted by Christian monks, they set up monasteries and turned their native taste for ornament to Christian tasks. They decorated the great parchment pages of Gospel books and carved stone crosses to replace the pagan cromleches which their forebears had erected. Celtic book illustrations were filled with the animal shapes and the interlaced lines of their own artistic heritage, as well as with patterns brought from Coptic Egypt, which showed clawing, desert birds among vine scrolls (see page 61). They are among the most intricate designs ever made, filled with a kind of whirling, explosive energy. Like the first Christians of Syria and Egypt, the Celtic monks were extensive travelers who journeyed all over Britain, down into Gaul and Spain to convert and teach the illiterate peoples. In the centuries that followed, bits of Celtic ornament appeared in distant lands, copied now in bronze or stone or parchment by local artists.

4. *Utrecht Psalter: Psalm 50.* About 830 A.D.

2. Viking style: *Borgund Stave Church,* County of Sogn og Fjordane, Norway. About 1150 A.D.

3. Viking style: *Animal-head Post from the Oseberg Find.* 800–850 A.D. Wood.

In the 8th century, Celtic culture was wiped out by Viking warriors from Scandinavia. The Vikings believed in demons of the forests and seas, and to ward them off, they carved dragons rearing from the prows of their ships, and from the beams of their houses. In Norway, Vikings who became Christians even decorated their timber churches with these dragon heads (*Figs. 2, 3*).

In Europe, the lively ornamented art of the barbarians slowly fused with Classical styles. The first impetus to this combined form was given by Charlemagne, who came to the Frankish throne in 771. Charlemagne wished to establish an imperial state which would link the formerly barbaric Gaul with Italy, the onetime center of Christianity and civilization in the West. Part of his plan was a revival of Classical art and learning. He built great monasteries where, for centuries to come, monks copied and so preserved the manuscripts of Greece, Rome, and Byzantium (see page 64). Here and there, the monks invented their own new styles of drawing and painting, partly based on the illustrations of these ancient books. The most interesting "Carolingian" manuscript which has survived is the Utrecht Psalter (*Fig. 4*). Every illustration drawn there seems lifelike, for even the robes and the leaves of trees appear to move in the wind. This work, which may have been passed from monastery to monastery, was imitated in many ways, even in such a difficult medium as rock crystal (*Fig. 6*).

6. Carolingian style: *The Crystal of Lothar*. 9th century. Rock crystal. *diam.* 7 $\frac{3}{10}$″.

5. *The Expulsion from Paradise*. Detail from the bronze doors of Hildesheim Cathedral. 1015 A.D.

In all these works of art, made during the so-called "Dark Ages," men were slowly learning again to draw and carve the human figure, in its dramatic and lively attitudes and its heroic postures. After Charlemagne's death in 814, Europe again fell into disorganization until the 10th century, when the Saxon King Otto forged together a new empire. Churches were built, and fresh Byzantine influences appeared. Otto III, too, was a great art patron. Early in the 11th century, one of his bishops in the town of Hildesheim directed the making of a pair of great bronze doors for the cathedral. The scene, shown at left (*Fig. 5*), modeled in high relief, might be a pen drawing from the Utrecht Psalter translated into bronze. The conquest of England by the Normans under William the Conqueror, in 1066, was the stimulus for the making of the famous Bayeux Tapestry (*Fig. 7* and pages 112–113), which shows such episodes of this heroic battle as the soldiers putting forth in boats with prows carved like those of the Viking ships. Celtic, and Viking, too, are the curious little animals and winged monsters which range along the borders.

7. *Bayeux Tapestry*. Detail from pp. 112–113, fig. 2.

1. *Bayeux Tapestry.* Scene showing the building of ships for the invasion of England by the Normans. Bayeux Cathedral, France. About 1066–1082.

2. *Bayeux Tapestry.* Scene showing the Normans suffering a setback at the Battle of Hastings.

3. *Bayeux Tapestry*. Scene showing the Norman invasion fleet crossing the Channel.

After the fall of Rome, few great building projects were carried out in the West, except for isolated structures built by Charlemagne. But as the 11th century drew on, serfs began to group together in villages. Goldsmiths, weavers, and other craftsmen formed guilds for their common protection. New walls and forts were built on the ruins of old Roman garrisons. Over new roads, traders passed. Pilgrims, too, set out to visit far-off churches, particularly one which was located at the farthermost tip of Spain where

1. *Nave of the Church of the Madeleine,* Vézelay, France. 1096–end of 12th century.

3. *Mont St. Michel.* France. 1203–1264.

the bones of St. James the Greater were said to have been found. As the "pilgrimage trails" became more traveled, certain churches along the way were enlarged and new buildings erected. The style of these new churches is called "Romanesque" because they are put together in the same way as Roman buildings: with great spaces covered with barrel and groined vaults as the Romans had built. The floor plan remained the same as that of the Early Christian basilica (page 60). Romanesque style differed from region to region in Spain, Italy, Germany, and particularly France where the finest Romanesque churches were built. In the south of France, near Italy, a building might be low and somber, with the general feeling of a Roman triumphal arch. In central France, a church like the one at Vezelay (*Fig. 1*) was higher and more luminous. Adjoining its central aisle, called the "nave," were clearly marked-off side aisles. Above them, a row of small windows, called the "clear-story," pierced through the thick walls. In the north of France, in Norman territory, Romanesque churches and monasteries were towering buildings not unlike feudal forts (*Fig. 3*).

Stained glass was probably first invented in the Near East and spread northwards through Italy in the early centuries of Christianity. Early examples, like the medallion below, were severe and rigid, with bold black lines painted upon the glass which was then held in place with thick lead bars.

Since the arches of the Romanesque building rested entirely on heavy structural walls, there was little space for windows. Instead, Romanesque walls were often decorated with frescoes, paintings made in water colors upon freshly applied plaster. Some, like Noah's Ark (*Fig. 2*), were painted from the Gospels by untutored artists.

2. *Wall Painting.* From church at St. Savin, Vienne, France. About 1080.

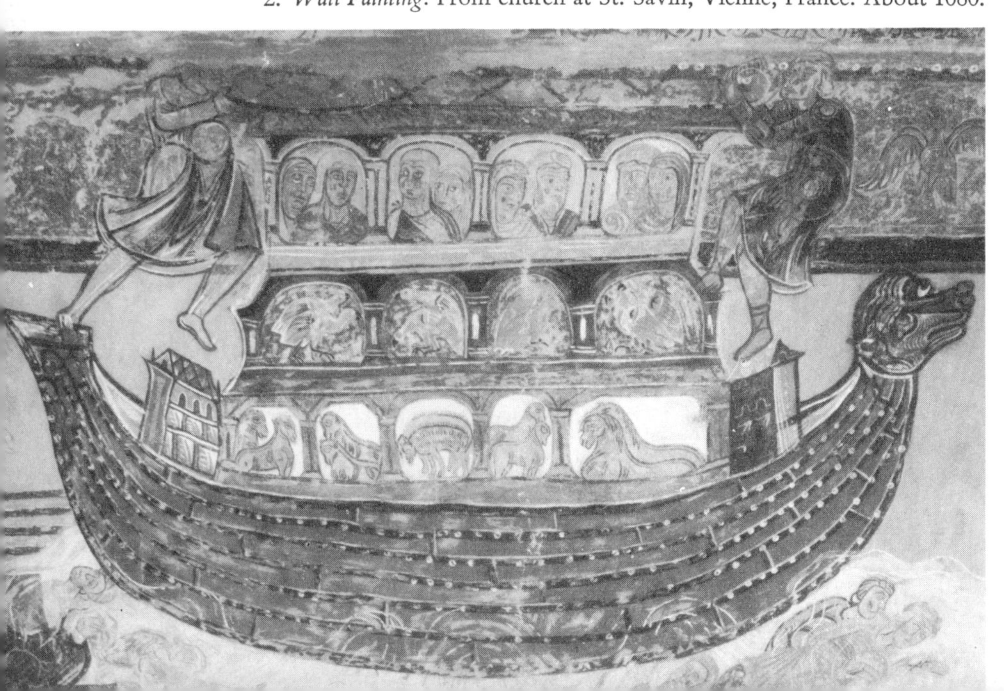

4. *Head of Christ.* End of 11th century. Stained glass.

The major ornament of Romanesque churches was sculpture, not life-size statues like the Classical manner of "graven images" to which the Early Christian Church was opposed, but sculpture ornament designed to teach the Gospels. The sources for these designs were mainly the precious manuscripts of the past, which were owned by local monasteries or lords. Also, from time to time, pilgrims passed by with their own books, illustrated in curious styles. Wandering sculptors, too, trod the pilgrimage trails, working where they stopped for shelter. In this way, many unknown hands were laid upon each Romanesque church, and patterns from far corners of the earth were mixed together, even winged lions from China and Syria and sharp-beaked birds from Ireland and Egypt. But the most impressive sculpture of each church was carved on the "tympanum," or half-moon over the doorway, which echoed the half-moon of the arches within. This front porch, like the billboard of a theater, was intended to stop the passerby and compel him to enter. So the sculptors chose an imaginary scene of terror: the Day of Judgment. This awesome scene included both the sinners and blessed, rising from their coffins to meet their fate; and above them towered a figure of Christ "In Majesty," in trancelike rigidity. To see the way these Romanesque figures took their places on the tympanum, see Figure 2 on page 116.

5. *Christ in Majesty*. From tympanum of Autun Cathedral. 12th century.

6. *The Damned*. From tympanum of Autun Cathedral. 12th century.

1. *Cathedral,* Chartres. 1145–1260.

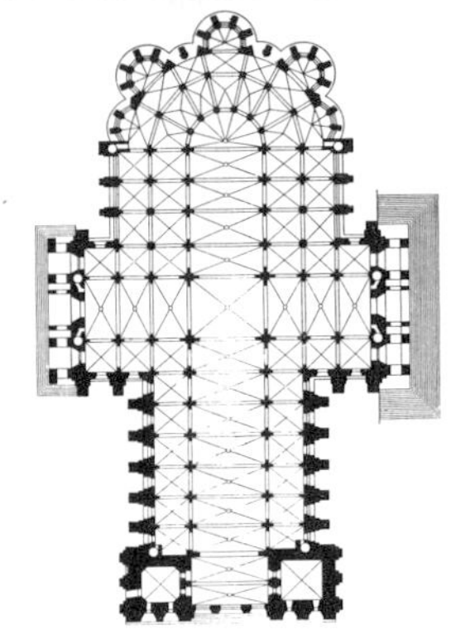

Floor plan, Chartres Cathedral.

Twelfth-century Europe saw kingdoms and classes united by the Crusades in a concerted effort to extend Christianity. Back from the Near East, the Crusaders brought fabulous tales of the wealth, art, and learning in Byzantium and Islam. Curiosity about distant lands was born again, and monks began to write books in the spoken languages, instead of in Church Latin. Universities were established and everywhere new ideas flourished, especially in France, which now had become the cultural center of the West. Architecture kept pace. Two architectural innovations led to a new style, that of the Gothic cathedral. These innovations were the pointed arch, which enabled builders to make much higher ceiling vaults, and the flying buttress. Instead of thick Romanesque arches made of great stone blocks, smaller stones set into thin, strong ribs bore the weight of the entire vault. Then, to support these high ribs, the builders propped another rib against them, at the point of greatest strain. This supporting rib, the "flying buttress," reached over the side aisles and was anchored in the ground outside the building itself. Now the wall could be opened up into tall windows, filled with stained glass. A crosspiece, the "transept," turned the structure into the shape of a cross. The design of the great western facade was standardized, with doors, towers, windows, all echoing exactly the structure within.

3. *Flying Buttresses.* Chartres.

2. *Western,* or *Royal Portal,* Chartres. About 1150.

4. *Interior of Chartres.* Diagonal view of nave and south transept.

The front of Chartres is still late Romanesque in style, with tall, unrealistic figures which seem to be carved after pen drawings in manuscripts. By the great front entrance, beneath the figure of Christ (*Fig. 2*), are the kings and queens of the Old Testament (*Fig. 7*). The worshipers had to pass between these figures to enter the church. The idea of carving the whole entranceway into a kind of theater in stone, making human figures of the columns, was originated by the Abbot Suger, head of the Abbey of St. Denis in Paris. It was Suger's plan that each bit of sculpture should take its place in a vast stone drama, so that everyone could study the Gospels, and the adventures of the Old Testament. The "Scholastic" philosophers from the new universities added their ideas for new subjects to be represented in the sculptures. The little figures on Chartres (*Figs. 5, 6*) range from ancient philosophers who predated Christ to symbolic representation of the months of the year, sins and virtues, and even to flowers of the fields.

The greatest Gothic cathedrals are Notre Dame in Paris and the cathedrals at Chartres, Reims, and Amiens. The task of building the first two spanned about a century. The last two were slowly built during the 13th century. The pictures on these pages are all of Chartres, the famous Gothic edifice whose 170 stained glass windows (see pages 118–119), and thousands of sculptures, large and small, make a monumental encyclopedia of the beliefs, hopes, and learning of the Middle Ages.

5. *Pythagoras.* Chartres.

6. *Harvester,* representing the month of July. West facade, Chartres.

7. *Kings and Queens of the Old Testament,* from West Portal, Chartres.

1. *Herod.* Stained glass window from the Basilica of St. Denis, north of Paris. About 1145.

Stained glass windows from the Basilica of St. Denis, the Cathedral at Chartres, and the Church of St. Pierre, also in Chartres, opened up the high walls of these Gothic churches.

2. *Rose window.* North transept, Cathedral, Chartres. About 1230.

3. *St. Andrew*. Stained glass window. Church of St. Pierre, Chartres. About 1300.

4. *St. Bartholomew*. Stained glass window. Church of St. Pierre, Chartres. About 1300.

1. *Resurrection of the Virgin.* Tympanum of Senlis Cathedral. End of 12th century.

As Gothic style progressed, sculptors grew freer with their tools and their ideas. Instead of copying manuscripts, some artists, thinking independently, began to choose models from life, basing their designs upon shapes and actions they had observed. Slowly, the sculptures which had lain closely against the cathedral walls began to move out in space, to take a step forward, as though shaking off a heavy weight. Although the angels' robes at Senlis Cathedral are still carved in thin, wiry lines, the figures move with extraordinary grace and freedom, turning to their task with concentration instead of standing stiffly to each side of the prostrate figure (*Fig. 1*).

3. French Bible illustration: *Saul Destroys Nahash and the Ammonites.* Paris. About 1250.

2. Gothic manuscript illustration: *The Shepherd David.* 13th century.

Other Gothic arts also progressed toward freedom and a kind of liveliness once favored by Greek artists. The Christian shepherd (*Fig. 2*) is still not executed with the grace and perfect anatomical detail of the Byzantine David on page 64, but the artist was trying to achieve that same spirit of kindly peace. However, while the smaller arts flowered, the Gothic cathedral itself, once a well-planned solution to an architectural problem, began to change in a less happy way. Ornamentation was carried to such lengths that it began to overgrow the structure. Amiens Cathedral, completed in the late 13th century, was touched with such ornamentation, like tongues of flame, and the style came to be called "Flamboyant."

5. *La Vierge d'Orée* ("Golden Virgin"). Amiens Cathedral. About 1250

The "Beautiful God" of Amiens is almost a free-standing sculpture (*Fig. 4*). On the south portal is the figure of Mary known as the "Golden Virgin," subject of the loving worship which grew in fervor during these centuries (*Fig. 5*). At first stern and supernatural like the young Ste. Foy (page 108), she gradually became a human figure with gentle features, crowned like a princess. No longer content simply to carve her elegant, gowned figure, the sculptor now has set her body in a graceful and natural hipshot pose.

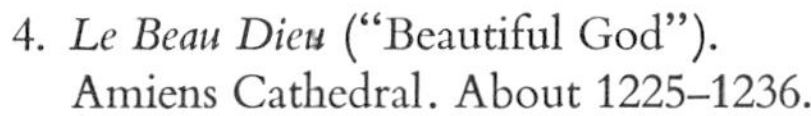

4. *Le Beau Dieu* ("Beautiful God"). Amiens Cathedral. About 1225–1236.

6. *Ekkehart and Uta.* Naumburg Cathedral. From the Western choir. 1250–1260.

Gothic sculpture had followed the same course as Greek sculpture had between the 6th and 3rd centuries B.C. At first rigid, and modeled in harsh, flat planes, the forms became more natural, then soft, relaxed, and meditative, and at last, aggressively scored with the hard marks of individual personality. (Compare the figures at right with those on pages 42–43.) The most naturalistic figures of Gothic cathedral art stand in the great Saxon cathedrals in Naumberg and Bamberg. Here, artists from the time of the Ottonian Empire had always kept a lively interest in the many facets of the human personality.

1. French Gothic: *Head of Christ*. Early 14th century. *h.* 9½″.

LATE GOTHIC NORTH

2. Matthias Grünewald: *Crucifixion.* From the Isenheim Altar. 1512–1515.

Medieval art had passed its zenith by the 14th century. Still, for a century more, the art of northern Europe remained Gothic in spirit and style. Here, art proceeded on two levels. In 1348, the arrival of the plague terrorized the whole Western world and produced a wild growth of art which today we might call "expressionistic," or even "surrealistic." Morbid concern with death and everlasting punishment, and the final agony of Christ, became new subjects for art, and were treated in the intricate style already evolved by stonecutters and painters. This morbid spirit continued into the 16th century.

At the same time, nations were being formed and a bristling nationalistic spirit prevailed. The Hundred Years' War, begun in 1337, aroused throughout Europe a sense of high courage and pride not seen since the Crusades two centuries before. Now, however, courage and pride were at the service of kings as well as the Church. And the greatest artists of all Europe laid their most precious work at the feet of their kings. From this international commerce of princes and artists arose what is called the International Style in painting, sculpture, and in the minor arts of tapestry-making and ivory carving. Elegant, mannered, and sophisticated, concerned with the trivial and delightful pleasures of everyday life, the International stylists set the stage for the great court arts which were to follow in Flanders, Versailles, and Vienna. But the boldest of the International artists lived, not in regal France, but in the Netherlands. For there, in the 15th century, oil painting was invented and the modern world's first school of portrait painting was born.

One third of all the people in Europe died of the bubonic plague. Reflecting the terror which followed in its wake, artists invented new images: Christ crucified, bloodstained, and torn by thorns was one (*Fig. 1*), very different in spirit from the transfigured *Christ in Majesty* of the 12th century. Another image was the *Dance of Death.* This morbid spirit lingered on into the 16th century in isolated regions, particularly in the Flanders and Germany of Bosch (*Fig. 3* and pages 124–125) and Grunewald (*Fig. 2*). Their works, though contemporary with the beginnings of the Renaissance in the North, are still medieval in detail and "expressionistic" imagery, as can be seen in Bosch's famous triptych, *The Garden of Worldly Delights* (page 124–125).

3. School of Bosch: *Christ's Descent into Hell.* First quarter 16th century.

1. Hieronymus Bosch: *Garden of Worldly Delights*. About 1500.

The 15th century saw a great flowering of the art of painting, which had been confined in the Middle Ages mainly to the decorating of manuscript pages or walls of churches. Even then, though, some book pages had begun to use the diminutive paintings independent of the text or the music (*Fig. 2*). The artists used tiny, pointed brushes and bright pigments made of powdered stones, berries, metals, and shells. They now could draw graceful limbs and features, dainty costumes adorned with patches of color. But they were also groping for an illusion of reality upon a flat surface. These late Gothic artists, who knew nothing of Classical painting, did not try to achieve this illusion as Greek and Roman artists had, with misty paint strokes and "impressionistic" shadows. Instead, they tried to build up small patchworks of landscape, figures, and buildings into a kind of mosaic diagram. The greatest of these painters were the brothers Limbourg, who worked for the dukes of Berry and Burgundy. The pictures in their *Book of Hours* (*Fig. 1*) are full-page scenes of court ladies and men, and the peaceable peasants who worked outside the castle walls. In an effort to add dimension the artists tried to make the fields appear to recede, and the tiny figures diminish in size as they retreated. All through Europe artists worked on such elegant, detailed pictures, precious enough to please the princes and ambitious enough to satisfy the artists. The painter of the Wilton Diptych laid gold leaf upon the wooden panel to make it as sumptuous as a Byzantine icon (*Fig. 3*); but his own interest is evident in the careful detail of the faces and postures.

1. Book illumination: Pol de Limbourg and his brothers: *Les Très Riches Heures of Duc de Berry*. Page of the month of March showing Chateau de Lusignan. About 1416.

2. *Pontifical of Metz:* "Bishop Dedicating a Church." 1302–1316.

3. English painting, by an unknown master: *Wilton Diptych* (left panel). King Richard presented to the Virgin and Child by his patron Saints. About 1395.

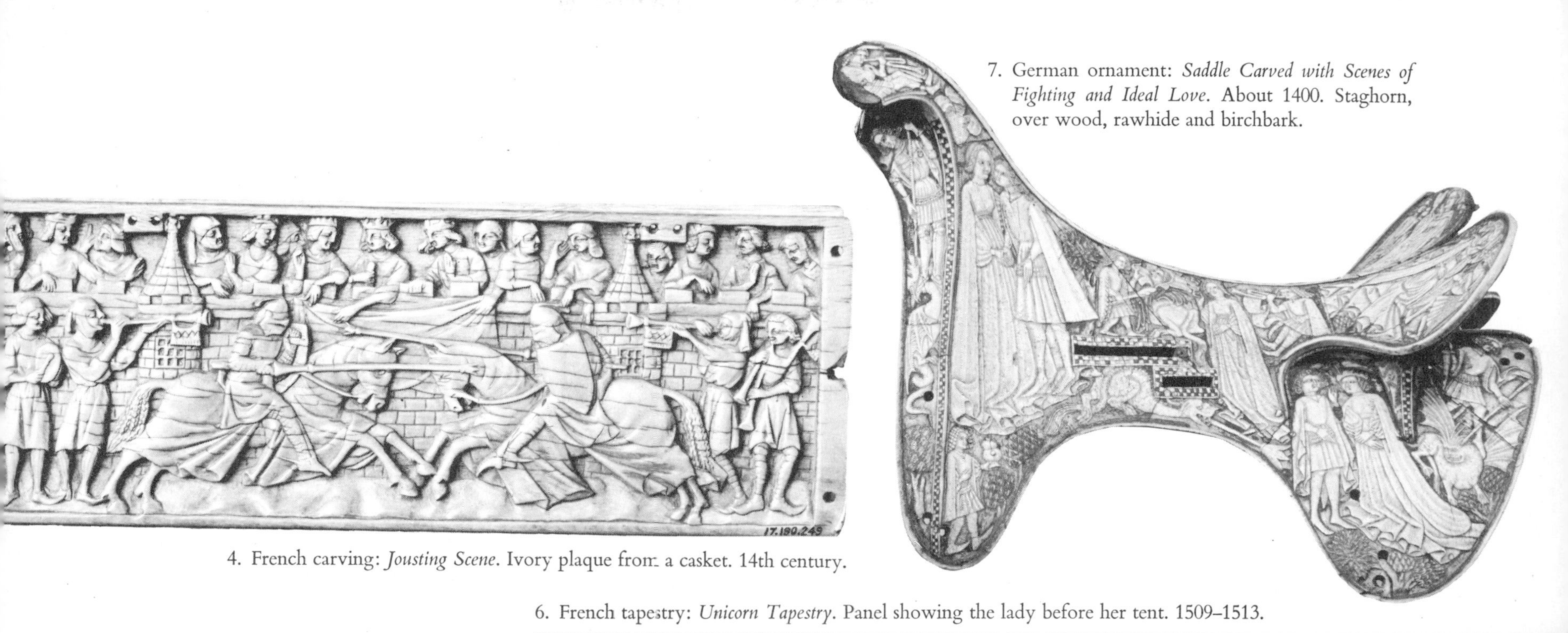

7. German ornament: *Saddle Carved with Scenes of Fighting and Ideal Love*. About 1400. Staghorn, over wood, rawhide and birchbark.

4. French carving: *Jousting Scene*. Ivory plaque from a casket. 14th century.

6. French tapestry: *Unicorn Tapestry*. Panel showing the lady before her tent. 1509–1513.

The International Style, elegant and dainty, touched many arts. Ivory carvers not only made stiff little holy figures for the devout. Now they carved scenes of love and chivalry on boxes, combs, and plaques for the courtiers (*Fig. 4*). Even saddles were intricately carved with heroic or romantic scenes (*Fig. 7*). Weavers made great tapestries to warm the clammy stone walls of the northern castles (*Fig. 6*). In these woolen tapestries, nobles stroll along flower-strewn pathways, acting out the popular legends and love stories of the time. Some of these patterns, like the "mille fleurs," or "thousand flowers," woven into the backgrounds, had been imported from the Near East by the Crusaders.

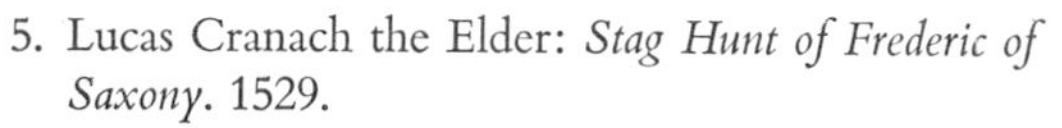

5. Lucas Cranach the Elder: *Stag Hunt of Frederic of Saxony*. 1529.

The International Style, like the "expressionistic" Late Gothic style (page 123), lingered on into the 16th century in Germany, in the work of such an artist as Cranach, who still fitted the tiny details of animals, men, rippled brook, and trees into an enamel-bright pattern.

During the 15th century, a great many painters with experimental ideas appeared in the country of Flanders. Although trained in the same techniques of the International Style as the artists in France and Germany, the Flemish were not the employees of the courts. Instead, they worked on commission for the rich businessmen and merchants of their thriving young country. Like their colleagues, they sought a more realistic way of portraying landscapes and portraits without using the bright, flat water colors of manuscript painting. For some time, many painters had experimented with a mixture of oil, rather than water or egg-white as a "binder" or liquid to hold the dry pigments. Finally, the painter Jan van Eyck perfected the method and made the first real "oil paintings." This medium allowed the artist to spread on layer after layer of color, bright and warm beneath, cool and pale near the surface. The transparent glow of these layers of paint made a blooming surface which was more subtle and alive than the water colors of the past. Now each Flemish artist worked on his own, specializing in particular problems of color, structure, or composition.

1. Flemish painting: Jan van Eyck: *The Madonna of Chancellor Rolin.* 1435.

Perhaps when Jan van Eyck painted the picture above, it seemed to him that the very horizons of his world, both actually and artistically, were stretching out beyond the boundaries of medieval thought. Here, he has swept open a great, sun-filled vista between the dainty Madonna and her devoted Chancellor. Although the hazy distance is painted with a breadth and airiness hardly seen since the Classical world, van Eyck lined up his figures precisely to left and right, and made his composition as equilateral and balanced as the twin towers of a Gothic cathedral.

2. Petrus Christus: *Legend of Saints Eligius and Godeberta.* 1449.

The Flemish world was one of down-to-earth shopkeepers and traders. These people were interested in the prosaic world around them, not in the fairy-tale romances of the French courts. So their artists, like Petrus Christus, often painted scenes of the very objects and rooms these men inhabited, their pipes and tools, their pet dogs, their shy brides. Here, a young couple is visiting a jeweler's shop. The artist has drawn each object with great care, even the figures reflected in the convex mirror at the right.

3. Hugo van der Goes: *Detail of Portinari Altarpiece.* 1473–1475.

4. *Maison du Roi in the Place de Ville* (market place). Brussels. First half of 15th century.

5. Rogier van der Weyden: *Portrait of a Lady.* 1455.

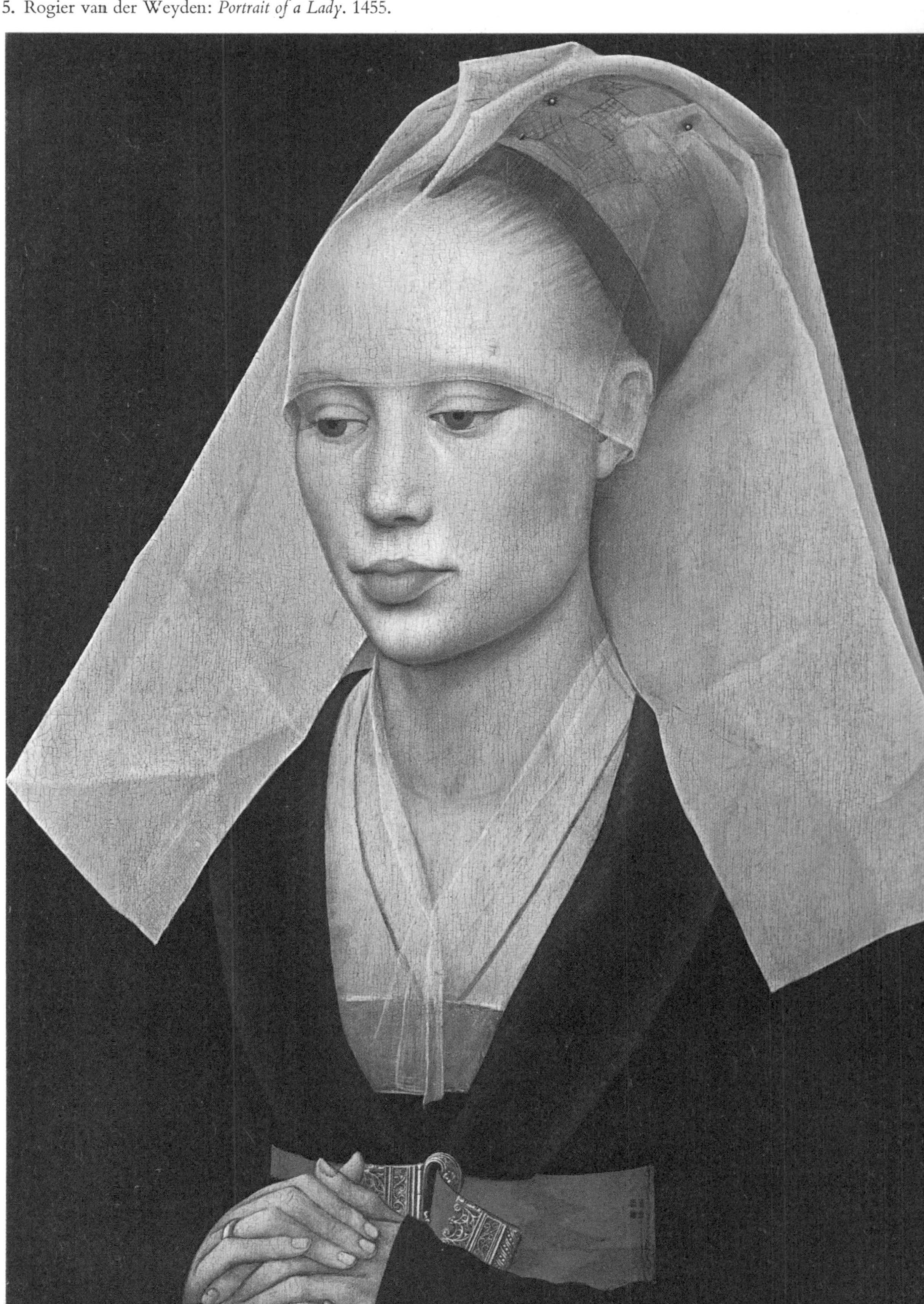

The huge altarpiece from which this tiny detail, above, is taken was brought from Flanders to Italy, where it stirred up great excitement among the Italian painters.

The human face has presented many tantalizing problems to artists. In some periods, painters cared little for the individual marks of personality and preferred to show the "ideal" or perfect beauty and serenity of the face. Greek artists of the Classic period made this kind of "ideal" portrait. Later, the Romans made portraits which included every detail, beautiful or ugly. In the Middle Ages, when art reflected the general concern with religious ideas, artists turned from human to divine figures, and human portraiture became a lost art. Now, however, with the beginning of the Renaissance, man once more became the primary subject of art. Artists usually worked for a patron. These patrons, prideful and prosperous members of the new society, wished to perpetuate their own memories. Sometimes, too, portraits were used as official introductions by people who were separated by great distances: perhaps a newly crowned king and the Pope, or a prince and the woman he was destined to marry. Flemish portraits showed the precise look of the sitter, but made little attempt to reflect the individual personality that would come later.

1. Sassetta: *Journey of the Magi.* About 1430.

THE ITALIAN RENAISSANCE

FLORENCE AND ROME

While northern Europe slowly pursued its course through Romanesque, Gothic, and International styles, Italy had embarked upon another course. There, Gothic painting, sculpture, and architecture differed radically from its northern counterpart; it was more tailored to human size, and less mysterious and awe-inspiring. In the 13th century two monks had founded orders whose philosophy was to bring the true Renaissance closer. St. Francis turned men's thoughts away from awe and terror, toward a greater affection for their fellows. St. Dominic's monastic order trained the Renaissance princes and made education a noble pursuit. While the special brand of Gothic art and thought produced in Italy foreshadowed much of Renaissance spirit, there were even more ancient and tangible sources. The ruins of Greek and Roman antiquity lay all about the countryside, surviving the Germanic invaders who had finally settled there and incidentally, added their driving energy to the native Italian stock. Italy, moreover, had never been cut off from the Mediterranean civilizations of Byzantium and Islam: trade always brought works of art, and even artists, from eastern workshops. From all these contacts with sophisticated arts, the Renaissance of the 15th century would grow. The true Renaissance—an extraordinary coincidence of genius, energy, and opportunity—centered around the Tuscan city of Florence, and the rich, enterprising merchant cities of Bruges and Ghent in Flanders. There, for the first time since Athens, artists, politicians, and scientists together affirmed the humanist principle that "wonders are there many, but none so wonderful as man." Each artist pursued his own interests, studied anatomy, perspective, and the sciences of color and vision, of engineering, and of weights and counterweights in space. As knowledge flowered, so did the invention of ideal images of man, the adventurer, the creator, the master of his own life. For a century, wave after wave of brilliant artists appeared. Then when the energy of the Renaissance seemed to flag at last, three of the greatest artists of Western civilization stepped forward, to open even greater vistas to a future still centuries away.

2. Duccio di Buoninsegna: *Temptation of Christ* from the *Maesta*. 1308–1311.

These three paintings were made in Siena, a medieval town where the Renaissance did not penetrate until long after Florence and other progressive cities had moved far ahead. In Siena, the Gothic-Byzantine style, invented for the painting of icons, lingered on. From the Greek heritage in Byzantine painting, the Sienese took their graceful way of drawing the human figure. From the oriental element in Byzantine painting, they inherited a delight in radiant color, particularly in gold-leaf backgrounds and crimson and green garments. Then, bit by bit, from more progressive artists of Florence and Flanders, Sienese artists learned to set figures within realistic landscapes, and to give them a sense of natural motion. The great master of the Gothic style in Siena was Duccio di Buoninsegna (*Fig. 2*). Duccio's figures move like graceful Classical ghosts among the spiny little hills, the minute architecture, and the glowing gold background.

3. Giovanni di Paolo: *The Expulsion*.

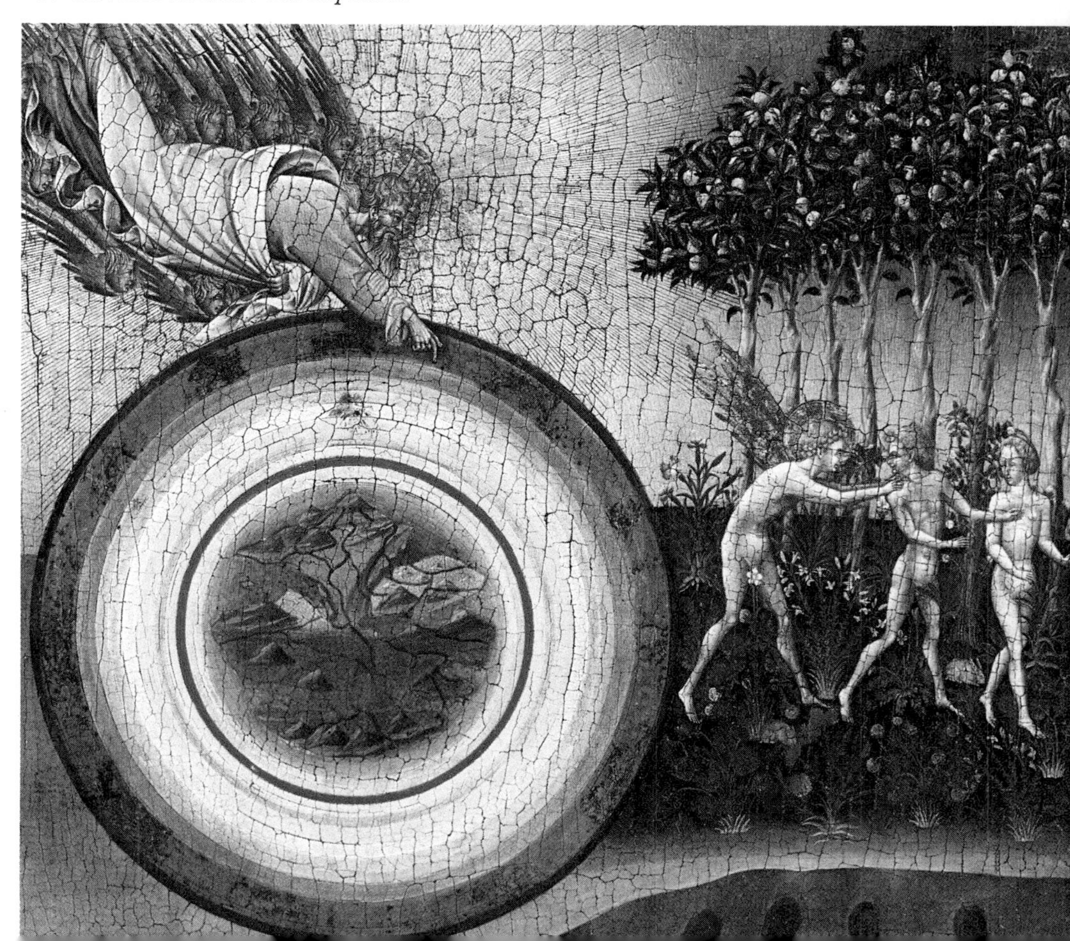

A century and a half later than Duccio, Giovanni di Paolo still worked in an old-fashioned style. His dainty figures move within a flower-strewn landscape like those of the International Style of France (see page 126). The subject of the painting at right was medieval, too. God the Father, as He watches the unfortunate Adam and Eve driven out of Paradise, points to a flat graph, which was the medieval Christian idea of the universe. The green circle at the center is the same Paradise which the artist has painted in detail at the right. The concentric outer circles are the realms of the sun, the stars, and the planets. For many centuries, medieval monks had developed this kind of false theory of the universe. One task of the Renaissance would be to rediscover the true facts, forgotten in the West since the Classical world had fallen.

The groundwork for the Italian Renaissance had already been laid by certain forward-looking artists of the Gothic age. Here, each facing pair of works—in painting, sculpture, and architecture—illustrates this fact. On this page are works of the 13th century; on page 133 are works of the 15th century. What the Gothic artists tried out, Renaissance artists carried to fulfillment. One of the great innovators in art was Giotto di Bondone (*Fig. 2*). Some said he was a poor shepherd boy who learned to draw on flat rocks in the fields. Whatever his origins, Giotto had learned to look closely at nature before he drew, to study the action of figures and animals, the way trees grow and hills recede. Then he set out to do what no northern Gothic artist had considered: he tried to eliminate each detail which would confuse his scene; he made his designs more and more simple, natural, and varied. In a modest, human way he has presented the great Gothic figure, Saint Francis, whose message, too, was one of simplicity and naturalness.

2. Giotto di Bondone: *St. Francis Preaching to the Birds.* Basilica of St. Francis, Assisi. Late 13th century. Fresco.

1. Niccolo Pisano: *Nativity*. Detail from pulpit in the Baptistery, Pisa. Between 1258–1278.

The pulpit which Niccolo Pisano designed in 1260 for his native town of Pisa was unique in that the artist took as models for his scenes the fragments of Roman sculpture he found lying about, rather than using medieval manuscripts or ivories as sources. The scene at left is one of the side panels from that pulpit. The particular Roman coffin, or sarcophagus, which Niccolo chose for his model some 800 years later, was probably made in the late years of the Roman Empire, when the art of sculpture had already begun to be adulterated by new styles filtering in from the Near East (see pages 56, 61). At that time, it had become acceptable to group several scenes together into one design to show a sequence of events. But the figures are realistically proportioned and draped in the heavy robes of Roman matrons.

3. *Cathedral and Campanile,* Pisa. 11th–12th centuries.

Italian Gothic architecture, unlike French, was horizontal in its general aspect. Structures were simple and delicate rather than monumental. The architects had perhaps been influenced by the Corinthian columns they saw surrounding the ruins of Roman temples. Instead of creating gigantic ensembles of sculpture which turned the church and cathedral porches into theaters of stone, these medieval architects often decorated their buildings with ranks of slender columns, and with black and white marble stripes. The effect was one of buildings designed to the proportions of men, instead of the superhuman edifices of the northern Gothic architects. The spirit of Greece seems to echo in these delicate, sun-washed cathedrals which dot the hills of Tuscany.

Nearly two centuries later, the Renaissance sculptor Donatello also looked at Classical carvings when he prepared to design a series of plaques for the altar rail of the cathedral of St. Anthony of Padua (*Fig. 4*). Like Niccolò Pisano, he organized his scene along horizontal lines, as though it had been taken from a rectangular sarcophagus relief. His figures, like Masaccio's, recede into the background, overlapping one another and turning aside as though a camera had caught them in action. Every detail contributes to the one central effect: a wild abandon which sweeps the mourning figures. This was an extraordinary work of art, even for the Renaissance, which more often showed figures restrained and serene. Donatello has drawn every figure into a panorama of agony, weaving flying hair and flailing arms into a unified composition. Perhaps, too, by making the tomb stand so quietly and stolidly in the foreground, he meant to suggest that the broken figure of Christ would endure this moment.

5. Masaccio: *Tribute Money*. 1427. Fresco.

4. Donatello: *The Deposition*. Terra cotta.

Giotto's style was reborn in Florence in the paintings of Masaccio, nicknamed Clumsy Tom because he was said to have forgotten to eat or to comb his hair when he was absorbed in his art. Masaccio went further than Giotto in creating a life-like scene upon a flat surface (*Fig. 5*). In a way, he had rediscovered the technique of painting the atmosphere which the Alexandrian Greeks had developed 1,400 years earlier. In the picture above, he opens the background, showing the sky and pushing back the horizon, which recedes like an actual vista. Masaccio had learned how to give the illusion of depth by placing figures one behind the other and by joining the bodies and scenery together in such a manner as to guide the eye into the picture. Then he went on to experiment with "aerial" perspective as well, the quality the earth's atmosphere gives to objects, making them mistier and bluer the farther they are from the viewer. A silky, glistening air flows between Masaccio's figures, separating them as though they actually stood in space. The figures themselves are still more "plastic" or solid than Giotto's, and are linked together into patterns by their outstretched arms and the sweeping folds of their garments.

Wide and low, the wings of Brunelleschi's orphanage stretch out, close to the ground. Across the sunny front porch, slender, wide arches are borne on unfluted Corinthian columns. The "Innocenti," too, has something of the quality of a Greek temple. In general, all Renaissance architecture followed the same ideal: man-sized scale, and balanced, harmonious forms. Instead of the soaring pointed Gothic arch, Renaissance architects preferred a gently rounded curve. Instead of the long, shadowy nave which gave an air of mystery to the northern cathedral, they preferred the enfolding wing plan of the Innocenti, or the circular ground plan.

6. Filippo Brunelleschi: *Orphanage of the Innocents*, Florence. 1421–1424.

Cathedral, Florence. 1296–1462.
(1) Dome—Brunelleschi
(2) Bell tower—Giotto
(3) Baptistery doors—Andrea Pisano and Lorenzo Ghiberti

In a sense, the Renaissance was born around the great cathedral in the center of Florence, in the main city square (*Fig. 1*). Built over the course of two centuries, the cathedral was first laid out in typical Italian Gothic style, without the towering vertical lines of French Gothic. Then, in 1334, Giotto was named town architect. He supervised part of the construction of the church and also designed the fanciful bell tower which rises at its right, inlaid with geometric designs in colored marble. Before the cathedral stands the octagonal Baptistery, which was roofed inside with a dome like the Pantheon's.

The final major work of construction was completed in 1437, when the architect Brunelleschi managed to erect the great dome upon the cathedral. None of his predecessors had been able to devise a way of building such a wide dome: Brunelleschi solved the problem by using Gothic ribs fixed at the base, and then filled in between with a webbing of brick. Two dome shells of dovetailed bricks were suspended one above the other with iron chains and prop poles. For extra height, the entire structure was mounted on a drum. The effect of this towering crown was so spectacular that Michelangelo later borrowed some of its details for his dome on St. Peter's Cathedral in Rome (page 154).

2. Filippo Brunelleschi: *Sacrifice of Isaac.* Trial panel for Baptistery doors, Florence. Bronze. 1402.

3. Lorenzo Ghiberti: *Sacrifice of Isaac.* Winning panel for Baptistery doors. 1402. Bronze.

In 1402, the city council of Florence decided to commission a new pair of doors for the cathedral Baptistery. The old pair had been fashioned by a member of the famous Pisano family of Gothic times (see page 132). Now the city, growing rich on the flourishing wool trade, decided to offer the challenge to the best and most progressive artists of the day. A competition was arranged, and sculptors were asked to design a trial panel, to be cast in bronze. The subject was to be the "Sacrifice of Isaac," chosen not only for its dramatic and religious interest, but also because it was a good test for an artist, for it would have to include a great many figures and objects, many in motion. The prize went to Lorenzo Ghiberti, who then worked on his doors for twenty-one years. When he finished this pair, he started work on another pair, which occupied him until the end of his life. Michelangelo found these last doors so beautiful that he called them the "Gates of Paradise." The doors were made, as were all major commissions at that time, in the artist's workshop, where he planned and supervised the project and was helped by many young apprentices, or student artists. By the time Ghiberti had finished his life's work, almost every sculptor of the Renaissance had worked with him in his studio at one time or another.

5. Lorenzo Ghiberti: *The Story of Abraham*. Detail from the *Gates of Paradise*. Baptistery, Florence.

4. Lorenzo Ghiberti: *Gates of Paradise*. Baptistery, Florence. About 1425–1452.

Compare Ghiberti's winning panel for the Baptistery doors in Florence (*Fig. 3*) with a panel by one of the losers, the same Brunelleschi who later specialized in architecture (*Fig. 2*). Both panels reflect elements of Gothic style, for each scene is set into a quatrefoil and arranged like a little picture on a manuscript page (see page 126, *Fig. 2*). Within this frame, however, each artist has approached his problem differently. Brunelleschi seems to have considered each figure by itself, rather like the disorganized figures in Niccolo Pisano's Pulpit (page 132). However, Ghiberti tried to pull the scattered details into a simple design. Ghiberti also did something that none of the other competing artists attempted: he planned to cast each scene in a single piece of metal, whereas Brunelleschi and the others cast their panels in many small parts or scenes, and then nailed them in place. In attempting this difficult casting feat, Ghiberti had to instruct himself in the art of "composition." He had to make each object flow into the one nearby, so that in casting, the parts would not break off. Each small detail had to be subordinated to the larger shapes. After Ghiberti's time, the "composition" of a work of art became as important as its detail and story. By the time Ghiberti designed his Gates of Paradise (*Fig. 4*), he dispensed with the constricting medallion and considered each block as a painting in bronze (*Fig. 5*). "I tried to imitate nature," Ghiberti explained, "to understand how objects strike upon the eye. These, I modeled upon different planes, so that those nearest the eye might appear larger, and those more remote, smaller in proportion."

1. Donatello: *David*. About 1430. Bronze. *h.* 60½″.

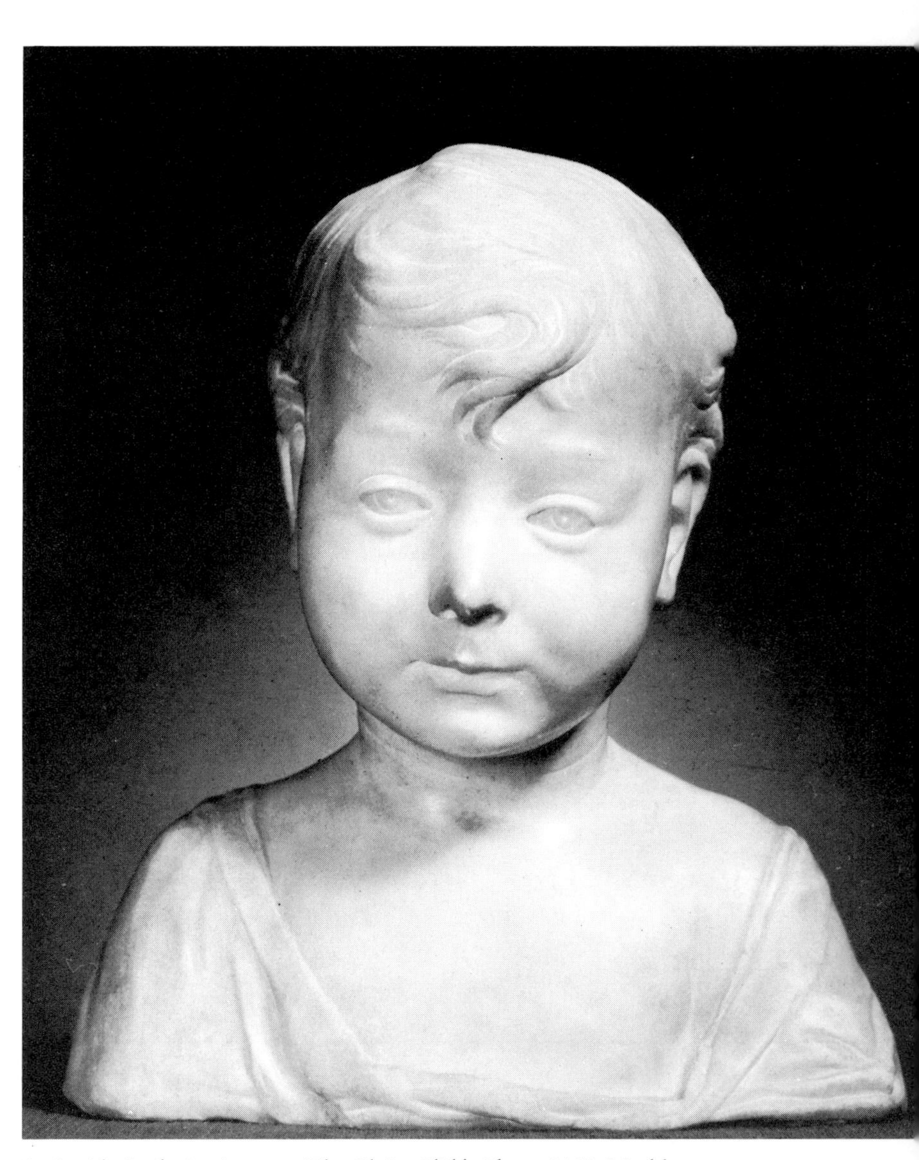

2. Desiderio da Settignano: *The Christ Child.* About 1460. Marble.

The works on these pages, from left to right, show how Renaissance sculpture evolved from a youthful stage in the work of Donatello, to a proud, self-assured maturity in the hands of Pollaiuolo and Verrocchio. Donatello himself had to learn, step by step, the ancient knowledge of anatomy and the physics of movement. With his friend Brunelleschi, Donatello went off to Rome, after both artists had lost the Florentine Baptistery competition. There he studied, measured, and tried to imagine how to reconstruct the broken statues and temples. People called the two young artists the "treasure seekers," thinking they were looking for ancient Roman coins. But Donatello and Brunelleschi were the first Renaissance archaeologists, and their discoveries opened the door for the inventions of style that followed. Donatello's figures are rather delicate in scale; their youthful bodies seem to harbor an intense but restrained energy. Many of his subjects were young heroes of legend who struck out alone against oppression: John the Baptist, St. George, and David. For, as Donatello struggled against one kind of medieval limitation, so, during this time, Florence was trying to win her independence from the Papacy and the Holy Roman Empire. Donatello's *David* was the first free-standing, nude sculpture made in the West since antiquity. The figure stood all alone, in its flower-decked helmet, in the palace courtyard of the artist's great patrons, the Medici (see page 142). Donatello also made the first equestrian statue since that of Marcus Aurelius was made in ancient Rome (page 54).

After Donatello, Florentine sculptors experimented with various ways of portraying the human body. Some, like Desiderio (*Fig. 2*), carved such delicate features that the skin of marble seems to have been only lightly touched, almost as with a paintbrush. One of the most famous of his followers was Luca della Robbia. He had invented a way of coating clay figures with glazes made of a secret blend of molten glass and oxide of tin. His greens, blues, purples, and whites gave the fragile clay more strength and also an air of lively reality. Many members of the della Robbia family worked together; the bust on the right is by Andrea della Robbia. From all over Tuscany orders flooded in for the family sculptures of delicate figures with downcast eyes and soft smiles, often surrounded by azure skies and wreaths of flowers (*Fig. 4*).

4. Andrea della Robbia: *Young Florentine Lady*. 1470–80. Glazed terra cotta.

5. Antonio Pollaiuolo: *Hercules and Antaeus*. Bronze. *h.* 18″.

3. Andrea del Verrocchio: *Colleoni* (a condottiere or military leader). Completed in 1496. Bronze.

By the late years of the 15th century, artists had mastered every step of carving and casting in bronze. Now they could tackle difficult problems of pose and dramatic personality. Pollaiuolo spent his life studying the human body in extremes of action. In painting, engraving, and sculpture, he explored ways of showing the body thrown out of balance, grotesquely strained and struggling. The small bronze group above represents the instant when Hercules, the legendary Greek hero, managed to defeat Antaeus, his enemy, by lifting him off the earth, from which he derived his great strength. Verrocchio made use of the same twisted, strained composition in his *Colleoni* (*Fig. 3*). With an arrogant twist of his shoulders, a stern thrust of his boots in the stirrups, this professional soldier and his strutting horse seem to symbolize the spirit and power of the century.

1. Masaccio: *Expulsion*. 1427. Fresco.

2. Paolo Uccello: *A Young Lady of Fashion*. Before 1450.

The works on these pages, from left to right, show a similar evolution, from youth to maturity, in Renaissance painting. Like his contemporary, Donatello, Masaccio pointed the way for later artists, and created images that were symbolic of the Early Renaissance spirit. His *Adam and Eve* are stocky, and almost earthy in their proportions and their dulled, claylike colors. They stride forth from their garden paradise like anguished but acceptant human beings, harshly expelled from their world of security. Their postures and expressions, the solidity of their bodies, and the filmy atmosphere of the background lend a reality to the scene very different from the one painted twenty years later by the Sienese artist, Giovanni di Paolo (see page 131), which was still Gothic in manner, for Paolo lived in an area yet untouched by the Renaissance. Masaccio's figures have something of the quality which Michelangelo later developed—a sense of art and man on the very threshold of a new age, of change, with terror and discovery on all sides.

After Masaccio, Italian painters explored every technical problem of their art and, like the sculptors, often specialized in the representation of individual personalities and tortuous movement. With the rise of a powerful merchant class, portraits were again in demand, as signs of success and wealth. At first, many Renaissance portraits were painted in profile form (*Fig. 2*), an idea copied from the Classical coins, to suggest the subjects' proud heritage from ancient Roman predecessors. Later, the full-face portrait became more popular. Uccello, who painted the portrait at left, was just as interested in painting scenes of battles and the hunt (pages 140–141), for in these he could let his imagination run freely, in studies of composition and space. Compare Uccello's animated, yet tightly knit scene of horses and men, their bodies almost scientifically adjusted into various perspectives, to the same subject by the Gothic-spirited German artist Cranach (page 127), full of "errors" of drawing. Antonio Pollaiuolo's paintings, like his sculptures, were essays in fast, distorting movement. The painting below (*Fig. 3*) shows the Greek nymph Daphne, at the very moment when she turns into a tree to escape from the god, Apollo. By posing his figures at the moment of violent action, Pollaiuolo could portray the utmost movement and tension. Yet this scene is more romantic and lyrical than most of his works; behind the flying figures, a gentle, river-wound landscape stretches into the misty distance. Only twenty years separate his painting from Uccello's; yet a great change in the style of landscape painting had taken place.

3. Antonio Pollaiuolo: *Apollo and Daphne*. 1475.

Signorelli was influenced by the work of Pollaiuolo, and his series of great frescoes of the Day of Judgment are writhing masses of human bodies in every position of agony and fear. In this corner of a fresco (*Fig. 4*), Signorelli packed a multitude of different positions and gestures, and he linked figure to figure, just as Masaccio had done earlier, by parallel patterns of arms, legs, and torsos, and colors which are repeated from body to body, making interlocking lines across the surface.

4. Luca Signorelli: Detail from *The End of the World*. 1500–1504. Fresco.

1. Paolo Uccello: *A Hunt in a Forest*. About 1460–1475.

1. Sandro Botticelli: *Pallas and the Centaur.*

In Florence and a few other cities, the Renaissance arts were stimulated and subsidized by individual families, some of the nobility, and others, brilliant and wealthy merchants. Between these cities and powerful families, swashbuckling skirmishes took place and the arts of war flourished alongside those of painting, sculpture, and architecture. At far right (*Fig. 6*), is an example of the kind of armor these Renaissance men wore. In Florence, the ruling family was the Medici, who were rich and cultivated bankers. One of the first heads of the family had sat on the jury which awarded Ghiberti the commission for the Baptistery doors (see page 134). One of the last members of the family, in the 16th century, became Queen of France. But the two greatest Medicis, who lived during the years which produced Donatello and Michelangelo, were Cosimo, "Father of His Country," and Lorenzo, "The Magnificent." Their portraits are at right (*Figs. 4, 5*), carved in relief upon large bronze medallions, popular at the time because they resembled Roman coins. The Medici palace in Florence (*Fig. 2*) was the center of Renaissance activity. Fortress-like on the outside and built out to the street in blocks of "rusticated" stone, it was like a museum within.

Donatello's *David* stood in the courtyard; fragments of antique sculptures stood all about. The artists and scholars of Florence gathered in this palace, dining, talking, and studying the past. Art and learning first flowered under the patronage of Cosimo. After the Turks overran Constantinople in 1453, a wave of Greek refugee scholars came to the palace and taught the Florentines to read the Classics in the original. Soon a special Academy was set up to study Greek and Roman art and ideas. This new study was called Humanism. Though many of the Humanists were also devout Christians, they hoped to bring about a fresher, more natural attitude toward art and life than had existed in the Middle Ages. To this end, they put on splendid festivals and pageants, often based on Classical myths or allegorical scenes. All the artists of the Medici circle collaborated on these pageants, designing scenery and costumes and marvelous floats in which even the horses were draped in tiger skins or golden armor. An impression of these pageants has come down to us in some of the paintings of Botticelli. His *Primavera* (pages 144–145), and *Pallas and the Centaur* at left, (*Fig. 1*), may be based on episodes from such events. The latter picture is a symbol of Renaissance wisdom overcoming the unruly past. Botticelli's style during those years was unique in virile Florence, for its almost feminine delicacy. The line with which he drew his figures (*Fig. 3*) is as lyrical and sensitive as a Chinese brush stroke.

2. Michelozzo: *Medici-Riccardi Palace,* Florence. 1444–1459.

3. Sandro Botticelli: *Dante and Beatrice Leaving Purgatory*. Illustration to Dante's *Divine Comedy, Paradise I.* 1492–1497.

6. *Armor of a Renaissance Prince*. German. 1460.

Under the leadership of the brilliant, imaginative, and luxury-loving Lorenzo, Humanist art and pleasures reached their zenith. But many people in Florence disapproved of the Humanist festivals and the splendid paintings, sculpture, and costumes which celebrated them. A picture like Botticelli's *Primavera* (pages 144–145), which portrays the coming of springtime as a Greek nymph passing through a grove, seemed too pagan for their tastes. As the year 1500 drew nearer, superstitious people began to fear the Day of Judgment as their predecessors had before the year 1000. Preachers railed against the pagan flavor of the Renaissance, with its paintings and sculptures of the nude human body, pagan nymphs and gods. The fiercest of these priests was Savonarola (*Fig. 7*). In 1497, the Florentines heaped most of their luxuries—what Savonarola called their "vanities"—into a great pyramid, which was publicly burned. Thus vanished many great paintings and sculptures by Renaissance masters, together with wigs, rouge, and false beards, jewels, mirrors, furniture, and brocades. Although Savonarola himself soon followed his "vanities" to the stake, his violent words seemed to hang in the air. The Florentine Renaissance was over; a new phase in art and ideas was beginning.

5. Florentine medal with portrait of *Lorenzo de' Medici, "Il Magnifico."* Attrib. to Niccolo Fiorentino. 1490. Bronze.

4. Florentine medal with portrait of *Cosimo Vecchio de'Medici*. About 1464. Bronze.

7. Florentine medal with portrait of *Savonarola*. Workshop of the della Robbia. About 1496.

Next pages: Sandro Botticelli: *Primavera*. About 1478.

The history of art, through antiquity and the Middle Ages, is mainly the history of styles and general ideas, to which many artists contributed. But after the 15th century, from the time of the High Renaissance, the history of art becomes almost entirely the story of great, individual geniuses. Their inventions and discoveries continued to contribute to the evolution of style in Western art, but it is their separate, personal styles which stand out.

Experiment and adventure, the study of movement and heroism—these characterized the Early Renaissance in its Florentine phase. Yet there was another side to the Renaissance too, which reached its climax around the end of the 15th century. This turn-of-the-century art reflected the kind of absolute calm and assurance that comes with complete mastery of a subject. In this respect, artists like Piero della Francesca, Bramante, and Raphael were what the world has come to call "Renaissance men." They were men who had mastered many subjects, and were also able to sum up in their work the many cross-currents of thought which underlay their age. These three men were born in Umbria, the central hilly district of Italy. The glistening sunlight and atmospheric hazes peculiar to this region seemed to influence the coloring used by these artists. Piero worked in several towns of Umbria; Bramante and Raphael worked in Rome, which, as the century turned, took over artistic leadership from Florence.

2. Donato Bramante: *Tempietto*. San Pietro in Montorio, Rome. 1502.

1. Piero della Francesca: *Madonna and Saints*.

Piero della Francesca was a painter, Latin scholar, and mathematician of the 15th century. He wrote a scientific treatise on perspective, and he studied the physics of light. Behind this enigmatic painting (*Fig. 1*) lie his studies of Greek and Roman philosophy, particularly in its revived phase which was called "Neo-Platonism" by the Renaissance humanists. One Neo-Platonic principle was that the perfect geometry in natural objects, like a seashell or an egg, is parallel to the perfect Christian community of Christ and the Madonna. Piero has painted a kind of visual study of this complex idea. He was fascinated, too, by light which he saw falling upon these figures, shearing them off from space as a chisel might cut stone. Here, St. John the Baptist and several saints surround the rocklike Madonna. The egg, symbolic of Christ Himself, hangs motionless over the Madonna and Child. The fanlike shell in back of the archway, beloved by Greek artists and later taken as a symbol of the Madonna, shelters the group. At the Madonna's feet kneels the Duke of Urbino, Frederigo da Montefeltro, art patron in his city as the Medici were in Florence, who commissioned this and many other works. On pages 148–149 are reproduced the four panels from a diptych, or hinged double-picture, which he commissioned Piero della Francesca to make on the occasion of his marriage. On one side of the diptych are portraits of the Duke—famous for the notch in his nose made by a lance wound—and his bride. On the other side are scenes of the pair being drawn in nuptial carriages.

Bramante was a painter as well as an architect. The austere temple at left was erected in Rome, on the spot where legend said St. Peter had been crucified. Bramante took the simplest Classical architectural elements: unfluted columns of the Roman Order called "Tuscan," an unornamented architrave and balcony, and a small dome. The Tempietto is a kind of solid symbol of Humanistic self-containment and control. This, however, gave way to another style almost at the instant it reached its climax. Four years later, Bramante was called by Pope Julius II to design a new plan for St. Peter's Cathedral, to replace the Early Christian basilica erected in Constantine's time (see page 60). The Pope decided upon a centralized architectural plan for the new edifice, instead of the long, mysterious hallway of the earlier medieval buildings. In accord with this, Bramante's design, altered later by Michelangelo (see page 154), was an enormous Greek cross, with a vast central dome lifted on massive piers. The human-sized vision of the Tempietto had already given way to a superhuman conception.

Politically the world had changed during Bramante's lifetime. By the century's end, Florence had fallen into political confusion, and power was now focused around the Papacy in Rome. Bramante, Raphael, and the Italian artists who followed them, all worked for the Popes, where they were often subject to willful papal "visions," and to papal efforts to turn the ancient Christian capital into a center of High Renaissance art.

Raphael was primarily a painter, though he was also the architect of several important Roman buildings. He was an archaeologist during the time of Pope Leo X (1475–1521), in whose service he investigated many of the antique ruins which stood about the city. In his youth, Raphael had studied in the town of Perugia, with a master, Perugino, whose special talent was for portraying sweet-mannered, gently swaying figures of saints in the soft, hazy atmosphere of Umbria. In many of his own paintings, Raphael still expressed this poised and serene world of the past. The gentle figures in this painting balance one another as harmoniously as two wings of a dove, their bodies as curving and graceful as Late Gothic saints. This is one of Raphael's early works, painted when he was only 21. In a later period, his style grew more solid and compact. At that time he painted the famous Madonnas—the Sistine Madonna, the Madonna of the Meadow, the "Belle Jardinière," and others—which were so beloved during the Victorian period. Still later, he painted a series of stony and imposing frescoes in the Vatican itself (pages 150–151).

3. Raphael: *The Marriage of the Virgin.* 1504.

1. Piero della Francesca: *Bridal portrait of Federigo da Montefeltro, Duke of Urbino*. 1465–1466.

2–3. Piero della Francesca: *The Triumphs of the Duke and Duchess of Urbino*. 1465–1466.

4. Piero della Francesca: *Bridal portrait of Battista Sforza, Duchess of Urbino*. 1465–1466.

·NEPHAS·
EST
VBI
REX
REGVM
CHRISTVS
SPINEAM
CORONAM
TVLIT
CHRISTIANVM
HOMINEM
AVREAM
GESTARE

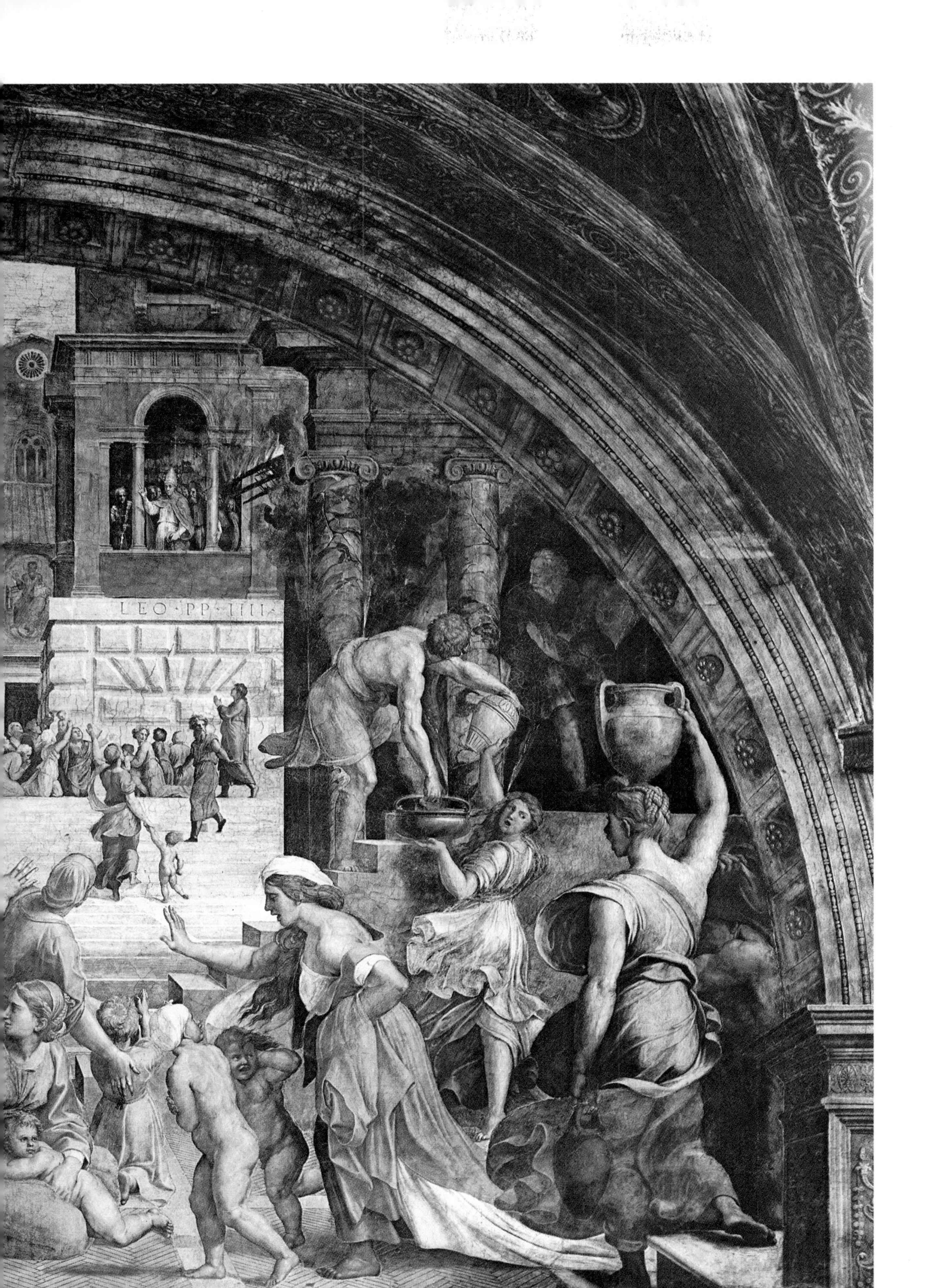

1. Raphael: *The Fire in the Borgo*. About 1514–1517. Fresco. Vatican, Rome.

1. Leonardo da Vinci: *Self-portrait.* About 1512. Red chalk.

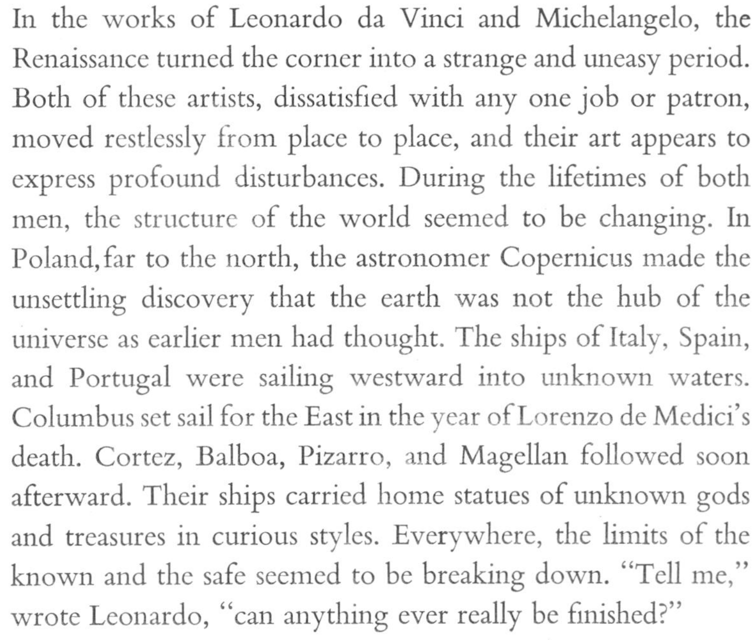

3. Leonardo da Vinci: *Studies of Horses.* About 1504.

In the works of Leonardo da Vinci and Michelangelo, the Renaissance turned the corner into a strange and uneasy period. Both of these artists, dissatisfied with any one job or patron, moved restlessly from place to place, and their art appears to express profound disturbances. During the lifetimes of both men, the structure of the world seemed to be changing. In Poland, far to the north, the astronomer Copernicus made the unsettling discovery that the earth was not the hub of the universe as earlier men had thought. The ships of Italy, Spain, and Portugal were sailing westward into unknown waters. Columbus set sail for the East in the year of Lorenzo de Medici's death. Cortez, Balboa, Pizarro, and Magellan followed soon afterward. Their ships carried home statues of unknown gods and treasures in curious styles. Everywhere, the limits of the known and the safe seemed to be breaking down. "Tell me," wrote Leonardo, "can anything ever really be finished?"

2. Leonardo da Vinci: *Lady with Ermine.* About 1483.

4. Leonardo da Vinci: *The Condottiere.* About 1480. Silverpoint drawing.

Leonardo was trained in the Florentine workshop of Verrocchio and later moved to Milan and Rome, finally ending his life in the service of Francis I in France. During his lifetime, he painted, made sculpture, and designed machinery and buildings. This colossal genius was interested in everything. He peered through magnifying glasses, watched storms and floods; he observed the grass growing, leaves uncurling, unborn babies. Everywhere he studied the facts of nature and recorded them in his notebooks, and everywhere he seemed to encounter uncertainty. Things grow, he saw, but they transform themselves, change, and wither away. Many of Leonardo's major paintings reflect this uncertainty. Staircases spiral off into the air as if they were ladders to nowhere (*Fig. 5*). The clear, sun-bathed atmosphere of Early Renaissance painting gave way to a veiled, smoky gloom, called "sfumato." Long after Leonardo's lifetime, other painters copied this sfumato effect to create a mysterious, unsettled impression.

Leonardo rarely brought a piece of work to completion, but those few which he did finish are drawn with a serpentine line of extraordinary power. In the picture at left (*Fig. 2*), the hand of the girl touches the throat of her pet mink with exquisite grace, while many conflicting thoughts seem to tighten the corners of her mouth. Many Italian artists after Leonardo imitated this suave, highly fluid line and the shadows of his flesh and textile tones; but without his genius, they found themselves employing only a hollow style, or "manner."

6. Leonardo da Vinci: *Grotesque Heads.* About 1490.

Leonardo da Vinci: *The Adoration of the Magi.* Uncompleted panel. Commissioned in 1481.

7. Leonardo da Vinci: *Study of an Embryo.* About 1512.

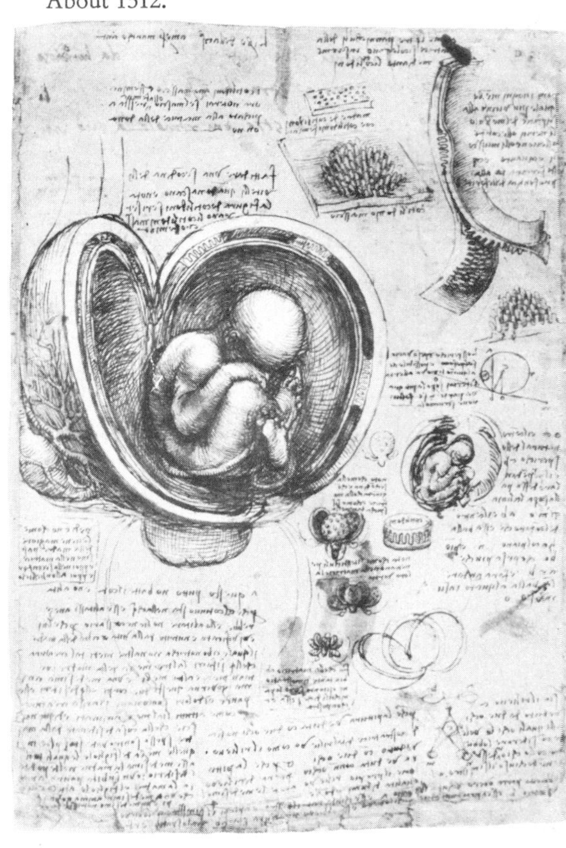

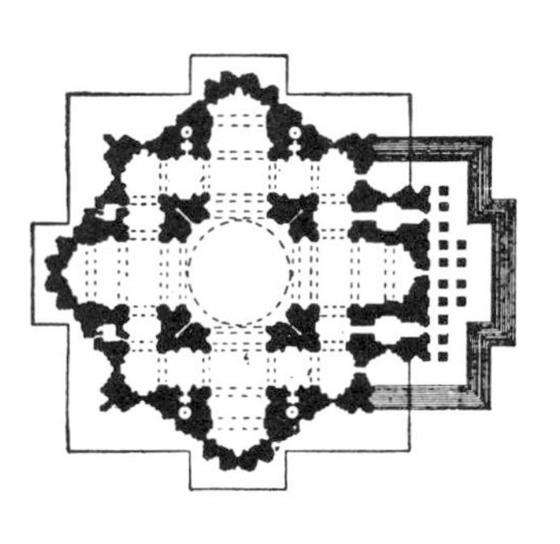

3. *St. Peter's,* Rome. Designed by Michelangelo. 1546–1564. (Floor plan at left.)

1. Michelangelo: *Self-portrait.*

Michelangelo was primarily a sculptor. When he turned to painting, he drew his figures with a monumental and stonelike coldness. When he designed architecture, like St. Peter's Cathedral or the Medici Tomb or the Laurentian Library steps in Florence, he wielded great sections of stone, marble and inlay, colossal columns, pediments, and arches as a sculptor might model clay. The primary quality of his art is crushing, boundless power. All of these elements can be seen in his greatest painting commission, for Pope Julius II (1443–1513), to decorate the Sistine Chapel ceiling in the Vatican. This chapel had been built in 1480 by the order of Pope Sixtus IV, and the famous frescoes on its walls had been painted from 1481 to 1483 by a number of gifted artists, notably, Botticelli, Signorelli, and Perugino, the teacher of Raphael. Michelangelo began work in 1508. In order to reach the height of the barrel-vaulted ceiling, he constructed a network of scaffolding, on which he lay to paint.

He divided the ceiling area into triangles and rectangles before beginning the complicated patterns of human figures. The whole ceiling of the chapel is separated into nine main panels—five large and four small—surrounded by a painted cornice which runs the length of the vault. This cornice is "supported" by caryatid-like forms of nude children standing on pilasters. The pilasters, a type of pier or column, flank the seated figures of the Old Testament prophets and sibyls who foretold the coming of Christ. The nine main panels tell the story of the Creation, the Fall, and other biblical episodes down to the Flood. The illustration on pages 156–157 shows about one third of the total area of the ceiling. The brooding, swirling figures seem to break out of their niches and overflow their frames, as though their universe were sprung apart. Every inch of space bursts with the same tension which, in the scene of the creation of man, leaps between the outstretched finger of the Lord and Adam's still-limp one (*Fig. 2*). All Michelangelo's later works repeat this curious "tension" between figures and their boundaries. If he worked in sculpture, the boundary was the rock itself. At the same time his incredible technical ability could enable him to finish a sculpture as exquisitely as this brooding Madonna (*Fig. 4*).

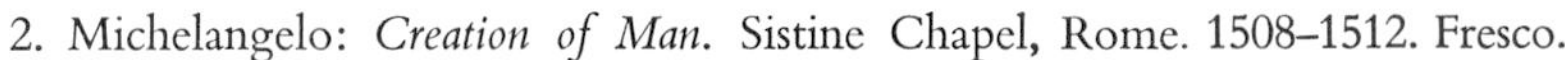

2. Michelangelo: *Creation of Man.* Sistine Chapel, Rome. 1508–1512. Fresco.

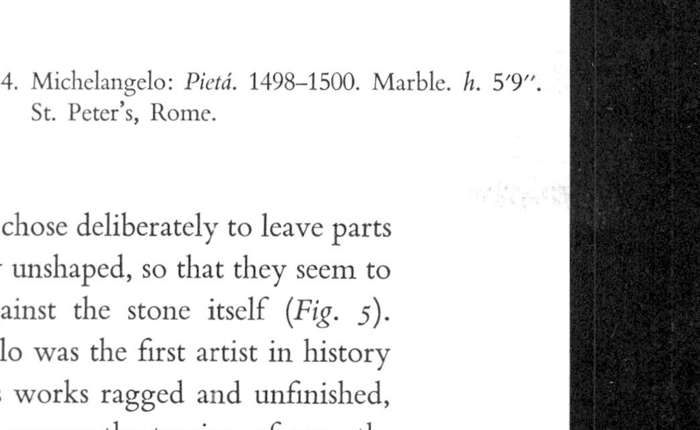

4. Michelangelo: *Pietá.* 1498–1500. Marble. *h.* 5′9″. St. Peter's, Rome.

Later, he chose deliberately to leave parts of the body unshaped, so that they seem to struggle against the stone itself (*Fig. 5*). Michelangelo was the first artist in history to leave his works ragged and unfinished, in order to express the tension of growth.

Thirty years after the completion of the ceiling, Michelangelo returned to the Sistine Chapel to paint the Last Judgment on the end wall, a pessimistic vision of humanity being hurled down to perdition by an angry God and a host of angels. This last effort reflected Michelangelo's deep concern with the disruptive force of the Protestant Reformation, which had begun in 1519.

Change and tension burst over Italy itself during Michelangelo's middle years. In 1527, Rome was invaded once again, this time by the armies of Charles V of the Holy Roman Empire, who was pressing his ancient claim to the city. In the North, the Reformation was already beginning to break off whole nations from papal domination. Michelangelo was able to survive these cataclysms. His last work was a model for the dome of St. Peter's, to surmount the new building based on Bramante's original plans. After Bramante's death, Michelangelo had reworked the plan, (*Fig. 3*); he gathered up the comparatively scattered spaces of Bramante's design and compressed them until they seem to swell upwards toward the great dome. The dome itself is a gigantic outgrowth of Brunelleschi's in Florence (see page 134), and is raised on a drum for extra height. But the drum on St. Peter's is a catapult for huge ribs which spring from pockets of black shadow, jutting upward between huge windows, cornices, and broken pediments. The outer dome is held in place by ten iron chains. Within the cathedral stand gigantic piers, 83 feet high, and the cupola rises 335 feet above the floor.

5. Michelangelo: *Pietá.* About 1556. Church of St. Rosalie, Palestrina.

Next pages: Michelangelo: *Ceiling of Sistine Chapel,* Vatican, Rome. 1508–1512.

1. Bronzino: *Portrait of a Young Man.* About 1535–1540.

2. Federigo Zuccari: *Window of the Zuccari Palace,* in the Via Gregoriana, Rome. 1590.

After Michelangelo's death, art in Rome and Florence underwent another change. The next generation of artists, in the mid-sixteenth century, are called "Mannerists," because they copied the manner of artists of the past, but without recreating the exuberant spirit of original discovery. The Mannerists had mastered every technical trick. By now, they could carve stone into fantastic shapes, cast gold and bronze into delicately balanced postures (*Fig. 3*), or fashion intricate pieces (*Fig. 6*). These artists and their elaborate works were much in demand in the kingdom of France, which was just now beginning to emerge from her long Gothic period. The Florentine metal worker and sculptor, Benvenuto Cellini, spent some time at Paris and Fontainebleau in the court of Francis I. At the same time in Italy, painters like Bronzino made portraits of their rich clients, with elegantly elongated hands and feet, and rather introspective, tired-looking faces, as though the sitters had seen a great deal of the world pass before their eyes. Now, in Italy, only Venice, at the top of its creative powers, was still producing works of art. But the 17th century was to bring Italian genius of a new type to the fore.

3. Giovanni da Bologna: *Mercury*. Bronze. About 1570. *h*. 5′9″.

5. Vesalius. *Secunda Musculorum Tabula*. 1543.

4. *Helmet*, made by Philip de Negroli, probably for Francis I. Milanese. 1543.

6. Benvenuto Cellini: *The Rospigliosi Cup*. Gold, enamel and pearls.

1. Titian: *Bacchus and Ariadne*. 1523.

VENICE

The Renaissance in Venice took a different form from that in Florence. It did not begin until the mid-15th century, and had reached its peak by the first half of the 16th. Its ideas were expressed mainly in painting, though a few Renaissance architects and sculptors lived in Venice.

There was little monumental sculpture made in Venice; instead, the workshops produced fabulous objects in glass, enamel, textiles, jewelry, leather, and in all the other rich materials beloved also by Byzantine and Islamic artisans. For Venice's connections had always been with the empires of the Near East and even China. Founded in the 6th century by refugees from the barbarians, Venice slowly grew richer by trade and plunder. As Mongols and then Turks swept through Persia, Syria, Egypt, and westward, Islamic artists fled into Venice with the secrets of their arts. Still today, Venetian glass and lace are world-famous. From these Oriental contacts, Venetian artists derived a love of color and sensuous, moving shapes; a love of splendid pageantry and mythology. When her artists cast off their lingering Gothic-Byzantine past, and turned toward the new techniques of Flanders and Florence, they combined the new with the old.

The masterpiece by Titian on the opposite page sums up many qualities present in 16th century Venetian painting: glowing colors which range from furry shadows to golden highlights; swirling figures whose limbs are linked into a long chain of twining shapes; and a dream-like spirit of unbounded pleasure in nature, song, dance, and poetry.

3. Gentile Bellini: Detail from the *Procession in the Piazza of San Marco.* 1496.

This is the central square of Venice as it looked to a painter of the old Gothic style in the late 15th century. When Renaissance painting techniques reached Venice, they came by way of the nearby town of Padua, an energetic Humanist art center which was built upon the ruins of an old Roman town. Many progressive artists had contributed their works to the city: Giotto came to paint a series of frescoes; Donatello's equestrian statue, the *Gattamelata,* stands in the main square. Mantegna, the leading Paduan artist, was influenced by such works of art and by the Roman ruins which lay about. His cold, chiseled manner of painting was brilliantly suited to experiments in perspective like the ceiling below. Mantegna's style was borne to Venice after he married the daughter of a leading painter, Jacopo Bellini, father of Gentile (*Fig. 3*), and also father of the more progressive Giovanni (page 162).

2. *Venetian Covered Goblet.* 16th century. *h.* 8⅞″.

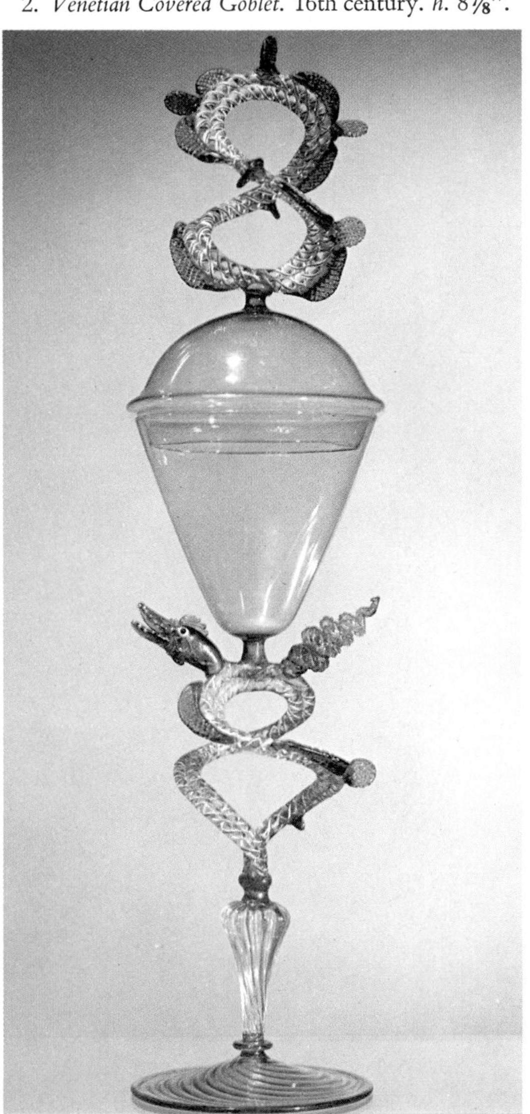

4. Andrea Mantegna: *Ceiling of the Gonzaga Bridal Chamber.* Ducal Palace, Mantua. Fresco. Finished in 1474.

The Venetian school produced some of the greatest painters of the Western world. In the centuries that followed, their techniques influenced the court styles of all Europe. When the splendidly robed princes of Flanders, Spain, or France posed for their portraits, they were painted in the pearly colors of Venice. Later artists like Renoir kept the Venetian tradition alive into modern times. Even more than their colleagues in other Italian cities, painters of the Late Venetian Renaissance loved to portray scenes from Greek and Roman myths, peopled with figures half-god, half-human, accompanied by musicians, and chariots and exotic animals.

During the lifetime of Giovanni Bellini, son of Jacopo and brother of Gentile (page 161), Renaissance style finally overtook Venetian art. Various influences speeded the change. Mantegna's cold, factual observations must have taught Giovanni and others how to observe an object carefully, then draw it clearly and precisely.

2. Giovanni Bellini: *St. Francis in Ecstasy*. About 1480.

1. Antonello da Messina: *The Annunciation*. About 1475.

Florentine painters like Uccello visited Venice, and the Sicilian painter Antonello da Messina (*Fig. 1*), brought the Flemish secret of oil paint. This new medium was much more suited to the Venetian taste than the cold, pale fresco of Florentine art. It was more radiant, more light-filled, more sensitive to subtle shades and shadows of tone. An artist could linger over his painting, softening or enriching the colors which remained wet and malleable for weeks on end. Though Giovanni retained Gothic elements—the knifelike line and meticulous small details of his paintings—a new naturalness seems to have infused his scenes. The real subject of his St. Francis (*Fig. 2*) may be a man finding himself in an awakening world: the funnel-like composition sweeps one's eyes beyond the small figure of the gentle saint, back into open fields and a light-streaked dawn sky beyond. When he painted the Madonna, as he did many times, Bellini frequently posed her before a curtain of splendid Venetian brocade, then pushed the curtain aside to disclose a soft summer landscape. Portraiture became a great specialty in Venice, for the rich oil colors appealed to the kings and princes of the many new empires being formed throughout the West.

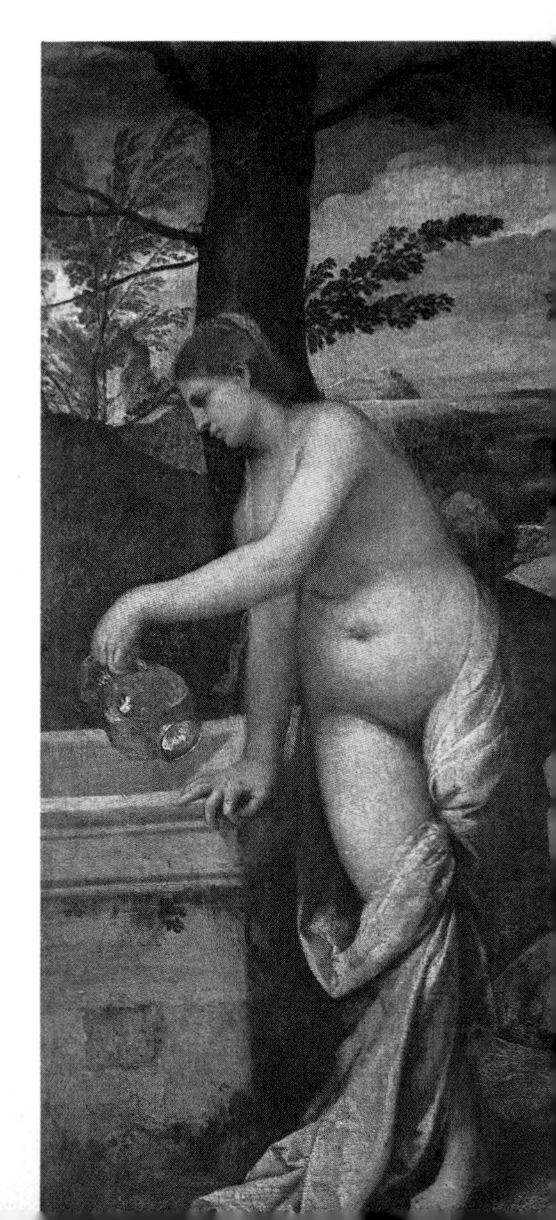

A series of extraordinary geniuses followed Bellini, as others had followed Masaccio in Florence. One of the greatest of these was Giorgione, one of Bellini's students. Giorgione's particular genius was for glowing color and an enchanted mood suggestive of ancient Greece. Compared with the rather cold linear forms of his teacher Bellini (*Fig. 2*), Giorgione's compositions were softened and warmer (*Fig. 3*), for by this time, the Venetians had learned to paint by laying areas of color next to one another, using very little line at all. Of course, they could only do this successfully after mastering the study of anatomy, so that correct shapes and proportions could be suggested, rather than actually drawn out. Also, the Venetians had now learned to vary the layers of transparent oil paint, spreading pearly whites above deep, warm oranges and reds, to capture glowing effects. In this moody country scene (*Fig. 3*) Giorgione placed two Venetian courtiers who, as they strum the lute and talk quietly, have evoked a dream of Greek nymphs. Even the edges of Giorgione's shapes are blurred, as though a mist had settled, blending together green and blue shadows and gleaming accents of a red velvet cloak or a patch of pearly skin.

4. Giorgione: *Laura*. 1506.

3. Giorgione: *Fête Champêtre*. 1477–1510.

1. Titian: *Venus with a Mirror.* About 1555.

Titian's lifetime spanned 99 years, from the early Venetian Renaissance of Giovanni Bellini, with whom he studied, to the unsettled era opened by the Italian campaign of Charles V, whom he painted (*Fig. 2*). Titian's work encompasses every changing aspect of Venetian style. As a comparatively young man, he painted such radiant panoramas as the *Bacchus and Ariadne* (page 160), and *The Three Ages of Man* (pages 166–167). In his middle years, revered in courts from Spain to England, he painted portraits of popes and kings, philosophers, and Renaissance women in their extravagant jewels and robes. He painted the nude with a resplendent beauty that no earlier painter had brought to this favorite subject. Often Titian posed these figures against a dark background built up in layers of glowing vermilions, dark greens, and browns, so that the ivory flesh tones stood out dramatically. The people he painted were full-bodied, imposing beings, at the height of their physical and spiritual power. Toward the end of his life, however, Titian's style began to change. Then, he often painted tragic religious subjects, such as this scene of Christ's Passion (*Fig. 3*). Serenity has vanished. Instead, great chalky shadows seem to billow through space. Beneath eerie flashes of white light, one can dimly make out moving bodies. Titian was anticipating the future: turbulence and storm, and emphasis upon theatrical, moody lighting effects were to become the major features of the new style just then being evolved in Rome.

2. Titian: *Portrait of the Emperor Charles V.* 1548.

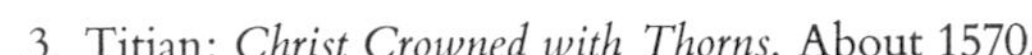

3. Titian: *Christ Crowned with Thorns.* About 1570.

4. Tintoretto: *The Last Supper*. 1594.

5. Tintoretto: *Bacchus and Ariadne*. About 1578.

More than Titian, his follower Tintoretto foreshadowed the art style known as Baroque. At times, Tintoretto was able to create a monumental composition, like the slowly revolving, light-bathed *Bacchus and Ariadne* (*Fig. 5*). But more often, his works were explosive studies of extraordinary perspectives, like the *Last Supper* (*Fig. 4*). Harsh greenish lights and wildly flying figures filled these paintings; the flat surface became a kind of stage proscenium through which fantastic actions could be observed.

1. Titian: *The Three Ages of Man.* About 1510–1515.

1. Carlo Crivelli: *Virgin and Child.* About 1470.

While the predominant direction of Venetian painting was toward soft color and moodier, more romantic scenes, some Venetian artists had continued in the austere, cold style of Mantegna and the Florentines. However, these painters, like Crivelli (*Fig. 1*) and Carpaccio (*Fig. 3*), added something which the serious, pioneering Florentines and Paduans had little time for: humor. Crivelli's dainty Madonna is posed like a Gothic sculpture. But the curious perspective which the artist made of the Child's downcast face is a Mantegnesque study; and the great horse-fly which he painted on the ledge was a deliberate attempt to mislead. It was simply a demonstration of technical virtuosity of which the painter was proud. This kind of painting is called "trompe-l'oeil," or "fool the eye." Carpaccio, too, drew and painted in a fastidious, linear, old-fashioned style; but the complicated patterns he made of the figures, flying before the gentle lion of St. Jerome (*Fig. 3*), and other storytelling groups, are among the most clever and varied of the Renaissance.

The world which Veronese painted was more often one of banqueting and pleasure than the mythological pleasures of Titian, or the religious banquets of Tintoretto, but the great scene below was, at first, given a religious title, the *Supper at Cana.* The painting below stretches across an entire wall; like the fly in Crivelli's painting, the balustrade and arches were painted to trick the observer into thinking he was seeing a real scene. When Veronese painted this picture, however, he found that the free spirit of Crivelli's and even Titian's days no longer existed. The Inquisition attacked him for putting non-religious figures like dwarfs, dogs, and monkeys into a supposedly holy scene. Only after a long trial and after he changed the picture's name were the charges against him dropped.

2. Paolo Veronese: *Feast in the House of Levi.* 1573.

3. Vittore Carpaccio: *St. Jerome and the Lion.* About 1507.

Color-filled Venetian painting appealed especially to the court painters of later Spain, Flanders, and France. But a Venetian architect, Palladio, became the favorite of the 17th- and 18th-century English landowners and their brothers in America, who had turned their backs on the luxuries of court life.

Like Brunelleschi and Raphael, Palladio learned his art in Rome. There he, too, studied and measured the Classical ruins and tried to make a system of proportions which other architects could follow. In 1570 he published a book of plans for all kinds of buildings, with details of ancient pediments, moldings, and columns. His own villas in the countryside near Venice were grand, symmetrical stone buildings. Often he used a central mass, domed and columned, with two wings on each side. This style, and others from his pattern book, were widely copied in England and America.

4. Andrea Palladio: *Villa Rotunda,* near Vicenza, Italy. Begun 1567.

THE RENAISSANCE IN THE NORTH

The early 16th century was the age of Henry VIII of England, Francis I of France, and Charles V of Spain, three monarchs under whom the Renaissance arts and ideas of Italy were finally introduced to the North. This was achieved by the personal patronage of the kings, and also by the independent travels of artists. Albrecht Dürer journeyed to Italy; Hans Holbein, to England; Leonardo da Vinci, to France. These men cultivated and spread the Renaissance point of view: a lively curiosity in the real world, and a will to push back the veils of superstition and terror which had kept the North backward in arts and ideas. New revolutions, however, beset this artistic development. The Reformation wracked Europe, and in 1517, Martin Luther published his articles of protest. Masses rallied to his side. In 1543 Henry VIII, too, broke from Rome. As the Reformation intensified, it was soon to give rise to the Counter-Reformation emanating from Rome itself, and to the new "Baroque."

1. Albrecht Dürer: *Self-portrait.* 1500

As the Renaissance permeated the North, the greatest change in art was a turning away from the expressionistic unreality of Late Gothic style toward a new kind of realism. Dürer, who was largely responsible for bringing the new ideas to his native Germany, was born thirteen years before Grünewald. Yet one has only to compare his pitiless, searching studies of the human face (*Fig. 2*) with Grünewald's nightmarish visions, to know that Dürer belongs more to the Italian tradition (see page 123). The son of a goldsmith, Dürer was trained in the Gothic style, and retained something of this manner, particularly in his woodcuts and engravings of Biblical subjects. But he was also fascinated by the Humanist ideas seeping north from Florence and Padua. He visited Italy and studied the work of Leonardo, Raphael, and Bellini. Like Leonardo, he was fascinated by the mystery of personality. These two men were among the first artists to draw their own portraits, not just as one of a crowd, but alone, gazing into a mirror, as though they sought some new frontier behind their own eyes. Dürer became a Protestant, and thought of himself as a prophet of the future, not only in his art, but also in his religious beliefs. So, if the *Self-Portrait* (*Fig. 1*), resembles, in its pose and intensity, some medieval images of Christ, Dürer probably intended the suggestion.

2. Albrecht Dürer: *Portrait of the Artist's Mother*. 1514. Charcoal.

The new fascination with realism affected Holbein, too, particularly in this devastating study of a dead man, which Holbein has called *Christ.* Compared with Grünewald's cadaverous image of Christ, painted only six years earlier, this work seems devoid of any devotion or sacred quality. Rather, it appears to be a cold-blooded study of any corpse. Yet Holbein could also be a meticulous and flattering portraitist. He spent most of his life in the England of Henry VIII, painting the king, his many wives, the intellectuals, scientists, statesmen, and artists who clustered around the court. There, Holbein painted these two typical young leaders of the international world. They were obviously interested in the new scientific discoveries of the day, for between them are globes and mathematical instruments, and a lute and a book of music. The curious form in the foreground, however, adds a different, perhaps disturbing note to the otherwise reasonable scene. Drawn with the technical agility of Mannerism (see page 158), this is a skull, pulled out of shape by a trick of perspective. One can see it correctly by squinting with one eye along the page from the lower left corner. This image harks back to the Dance of Death subject of Late Gothic art; it is a reminder both to the onlooker and to the subjects of this portrait, that despite their new knowledge, death still exists. In another clue to the personalities of these men, Holbein set a tiny crucifix almost out of sight in the upper left corner. Probably this indicates that the subjects were Catholics, as Holbein himself remained, although they lived in a country which was soon to break away from Rome.

3. Hans Holbein the Younger: *Christ in the Tomb.* 1521.

4. Hans Holbein the Younger: *The Ambassadors, Jean de Dinteville and Georges de Selve, Bishop of Lavour.* 1533.

1. Jean Clouet: *Portrait of Francis I.* About 1524.

In 1515 Francis I came to the throne of a unified France, which left him comparatively free to cultivate the arts. Like his now-enemy, now-ally Charles V, he fell in love with Italian Renaissance style. Leonardo da Vinci worked for him, designing architecture, fountains, costumes, and other objects. Cellini contributed ornaments for the royal table, statues, and armor. Under Francis, the fortified medieval castles which lined the Loire River were expanded into great chateaux, and new ones were built for the multiplying members of the court. At the Chateau Chambord (*Fig. 2*), wide windows break the walls, letting sunlight pour in. Elegant staircases, archways, and gardens laid out like geometric diagrams adorned this and other chateaux. Classical columns were added to gateways, and the Gothic spires which remained from past centuries were counterbalanced by horizontal wings and rows of pilasters in the Italian style. Francis' taste for painting was not quite so progressive. His court painter, Clouet, though an excellent observer and master of careful, well-constructed portraits, still drew in a rather fastidious, impersonal Gothic manner. Later, Francis set up his own school at Fontainebleau and imported a group of Italian artists to teach his own artists. But as often happens when artists set out to adopt a foreign style without painstakingly re-inventing it for themselves, the Fontainebleau artists took over only a weak version of Mannerist painting, and produced such faintly ludicrous, overrefined works as this mythological boudoir scene (*Fig. 4*). Partly Mannerist, partly a genuine explorer of Classical form was Francis' sculptor, Goujon. The languid Diana (*Fig. 6*) is said to be a portrait of the beautiful Diane de Poitiers, mistress of Francis' son, Henry II.

3. *Double-barreled Wheel Lock Pistol.* Made by Peter Pech of Munich for Emperor Charles V. About 1540.

2. *Chateau of Francis I.* Chambord, France. 1526–1544.

4. Fontainebleau School: *Birth of Cupid.* 1540–1560.

6. Jean Goujon: *Diane.* Chateau d'Anet.

England was never so progressive in the visual arts as the countries to the south were, but already it had challenged the world in literature. For by the end of the 16th century, the Classical tales and Italian legends of Shakespeare were among the finest examples of Renaissance style north of Italy itself. In 1520, Francis was visited by his English counterpart, Henry VIII. Astonished at the luxurious Italianate art he saw in France, Henry determined to bring the Renaissance to his own court. But in spite of his ambitions, English art changed but little for another century. The King tried to stimulate new architecture by closing the monasteries and using their funds for public construction. But the Tudor-style houses built in his time, and in that of Elizabeth who followed, were still dark and gloomy, with clammy rooms, low roofs, and dark wood beams. What painting Henry and Elizabeth were able to stimulate, apart from that of the visiting Holbein, were mainly miniature portraits of the rulers and their pompous courtiers, uncomfortable in stiff lace and jewels.

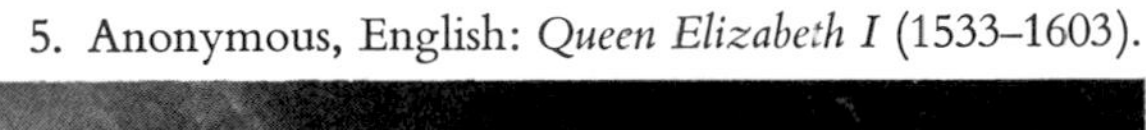

5. Anonymous, English: *Queen Elizabeth I* (1533–1603).

7. *Ship Pendant.* German, about 1600. Gold, enamel, crystal and jewels.

One of the last great artists of the Northern Renaissance was Pieter Brueghel. Like his Late Gothic countrymen (see pages 128–129), Brueghel recorded the smallest details of the world before him: farmers and their harvested fields, hunters in the winter snow, or children at play (*Fig. 1*). Then, too, he visited Italy and learned how to use the new Renaissance techniques—of composing long panoramas with each plane receding into the distance, and of drawing scattered details into vast, curving patterns.

As in the work of Bellini (see page 162), man appears to be a perfectly integrated part of the panorama. The two tiny figures in the lower left corner of the drawing at right belong to this landscape in the same way that the tiny figures of a Chinese scroll are an integral part of their mists and quiet valleys (pages 90–91). No Northerner before Brueghel had seen landscape with such breadth. In composition, Brueghel foreshadowed the new Baroque style, which was born in Italy at the end of his lifetime.

2. Pieter Brueghel the Elder: *Waltersburg*. 1554. Pen and brown ink.

1. Pieter Brueghel the Elder: *Children's Games*. 1560.

As Brueghel trod the roads between Italy and his homeland, the Netherlands, he saw not only beautiful and majestic landscapes, but scenes of terror and massacre, as well; for in 1556, Philip II had ascended the throne of Spain and the Netherlands, and had given his support to the Inquisition which was attempting to keep the Protestant section of the Netherlands from breaking away from Spain. Philip's emissary, the Duke of Alba, was sent to crush the opposition. Under the Duke's iron hand, Netherlanders were massacred and broken on the wheel or hung from gallows on the hilltops. Some of Brueghel's paintings show these tall gallows poles leaning in the wind, bearing shreds of clothing and bones. But they, too, like the figures of soldiers and peasants alike, are so closely knit into the vast landscape that they seem no more important to its rhythm than the flight of birds or the fall of snow.

THE BIRTH OF BAROQUE

ROME

Baroque style was initiated in Rome late in the 16th century and spread across Europe during the next two hundred years. At first, it was a deliberate propaganda weapon for the Counter-Reformation. The Council of Trent, which laid down rules for this new holy war, established a new principle for art. There was no place in this new scheme for the Humanist researches or pleasures, or for scholarly, private investigations. Art must have only one end: to stamp out heresy and bring the people back into the churches. It should excite their hearts and minds, and inflame their senses with colors, shapes, and sounds. These principles were quickly put to use as a surge of church building continued under the Jesuit Order, established in 1534 by the fiery Spaniard, Ignatius Loyola.

One of the first Baroque-style edifices was the "Gesù," the mother church of the Jesuit Order, begun in Rome in 1568. In architecture, the style first took root. Soon, every form of art was woven into a great religious panorama. Music totally unlike the plainchants of medieval monks, or the simple, Greek-style songs of the Renaissance, began to be composed. In Baroque "polyphonic" music, many voices joined in singing different, spiraling lines of melody. These complex sounds, woven into rich patterns, were supported by the reverberations of great Baroque organs. The same hunger for theatrical effects influenced architecture, painting, and sculpture. In whatever medium it expressed itself, the Italian Baroque style cried out for sudden contrasts of light and shadow, for massive forms which escape their boundaries breaking out into space. Materials were made to transform themselves into others, like Daphne's fingers into leaves (page 179, *Fig. 4*), or an entire ceiling into clouds (page 180).

1. Giovanni Lorenzo Bernini: *Piazza before St. Peter's,* Rome. Begun 1656.

2. Giacomo Barozzi da Vignola: *Church of the Gesù*, Rome. Begun in 1568.

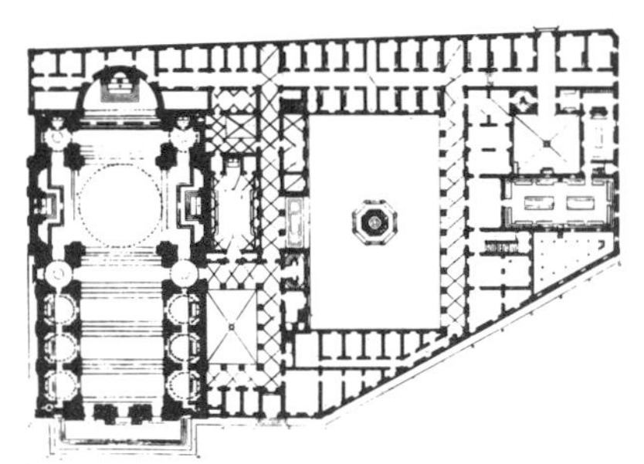

3. Floor plan: *Church of the Gesù*, Rome.

The architect Vignola actually based his plan for the Gesù (*Fig. 2*) upon a much earlier church by the Renaissance architect Alberti. However, he has emphasized the design of scrolls which join the lower horizontal section of the façade to the central tower; and within the church, too, Vignola straddled the old and the new, by setting a great dome over the intersection of nave and transept, and by sheathing the walls with varicolored marble to enhance their splendor.

Gothic architecture had overwhelmed man by its soaring lines and long naves; Renaissance architecture with its low, horizontal lines and circular plan, gave back to man his Classical position of importance. The Baroque attempted a marriage of these two styles, drawing the entire floor plan into an oval, surmounted by a great dome. Twin towers might be added, like those of Gothic cathedrals, only more stolid and pierlike. Later, the walls were made to roll in and out so that space itself seemed alive, compressed like water between the rocking walls (*Fig. 4*).

A further step was taken by Borromini, who broke the façade of his San Carlo into great curves and swags, as though he modeled its heavy columns and balustrades in soft clay. The moving genius of Italian Baroque style was Bernini. His piazza in Rome (*Fig. 1*), is the summation of Baroque space. Its two great winging arms, flung out before the cathedral designed by Bramante, with Michelangelo's dome, encompass a space big enough to hold thousands of worshipers.

4. Francesco Borromini: *Church of San Carlo alle Quattro Fontane*, 1638–1646. Facade, 1665–1667.

1. Michelangelo da Caravaggio: *Conversion of St. Paul.* 1601.

In Baroque Italy, there was no longer any place for the serene, softly lit works of such artists as Raphael or Titian. The new taste, which artists like Michelangelo and Tintoretto had foreshadowed, was for pictures showing violent movement and sudden, shocking contrasts of light and shadow. A spokesman for this new style was Caravaggio, a revolutionary who pitched his art against both the serenity of the Renaissance and the artificial works of his own Mannerist contemporaries. It was Caravaggio's wish to show the ugly or grotesque side of reality, with its coarse details and sprawling gestures. In a sense, he was reviving an idea of the Late Gothic North: the representation of wracked and tortured bodies. To make his pictures even more compelling, Caravaggio set his scenes so that one beam of white light raked into the darkness, cutting like a blade over flesh and bone. He meant this forced, theatrical light to be as shocking as a spotlight beamed onto a dark stage. He invented this technique for religious pictures of peculiar and novel power (*Fig. 1*). But like his other Baroque contemporaries, Caravaggio also displayed his mastery of artistic techniques by painting secular scenes in which light sprayed across a series of objects—flesh, glass, and flower petals—reverberating like a chord of music (*Fig. 2*).

2. Michelangelo da Caravaggio: *Boy Bitten by a Lizard.* 1592–3.

3. Giovanni Lorenzo Bernini: *The Ecstasy of St. Theresa.* 1645–1652. Marble, life-size.

4. Giovanni Lorenzo Bernini: *Apollo and Daphne.* 1622–24. Marble, life-size.

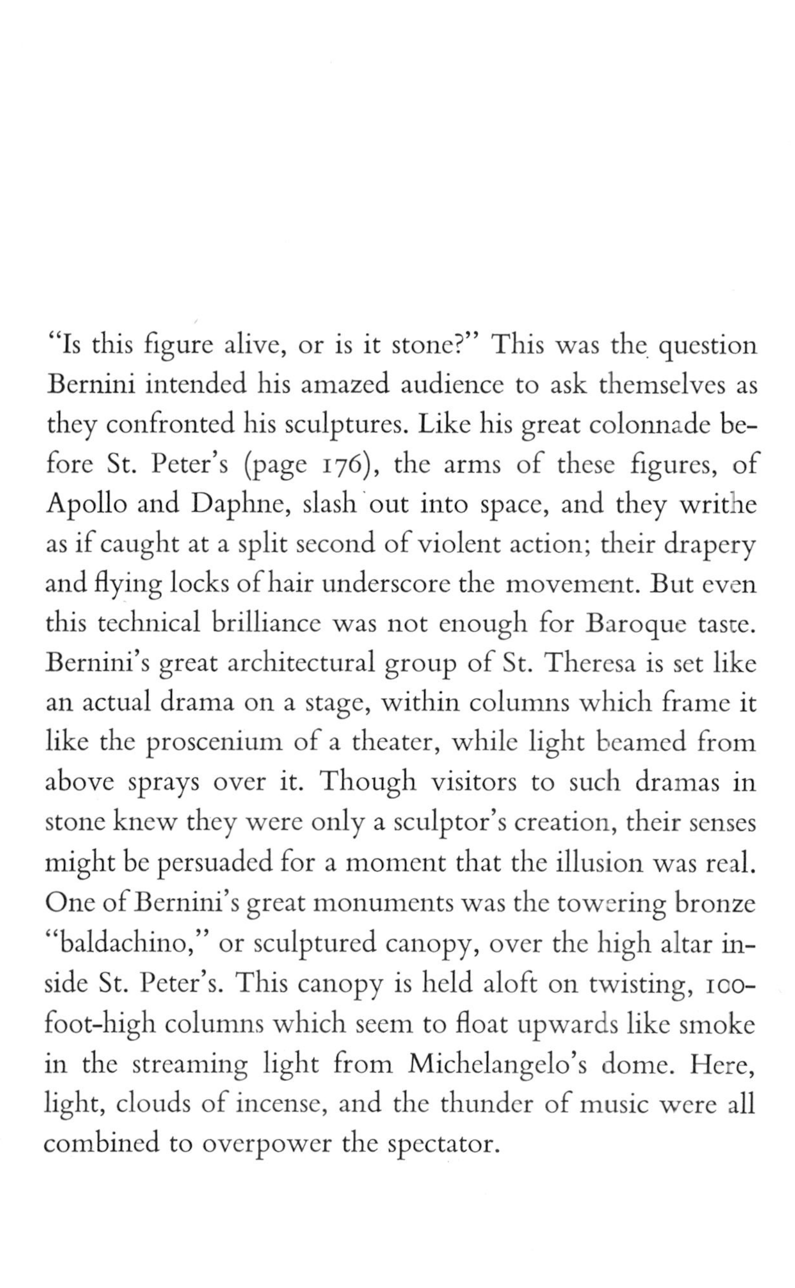

"Is this figure alive, or is it stone?" This was the question Bernini intended his amazed audience to ask themselves as they confronted his sculptures. Like his great colonnade before St. Peter's (page 176), the arms of these figures, of Apollo and Daphne, slash out into space, and they writhe as if caught at a split second of violent action; their drapery and flying locks of hair underscore the movement. But even this technical brilliance was not enough for Baroque taste. Bernini's great architectural group of St. Theresa is set like an actual drama on a stage, within columns which frame it like the proscenium of a theater, while light beamed from above sprays over it. Though visitors to such dramas in stone knew they were only a sculptor's creation, their senses might be persuaded for a moment that the illusion was real. One of Bernini's great monuments was the towering bronze "baldachino," or sculptured canopy, over the high altar inside St. Peter's. This canopy is held aloft on twisting, 100-foot-high columns which seem to float upwards like smoke in the streaming light from Michelangelo's dome. Here, light, clouds of incense, and the thunder of music were all combined to overpower the spectator.

1. Andrea Pozzo: *The Entrance of St. Ignatius into Paradise*. St. Ignatius, Rome. About 1702.

2. *Baroque Harpsichord*. Italian. 17th century.

3. Niccolo Salvi: *Fountain of Trevi*. Rome. 1732–1762.

As the Baroque style gathered force in Rome, it sent out waves of influence throughout Europe. Works of art were made with greater and greater scale and virtuosity, as though the artists would stop at nothing to turn stone into sunlight or bronze into water. In Rome and neighboring cities, a school of "trompe-l'oeil" ceiling painters developed. These artists expanded upon the optical tricks used by some Venetian artists, such as Veronese (page 168). Their techniques, sharpened by apprenticeship in the Mannerist schools (page 158), now were lavished upon pictures which made space seem to explode into infinite vistas. Pozzo, who was a Jesuit, marked a small spot upon the floor beneath this awesome ceiling, at which precise point the spectator must stand in order to understand its complex perspectives. In this way Pozzo meant to say that each man must cast his whole being into the hands of the Church.

This extravagant play of materials and effects continued in popularity into the 18th century, but by this time, the crest of the Baroque wave was riding over other parts of Europe.

1. El Greco: *Burial of Count Orgaz.* 1586. 15′10″ by 11′9″.

CATHOLIC BAROQUE

SPAIN, FLANDERS, AND VERSAILLES

As the Baroque style spread through Europe, it took somewhat different forms from country to country. But universally, the Baroque style continued to be preoccupied with dramatic light and shadow, and a fondness for panoramic space linked in strong patterns. Sometimes, the Baroque continued to express the fervid, mystical emotions which had initially produced it in Rome. At the same time, chiefly in France, the Baroque style was taken up by artists of a more reflective and philosophic attitude. For, curiously enough, one element of the Baroque ran parallel to scientific thought. The 17th century was an age of abounding scientific genius, and Newton and Kepler were two of many scientists and astronomers whose major investigation was that of light. Did it consist of waves, or particles, they asked; was it a stream of Divine Grace or a function of mathematics and physics? Reflecting this scientific concern, the spreading Baroque style began to put forth one more current: dispassionate, or poetic studies of light streaming through space.

At the same time, a new outlet for the artistic imagination was opening, into dreams of an ideal world, a golden stage of nature upon which strange dramas might occur. Thus was born the first intimation of the Romantic movement, which was to mature two centuries later. And while some artists dreamed of sublime landscapes, sun-washed and serene, one king found a way to bring them to life. Louis XIV, who ascended the French throne in 1643, turned the new astronomical theories to his own exaltation, by calling himself the "Sun King," center of the universe. Now the Baroque splendor and excitement, and breathtaking contrasts of light, pattern, and materials which hitherto had been confined to individual works of art, were all summoned to his presence in a stupendous panorama of glass and stone, gardens, paintings, and sculpture.

2. *Altar of the Transparente,* Toledo Cathedral. Completed 1732.

El Greco was independent enough not to belong to any one school of painting. Yet his art is as clearly Baroque in feeling and style as is the fantastic Altar of the Transparente (*Fig. 2*), which was constructed over a century after his lifetime. Here, boiling clouds and flying angels carved out of colored marble and spotlit from across the shadowy nave are a last achievement of Baroque sculpture. Church décor of this sort reached its climax in later 18th-century monasteries and cathedrals of Germany (see page 208); but here, the work has been set with more awesome effect into the gloomy interior of a 13th-century Gothic cathedral.

In El Greco's time, Spain was a land torn between terrors of the Inquisition and the religious fervor inspired by visionaries like St. Theresa. Into this whirlpool of mysticism, the artist had been drawn from his birthplace, Crete, where he had learned the Byzantine manner of icon painting: sharp, angling shapes bathed with golden light. In Venice he studied the soft, rushing brushwork of Titian and the explosive compositions of Tintoretto. At about the time he arrived in Spain, St. Theresa had written of an angel she had seen in a vision, "Very beautiful . . . and his face was so aflame he appeared all on fire." Again, she wrote, "My bones are all disjointed!" These words might be descriptions of El Greco's own figures, wracked, their bones broken and drawn out into writhing, flamelike patterns (see page 184).

In the complex painting shown at left, the nobles on the lower level are clustered together and as accurately drawn as figures in any Italian Renaissance group. But in the realm of heaven, above them, El Greco has let his visionary imagination run free to distort and recombine his forms in a glowing, electric apotheosis of Baroque design. In the painting on page 185, El Greco, who envisioned such extraordinary forms, has depicted what must have been a moving episode for him or any artist: the moment when Christ healed the blind man.

LAVDAMVSTE BENEDICIMV

2. El Greco: *Christ Healing the Blind Man.*

1. El Greco: *Adoration of the Shepherds.*

1. Peter Paul Rubens: *The Garden of Love.* About 1638.

Rubens and Velasquez carried the Baroque style of painting to its highest point. While in his twenties, Rubens spent eight years in Italy and then returned to his native Antwerp to set up the most productive artist's workshop in the Western world. There, assisted by many apprentices, he turned out portraits, religious paintings, and mythological scenes as well as designs for tapestries, triumphal arches for parades, and chariots and costumes for festivals. He made a set of mural-size paintings which showed the arrival of the Italian Marie de' Medici in Marseilles, for her marriage to King Henry IV of France. These pictures hung in the Luxembourg palace within Paris, and were a living lesson in the Baroque style to French painters of succeeding generations. Like his Flemish predecessor Brueghel, Rubens loved to paint the swirling interchange of bodies dancing through space in long, spiraling patterns. But his manner of painting was far more advanced than Brueghel's, for he had mastered the Venetian technique and carried it to its ultimate point. No one before or since has painted such living flesh tones, glowing and flickering through ivory highlights, nor such silks, satins, and flower petals, gleaming like mother-of-pearl in candlelight.

2. Peter Paul Rubens: *Head of a Child.* 1616.

1. Diego Rodriquez de Silva y Velasquez: *Maids of Honor* (*Las Meñinas*). 1656.

If one side of Spanish Baroque temperament expressed itself in ecstatically moving forms, another side chose austere formality. The Escorial (*Fig. 3*), was Philip II's residence, a grim enclave of monastery and church buildings, located in desolate country outside Madrid. By the time Velasquez became Court Painter to Philip IV, this building had been given up in favor of another palace. Yet its severe architecture and unadorned silhouette have some of the impersonality of Velasquez' painting. In Velasquez' lifetime, the power of the Spanish Empire was declining. The Spanish Armada had been defeated by England in 1588, and by 1648, the crown had been forced to grant independence to Holland.

3. *The Escorial,* near Madrid, Spain. 1563–1584.

2. Diego Rodriquez de Silva y Velasquez: Detail from *Portrait of a Young Spaniard.* About 1628.

The atmosphere in the court of Philip IV was both grim and sad. Velasquez' method of working, too, was as austere as Rubens' was lavish. Sometimes Velasquez traveled to Italy, and there had a chance to paint the extraordinary face and figure of the Pope. But more often, he spent his days in the palace, painting the long-faced Spanish princesses and their pet dwarfs and dogs (*Fig. 1*). Rubens' brush was loaded and streaming with glossy paint; Velasquez wiped his until it was almost dry. Then he drew it over layers of dark underpaint, catching the curious, still light which cut through shadows and fell in dry grains upon red velvet, blond hair, jewels, and a mirror. Nor did Velasquez gather his pictures together, as Rubens did, in great moving clusters of shapes. Instead, he set the figures here and there, almost at random. Then he pulled the design together with accents of light and color, so that, for instance, a section of dusky background would be balanced by a highlighted figure. This fascinating composition shows the painter himself, with the royal children. In a mirror in the background, the king and queen are reflected. For Velasquez, nothing was so compelling as this patient kind of study, of light dissolving shapes into brushstrokes of pale paint.

1. Nicolas Poussin: *The Gathering of the Ashes of Phocion*. 1648.

3. Nicolas Poussin: *The Holy Family*. Drawing. About 1647–48.

2. Detail of (1).

Poussin and Claude Gellée (also known as Claude Lorrain), were the French counterparts of Velasquez and Rubens: all belong to the Baroque Age, although to different sides of it. Poussin's style, like Velasquez', is cold and rational. His paintings are clearcut studies of shapes set within deep space; the mood created by these forms may be one of harmonious serenity. Claude's art, by contrast, is full of dramatic shadows and unexpected events. Both these French masters spent their working years in Rome, which was not only the fountainhead of Baroque style but also the home of the Late Renaissance. Poussin was influenced especially by such works of Raphael's as the Vatican frescoes. Carefully composed, Poussin's great landscape and figure paintings generally focus upon some central image, or a major figure toward which all the other elements are drawn by stately diagonal lines or swinging chains of linked bodies (see pages 192–193). Thus, the eye is drawn in a slow sequence, from shape to shape in the painting above (*Fig. 1*), until it comes to rest upon the stately Classical temple in the background, just as a series of musical chords will finally resolve themselves into a dominant one. In the detail at left from this large painting, one can see how each shape is clearly delineated, like a stone block in sunlight. Later French painters like Corot and Cézanne would learn from Poussin's manner of painting. Yet in spirit these works belong very much to the France of Poussin's time, in which court playwrights like Racine and Corneille were composing dramas based on Classical themes in which their heroes spoke in stately, balanced measures.

4. Detail of (5).

Claude, too, composed light-filled landscapes set with ruins of Roman temples. But the light itself is golden instead of cold white; it blurs and softens the edges of things instead of marking them off sharply; and it falls, here and there, upon strange, half-recognizable shapes—a moss-covered tower, a fragment of ruined columns, a plunder-laden ship from some Oriental port. The manner in which these two artists observed nature differed profoundly.

For Poussin, a study drawing (*Fig. 3*) was almost a scientific aid to the understanding of solid forms in light. For Claude, however, the drawing (*Fig. 6*) was an expression of the ebb and flow of the elements, swept onto the paper in dark washes from a loosely held brush. Then, once back in his studio, Claude made more imposing, carefully organized works, with all the forms majestically drawn together toward a single focus deep in the background. Poussin, however, usually set an elegantly drawn subject just at that focal point; Claude might leave the space entirely open, as though only distant horizons lay where the eye finally rested (*Fig. 5*). This kind of composition may leave one feeling vaguely suspended, as though the last note in a scale hung in the air, unsounded. In this, Claude prefigures the Romantics of the 19th century. But before then, his art was to have its influence upon the landscape painters of Holland and England (see pages 200, 222).

5. Claude Lorrain: *The Embarkation of the Queen of Sheba.* 1648.

6. Claude Lorrain: *Ship in a Tempest.* Ink and wash drawing.

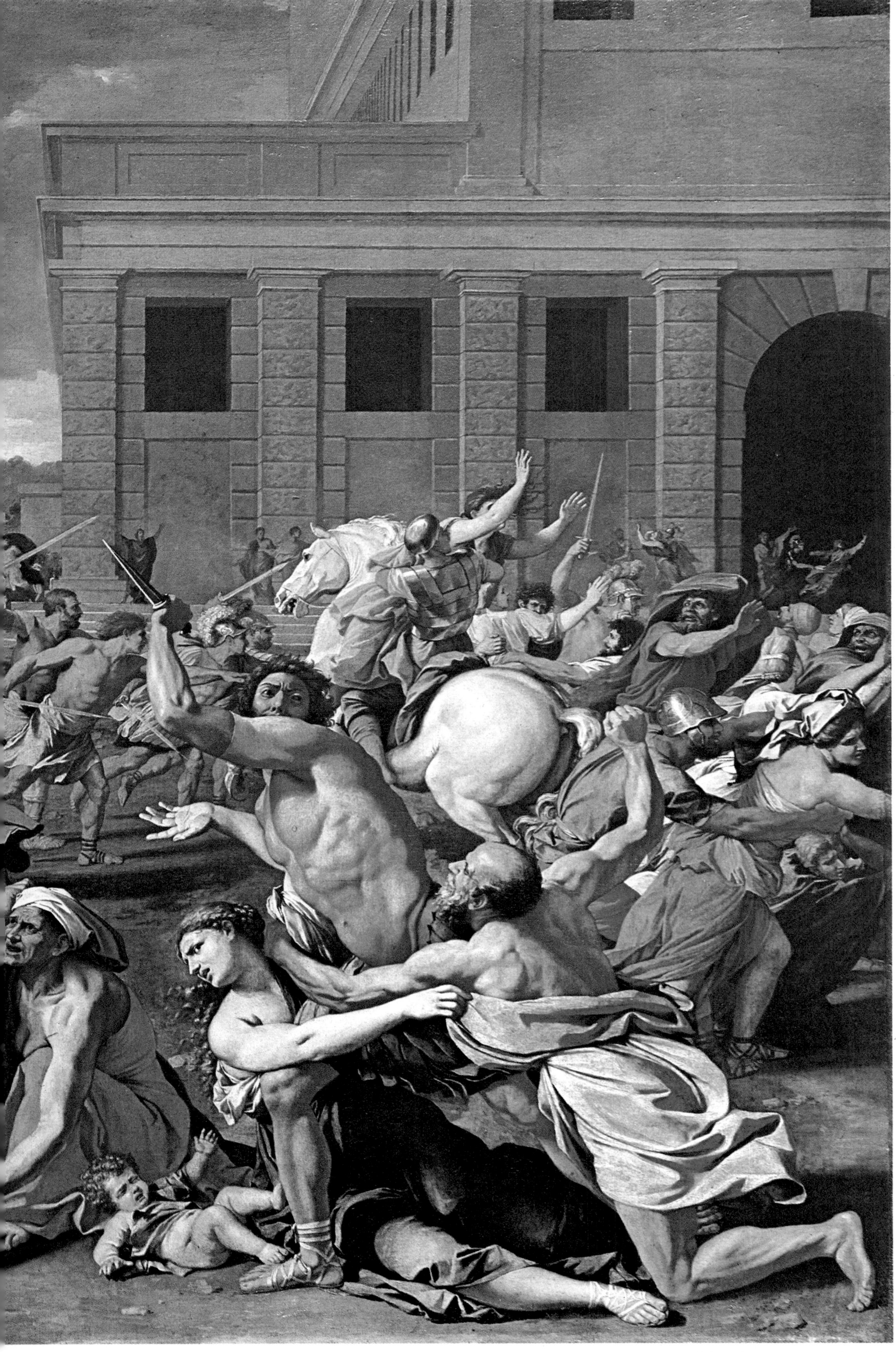

1. Nicolas Poussin: *Rape of the Sabine Women.* Before 1637.

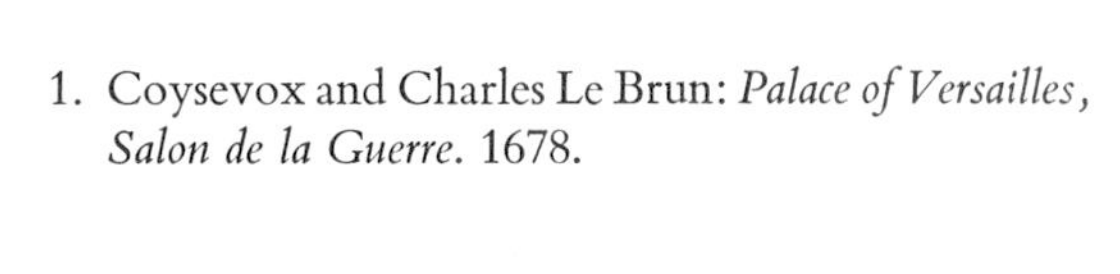

1. Coysevox and Charles Le Brun: *Palace of Versailles, Salon de la Guerre*. 1678.

2. *Parade Helmet of Louis XIV*. About 1700.

In Italy, Spain, and Flanders, artists working in the Baroque style made use of dramatic lights and shadows, and deep space drawn into stately patterns. Louis XIV of France brought these abstract elements to life in his grandiose palace at Versailles. All the greatest artists of the land were swept into his service, and entire factories, including the famous Gobelins, were purchased to turn out tapestries, furniture, porcelain, and other objects for the palace. These were designed in a style which today bears the king's name, "Louis Quatorze," just as later styles bear the name of his two successors, Louis Quinze and Seize. Louis Quatorze furnishings have something of the ponderous weight and mass of medieval oak furnishings, here translated into massive bronze and gold leaf, painted stucco, and colored marbles. The wall at left, for instance, has been turned into a pageant of ornament, with gilt angels, wreaths, stucco figures, all paying homage to the Sun King himself carved in relief. So brilliantly did Louis XIV organize the artistic activities of his kingdom, that for the next 200 years, French styles led the world in painting, architecture, furniture design, fashions, and other arts.

3. Charles Le Brun: *Four faces—Admiration, Crying, Smiles, Despair.*

Under Louis XIV, an Academy was set up in France which classified all the known techniques and styles, just as scientists were then doing in their sphere, and dictated standards of achievement. The first director of the Academy was Charles Le Brun, architect and painter. In these drawings, Le Brun showed his talent for classifying, making a study of various expressions of which the human face is capable.

The town of Versailles, outside Paris, had been the site of a small hunting chateau for King Louis XIII. Under the Sun King, the chateau was enlarged, magnificently furnished, and made the center of his brilliant court life. The architect Jules Hardouin Mansard created a sweeping structure in Italian Renaissance style, divided into three horizontal ranks. The lower one was "rusticated" like the Medici Palace in Florence (page 142); the central one was faced with elegant Ionic pilasters and columns; and the top one bore a row of small windows, a balustrade, and a rank of ornamental sculpture. Within the building, Charles Le Brun designed great chambers faced with mirrors and inlaid marble, to be lit by thousands of candles. In front of the palace, magnificent gardens were designed by André Le Notre. Like a Poussin vista, fountains, orange groves, and geometrically arranged flower gardens were spread out, and sculptures by Italian Mannerists like da Bologna (page 159) added to their magnificence.

5. *Garden of Versailles at the Time of Louis XIV.*

4. André Le Notre: *Garden of Versailles.* 1662–1682.

1. Rembrandt van Rijn: *The Sampling Officials of the Drapers' Guild*. 1662.

PROTESTANT BAROQUE

HOLLAND, ENGLAND, THE COLONIES

Seventeenth-century Holland had no need for the grandiose arts of Baroque Italy, Spain, or France. There were no courts to pay for such magnificence, nor Catholic churches to be decorated with religious images. The Protestant point of view went back to Moses' law against graven images. John Calvin himself put it this way: "Man should not paint or carve anything except what he can see around him, so that God's majesty may not be corrupted by fantasies." So it was to the objects in the world around him that the Dutch painter turned. Portraits of individuals and of assembled guild members, officers of clubs and institutions were very popular. So were landscapes of the placid Dutch countryside; and so were still-lifes and "genre" scenes, intimate glimpses of middle-class home life. A great flurry of picture production went on in Holland along these rather modest lines; and several geniuses were born into this world too, who ranked alongside other Baroque masters of Flanders and southern Europe like Rubens, Velasquez, and Bernini.

Across the Channel in England, the reigning genius of the century was the architect; in the other visual arts, England was still slowly absorbing the Italian Renaissance and Baroque lessons and transmitting them far afield, to her colonies in the New World.

Rembrandt was the greatest artist of the Baroque North. His art, like that of Titian, Michelangelo, and Leonardo, overleapt boundaries of place and style and foreshadowed many future developments in art. He first won considerable success in his portraits of sleek, well-scrubbed Dutchmen and their wives. In these years, Rembrandt was married to the lovely Saskia, whom he often painted in mythological or poetic costume. In this picture (*Fig. 2*) she wears the headdress of Ceres, the Roman goddess of the fields. After Saskia's death, Rembrandt gradually withdrew from the world of commissions, although now and then he was called on to make a group portrait, like *The Sampling Officials of the Drapers' Guild* (*Fig. 1*). But his subjects are no longer scrubbed and tidy. Now, deep golden shadows wash the faces, light-splashed and drawn into moving patterns like those of Italian Baroque paintings. These faces do not seem complacent; they are men troubled and saddened by experience. At this time, Rembrandt found many moving subjects among the Jews in Amsterdam's Ghetto; and within the deepening shadows of his own face, he examined the gradual encroachment of age and melancholy. Like his contemporary in Italy, Claude Lorrain, Rembrandt loved suggestions of exotic foreign lands: turbaned Arabs or costumed Romans with great golden swords (pages 198–199); strange architecture reaching up into the dark sky. He broke the rigid Protestant rule against religious subjects and painted many scenes of the Old and New Testament.

In these foreign and forbidden images, Rembrandt must have found intimations of a wider, moodier, more heroic world than the Dutch one he had apparently outgrown. As this mood of estrangement deepened, his pictures grew darker. Billowing shadows congeal behind the figures, forcing them into the foreground. Sometimes Rembrandt built ridges and bumps of paint like clay onto the canvas to make the surface richer. This kind of surface is called "impasto." Many later painters used it to enrich the effect of their lights and shadows. Rembrandt never ceased to be absorbed by the natural world around him. If his paintings could be so very complex and full of mysterious suggestions of forms, his drawing could be as simple and precise as a Sung ink sketch (*Fig. 3*). In years to come, Rembrandt's art was despised for its dark and somber unquiet; not until the 19th century, when the Romantic Movement reawakened interest in dark colors and brooding subjects, was Rembrandt's genius acknowledged.

2. Rembrandt van Rijn: *Saskia as Flora.* 1634.

3. Rembrandt van Rijn: *A Winter Landscape.* About 1647.

1. Rembrandt van Rijn: *The Oath of the Batavians to Claudius Civilis*. 1661–1662.

1. Frans Hals: *The Jester*. Before 1626.

The wide, flat Dutch countryside, where cows browsed among mossy trees and afternoons were quiet and blue, drew many Dutch painters into landscape art. Jacob Ruisdael was the greatest of these. His pictures reflect the same preoccupation with light-filled nature which Poussin and Claude felt for their Roman hillsides. These landscapes, with clouds towering in the still sky, and golden tree-stroked fields at each side, are more loosely composed than Poussin's images, less poetic and romantic than Claude's. But they are painted with a serene and penetrating seriousness which was to have a strong influence on English painters two centuries later.

One of the main portals through which Italian Baroque style entered Holland was the workshop of Peter Paul Rubens in Flanders. The Dutch painter Frans Hals had known and admired Rubens when both were students. Later, after the example of Rubens' work, Hals developed a particular zest for painting and a brushstroke that made him famous. With a square, loaded brush, he slapped on color, drawing in brisk, angular dashes that seem almost alive. His specialty was the portrait, and though his moment of popularity was brief, he made some of the most personal, lively images in history, catching the glint of his sitter's eye, the rumpled fabric of his shirt, the turn of his shoulders (*Fig. 1*). But like Rembrandt, Hals had independence of style which appealed little to Dutch taste, and he died in poverty. In Holland, which was overpopulated with painters anxious to please the common taste, these great artists went unappreciated in their own day.

2. Jacob van Ruisdael: *Wheat Fields*.

The Baroque always had two sides: the emotional moods of Rubens and Rembrandt, and the quiet, examining, cold style of Velasquez and Vermeer (*Fig. 3*). Vermeer set up his easel in a cubelike Dutch parlor, between whitewashed walls, heavy furniture, and Turkish rugs. Then, deliberately, without letting a breath of emotion stir his eye or brush, he composed each object into a frozen pattern. Like every Baroque artist, Vermeer let light pour in upon the scene. For him, it was the clean, white light of the Dutch midday, not the tumultuous shadows of Rembrandt's nights. Vermeer's shafts of sunlight crumble across the grainy surfaces of rugs and cloth, slip in knife-swaths across strips of wood and polished brass, and arch across the pale, high brow of his model. Each shape was adjusted to balance another one: the map, a symbol of the passionate Dutch curiosity about the world; the curtain falling across the whole scene.

3. Jan Vermeer: *The Artist in His Studio.* About 1670.

If a dark patch, such as the painter's clothing was shown, then a light and luminous area must balance it, like that of the young girl's face and heavy book. The subjects which Vermeer selected for these careful studies were few in number, and had none of the exotic, dramatic overtones of Rembrandt's work. He may have painted his own daughter, for the same pale, highbrowed girl appears in several works: here she wears a crown and carries a long horn. Perhaps she is dressed as the Muse of Poetry, or Art. Many times Vermeer painted this same room; it may have been his own. Some scenes show a piano; others, a work table. Possibly the figure in this painting is Vermeer himself, but no portrait of his face has been preserved. Most likely, his taste for impersonal and austere subjects would not have led him to paint his own features. Like Rembrandt's "romanticism," Vermeer's "constructivism"—as we might call it today—was far ahead of the taste of his time. He was little known during his own life and forgotten afterward, until, in the middle of the 19th century, some artists grew interested in this kind of severe, correct study of light and dark shapes in space. Then Vermeer's paintings began to be rediscovered and are now considered masterpieces.

1. Anthony van Dyck: *Children of Charles I.* About 1635.

Until the 17th century England had projected most of her creative genius into literature and had remained behind other European countries in the visual arts. As the 17th century drew on, however, English art began to advance. Within court circles the Flemish Van Dyck, who painted the children of King Charles I, (*Fig. 1*), now replaced the influence of Holbein.

2. Inigo Jones: *The Banqueting Hall, Whitehall.* London. 1619–1622.

3. Christopher Wren: *Steeple of St. Mary-le-Bow.* London. 1680.

England's first "modern" artist was the architect Inigo Jones. After spending some time in Italy where he studied Palladio's villas, he returned to the courts of James I and Charles II. There, he designed many buildings, the most elegant of which is this Banqueting Hall (*Fig. 2*), a perfect Italian Renaissance model. Christopher Wren, Jones' follower, brought the Baroque style of architecture to England. He had lived in Paris during the splendid years when Mansart, Bernini, and others worked for Louis XIV. From them he derived a taste for grandeur of scale, (*Fig. 4*). After the great fire of London in 1666, he was called upon to design many new buildings, especially churches, for the devastated city. One of Wren's trademarks was the delicate "steeple" which he set upon almost all of his smaller churches (*Fig. 3*). This steeple design was widely copied in America during the next century, on the white churches of New England.

4. Christopher Wren: *St. Paul's Cathedral.* London. 1675–1710.

5. Francis Bacon: Title page of *Instauratio Magna*. 1620.

8. Anonymous, American: *The Mason Children*. 1670.

During the course of the 17th century, leadership in world trade gradually passed from Holland to England, as the British Navy became the most powerful on the seas. Now England felt her boundaries expanding physically as well as in the realms of politics, poetry, and architecture. Science, too, led by Sir Francis Bacon, one of the great modern philosopher-scientists, forged into new fields. This frontispiece engraving (*Fig. 5*), from one of Bacon's treatises, sums up what many men of the 17th century may have felt as they saw new horizons appearing beyond the seas.

In the Dutch and English colonies of the New World, men were struggling to build a society like that which they had left behind. In the British colonies of New England, the new settlers lived in rather dark, hutlike houses (*Fig. 6*) whose shape reflected the style of the old Tudor houses of their homeland. During the austere New England winters, the settlers clustered tightly around the great central fireplaces of these houses, turning their backs on the hostile world around them. In the Dutch colonies of the mid-Atlantic coast states, the landowners were richer and lived in a temperate and fertile region. The buildings and houses they built were more luxurious

6. *Parson Capen House,* Topsfield, Massachusetts. 1683.

structures, with some of the Italianate proportions of the buildings of Jones and Wren, shown on the left. Even though no columns or pilasters adorn this plain brick hall (*Fig. 7*), the wall and windows are broken into regular, rhythmic patterns.

There was little original painting done in the colonies during this century. The rich plantation owners sent for portraits from the homeland, as did those New Englanders who could afford them. But here and there, along the Hudson River and up into the north, journeymen artists, called "limners," wandered with stocks of half-painted canvases, ready to paint in the features and, perhaps, the hands to make recognizable, individual portraits. The limners worked in whatever style they had brought with them from their homes in Europe: the Dutch-born might work in the watered-down Baroque style; the English-born might paint in the stiff, intricate, dying style of old Tudor England, or with the remembered elegance of Van Dyck.

7. *College of William and Mary,* Williamsburg, Virginia. 1695–1702.

1. Antoine Watteau: *Embarkation for the Island of Cythera.* 1717.

THE EIGHTEENTH CENTURY

2. Detail of (1)

ROCOCO AND NEO-CLASSIC

The 18th century saw Baroque style undergo a change. Beginning in the court of Louis XV, the magnificent concepts of the Baroque were transformed into a frothy, decorative style called the "Rococo," from the French word, "rocaille," meaning decorations made of seashells. Rococo style invaded church architecture, too, along the Danube cliffs of Austria, where the Hapsburg rulers, descendants of the Holy Roman Empire, built monasteries and churches crowned with rippling towers and onion-shaped domes. But after the middle of the century, just as in the 17th century, scientific interest had influenced Baroque style, science now brought about a union of archaeology and art which produced the Neo-Classic style. For among the great scientists of this "Age of Reason," were archaeologists, who uncovered the ruins of Pompeii and Herculaneum, and "encyclopedists," who classified and marked down all known facts in many fields. The mania for classifying and examining spread into art itself. Some painters made point-by-point studies of ruins and vistas. Others used newly discovered facts to reconstruct their own Neo-Classic scenes. The Neo-Classic style was given official note by the French court of Louis XVI. Men of such diverse ideals as Napoleon, Jefferson, and Washington were all Neo-Classic in their tastes, as their columned homes and classically styled portraits indicate. This style was given its ultimate expression in the paintings of Jacques Louis David.

4. *Marie Antoinette's Harp.*

5. Meissen figure: *Harlequin with Jug.* About 1738. *h.* 6½″.

These are some of the delicate treasures of Rococo style, made for Louis XV and his courtiers. In the Palace at Versailles, heavily gilded moldings were replaced by simple pastel-colored panels painted with spider-tracings of ornament, like the design for a decoration by Watteau (*Fig. 3*). In the place of Bernini's powerful, space-enclosing sculptures, small porcelain figurines like this German one came into vogue (*Fig. 5*). The court presented comedies from Italy, peopled with shy, gentle characters like Pierrot and Pierrette and costumed harlequins (pages 206–207), who are still part of our language today.

6. *The Imperial Coach of the Viennese Court.* 18th century.

3. Antoine Watteau: *Colombine and Harlequin.*

As Rubens had given the Baroque its most splendid expression, so Watteau brought the Rococo style to its highest development. As a student, Watteau had worked in the Luxembourg Palace among Rubens' great Medici series (see page 187); from these, he learned to employ the flickering Venetian style of painting so brilliantly that he was named the official painter of Louis XV's theatrical "fêtes galantes," the wonderful evening parties held in the gardens of Versailles (*Fig. 1*). Follow the line of these figures, as it curls over a hillock and down into the harbor valley; notice the garland-like arrangement of the figures, then the flying skein of cupids twining about the ship's mast; all these rippling lines seem to echo the curling shapes of flowers or shells. Yet, there is a touch of sadness in the misty shadows of the garden, and in the colors with which Watteau touched the silks and powdered wigs of his dancers—oranges, violets, and shadowy greens, bathed in a soft light. In Watteau's followers, this sense of foreboding would be felt even more strongly, although on the surface, Rococo style continued to express a trouble-free delight in pleasure.

1. Antoine Watteau: *Italian Comedians*. 1720.

In South Germany and Austria, a series of magnificent churches, monasteries, and palaces were erected in a style embracing both the Baroque and Rococo. Here, the great age of architecture, begun during the Italian Renaissance, finally came to an end. In the future, there would be no need for palaces; two hundred years would pass before a new architectural style would be born.

The design by Neumann for his great "Church of the Fourteen Saints" (*Fig. 1*) is the summation of Rococo architecture: the intersecting ovals of the floor plan create a curving, rolling space brilliantly echoed in the exterior by the rippling Baroque towers. One can compare these towers with those of the austere Spanish Escorial (page 189) to see how Rococo taste has added a froth of broken, twisting, curling ornament.

1. Balthasar Neumann: *Church of Vierzehnheiligen* 1743–1771. Floor plan below.

In Renaissance buildings space had been divided into rather set and plain areas, and staircases were pushed back into corners. But in the German Rococo building, the staircase became the heart of the design, sometimes swirling upward like the inner chambers of a shell, sometimes open and turning back on itself, as in the majestic example at right. Light streams from the windows across these white walls into the arched recesses of the stairwell, across the stucco garlands, angels, and classical figures which ornament the walls. The ceiling is in the "trompe l'oeil" style perfected in Baroque Rome and Venice (page 180). It was painted by the Venetian Tiepolo, who was called to Germany to put the crowning touch upon this royal palace.

2. *Blackamoor*. Venetian. 18th century. Colored marble.

Part of Rococo delight in make-believe was an enthusiasm for Oriental and exotic arts. Sometimes, as in this "Chinese Room" from the splendid Hapsburg palace in Vienna (*Fig. 4*), these objects were set directly into a Rococo framework. Here, Chinese porcelains, paintings, embroideries, and lacquer objects are fixed into curling gilt frames, just as a jeweler might set a stone into a golden ring. The Blackamoor from Venice (*Fig. 2*), too, was made to pique the imagination by its suggestion of far-off lands.

3. Balthasar Neumann: *Grand Staircase at the Palace of Wurzburg*. 1720–1744. Ceiling frescoes by Tiepolo.

4. *The Chinese Room*. Schönbrunn Palace. Vienna. 18th century.

5. Ignaz Günther: *Female Saint.* South Germany. 1755. Painted limewood. *h.* 5′.

Under the impact of the Rococo style, Venetian painting flourished again. Several of the greatest artists of the day worked in this city which reflected the color and fanciful movement of Rococo. Among these men who restored Venice to its former position in the arts were Tiepolo and Guardi. Yet, the Rococo was an international art style. Tiepolo (*Fig. 6*) and the unknown northern carver of this limewood saint (*Fig. 5*) achieved almost the same kind of ethereal, air-blown motion and frothy, insubstantial form.

6. Giovanni Tiepolo: *Drawing of "Helios."* 1696–1770. Black crayon, pen and wash on white paper.

The deliberate, analytical side of the Baroque movement proceeded toward the Rococo in another way. It too grew more filmy, delicate, and playful, but remained a style of precise, scientific observation. One of the greatest of these Rococo observers was Guardi, many of whose paintings were taken home by tourists, just as we might take picture postcards to remind us of views and monuments. Here, Guardi has painted the magnificent Venetian Baroque Church of the Salute, which rises beside the Grand Canal in Venice (*Fig. 7*). Guardi painted each scene with precise detail and in perfect scale. Yet he went further, bathing his scenes in Rococo light, air, and pale color, touching tiny dabs of dark color on the blue sheen of water and sky. This delicate style would later make Guardi of great interest to the French Impressionists.

7. Francesco Guardi: *Santa Maria della Salute and the Grand Canal.* About 1782.

1. William Hogarth: *The Graham Children*. 1742.

In England and France, during the 18th century, a growing body of artists and intellectuals turned their backs on the extravagant court styles. Hogarth in England and Chardin in France were two who resisted the artificial manners of the court artists, although they, too, painted in the delicate, light-washed Rococo method. Their subjects, however, were more like those of the 17th-century Dutch: peasants or middle-class families, set in commonplace homes or even in the tumbledown recesses of a hut. Hogarth could be a brilliant and scathing caricaturist, mocking the false manners and wretched distortions in the daily chores and pleasures of the society he saw (*Fig. 2*). Chardin, a much milder man, was beloved by thousands of middle-class French families who bought engravings of his works, such as *The Blessing* (*Fig. 5*). Today, Chardin is admired for the extraordinary way in which he painted the lights and shadows of candle and lamp falling on the surfaces of humble household objects. As small and delicately boned as any courtier, Chardin's figures are, however, the simple and sober middle-class city dwellers. In the new era which was beginning, these people would be the new patrons of art, replacing the kings of the Rococo period. For a brief period, a few great artists were able to serve the rather sentimental taste of the people, but in the next century the continuing demand for this kind of homely painting forced most of the great artists into radical

3. Thomas Chippendale: *Drawings for furniture.*

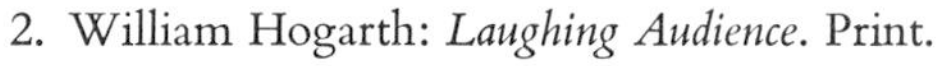

2. William Hogarth: *Laughing Audience*. Print.

4. Jean-Baptiste Chardin: *Blowing Bubbles.*

5. Jean-Baptiste Chardin: *The Blessing.* 1740.

positions of rebellion. During the 18th century, English decorative styles followed those of France and Italy, as wave after wave of influence continued to cross the Channel. Some designers worked in typical Italian Renaissance style; others, who gave a more original flavor to English art, experimented in far-flung fields along the line of Rococo taste for the exotic and fanciful. Chippendale, for instance, published a book of patterns for tables, chairs, and mirrors, in styles which included Chinese, Classic, Rococo, and Gothic elements (*Fig. 3*). On this mirror frame, a great plumed bird has alighted; a fat Chinese Buddha sits above; a Chinese maiden touches her hair below; plum blossoms, chrysanthemums, icicles, shells, and swags complete the circle. A famous English landscape architect, Sir William Chambers, wrote a book on Chinese gardens, which so delighted the English home owners that many built just such wild, rambling bowers behind their mansions. One English writer, Horace Walpole, preferred the Middle Ages. His mansion, called "Strawberry Hill," was a "Gothic" building, down to the last spire, pinnacle, and pointed window. This lingering taste for bizarre and exotic arts would stimulate the Romantic movement of the next century. But for a time, in England as on the Continent, it was submerged by another style, the Neo-Classic, based on Greek and Roman models (see pages 212–213).

1. Giovanni Paolo Panini: *Renaissance Rome.* 1757.

The new passion for recording facts led one Roman artist, Panini, to paint a series of huge canvases, which were really encyclopedias of objects. This canvas (*Fig. 1*) portrays over fifty actual ruins which are still standing in Rome, as well as famous statues which had then been excavated. In another century, the camera would do this kind of job.

While one group of English designers and architects explored the odd, exotic, and Oriental fields, others joined the Neo-Classic movement. In 1768 Sir Joshua Reynolds established the Royal Academy of Arts in London to uphold classical standards of craftsmanship and style. Josiah Wedgwood made this line-for-line copy (*below*) of a newly discovered Roman glass vessel. He later designed the Neo-Classic dinnerware which still bears his name. The architecture of the time was named "Georgian," after the four kings whose reigns spanned the century. Georgian homes were smaller versions of the Palladian villas, which were in turn based upon Palladio's careful studies of Roman ruins (page 169). The Georgian design, of imposing columns upon a small central porch between balanced wings, has often been copied in America, usually in brick and wood houses, that are still called "Georgian." Furniture was made for the English Georgian homes by such designers as Robert Adam, who had made a careful study of Roman ruins and decorations. His dainty chairs and tables were direct copies of the wall paintings of Pompeii.

3. Thomas Wedgwood: *Copy of the Portland Vase.* English, 18th century. *h.* 10″.

2. Sir Joshua Reynolds: *Col. George K. H. Coussmaker.* 1782.

Perhaps the aura of melancholy in some of the works of Watteau was his response to a new force now gathering beyond the artificial boundaries of Versailles. This new intellectual and artistic force was the search for knowledge, the plain, objective truth of history, of science, and of human nature and destiny. In art, this search led to the development of the Neo-Classic style, which strove to impart to its representations of contemporary subjects some of the classical dignity which the 18th-century rationalists admired in the records of ancient Greece and Rome (*Figs. 2, 4, 6*). The new art style also endeavored to report in encyclopedic detail the facts and objects of the physical world. Where, before, Mantegna had painted the ruins of Classical Rome, and Poussin and Claude had created imaginary reconstructions of these ruins, now hordes of scientists began to excavate the remains of Pompeii and Herculaneum, bringing to light, for the first time, a fairly complete and accurate picture of Classical life and art. An enthusiasm for reviving and copying the ideas and art of ancient civilizations was fired by the writings of a German archaeologist, Heinrich Winckelmann, and others.

4. Gilbert Stuart: *George Washington.*

In America, the public taste also developed for art done in the Classical manner. Of the American artists, Copley was the greatest, for although his figures are often set in the grand manner, against somber backgrounds of swathed Classical draperies, the figures themselves have an intimacy of personality which puts them closer to the work of Chardin than that of the mannered Reynolds. Gilbert Stuart painted in America, but his portraits reflected the "grand manner": Washington stands here (*Fig. 4*) like the young Augustus in Rome (page 54). The Neo-Classic ideal persisted into the 19th century in America and led such an artist as Greenough to depict Washington, bare-chested in a Roman toga, gesturing like a Classical hero (*Fig. 6*).

Architects in the New World also drew on Classical models which had been filtered through English hands. On the church below (*Fig. 8*), in Old Lyme, Connecticut, a steeple in Christopher Wren's style (page 202) tops a Georgian porch with Ionic columns. When Thomas Jefferson built his mansion at Monticello (*Fig. 7*), he chose a domed Roman plan like the Pantheon. For homes like these, the American craftsman Duncan Phyfe designed furniture based on English models, and silversmiths such as Paul Revere made cups, bowls, and trays in austere, unornamented shapes.

6. Horatio Greenough: *George Washington.* 1832–1841.

5. John Singleton Copley: *Daniel Crommelin Verplanck.* 1771.

7. Thomas Jefferson: *Monticello.* Charlottesville, Virginia. 1796–1806.

8. *Church at Old Lyme.* Connecticut.

1. *Marie Antoinette's Salon.* Versailles.

3. *Marie Antoinette's Hameau or Shepherd's Hut.* Versailles.

The works on these pages document a change in the intellectual and political fabric of the Western world. Often, the brilliant sculptor, Jean Houdon, came to the court of Louis XVI to model the Dauphin or one of the royal entourage. But Houdon also had sitters whose ideas were to combine to overthrow the monarchy: among them Voltaire, Rousseau, Washington, and Franklin.

4. Jean-Antoine Houdon: *Voltaire.* 1781.

In France, the Neo-Classic style was given royal approbation by King Louis XVI. Compare the austere, perpendicular lines in the salon of Louis XVI's queen, Marie Antoinette (*Fig. 1*) with the typically Rococo salon on page 210. The legs of these tables and chairs are straight and fluted like Classical columns; the walls are paneled with simple Classical designs based on Pompeiian models. But although this was the official Louis Seize style, the Austrian queen, Marie Antoinette, preferred her "English garden," where nightingales sang amid artificial hills and lakes. She even had this make-believe shepherd's hut built, where she and her ladies might dress in thin muslin costumes and play at being milkmaids (*Fig. 3*). The greatest painter of the dying era was Fragonard. His breathtaking picture below might show the Queen herself, drifting in a fabulous boat upon a royal lake, while a flashing storm rolls onward in the distance. Fragonard did not often paint such moody pictures as this; more often, he delighted the court ladies with fanciful, gay pictures of their games and love matches.

2. Jean-Honore Fragonard: *A Fete at Rambouillet.* About 1780.

5. Jacques Louis David: *Oath of the Horatii.* 1784.

In 1789, mobs from the slums of Paris rose up in revolt and stormed the Bastille, a huge prison at the heart of the city. After the devastation and upheaval of the French Revolution, life and art would never again be the same in France.

As Marie Antoinette was being carted to the guillotine through the streets of Paris, she was sketched by a painter among the crowd named David (*Fig. 6*). A friend of the Revolutionaries, David became the artistic spokesman for their ideas and ambitions. To give shape to their heroic ideals, David painted scenes of Roman warriors and heroes, like the militant, fearless youths who died in the attempt to keep Rome safe from invasion (*Fig. 5*). David drew his figures in a clear, cold line, and painted in ashen, stonelike colors. Every piece of furniture, the armor, the costumes, and even the coiffures of the figures were carefully drawn from exact archaeological reports of the time.

With the end of the Revolution and Napoleon's accession to power, David turned from his glorification of the revolution in classical terms to painting flattering portraits of the new emperor and his victories. Like Alexander the Great, Charlemagne, and Louis XIV, Napoleon during his reign stimulated the invention of a new art style; Neo-Classicism remained the order of the day, and in Paris many buildings in this style were constructed during the years of the first empire. A more significant contribution to art was Napoleon's establishment of a national museum in the old royal residence, the Palace of the Louvre. Into this museum, which was the first one open to the public, were swept all the art treasures that the French legions had confiscated during their campaigns through Europe and Egypt. In addition, the new museum housed the many private French collections of art, which, like their owners, had been scattered by the revolution.

6. Jacques Louis David: *Marie Antoinette on Her Way to the Guillotine.* Drawing. 1793.

1. Francisco Goya: *The Execution, May 3, 1808.* 1814.

NINETEENTH CENTURY

REVOLUTION, ROMANTICISM, AND THE SCHOOL OF PARIS

Revolution, which altered the face of Europe in the 19th century, extended into art as well, changing its look and even its meaning. The Rococo style had belonged to the courtly past, but in this century of revolution, there were fewer and fewer of those royal patrons who commissioned tapestries, porcelain, furniture, and portraits. The new patrons came from the middle class, a society of factory owners, small businessmen, lawyers, and journalists. A few were bold and adventurous; but most were relatively conservative, with little time to spend on art, and without a background of artistic cultivation. In the main, they liked art that reminded them of the bravery of their ancestors: paintings, sculpture, and buildings in the Neo-Classic style.

So a lively industry grew up in Europe, supplying this artistic demand, in a style which we call "academic," because originally it was the officially approved style of the French and English Academies. Most 19th-century architecture was "academic"—not only Neo-Classic, but a jumble of styles which appealed now to one, now to another set of patrons: in London, the Houses of Parliament were built in Gothic style; in Paris, the Opera was Baroque. But some painters and sculptors, daring to break free of the commercial taste, diverged into new channels. Some steered close to politics, adding their pleas for justice to those of the political revolutionaries. Others, seeking an escape from the drab world, created a style in art and ideas called Romanticism. The greatest creative minds of Europe —Goethe, Byron, Keats, Beethoven, Wagner, and others— became a part of this movement, along with the painters and sculptors. Exotic lands, extravaganzas of feeling, color, and sound—all these were part of the Romantic ideal. Another avenue of escape was that of the natural world, the peaceful poetry of Wordsworth, and the painting of Poussin and Ruisdael. And, as in previous centuries when artists probed the natural world, they reflected the scientific advances of their day. As scientists invented the camera, the telephone, the wireless, and discovered the X-ray and the significance of radium, so painters moved from the Romantic to Realism, to Impressionism and finally, to the private visions of the great Post-Impressionists, whose art breaks into worlds not even yet entirely explored. The 19th century in Europe was an epoch of great, independent geniuses breaking frontiers; but in their own time, their art ran counter to what society demanded, and the radical artistic inventions and styles alienated them from security.

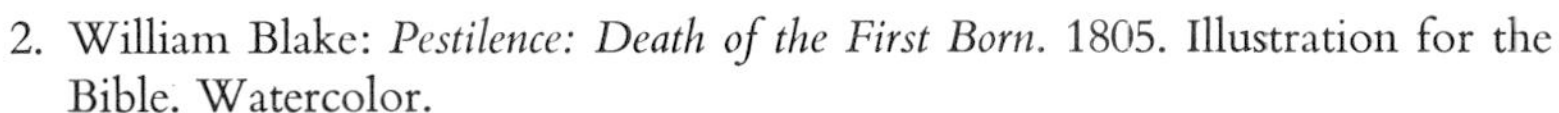

2. William Blake: *Pestilence: Death of the First Born.* 1805. Illustration for the Bible. Watercolor.

3. Francisco Goya: *The Clothed Maja.* 1796–1798.

Goya and Blake lived at opposite ends of Europe, and had little in common; yet each in his own way bridged the past and present. Goya, like Velasquez, was court painter to the royal family of Spain. When Goya wished, he could paint in the gauzy, light-streaked Rococo style, as in this portrait of the Duchess of Alba (*Fig. 3*). At other times, however, Goya could paint with devastating realism, as in the picture on the opposite page: a massacre of Spanish townspeople by the invading troops of Napoleon. A murky sky hangs above this scene; blood seems to have been scooped onto the canvas; the figures are gashed in choppy strokes of the brush. This kind of painting was Goya's own revelation and had nothing to do with his commissioned works. His thousands of etchings and engravings range over the whole of man's experience. The figures in the picture below (*Fig. 4*) dance in a circle like Rococo figures; but over them broods a pitch-dark sky and they seem to have the faces of witches.

4. Francisco Goya: "Three Majos and Three Majas Dancing." From *Los Proverbios,* edition of 1864.

Blake had been schooled in the academic Neo-Classicism of England; it was this cool, linear style which he used as he cried out against the evils which afflicted his own land: the social iniquities that accompanied the Industrial Revolution, the excesses of Puritanism, and what he saw as the godlessness of modern men. Perhaps Blake was partly mad: his drawings seem as though an uncontrollable rhythm underlay the sweeping parallel lines. But if this was the case, his kind of insanity lent formidable power to his drawings and his poetry. The outreaching scaly figure, at the left, was one of Blake's many illustrations for the Bible.

1. Adolphe Bouguereau: *Two Sisters.* 1871.

3. Jean Baptiste Corot: *Woman with the Pearl.* 1868–1870.

The faces shown in Figures 1, 3, and 4 illustrate the radical change in French 19th-century painting. Bouguereau was the most popular academic painter of the time, drawing as meticulously and carefully as his Neo-Classic masters, but adding easy, sentimental touches which enraptured the public. Actually, the final blow had been dealt to his brand of academic figure-painting around 1839 by the invention of the camera, an instrument which fascinated the public as much as it did the artists. For, suddenly artists saw how far from the truth their drawings really were, no matter how hard they had worked to discover nature's laws and proportions. Delacroix once held a photograph of a naked body next to a figure by Raphael. Even that impeccably painted body seemed to be wrongly proportioned in comparison to the image upon the photographic plate. If all these centuries of study and progress had led to nothing but error, these artists asked themselves, was it not likely that art itself had been going in the wrong direction? Was there not a "realer" way to see and paint the world? Corot, when he turned to figure-painting, dealt with masses of bone and flesh just as he otherwise did with sky, earth, cement, and water (see page 223): he built up the shapes in hard, thick blocks of dark and light color, until he seemed to hew the figure out of earth itself. Manet went further still. Like Velasqúez, he used a dry brush to lay on gauzy layers of cold color. With such strokes, he flattened out a face into frayed bits of form, which almost dissolve in flakes of light. Like Goya (page 216), whom he admired and often copied, Manet was fascinated by sudden, shocking contrasts of white flesh against dark shadows, or oddly tinted fabrics like the mauve, pink, and yellow scarves of his Spanish-style bullfighter (*Fig. 6*). In each of these works, Manet has placed the figure against a starkly contrasting background, so that flesh and costume seem to jut forward, just as each plane of the Corot head juts off from its connecting plane. Art was approaching a new level of "realism," and the public, which found these ways of breaking down the human form both brutal

2. Gustave Courbet: *My Studio.* 1855.

called Romanticism. The greatest creative minds of Europe—Goethe, Byron, Keats, Beethoven, Wagner, and others—became a part of this movement, along with the painters and sculptors. Exotic lands, extravaganzas of feeling, color, and sound—all these were part of the Romantic ideal. Another avenue of escape was that of the natural world, the peaceful poetry of Wordsworth, and the painting of Poussin and Ruisdael. And, as in previous centuries when artists probed the natural world, they reflected the scientific advances of their day. As scientists invented the camera, the telephone, the wireless, and discovered the X-ray and the significance of radium, so painters moved from the Romantic to Realism, to Impressionism and finally, to the private visions of the great Post-Impressionists, whose art breaks into worlds not even yet entirely explored. The 19th century in Europe was an epoch of great, independent geniuses breaking frontiers; but in their own time, their art ran counter to what society demanded, and the radical artistic inventions and styles alienated them from security.

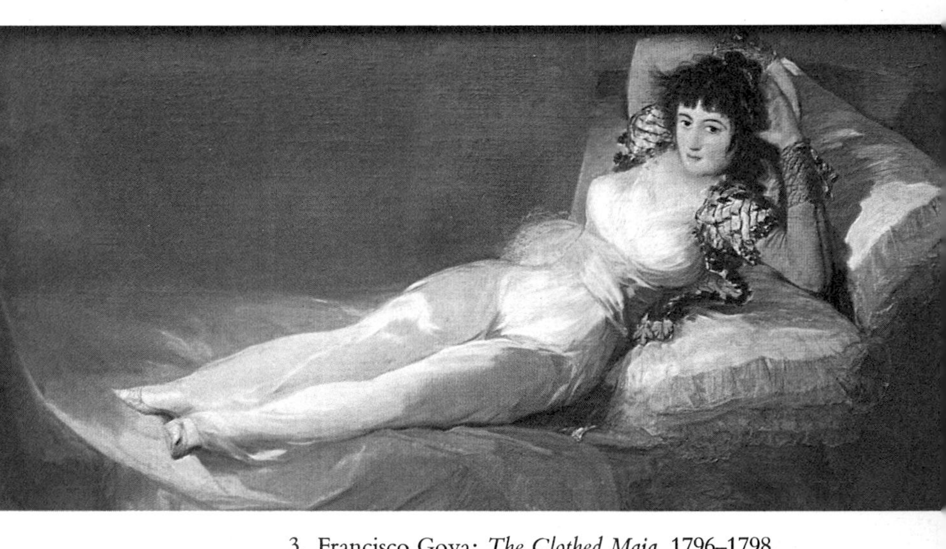

3. Francisco Goya: *The Clothed Maja*. 1796–1798.

Goya and Blake lived at opposite ends of Europe, and had little in common; yet each in his own way bridged the past and present. Goya, like Velasquez, was court painter to the royal family of Spain. When Goya wished, he could paint in the gauzy, light-streaked Rococo style, as in this portrait of the Duchess of Alba (*Fig. 3*). At other times, however, Goya could paint with devastating realism, as in the picture on the opposite page: a massacre of Spanish townspeople by the invading troops of Napoleon. A murky sky hangs above this scene; blood seems to have been scooped onto the canvas; the figures are gashed in choppy strokes of the brush. This kind of painting was Goya's own revelation and had nothing to do with his commissioned works. His thousands of etchings and engravings range over the whole of man's experience. The figures in the picture below (*Fig. 4*) dance in a circle like Rococo figures; but over them broods a pitch-dark sky and they seem to have the faces of witches.

2. William Blake: *Pestilence: Death of the First Born*. 1805. Illustration for the Bible. Watercolor.

4. Francisco Goya: "Three Majos and Three Majas Dancing." From *Los Proverbios*, edition of 1864.

Blake had been schooled in the academic Neo-Classicism of England; it was this cool, linear style which he used as he cried out against the evils which afflicted his own land: the social iniquities that accompanied the Industrial Revolution, the excesses of Puritanism, and what he saw as the godlessness of modern men. Perhaps Blake was partly mad: his drawings seem as though an uncontrollable rhythm underlay the sweeping parallel lines. But if this was the case, his kind of insanity lent formidable power to his drawings and his poetry. The outreaching scaly figure, at the left, was one of Blake's many illustrations for the Bible.

1. J. A. D. Ingres: *Mademoiselle Rivière*. 1805.

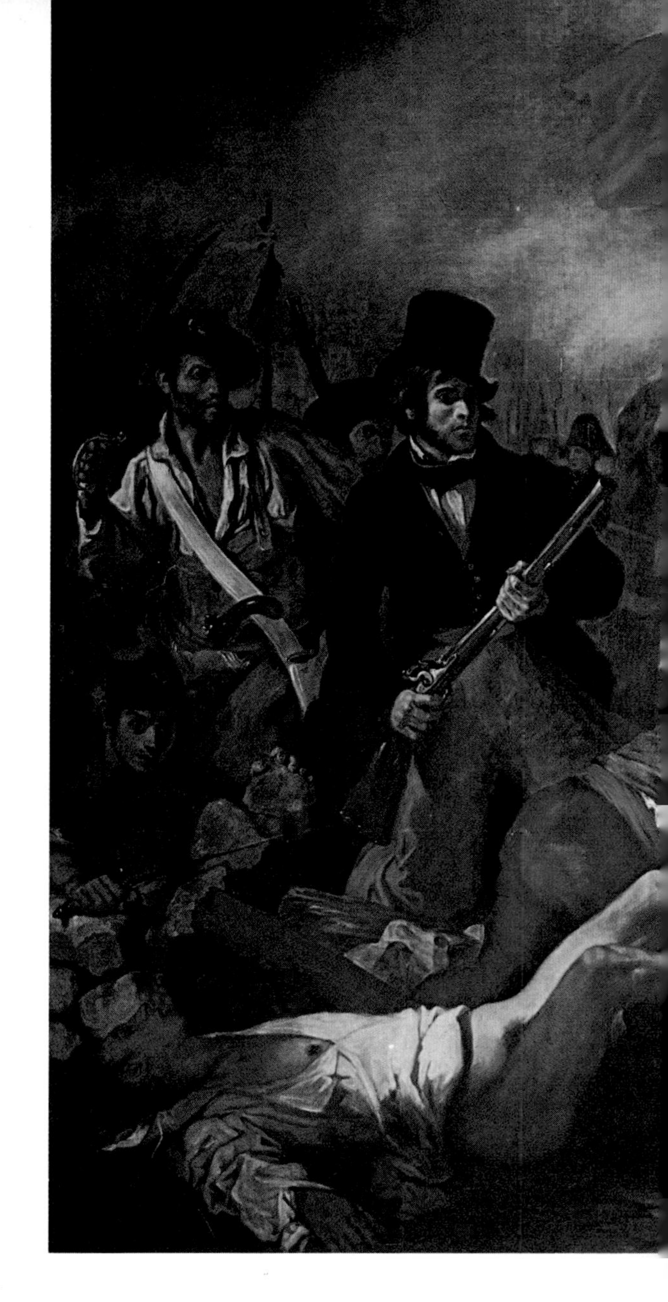

Romanticism was characterized by an emotional preoccupation with the exotic, and the sensual, in contrast to the more formal conventions of Neo-Classicism.

Ingres' art straddles these two worlds: the correct and academic Neo-Classicism of David, and the brooding, exotic spirit of Romanticism. Ingres was attacked from both sides: the academic Neo-Classicists called his work "Gothic," by which they meant barbaric. Delacroix and his friends railed at his cold and expressionless style. Yet Ingres proceeded to make some of the most elegant and enigmatic portraits in history. Mlle. Riviere (*Fig. 1*), is formally posed within the frame like a Flemish or Italian model, before a landscape which echoes her placid mood; but in this portrait, Ingres has made an extraordinary pattern of sensual curves, which seem to contradict the shy stare of the figure. The curves, originating in the fur boa which seems to clasp Mlle. Riviere like a serpent, repeat themselves again and again, across her face, her brows, her arched nose, and down the front of her pleated gown. More coolly exotic is the *Odalisque* (*Fig. 2*), reclining languorously in a harem. Like many painters of the Romantic school, Ingres often sought escape from the austere and prosaic personalities he was commissioned to paint, by portraying scenes of far-off and exotic lands.

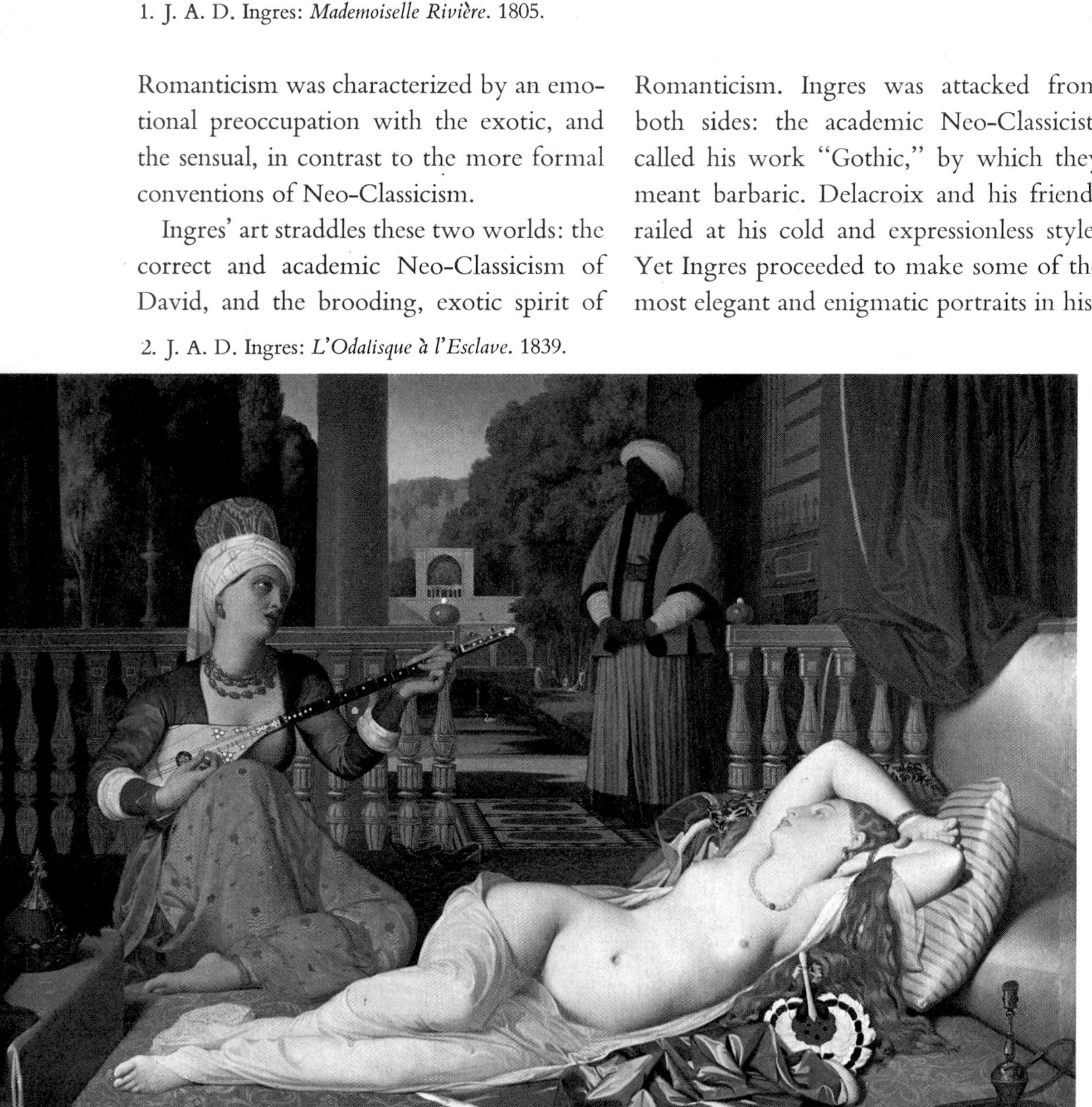

2. J. A. D. Ingres: *L'Odalisque à l'Esclave*. 1839.

Delacroix broke completely with even such questionable Neo-Classicism as Ingres', whom he attacked violently for his coldness. Instead, he tried to create a new art as full of expression and movement as the art of Rubens. So explosive did Ingres find the

3. Eugène Delacroix: *Liberty Leading the People*. 1830.

5. François Rude: "*Marseillaise*" (*Chant du Depart*), Relief from Arc de Triomphe, Paris.

6. Eugène Delacroix: *Algerian Women in their Apartment*. 1834.

work of Delacroix that he once remarked, as he entered a gallery full of the younger man's paintings, "I smell gunpowder!" Romantic painting as created by Delacroix and Géricault can be compared to the music composed by Beethoven in the later years of his life. Before Beethoven, the Baroque and Rococo music of Bach and Mozart had employed pure lines of melody, curling and twining throughout the composition, like the lines in a Watteau painting, or a church plan by Neumann. Beethoven, however, changed the very sound of orchestrated music, adding many instruments to make a deeper, richer musical fabric. Out of these storms of sound, beating melodies rush forth, exploding into crashes of cymbals and drums. Romantic style in painting expressed itself in similar ways. Jumbles of forms in both these paintings (*Figs. 3 and 4*) swarm together in dark shadows, rising up to peaks of bright color and upward-reaching figures, falling back again into dark paint strokes and almost unfinished shapes. Each of these works was based upon an actual contemporary event; Delacroix chose a reported incident during the overthrow of the Bourbon monarch in 1830; Géricault showed the rescue of the survivors of a terrible shipwreck. Rude's sculptured group on the imposing Arch of Triumph in Paris echoes these same heroic gestures and sweeping actions (*Fig. 5*). Another side of Romanticism had been foreshadowed a century earlier in the Oriental and exotic touches used by some English designers like Chippendale (see page 210). Delacroix, too, traveled to Morocco, bringing back memories of harems, tiger hunts, and strange faces (*Fig. 6*), very different from the faces and colors of the new industrial world.

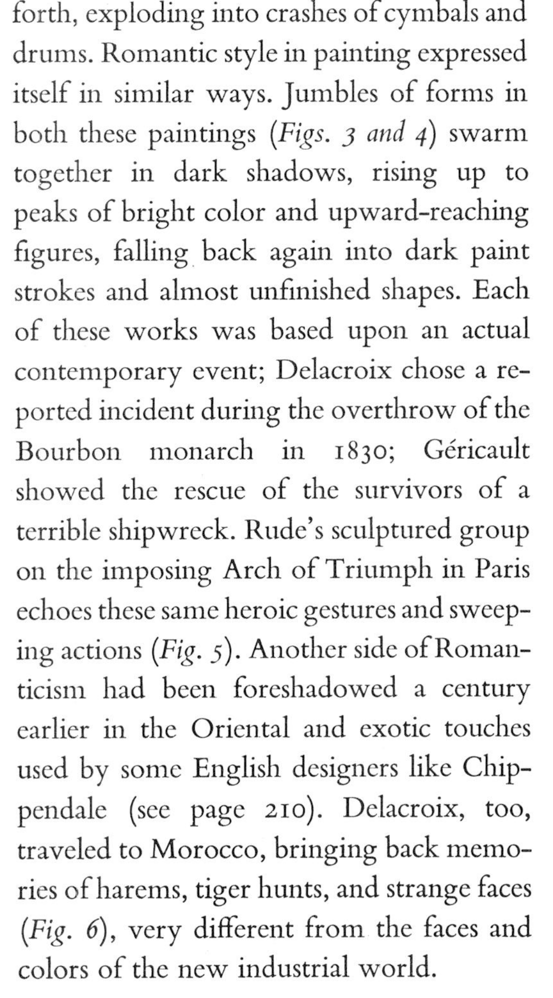

4. Theodore Géricault: *The Raft of the Medusa*. 1818–1819.

1. Adolphe Bouguereau: *Two Sisters*. 1871.

3. Jean Baptiste Corot: *Woman with the Pearl*. 1868–1870.

The faces shown in Figures 1, 3, and 4 illustrate the radical change in French 19th-century painting. Bouguereau was the most popular academic painter of the time, drawing as meticulously and carefully as his Neo-Classic masters, but adding easy, sentimental touches which enraptured the public. Actually, the final blow had been dealt to his brand of academic figure-painting around 1839 by the invention of the camera, an instrument which fascinated the public as much as it did the artists. For, suddenly artists saw how far from the truth their drawings really were, no matter how hard they had worked to discover nature's laws and proportions. Delacroix once held a photograph of a naked body next to a figure by Raphael. Even that impeccably painted body seemed to be wrongly proportioned in comparison to the image upon the photographic plate. If all these centuries of study and progress had led to nothing but error, these artists asked themselves, was it not likely that art itself had been going in the wrong direction? Was there not a "realer" way to see and paint the world? Corot, when he turned to figure-painting, dealt with masses of bone and flesh just as he otherwise did with sky, earth, cement, and water (see page 223): he built up the shapes in hard, thick blocks of dark and light color, until he seemed to hew the figure out of earth itself. Manet went further still. Like Velasqúez, he used a dry brush to lay on gauzy layers of cold color. With such strokes, he flattened out a face into frayed bits of form, which almost dissolve in flakes of light. Like Goya (page 216), whom he admired and often copied, Manet was fascinated by sudden, shocking contrasts of white flesh against dark shadows, or oddly tinted fabrics like the mauve, pink, and yellow scarves of his Spanish-style bullfighter (*Fig. 6*). In each of these works, Manet has placed the figure against a starkly contrasting background, so that flesh and costume seem to jut forward, just as each plane of the Corot head juts off from its connecting plane. Art was approaching a new level of "realism," and the public, which found these ways of breaking down the human form both brutal

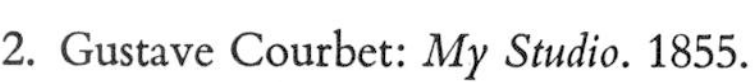

2. Gustave Courbet: *My Studio*. 1855.

4. Edouard Manet: *Woman with an Umbrella.* About 1872.

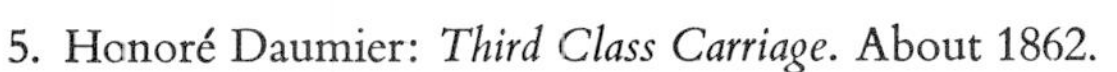

5. Honoré Daumier: *Third Class Carriage.* About 1862.

6. Edouard Manet: *Mlle. Victorine in the Costume of an Espada.* 1862.

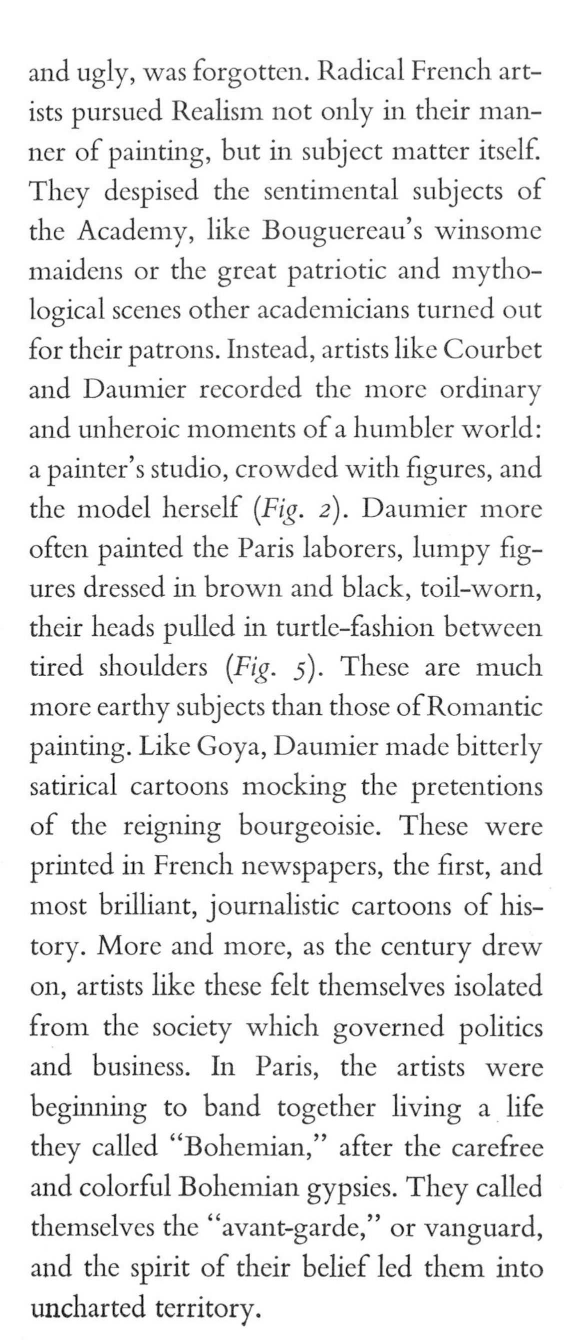

and ugly, was forgotten. Radical French artists pursued Realism not only in their manner of painting, but in subject matter itself. They despised the sentimental subjects of the Academy, like Bouguereau's winsome maidens or the great patriotic and mythological scenes other academicians turned out for their patrons. Instead, artists like Courbet and Daumier recorded the more ordinary and unheroic moments of a humbler world: a painter's studio, crowded with figures, and the model herself (*Fig. 2*). Daumier more often painted the Paris laborers, lumpy figures dressed in brown and black, toil-worn, their heads pulled in turtle-fashion between tired shoulders (*Fig. 5*). These are much more earthy subjects than those of Romantic painting. Like Goya, Daumier made bitterly satirical cartoons mocking the pretentions of the reigning bourgeoisie. These were printed in French newspapers, the first, and most brilliant, journalistic cartoons of history. More and more, as the century drew on, artists like these felt themselves isolated from the society which governed politics and business. In Paris, the artists were beginning to band together living a life they called "Bohemian," after the carefree and colorful Bohemian gypsies. They called themselves the "avant-garde," or vanguard, and the spirit of their belief led them into uncharted territory.

The development of painting may be traced by studying the manner in which painters apply their paints: the kind of brushstrokes and lines they use, the consistency or quality of their paints, and the kind of light they describe. From time to time, however, changes occur in the kind of subject which painters choose to show. In the Middle Ages, painters rendered religious subjects, and as the Gothic Age drew to a close, portraiture was reborn. Renaissance artists loved Classic themes, and in the Romantic decades, artists elected heroic episodes from their own world. One subject to which artists of many ages have returned again and again is the landscape. Landscape painters in Rome (page 58), in Late Gothic Flanders (page 128), in Florence (page 148), and in Rococo France (page 204), treated the subject in various ways, as did the landscapists of Sung China (page 90), or Persia (page 75). The Venetian Bellini (page 162) saw landscapes bathed in a golden light, as though all of nature was a part of the same divine handiwork. Hieronymus Bosch saw landscape as a monstrous, imp-ridden hell (page 123). To Poussin and Claude, landscape painting was a stage on which splendid Classical and Oriental dramas might be enacted. In the 19th century, many artists again began to paint landscapes.

2. John Constable: *Dedham Mill*. 1820.

The kind of landscape painting that was evolved by Constable and Turner, two English painters of the same period, had an even greater influence upon the next generation of French artists than Delacroix's Romanticism. The new landscape vision was born among poets and painters in the England that Wordsworth knew. The natural world now beckoned these artists as a subject to be loved and studied, as once the human body had been. Constable approached his easel with a much more passive attitude than Poussin, who grandly plotted sweeping arcs and diagonals through space to make his monumental structures. Constable merely tried to set down forms just as he saw them, without the flourish and sweep of Claude's drawings. His approach was more like the Dutch Ruisdael's. Most important, Constable's patient scrutiny of the landscape sometimes led him to make sketches in a new way: by setting flat strokes of color beside each other, like blocks, and then touching on white dashes for highlights where the sun struck a reflection. Turner used his paints in a still more extraordinary way. He painted scenes of ships, like the one below, of harbors, and of fields under burning skies which swallowed each detail into a mist of flaming color. Both Constable and Turner were searching for ways of knowing the world other than in the traditional drawing.

1. Joseph M. W. Turner: *The Fighting Temeraire*. 1838.

In the 1830's in France, a group of painters gathered in the forest town of Barbizon near Paris to paint landscapes. They daubed their canvases quickly, with loose brushstrokes, making studies in the manner of Constable. Their first break with tradition was to paint outdoors, directly from nature. Because the French forests are filled with a silvery mist which softens the outlines, the Barbizon pictures, too, were faintly milky, as though an invisible veil wrapped the scene in a single, pale tone. But the Barbizon artists tried to keep from "romanticizing" their subjects, or making them deliberately poetic. The outstanding member of the group was Corot. Often he traveled to the south, particularly into Italy. There, in the clear light around Rome, he made pictures

3. Claude Monet: *Impression–Sunrise*. 1872.

4. Jean Baptiste Corot: *View of Rome*. 1826–1827.

with cool swaths of color, very much like Constable's sketches. This technique of seeing things in pure blocks of shadow and light, and of painting them sharply, without modeling the edges or surfaces, gave an extraordinary hardness and luminosity to Corot's work. His technique was to break down the world into its parts, as one might take the plaster off a wall and expose the bricks behind. Once artists began to break down reality, they embarked upon an extraordinary voyage of discovery. The next daring step in landscape painting was taken by Monet, who in 1872 exhibited this painting of a sunrise (*Fig. 3*). A critic mockingly called the group to which Monet belonged the "Impressionists," after the title of the painting, and the label stuck. Impressionism was actually a radical development of Corot's style, breaking down solid objects into the mysterious element, light, that painters had loved since the Venetian Renaissance. And once again, art paralleled scientific development. As scientists began to find that the world could be broken down into smaller parts, almost infinitely, art reflected the new scientific discoveries. Monet and his Impressionist colleagues made pictures which look like mosaics of paint dabs. Seen close up, the pictures made no sense at all to the outraged Paris public which crowded the exhibitions. But if one stood a few feet away, the pictures fell into place, flickering and vibrating, all in motion like water under sunlight. Monet, the most persistent Impressionist (*Figs. 3, 5, 6, 7*), painted the same subjects at various hours. He watched the light change from moment to moment, through daybreak and hot noon until twilight, growing blue and violet, blurring the edges of objects. His later pictures, painted in his pond-filled garden, show the trees, rivers, and water lilies deprived of their substance and revealed only as radiating light.

5. Claude Monet: *Haystack*. 1891.

6. Claude Monet: *Gare St. Lazare*. 1877.

Next pages: Claude Monet: *Terrace at Le Havre*. 1866.

7. Claude Monet: *Houses of Parliament, Westminster*. 1903.

Claude Monet

1. Antonio Canova: *Cupid and Psyche*. 1793. Marble.

2. Auguste Rodin: *Cupid and Psyche*. About 1893. Marble.

3. Auguste Rodin: *The Burghers of Calais*. 1884–1886. Bronze.

Toward the end of the 19th century Impressionism, as a schoolroom of modern art, developed a wide split, and two opposed modes (or tendencies) evolved. One was in the Romantic tradition, with the emphasis on the emotional, while the other appeared austere, analytical, and probing. Renoir (page 228) and Cézanne occupied these contrasting positions, and in the art of sculpture, Rodin and Maillol offered the same contrast. Not since Rubens and Velasquez had such clearly opposed geniuses come forth to give their interpretations of a single style. Together with Monet, Renoir learned to paint the dappled sunlight bathing a scene, turning the faces of figures lavender, pale green, apple red. But it was the splendidly carefree, ebullient life of the Bohemian artists and their friends which Renoir painted in glowing scenes: figures dancing, dining or promenading in swirling lines flow through the canvas space, then turn back on themselves like the lines of movement in a Rubens or a Watteau. Affection and radiant life are the spirits which Renoir's paintings evoke: although he mastered the broken effects of Impressionism, he never distorted his figures in unlovely ways, but even in his long search for style, occasionally went back to an old-fashioned, linear, Neo-Classic way of drawing. Rodin's art, like Renoir's, seems to return in spirit to the more emotional Romantic age, yet it also embodies the broken effects of the new art. Like Michelangelo, Rodin often left parts of his sculptures unfinished, buried in ragged clay or stone. From this great mass, the figures seem to heave upwards, veiled and struggling, to cast their limbs about and sink back into darkness. Sometimes Rodin chose subjects from the past, Greek nymphs like those above, which still were the popular subjects of academic sculptors and painters. Canova (*Fig. 1*) was the most famous academician of his time; like Bouguereau, he had an unquestionable mastery of technique. Yet when Rodin approached the same subject, he changed Canova's artificial scene into a rough, scrambling moment of life. Rodin also made monumental portraits. In spirit and in treatment, his burghers may remind one of Rembrandt's guild members (page 196): each, a shadowed human being, groping forward out of the darkness of surrounding space and material, as though they were joined together in a slow dance.

Cézanne, too, had learned from Impressionism how to compose a picture from separate bits of color. But instead of laying these fragments on the canvas in a flickering haze, he attempted to create a structure as balanced and substantial as one by Poussin: to "do Poussin over again from nature," as he said. He wanted to make pictures as cold and hard as those of the Baroque master, perfectly blended and harmonious. But he was not satisfied with the artificially composed images of Poussin's paintings, but wanted, rather, to paint from nature, using the colors and shapes he observed. As he peered into the distance, Cézanne noted trees leaning across his line of sight, and hills receding, step by step into the pale distance. The marks he made on the canvas were mere indications of what he saw. He tried to make one brushstroke recede behind another by painting it darker or cooler in color. When he drew the human figure (*Fig. 6*), he sought out the same relationships of position in space: he did not care to model the colors smoothly, nor to make the lines of the body flow into one another, as Ingres might have done, or as even Renoir did with his warm tones. If he painted a round or curving surface, he applied his brushstrokes as one might set bricks into a stepped-back wall, each one flat and straight but receding behind its neighbor. Cézanne did not care any more than Renoir for the infinite tiny details and distortions which make an object individualistic. Compare his painting of harlequins (page 231) with Watteau's on the same theme (page 206). At first glance, the composition may look less balanced and tightly knit than the formal 18th century one, where the central figure stands as erect as a column, entwined with garlands of human faces. Cézanne has constructed his of bent, leaning, angular fragments of forms, pressing together as heavily as broken stones in an old wall. Vast and labored structures, Cézanne's paintings are monuments to the modern, passionately analytic viewpoint, and they became the inspiration for much 20th-century art.

Maillol in his own way dealt with the same kind of massive, static shapes which obsessed Cézanne, though he went back to Classical sources for his subjects and for the shapes and weights of his figures.

5. Paul Cézanne: *Landscape with Viaduct*. 1885–1887.

4. Aristide Maillol: *Leda*. 1902. *h*. 11½″.

6. Paul Cézanne: Study from a cast of *L'Ecorché*.

Next pages: Renoir: *Luncheon of the Boating Party*. 1881.

1. Paul Cézanne: *Still Life: Jug and Fruit.* 1890–1891.

2. Paul Cézanne: *Card Players.* 1890–1892.

3. Paul Cézanne: *Mardi Gras* (*Shrove Tuesday*). 1888.

Since the beginning of the 19th century, painters had labored in many ways to draw closer to the heart and body of nature, to paint her tones and relationships with as little distortion as the human eye and hand could achieve. Now, as the century drew to a close, a few painters began to draw back from that rigorous, demanding position and to return to a kind of art which had existed before: the making of stunning patterns upon a flat picture surface. Seurat (page 234) and Gauguin were artists of this sort, although each started out as a student of nature in the Impressionist schoolroom. Seurat carried the Impressionistic technique to its extreme. Inch by inch, he covered his canvases with tiny points of color, building up shapes like wooden dolls in profile against the grainy, unreal flatness of his background. Gauguin had studied not only Impressionism, but medieval art, tapestries, enamelwork, and Japanese prints as well. In his hands, the Impressionist brushstrokes flattened out like ink blots crawling over glass, or wide, stitched sections of embroidery. Restlessly, he tramped over much of France, north to Brittany, south to the sun-wracked Midi; at last, he set sail for Polynesia, where he painted his greatest works, and died, almost forgotten.

1. Paul Gauguin: *Self-portrait.* 1889.

2. Paul Gauguin: *I Raro Te Oviri* (*Under the Pandanus*). Tahiti. 1891.

Next pages: Georges Seurat: *A Sunday Afternoon on the Island of La Grande Jatte*. 1884–1886.

1. Vincent van Gogh: *The Zouave.* 1888.

Like his friend Gauguin, and later Degas and Toulouse-Lautrec (page 241), Van Gogh was also impressed by Japanese compositional manner. *The Zouave,* left, is an experiment in this style. Every line and pattern—the flat bricks of the floor, the hat, and posture of the flame-skirted figure—all wrench the eye in a dynamic, oblique direction, from left to right. As his exhilaration with this new art increased, insanity kept pace, and recurring breakdowns swept him rapidly away from the holds he clung to in the visible world. At moments, frenzy and ecstasy made him paint a scene such as the *Starry Night* (*Fig. 3*), in which thick whiplashes of color stir the dark body of a tree and make the hills, valleys, and stars sweep like rapids rushing toward the sea. During more lucid periods, however, he could paint a landscape like the one on page 238, a fragile weaving of deft, quivering brush-

The story of Van Gogh's life has become a legend. His dedication of purpose, his extreme sensitivity to colors and shapes, and his final agonized battle against insanity, all become a part of our image of this great Dutch painter. Yet Van Gogh's source of both agony and accomplishment was his consciousness of the distance between the world and his personal image of it. Each of his paintings was a labored effort to bring himself back into focus upon the facts of nature. He did not, like Bosch, paint the monsters and swamps of nightmares, nor did he, like Grünewald, paint the human body attacked by leprous disease. Instead, through the most agonizing extremes of illness, he continually labored to bring himself back into focus upon the facts of nature, to paint landscapes, bowls of flowers, the corridors of the hospital where he was confined, the faces of his gentle doctor, his neighbors, his artist friends. When, in his early days, Van Gogh drew this peasant wracked by sorrow (*Fig. 2*), he recorded the facts as accurately as his untaught hand allowed him to do, drawing the bunched muscles, thick hands, and wasted shoulders. During a brief sojourn in Paris, Van Gogh met the Impressionists and Post-Impressionists; later in the south of France, he absorbed their phenomenal new vision and, under the burning southern sun, gave vent to his passion for color and light.

2. Vincent van Gogh: *Old Man in Tears.* 1882.

3. Vincent van Gogh: *The Starry Night.* 1889.

strokes and pale colors. In the last year of his life, just before he committed suicide, Van Gogh painted *White Roses* (*Fig. 4*), fragile and pale, bunched together in the most lyrical, casual way. Then, on closer examination, one sees the bouquet charged with tension like a cluster of coals about to burst into flame. In these uncontrolled swings between reality and wild distortion, Van Gogh's genius expressed and destroyed itself. After his lifetime, many schools of artists used this language of formal distortion to express their own troubled or ecstatic feelings. But because they did not possess his peculiar genius, their works seldom compare in intensity with his.

4. Vincent van Gogh: *White Roses.* 1890.

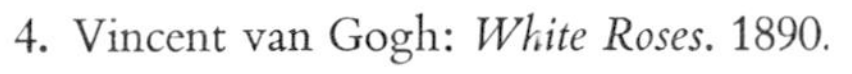

Next pages:
Vincent van Gogh:
Landscape at Arles. 1889.

1. Edgar Degas: *Rehearsal of the Ballet on the Stage.*

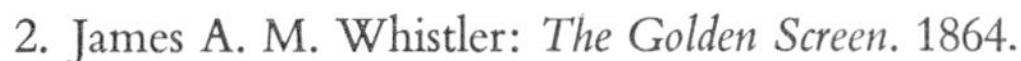

2. James A. M. Whistler: *The Golden Screen.* 1864.

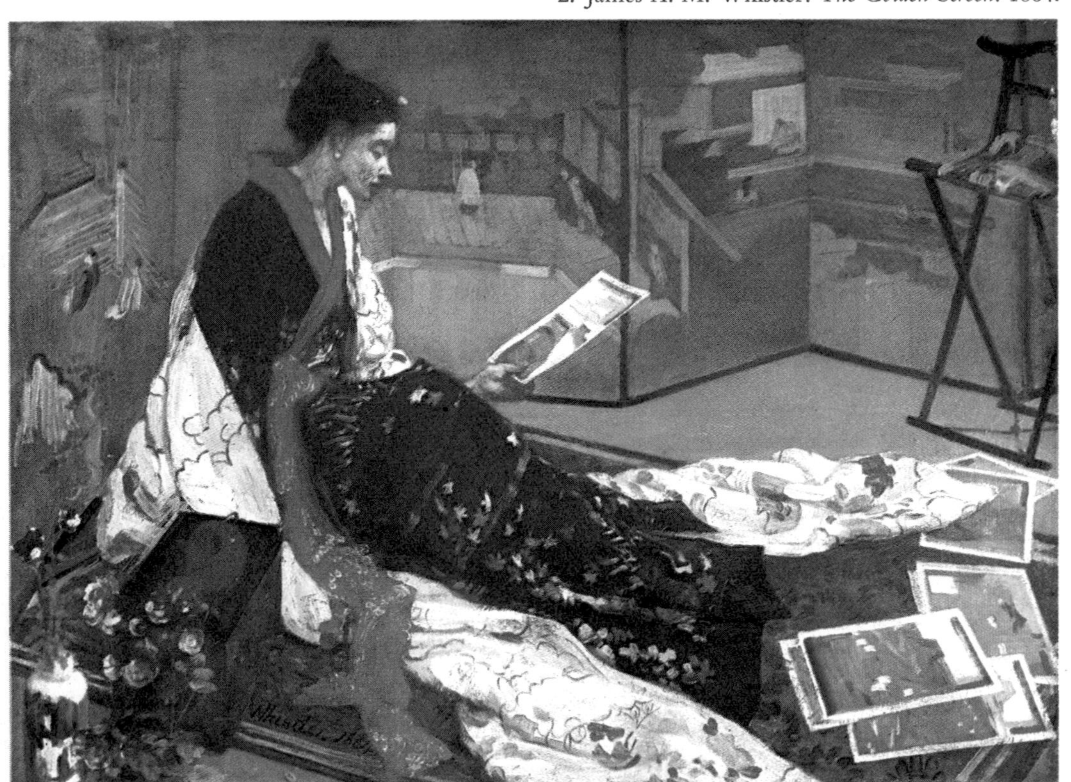

From time to time, since its popularity in the Rococo period, Oriental décor became fashionable in Europe. Around the middle of the 19th century, the fashionable ladies of London and Paris again began to order Japanese furnishings, fans, kimonos, and porcelains. At the same time, examples of Japanese prints began to turn up, some stuffed into the corners of packing crates, others imported by booksellers and travelers. At first, the prints seemed oddly composed and out of balance (see page 102). To Western eyes, accustomed to seeing figures arranged in regular order above and behind a horizontal floor plane, these prints came as a shock and a revelation. Often a picture seemed too big for its space, almost falling out of the edge of the frame. Other patterns were tilted, as though the artist had suddenly opened his eyes upon a scene rushing by.

Astonishingly, the design of these prints seemed to match the impression given by that phenomenal new device: the camera. For it, too, could give a sudden, off-balance, candid view of the "ukiyo-e" or "floating world," as the Japanese print-makers called it. Many painters now began to try compositions of this sort. Among them were Degas and Toulouse-Lautrec in Paris, and the American, Whistler, in London. Degas placed his easel before groups of ballet girls, dancing, bathing, dressing. He painted their light-frazzled bodies, their dresses and their

3. Henri de Toulouse-Lautrec: *Yvette Guilbert*. 1894.

glancing feet against the darkness of a theater. In each work, he tried to find a new angle of vision, oblique, as if seen from above, or even from very close up. For the scene above, he placed himself in a box by the stage. Probably he sketched very quickly, as Hokusai did when he drew his sketches of fat men in their baths, hardly rearranging a form or a shadow, except to emphasize the light that cuts through the gloom. Degas made extraordinary use of the great, yawning area of empty space—just as Van Gogh did in his study of the Zouave (page 236), to sweep the eye diagonally across the scene. Whistler left America behind forever in his search for a more congenial artistic atmosphere and found it in London and Paris, where he painted delicate studies of personalities such as the one at left (*Fig. 2*), cast into Japanese postures and costumes. Sometimes Whistler even called his pictures "Nocturnes," or Studies in Color, to suggest that these color patterns were all that really mattered to him.

For scathing accuracy with the pencil, no artist of the 19th-century Bohemians could touch Toulouse-Lautrec. Crippled and dwarfed, he was as isolated from the society which he painted as Van Gogh was from the mild people of southern France whom he portrayed. But while Van Gogh's emotions flooded his work, Toulouse-Lautrec kept a firm control over his biting lines and acid colors. When he chose, he could use his pencil like a whip, exaggerating here, underplaying there, catching in a few strokes the personality of the extraordinary Yvette Guilbert, or the bland, bizarre faces of the drinkers at the Moulin Rouge, the famous Paris dance hall. Toulouse-Lautrec was a master of composition as well. His theater posters are still models of poster art; no eye could escape being drawn by their tense and contrasting patterns of flat shapes. A picture like the *Moulin Rouge,* with its figures arranged behind the slashing orange balustrade, is a *tour de force* of sheer pattern. The white, ratlike face of the bearded man in the center is the focus of a spray of caricatured images, from the frozen mask of the girl at the right, to the turtle-like gentleman in the far distance. Hokusai or any other Japanese printmaker would have understood this devastating, off-balance kind of composition. Since the beginning of the century artists had moved further and further away from the kind of realism which a Renaissance man would have understood. Each artist, or school of artists, now looked at reality from his own vantage point, omitting whatever did not concern him, and concentrating on elements that did. Thus, out of all the manifold aspects of nature, artists had begun to "abstract" particular ones. In the next century, abstract art would be carried to new extremes.

4. Henri de Toulouse-Lautrec: *At the Moulin Rouge*. 1892.

The outstanding artists of the American 18th century had gone to Europe to learn to paint and make sculpture in the "grand" manner of the academies. But toward the 19th century, another kind of art began to appear in America. Artists now made images of their own new world just as it looked, without trying to make it into an echo of Rome or London. Some artists like Peale (*Fig. 2*) approached their subject as a classifying scientist of the 18th century might have done. Here, Peale has painted his own portrait beside what was the first "natural history museum" in America—shelves of stuffed birds and bones that he had collected himself. Other gifted scientist-painters were Audubon, whose pictures of birds and small animals have never been surpassed, and Catlin, who drew many studies of the different Indian tribes, their costumes, dances, and camp sites.

1. Albert Pinkham Ryder: *The Forest of Arden.* Painted 1888, finished 1897.

AMERICA

In America at the turn of the century, the Neo-Classic ideal still claimed the imaginations of its leaders and its artists. At the same time, the 19th century saw the beginning of a particularly American style of "realist" painting and sculpture. This new Realism expressed all the exhilaration of the young nation, and especially the eagerness it felt for its unexplored regions in the West. There were many variations but it differed from European Realism in that it was not concerned with the breakdown of reality into its basic structure, but rather with the recording of nature in its outwardly correct garb. This vein of American art persists today, although in a minor current. Elsewhere, it has changed into journalism or caricature, or, under the influence of European styles, into various pattern-arts which have in their turn, influenced the American arts of advertising and design. Even more important, however, was the birth of a new architectural concept which was to produce the great skyscrapers of the 20th century.

2. Charles Willson Peale: *The Artist in His Museum.* 1882.

3. George Catlin: *Wah-pa-ko-läs-kuk, The Bear's Track.* One of Kee-o-kuk's warriors, Sauk tribe.

6. John James Audubon: *The Black Rat.* 1842.

On into the 20th century, when European art was plunging ahead into extraordinary fields of abstract and expressionist art, some of the foremost American painters continued to record the scenes around them in a factual manner. Bellows' brilliant study of boxers, entitled *Stag at Sharkey's,* is typical of these.

4. Thomas Eakins: *The Gross Clinic.* 1875.

After the Civil War ended in 1865, a strong American society patterned after Victorian England grew up in the Atlantic Coast regions around New York and Philadelphia. There, artists such as Eakins painted the dour faces of these hard-working citizens, unvarnished by Romantic idealism or by the artificialities of European Neo-Classicism. The famous picture at the left (*Fig. 4*), shocked many of the conventional people of the day, who thought that a surgical operation was no fit subject for art.

7. George Bellows: *Stag at Sharkey's.* 1907.

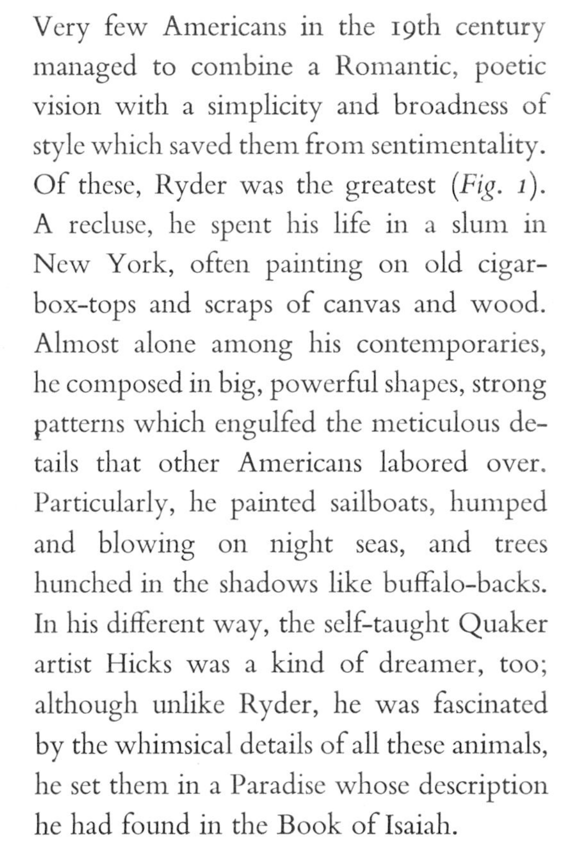

Very few Americans in the 19th century managed to combine a Romantic, poetic vision with a simplicity and broadness of style which saved them from sentimentality. Of these, Ryder was the greatest (*Fig. 1*). A recluse, he spent his life in a slum in New York, often painting on old cigar-box-tops and scraps of canvas and wood. Almost alone among his contemporaries, he composed in big, powerful shapes, strong patterns which engulfed the meticulous details that other Americans labored over. Particularly, he painted sailboats, humped and blowing on night seas, and trees hunched in the shadows like buffalo-backs. In his different way, the self-taught Quaker artist Hicks was a kind of dreamer, too; although unlike Ryder, he was fascinated by the whimsical details of all these animals, he set them in a Paradise whose description he had found in the Book of Isaiah.

5. Edward Hicks: *The Peaceable Kingdom.* About 1830–1840.

1. Albert Bierstadt: *The Buffalo Trail.* 1896.

An American "Romantic" landscape style, indirectly inspired by the Italian paintings of Claude, was created in the early years of the 19th century by artists working in the lush, hazy valleys of the Hudson River. The American artists of this school loved the moody Italian way of painting, in glowing layers of transparent color. They added local touches, like these buffaloes, or perhaps an Indian tepee touched by the last rays of sunset.

4. George Caleb Bingham: *Fur Traders Descending the Missouri.* About 1845.

2. Winslow Homer: *Hound and Hunter.* 1892.

George Caleb Bingham, too, brought a Romantic spirit to the region of the Middle West, then a lonely land peopled by fur trappers and merchants. Unlike the Hudson River painters, however, Bingham was able to subordinate technical effects to his sense of theater and design. This group, from the owlish-looking fox hunched at the left, to the oarsman at the right, seems to be frozen in a mysterious drama. Bingham has stressed the unreal effect by isolating the clearly drawn figures before a shrouded, misty background. In a few decades the Surrealist painters of Europe would use the same technique to create their disturbing dream pictures.

3. Edward Hopper: *Gas.* 1940.

Today, many American artists have departed from realism of this kind, but of those who continue in the realistic tradition, Edward Hopper (*Fig. 3*) is outstanding. Grave and serious, Hopper makes pictures as clearly composed as a Dutch landscape. This haunting mood is created by the white light, the blank spaces, and dark, angling shadows which Hopper locks together like segments of a picture puzzle.

Winslow Homer began as a Civil War artist-journalist, then grew more famous when he turned to water colors of sailboats on the dark blue waters of Maine. He became a master of composition, and an earthy feeling for paint, stroked on in bold, thick strips. In composition, this work (*Fig. 2*) seems rather like Bingham's *Fur Traders.* Yet it substitutes for Bingham's ghostly "Sur-realist" view, a concentrated, unexaggerated Realism which has been one of America's main contributions to modern art.

5. Henry H. Richardson: *Marshall Field Warehouse*. Chicago. 1885–1887.

In America in the early 19th century, as in England and France, a jumble of borrowed architectural styles cluttered the skylines of nearly every town and city. Renaissance and Gothic buildings, Greek and Roman structures stood side by side. No new architectural vision had yet emerged in this world which was just beginning to learn how to handle steel, iron, and cement. At last, however, a trio of innovators attempted to scrape down through the accumulation of ornament and shapes to invent a style which would be consonant with the new building materials. Henry Richardson (*Fig. 5*) was one of the first of these searching architects. He felt that only the Romanesque style fittingly expressed the youth and virility of his young country. But perhaps even more than Romanesque lines and solid spaces, Richardson's buildings express his fascination with heavy, rugged materials. Pseudo-Gothic houses, like those painted by Charles Burchfield (*Fig. 6*), might have been made of paper or clay, but Richardson's stone blocks have been handled without artifice, and without trying to imitate anything else. Louis Sullivan was the next experimenter with original architectural shapes. Today perhaps, this great arching portal, below, reminds one of a Romanesque or even Islamic doorway, but at the time that it was built, it was considered astonishingly simple.

6. Charles Burchfield: *Promenade*. 1928 or 1929.

7. Louis Sullivan: *Transportation Building, Golden Portal*. World's Columbian Exposition, Chicago. 1893.

Two inventions had given the new architecture a boost: structural steel, which could bear heavier loads than iron, and, at the turn of the century, poured-concrete construction. Now architects could set together great slabs of solid concrete, poured on the spot, reinforced from within by a grill or network of fragile iron rods or wire. The great explorer in this new medium was Frank Lloyd Wright. Like so many of his contemporaries, Wright had felt the influence of the Orient. Now that he had a material which could be used as simply as Japanese wood and paper and yet withstand the arduous Western climate, he began to design buildings as starkly laid out as Japanese houses of paper and wood. His early designs, around the turn of the century, were *tours de force* of this style. Not a vestige of Gothic, Greek, or Renaissance ornament is added; only the flat lines of walls and roof repeating the horizontal lines of the earth, the vertical lines of trees and human beings. The church plan (*Fig. 8*) has been put together as cleanly as a painting by Vermeer or Cézanne. Wright's next innovations belong to the international world of style (page 261).

8. Frank Lloyd Wright: *Unity Temple*. Oak Park, Illinois. 1903.

1. Henri Matisse: *The Hindu Pose*. 1923.

TWENTIETH CENTURY

ART BECOMES INTERNATIONAL

Since the Renaissance, Western art has usually followed two paths, which seem to reflect two of the basic ways in which Western man observes the world. One way is cold, formal, and analytical. Painters of this school set their figures, frozen into immobility, within cool light. They shift these figures back and forth to build a tight composition in space, ignoring the ruffling, distorting effect of emotion. Piero della Francesca, Poussin, Vermeer, David, and Cézanne were all this kind of painter. The other way is emotional and fervent. Painters in this style may use darker, warmer colors, stroked into complex, changing patterns and forms in deep, shadowy space. Changing lights gleam from rippling muscles and rich fabrics; flux and change inhabit these works; no form is steady or secure; everything is in motion. Titian, Rubens, Watteau, Delacroix, and Renoir were artists of this school. Rodin was such a sculptor. Twentieth-century art, too, follows these separate attacks upon reality. Eddies of style have followed upon one another during this half-century, just as, politically, decades of peace have given way to decades of war. Some artists have expressed the turbulence and insecurity of this world; others have built works and buildings of the purest geometrical shapes, as permanent and emotionless as mathematical diagrams. Perhaps the only art style which does not exist today is the kind of humanistic naturalism which existed during the Renaissance, based upon the idea of man as controller of his universe. Instead, art has advanced from naturalism toward abstraction to describe ultimate space and innermost forces. It is too early to know what school of art will characterize our century, but there is a language of the present day hidden in the forms and materials of 20th-century art, just as the explosion of Hellenism was reflected in the *Winged Victory's* posture, or the birth of Humanism in Masaccio's *Expulsion*.

3. Pablo Picasso: *Artist and His Model.* 1931. Etching.

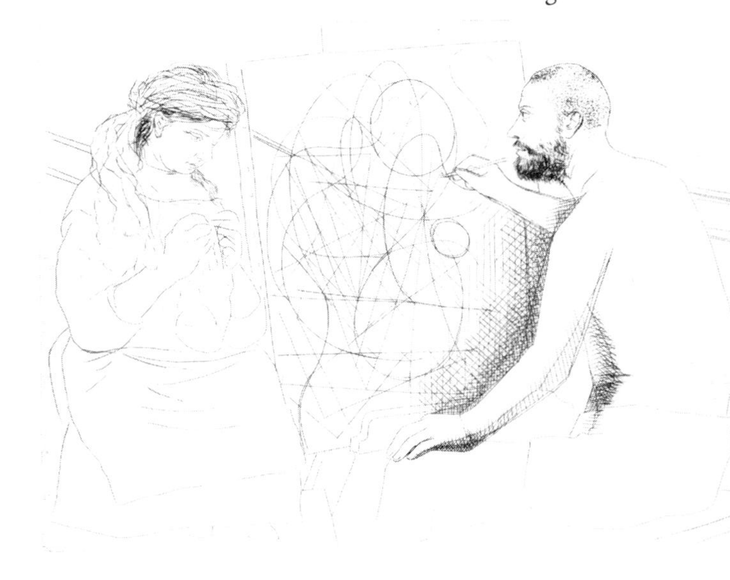

2. Henri Matisse: Pages from Mallarme's *Poésies,* with etched illustration. 1932.

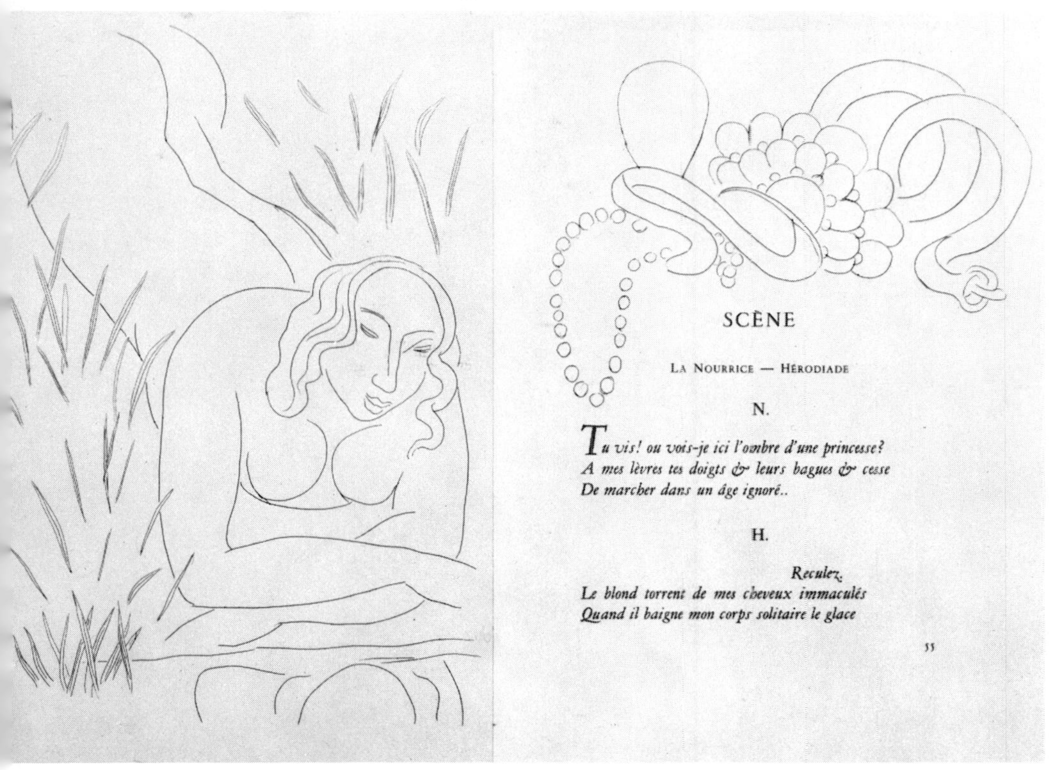

SCÈNE

LA NOURRICE — HÉRODIADE

N.

Tu vis! ou vois-je ici l'ombre d'une princesse?
A mes lèvres tes doigts & leurs bagues & cesse
De marcher dans un âge ignoré..

H.

Reculez.
Le blond torrent de mes cheveux immaculés
Quand il baigne mon corps solitaire le glace

55

On this page, and on pages 248–9, 251, and 252 are works by the two greatest artists of the first half of the 20th century. Together they sum up a great deal of artistic experiment and theory which has gone before. Each artist made his special contribution—Matisse in the field of expressive color (*Fig. 1* and page 251, *Fig. 6*), Picasso in the field of abstract form; yet each went farther. Matisse made tiles and textiles, book illustrations, stained glass windows, paper cutouts, and sculpture. Sometimes a line as willowy as Botticelli's expresses his fervor, as in the book illustrations at left; at other times, he made purely abstract works of flat color. Picasso, too, has worked in many media: today he turns from ceramics to metal work, from painting to the graphic arts. In the fascinating etching above, Picasso has made a witty and revealing comment on the modern artist's occupation: his eyes fixed on the model, he translates what he sees into "abstract" lines on the canvas.

1. Pablo Picasso: *Night Fishing at Antibes*. 1939.

1. Edvard Munch: *The Cry*. 1895. Lithograph.

3. Ernst Barlach: *Crippled Beggar*. 1930. Vitrified clay. *h*. 82″.

2. Ernst L. Kirchner: *Dodo and Her Brother*. 1905–1906.

One of the most vital of 20th-century styles is Expressionism, which was foreshadowed at the turn of the century by the Scandinavian Munch (*Fig. 1*). Snakelike lines thread through *The Cry*, like high-tension cables. What was Munch expressing? Perhaps it was the same sense of anguish and crumbling of old traditions that made the German poet Nietzsche write at about the same time: "I felt a cry in the whole universe!"

In the year 1904, two painters living as far apart as Dresden and Paris, made the same discovery: in the dusty cases of scientific museums, they came upon African statues (see pages 12–13), which had been brought to Europe during the previous centuries. These jagged, hacked-off statues suggested a more brutal and stronger art, expressive of dark terrors and energies. Also, these figures suggested new ways of using materials, a block of wood cut deeply in sharp, diagonal slashes (*Fig. 3*), or paint scored in rhythmic, angular strokes. Both the artists, Maurice de Vlaminck and E. L. Kirchner (*Fig. 2*), helped to form groups which soon began to exhibit pictures in the new Expressionist style. Kirchner's group in Germany was called "The Bridge." Later, this gave way to the "Blue Rider" group. Vlaminck (*Fig. 4*) and his friends in Paris were called the "Fauves," or "wild beasts." They all painted in much the same way, garishly colored landscapes and still-lifes, and men and women, bent by storms of howling color stroked onto the canvas in brittle, flat shapes. Contrasts of acid green, sapphire blue, citron and lavender, which earlier painters found repellent, these artists used deliberately.

In the 20th century, art has gradually become international in a way unknown since Greek style pervaded the entire Mediterranean world. With all the world of art history suddenly opened up to them, artists were, for the first time, able to select styles and motifs out of the past which seemed congenial to their way of looking at the world. Rouault, for instance, looked to medieval stained-glass windows. He took more up-to-date subjects—judges, kings, clowns, and others who seem to bear the burden of modern ills and sorrows—and painted them in such dark, glowing colors, flat to the surface, separated by thick black lines like the leading in 12th-century glass.

4. Maurice de Vlaminck: *Tugboat on the Seine*. 1906.

5. Georges Rouault: *The Seated Clown*. 1945.

Expressionism at first reflected violent and anguished feelings, whipped up by the emergence of Germany among the militant, nationalistic modern systems. Though he began his career as a Fauve, Matisse was soon carried beyond this angry style. He retained, however, his love of color and pattern, but gradually tempered it in a gentle art of dancing figures and bright gardens, luxurious patterns and semi-Oriental subjects like *The Hindu Pose* (page 246). The other great patternmakers in Western art were the craftsmen of Islam, and in many ways Matisse's art reminds one of that luxurious world, for he too worked in many decorative mediums, particularly tile and glass, in addition to painting. This little chapel (*Fig. 6*), which he designed toward the end of his life, is a luminous summation of his work. Colored light from the windows falls into the cool interior, unadorned except for several figures sketched in black upon white tile, and the simple stone altar appears as rough and cool to the touch as a field stone.

6. Henri Matisse: *Chapel of the Rosary*. Vence. Architecture, stained glass windows, tile figure of St. Dominic and altar decoration by Henri Matisse. 1950–1951.

1. Pablo Picasso: *Les Demoiselles d'Avignon*. 1907.

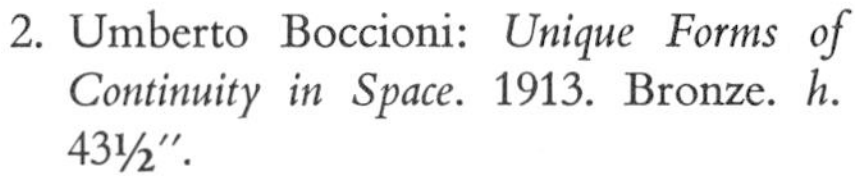

2. Umberto Boccioni: *Unique Forms of Continuity in Space*. 1913. Bronze. h. 43½″.

3. Georges Braque: *Man with a Guitar*. 1911.

4. Pablo Picasso: *Head of a Woman*. 1951. Bronze. h. 21⅛″.

The discovery of African sculpture led to another radical modern movement of the cold and analytic mode: Cubism. When Pablo Picasso painted his canvas of the *Young Ladies of Avignon* (*Fig. 1*), he took the design of angles and sickle-shaped curves from African art and transplanted it to the heads at the right of the picture. He did not make this extraordinary and, in ways, ugly picture to "express" any particular feeling about his subject. Rather, he felt that the African manner of looking at a figure revealed some new facet of its structure. In other words, Picasso had returned to Cézanne's method of viewing a scene in flat, interconnected planes, and then of duplicating those planes upon the flat canvas. Soon, artists like Picasso and Georges Braque began to paint almost entirely unrecognizable designs of these flat planes, sliding together, sometimes obscuring one another and sometimes so transparent that one shape appeared beneath another. This phase, "Analytical Cubism," was a more radical departure than had ever been attempted. Painters no longer tried to give a semblance of reality, but worked with pure "abstract" patterns.

The sculpture shown above (*Fig. 4*) gives a clear idea of the Cubist technique. Taking a solid, three-dimensional subject, Picasso has analyzed each of its surfaces and profiles into the separate forms which make it up. If Picasso were to paint a Cubist picture of this head, he would paint the various surfaces and geometric shapes as if they were spread out flat.

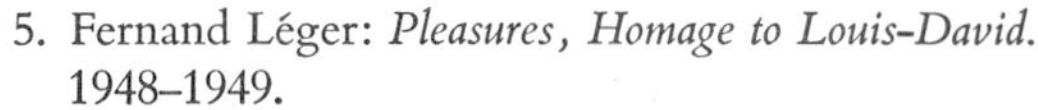

5. Fernand Léger: *Pleasures, Homage to Louis-David*. 1948–1949.

6. Back view of (4).

7. John Marin: *Sunset, Casco Bay*. 1919.

One group which shot off from the main avenue of Cubism tried to turn that cold technique to a more expressive end. This was the Italian Futurist group. "A fast automobile is more beautiful than the *Victory of Samothrace,*" wrote the Futurists around 1910; they wished to show the rocketing speed of modern life and the shearing passage of figures through space, as in Umberto Boccioni's striding man (*Fig. 2*).

The Cubist technique of dividing a figure or scene into its component parts became a common language among many painters of the next decades. The most individual of them adapted it to their own interests. Fernand Léger, for instance, saw his figures as thick, columnar shapes rather like those in machines. More and more, the Cubist way of looking at the world seemed appropriate to our industrial age. In America a Cubist style appealed even to such a delicate, poetic artist as John Marin. He has broken the rays of sunlight in this water color into geometric shapes (*Fig. 7*), which crisscross over the flat screens of sea and earth. In England, too, the technique is used today by artists such as Graham Sutherland (*Fig. 8*), to analyze and reassemble the shapes of his subjects. Today, Cubism is one of many new ways of seeing and composing; it can be radically interpreted from artist to artist as the different works on these pages show: from the undulant, smoothly polished, interlocking surfaces of Moore's sculpture to the harsh figure of Sutherland's painting.

8. Graham Sutherland: *Crucifixion*. 1946.

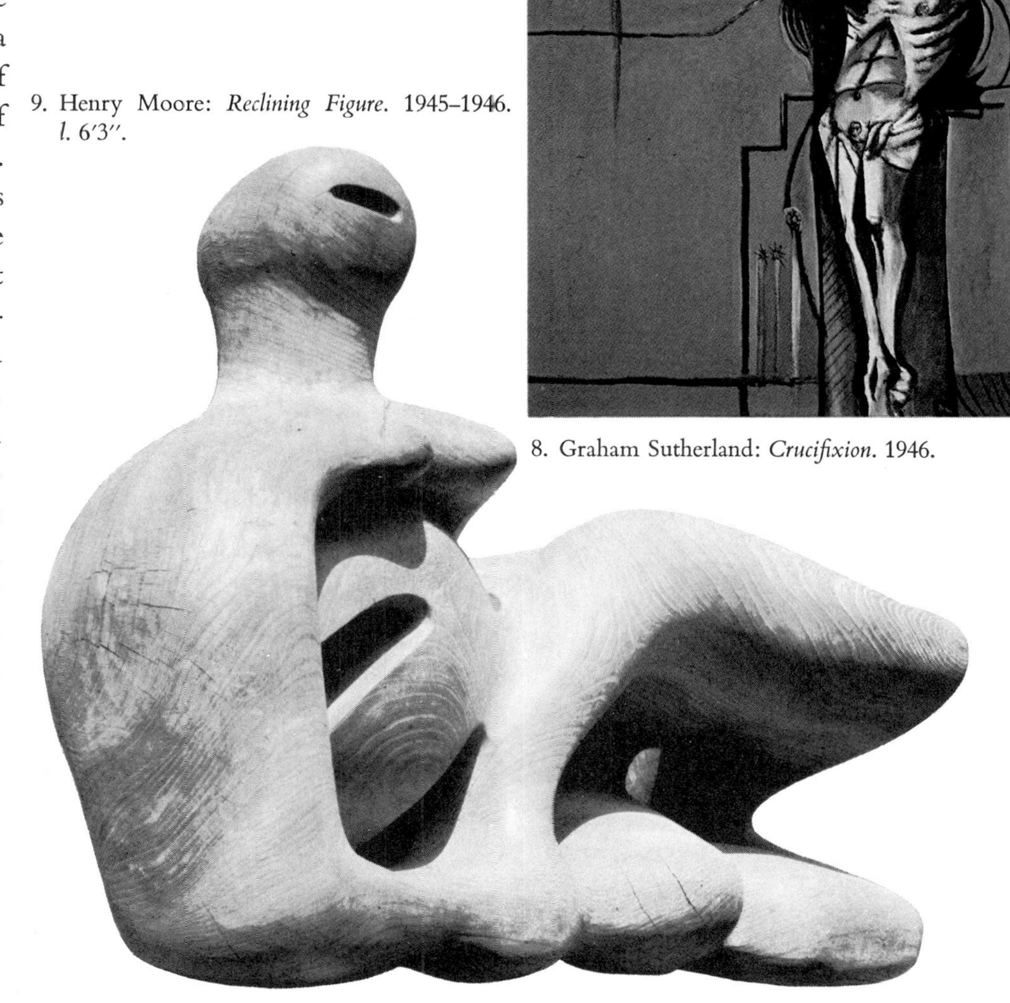

9. Henry Moore: *Reclining Figure*. 1945–1946. *l.* 6′3″.

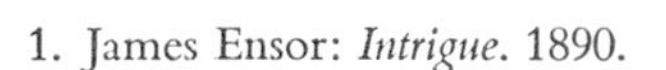
1. James Ensor: *Intrigue*. 1890.

As scholars and artists were gradually discovering the arts of unknown peoples and realizing their applicability to the modern way of seeing, so, on another level, a hitherto unknown area of life was opened up during the early decades of the century. This was the human unconscious, gradually charted by Freud and other students of human psychology. The revelation had deep effect upon the arts. The Surrealist movement, in painting, sculpture, poetry, even music and the drama, was a broad attempt to interpret this whole strange world of man's inner life. As early as 1890, the Belgian Ensor painted this weird group of grotesque faces (*Fig. 1*), which seem to express a much grimmer nightmare than even Munch drew. In 1912 De Chirico painted this dreamlike scene (*Fig. 3*), filled with images which had no rational explanation: a cane balanced against a wall, a headless statue facing seawards. More effective was the way the scene was painted, in flat, empty areas emphasizing loneliness and unreality. Salvador Dali's pictures carried this style to its extreme (*Fig. 2*).

3. Giorgio de Chirico: *The Autumnal Meditation*. 1912.

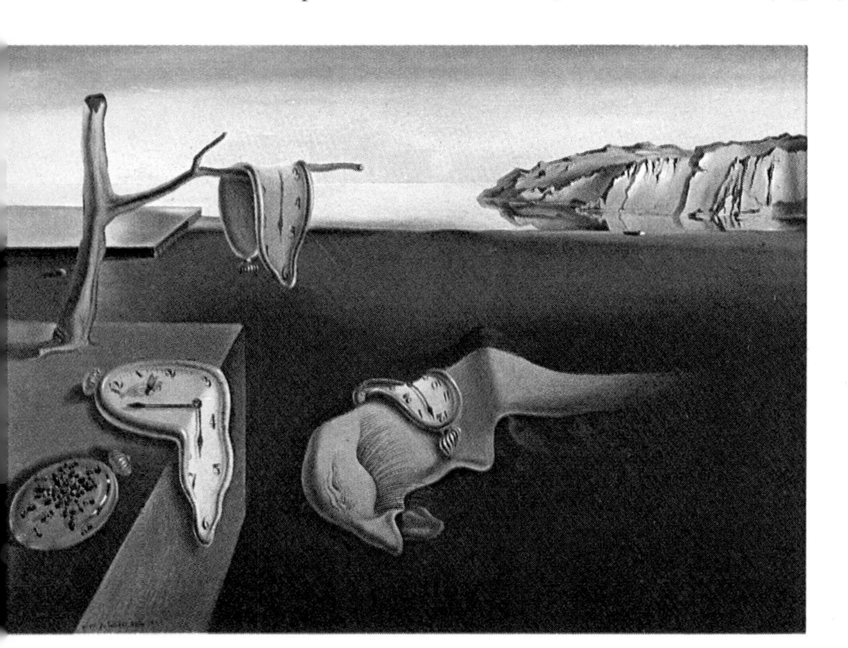
2. Salvador Dali: *The Persistence of Memory*. 1931.

4. Paul Klee: *Child Consecrated to Suffering*. 1935.

5. Balthus: *The Golden Days*. 1944–1946.

6. Mario Marini: *Horse and Rider*. 1950. Bronze. *h*. 71″.

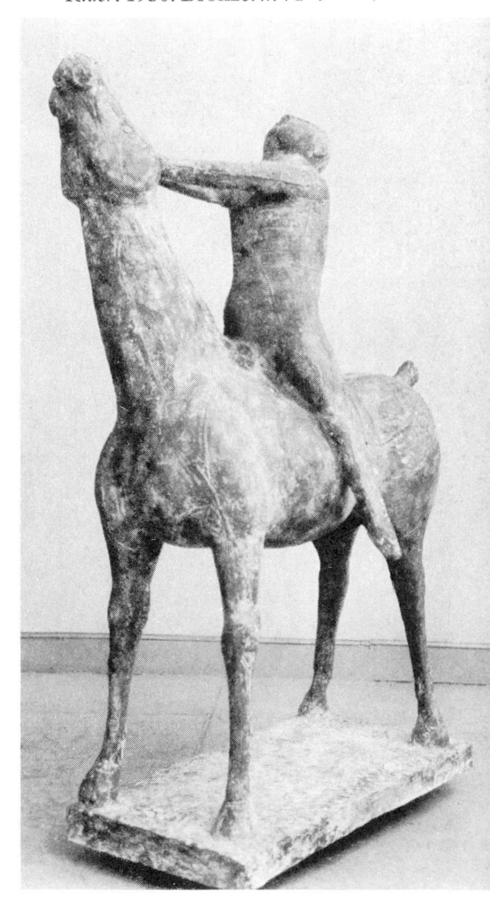

The great years of Surrealism were the late '20's and '30's in Paris. There, a crowd of artists gathered from many countries. They wrote plays and acted in them, composed music, designed costumes and stage sets, painted and wrote poetry. At this time, as the arts began to converge, and each depended on others to help search out ephemeral meanings, such an artist as Paul Klee began to make what were really painted poems, pictures of these unconscious thoughts and feelings with curious poetic titles (*Fig. 4*). Now, a new fascination added fuel to Surrealism: children's art, and the primitive materials, gestures, and forms which children and insane people create. Klee and others sometimes painted on scraps of burlap, or old paper, or glass. Bit by bit, boundaries which separated the "fine arts" from other created objects and interests were breaking down.

7. Alberto Giacometti: *Figure in a Box*. 1950.

The Post-War decades in Europe and America have seen Surrealism persist as one way of expressing the shock and turmoil of modern life. Some artists, like the French Balthus, paint in as traditional a manner as De Chirico or Dali, communicating a haunted mood with groups of enigmatic figures. Other artists, like the Italian Marini, the Swiss Giacometti, and the Polish-born Lipchitz, draw upon newer techniques of composing the figure. One can say of most works of Surrealist intent that they express a particular complex of literary or psychological ideas. Surrealism is, for the most part, a very modern kind of "story" art, making bitter or melancholy comments upon the contemporary world. Of these four, Giacometti, perhaps, has made a particularly relevant image (*Fig. 7*). The two boxlike caverns which confront and lie behind the tiny, stalking figure enclose him just as mysteriously as we may feel time and the universe enclosing ourselves.

8. Jacques Lipchitz: *Mother and Child II*. 1941–1945. Bronze. *h*. 50″.

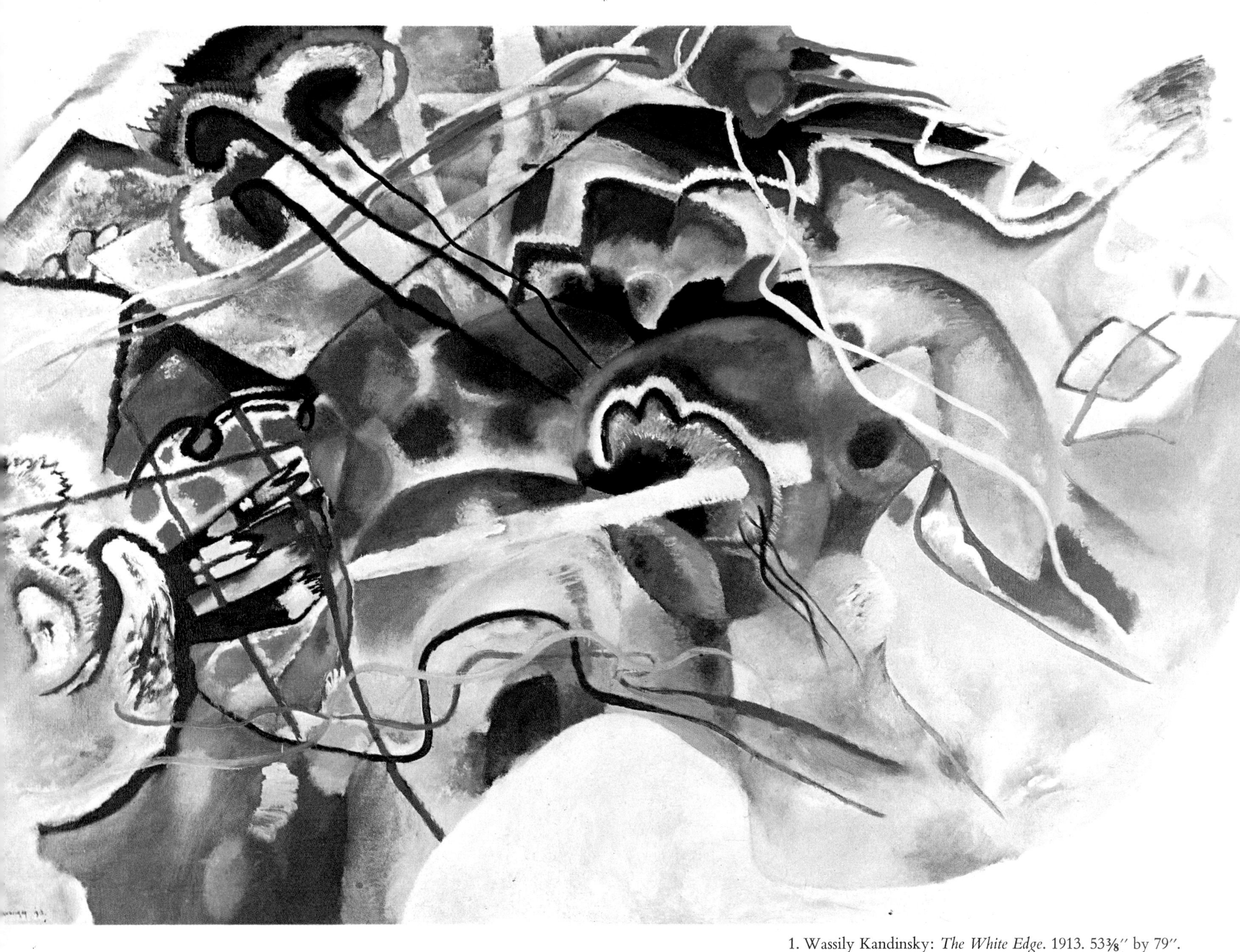

1. Wassily Kandinsky: *The White Edge*. 1913. 53⅜″ by 79″.

Wassily Kandinsky was born in Russia, but early in life he became a friend of the German Expressionists (page 250) and later the Parisian *avant-garde*. As early as 1910, Kandinsky began experimenting with a new kind of painting which had no literal subject at all. It was, instead, simply an abstraction of colors and shapes, bending, flowing, entwining, and melting into one another like strands of music. Later, Kandinsky met a group of other Russian artists, called "Constructivists" (page 261), and his style became colder, more geometric and analytical, built of squares, triangles, and short straight lines set into tight patterns. He called this style "Non-Objective." It was Kandinsky's observation that colors and shapes had each their own rhythm, "weight," and importance in a picture; that they could be woven into entirely subjectless compositions as valid and complete as music, or a mathematical progression. The picture above is one of his masterpieces, a huge painting which absorbs the observer into its clouds and recesses of floating color. The white scoop-edge which gives the picture its name, compresses the central mass, forcing each color and shape into position. One can study this picture for a long time, following the various lines and tones as one might watch a dense sky boiling and changing pattern from moment to moment.

Mondrian's painting is composed of the same elements which went into Kandinsky's painting: pure colors, placed upon a canvas without any direct reference to a subject in the real world. Yet it is obvious at a glance that an entirely different spirit, and even "subject," underlies this abstraction. If Kandinsky's work is emotional, filled with change and turbulence, then Mondrian's might be said to be cool and completely "finished." One might point to another famous pair of contemporaries, Rembrandt and Vermeer, who, in radically different ways, both expressed the Baroque spirit of their time. Actually Mondrian was a native of Holland; is there something of the quality of a Vermeer in these still, straight lines, these contrasts of flat, bright color? Yet, there is enough staccato variation in this picture to give it a very modern mechanical vitality, like the sounds and flashing lights of Broadway, for which it is named. In the next four pages are grouped several modern works of art by artists who may be said to follow the mode of either Kandinsky or Mondrian, working in the Expressionist spirit.

2. Piet Mondrian: *Broadway Boogie Woogie.* 1942–1943.

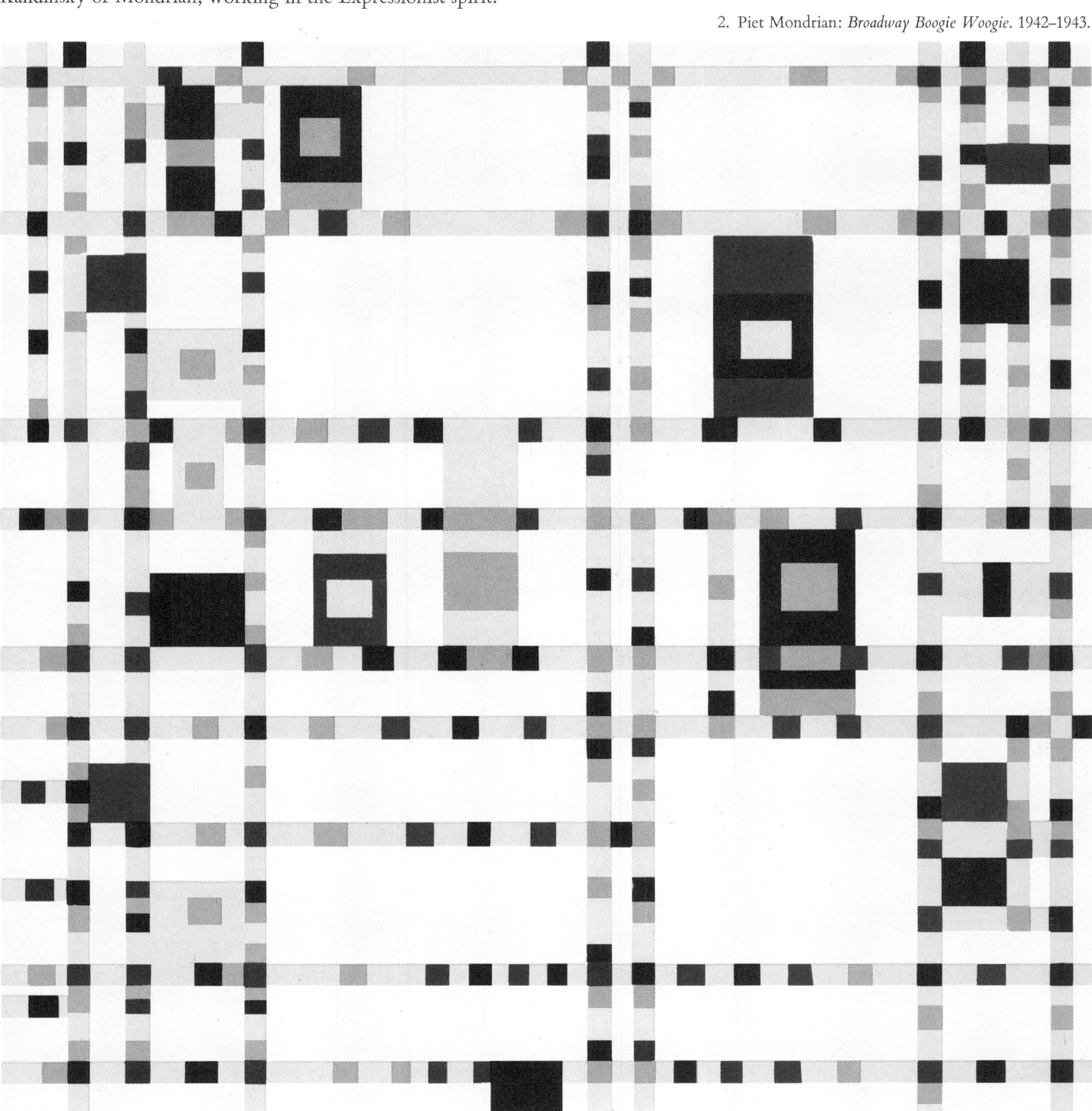

1. Jackson Pollock: *Number 12.* 1952.

In different ways, all the works of art on these pages are related to Kandinsky's abstract vision. The "Abstract Expressionism" of Willem de Kooning and Jackson Pollock, the "direct metal" sculpture of Theodore Roszak, the pinched and ploughed, Rococo-spirited image of Nakian, and the humped, hooded, monumental church of Le Corbusier—each of these contemporary works is an arrangement of abstract shapes, lights, colors, spaces, and forces which expresses something of the constant movement and shifting interrelations of our times.

2. Willem De Kooning: *Two Women in the Country.* 1954.

Abstract Expressionism is the name given to the new style of art which evolved in America in the 1940's under the indirect influence of Kandinsky, and has since spread all over the world, wherever artists are free to experiment with radical and often unpopular ideas. Artists like Pollock and de Kooning have renounced all effort to make their pictures images of the real world: they do not hollow out the picture space with perspective lines, nor build figures, landscapes, solid bodies within such space. They treat the picture surface as though it were the surface of a wall or a bowl—simply a flat sheet to receive a covering. Then with a welter of lines and colors freely disposed over the surface, these artists attempt to build up focuses of intensity, whorls of greater weight or brilliance which give a loose, scattered structure to the canvas. De Kooning may introduce figures which half-evolve, half-vanish in the buckling ranks of paintstrokes he lays down. Pollock created no image at all, simply gathering and dispersing energies—much the same kind of universe that astrophysicists contemplate when they survey the galaxies of the outer universe. The idea is not new: Zen artists of China and Japan had a style they called "flung ink," which achieved the same effect on soft white silk or paper.

It is difficult for contemporary architecture to have the freedom and movement of these paintings and sculptures, so most new building has followed a path closer to engineering (page 260). One exception is the recent work of Le Corbusier, French architect who has built important structures in France and India. There is no regular, intellectual plan to the enormous masses of Le Corbusier's church. Through thick white walls, under this amazing roof, light enters in heavy clots, gathering intensity and shape. For one who might wish to make references to modern science, these packages of light might be imagined as quanta of energy, irregular in location but maintaining a constant level. However, the comparison is not essential, for this building is as astonishing in pure volume and mass as the complex of St. Peter's and the Bernini arcade. Other architects, particularly in Italy and South America, are experimenting in this kind of free-form design today.

5. *Interior of Notre Dame du Haut.*

3. Le Corbusier: *Notre Dame du Haut.* Ronchamp. 1955.

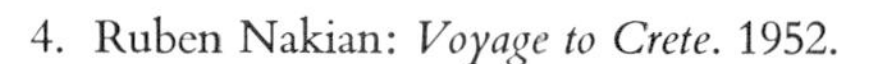

4. Ruben Nakian: *Voyage to Crete.* 1952.

6. Theodore Roszak: *Thorn Blossom.* 1948. Steel and nickel silver. *h.* 33½″.

Just as paint and space have become, curiously, the new "subject" for Abstract Expressionist painters—instead of the faces, hills, and flowers which that paint might have represented—so the material of sculpture too has become a kind of new focus of interest. Roszak and other contemporary "direct metal" sculptors work directly with the molten metal. They may weld parts together, heating them with blowtorches until the bronze is twisted into these vicious shapes, pockmarked like a meteor which has plunged through space. Or, a sculptor like Nakian may work directly in plaster or clay, pinching it into shape, dragging his fingers through it. Other sculptors work with great chunks of wood in the same way, carving out and polishing segments which are then joined together into abstract conglomerations of mass.

1. Howells and Hood: *Tribune Tower*. Chicago.

2. Eliel Saarinen: *Second Prize Design for Tribune Tower*. Chicago. 1922.

3. Walter Gropius: *The Bauhaus*. Dessau, Germany. 1925–1926.

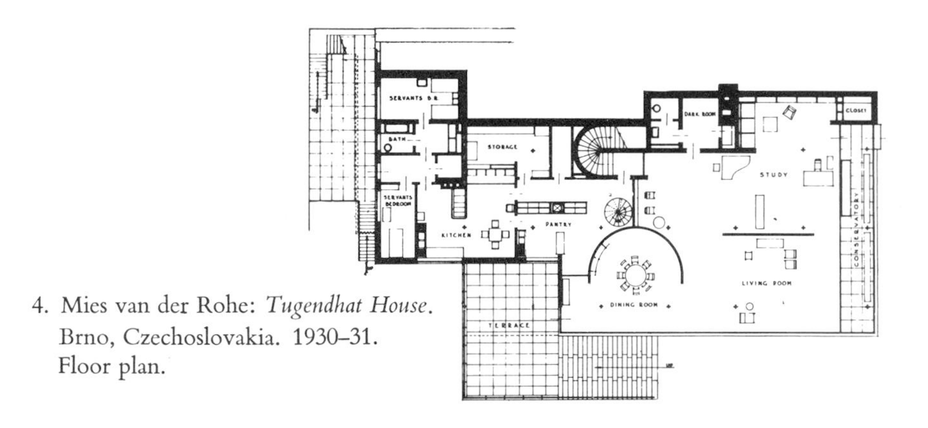

4. Mies van der Rohe: *Tugendhat House*. Brno, Czechoslovakia. 1930–31. Floor plan.

5. Constantin Brancusi: *Bird in Space*. 1925. Bronze.

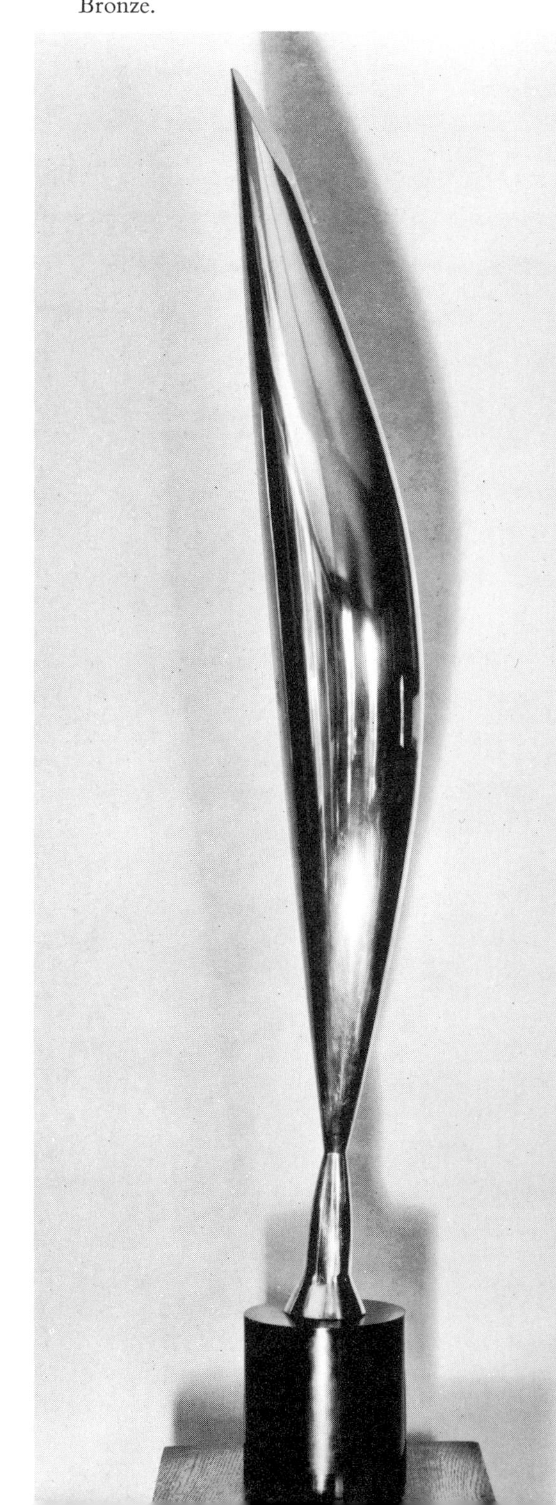

The buildings shown here trace the emergence of the International Style of architecture, which has been the outstanding product of modern engineering art. In the early 1920's, new developments in building had already led to the skyscraper. But as though they were swimmers afraid to abandon familiar shores, these first skyscraper designers clung to the old ornaments which they had inherited from history and the eclectic 19th century. The Chicago Tribune tower is crowned with a cage of Gothic pinnacles and arches which no eye can see. Already, though, advanced architecture was on the way: other building plans were entirely unadorned, an up-shooting rank of vertical piers and windows. A great lift was given to modern design by the German Bauhaus, a school of architecture and related arts established in Dessau in 1919 by Walter Gropius. Bauhaus students were taught to make use of all the new machines of the industrial world, to master all the materials at their disposal, and to invent designs which were as logical to these techniques as the log cabin had been to the woodchopper's ax. The Bauhaus wished to make a complete break with the past. Artists from all Europe came to this lively center, and the styles invented there quickly became international. In Mies van der Rohe's plan for a house (*Fig. 4*), empty space is made to flow smoothly from room to room through open passageways; Mies and his colleagues tried to divide the stiff, cramped spaces of old-fashioned homes into areas more comfortable for the human body. From these experiments, the new American style of open-plan "ranch house" has grown. Frank Lloyd Wright continued his radical experiments: the extraordinary house, called "Falling Water" (*Fig. 6*), was built of self-supporting beams cantilevered from a central pier, which made it unnecessary to have cumbersome, view-obstructing corner piers. The Lever House (*Fig. 8*) and the Seagram Building in New York City, and many other recent structures in America and Europe are all refinements of these International Style explorations.

Many artists of our time were influenced by Bauhaus experiments in their attempts to refine and use the newest materials, to make tight, clean structures midway between engineering and poetry. Where contemporary artists in the various Expressionist styles deal with masses in movement and change (pages 250–251), these artists work with forces in absolute geometrical balance.

4. Alberto Giacometti: Detail of *Portrait of Prof. Yanaihara*.

GLOSSARY OF ART TERMS

ABSTRACT ART A school of art which believes that shapes and colors, and their arrangement in a painting or sculpture, are of primary importance. Further, these elements are independent of the subject of the work of art, if indeed there is one. Abstract art has often produced works entirely unrelated to natural forms (called non-objective art); more often it simplifies or distorts them, but at least suggests them. Since 1910 abstract art has dominated Western art. Cubism is the earliest example of abstract art; the paintings of Kandinsky and Mondrian (p. 256, 257) are examples of its latest forms.

ABSTRACT EXPRESSIONISM A form of art characterized by paintings of enormous dimensions, executed very freely with splashing and dribbling of paint on the canvas. A strong dependence on accident and chance is assumed by the artist, and there is a deliberate avoidance of geometric forms as well as objective images. It combines certain elements of Surrealism, Expressionism, and the general tenets of Abstract Art. Abstract Expressionism is the dominant post-World War II development in painting, introduced in New York by Jackson Pollock (p. 258), and in Paris by Dubuffet.

ACADEMY A place for advanced training, or an association of learned men devoted to the advancement of art or science. An art academy may be a private gathering of student or professional artists. Official or public academies were originally established in the 16th and 17th centuries to free artists from the restrictions of the craft guilds. The academies obtained royal support but this resulted in new stylistic restrictions, as in the French Academy under Louis XIV. By the 19th century a new revolt began and is still under way.

ACANTHUS A bushy, handsome plant common to most Mediterranean countries. Its elongated leaves with deep, gracefully curved cuts, served as the models for the leafy ornamental forms seen on Corinthian columns.

Corinthian Column in Museum at Epidauros, Greece. Acanthus design. (Philip Gendreau)

ACROPOLIS The Greek word for "high city." From the earliest times, the Greeks built their towns around fortified hills or citadels, upon which their chief temples were located. The most famous acropolis is that of Athens, where the Parthenon (447–432 B.C.) is located (pp. 44–45).

ALEXANDER MOSAIC A large floor mosaic made of tiny cubes of colored marble, discovered during the excavations of Pompeii. The panel shows Alexander's victory over the Persian King Darius in 333 B.C. The Alexander mosaic is almost certainly a Roman copy of a Greek work (p. 46, 48).

ALHAMBRA A Moorish palace built in the late 13th and early 14th centuries in Granada, Spain. It is an outstanding example of the magnificent late Islamic art in Europe. Situated on high land and commanding a broad view, the Alhambra is, in the true Islamic tradition, at once a pleasure palace and a fortress. In design, it is a series of rectangular courts of various sizes. The well-balanced arrangement of the rooms echoes the intricate, repeated geometric designs that cover the ceilings, walls, and floors, in the dazzling colors of glazed tiles and molded ornamentations. After 1492, when the Moors were driven out of Spain, the buildings suffered heavily from repeated destruction and from an earthquake in 1821. They were restored, however, in the 19th century.

ALTAMIRA A cave in northern Spain, near Santander, where a large number of prehistoric paintings of animals are preserved. The pictures are painted directly upon the roof of the cave and may date from about 12,000 B.C. Like the Lascaux cave paintings in France, they depict magical images which were believed to help prehistoric man in his hunting. They show a highly developed artistic sense (p. 11).

ALTARPIECE A painting above an altar. The term is most frequently used in reference to the altar decoration of the Middle Ages, which consisted of double or quadruple hinged wings. The outer wings could be folded shut, showing another scene painted on the reverse side. These paintings often depicted specific feasts or events in the life of a town or church's patron saint. Outstanding examples are Grünewald's Isenheim Altarpiece (p. 123) and Van Eyck's Ghent Altarpiece.

AMBULATORY A semi-circular corridor around the main apse of a church (see GOTHIC PLAN). The ambulatory was added to churches in the Middle Ages for pilgrims who wanted to see the relics behind the altar or in the crypt beneath the altar. The addition of the ambulatory also increased the number of radiating chapels with their small altars for worship. The ambulatory became a standard part of Romanesque and Gothic church architecture.

AMIENS CATHEDRAL The largest French cathedral and the most famous example of French Gothic architecture. The nave of the cathedral was begun in 1218, and the eastern end, containing the altar and choir, was completed about 1270. The lofty vaults are 139 feet high and enclose an area of over seven million cubic feet. One of the most classical of cathedrals, Amiens was built on a cross-shaped plan. The main apse is three stories high and contains a glazed arcade in the wall above the choir. Sculptures on the three west portals reflect the medieval universe with a Last Judgment scene, statues of kings, prophets, saints, and lively reliefs of monthly activities. The statues of the *Beau Dieu* and the *Vierge d'Orée* of the south portal have long been famous (p. 121).

ANATOMY The structure of living bodies, both plant and animal. In art, the term is applied almost exclusively to the human body. Possibly the first artist to study anatomy for artistic purposes was Leonardo da Vinci. Leonardo practiced dissection, the separation and examination of the parts of the body, because he believed that a thorough knowledge of the body's internal structure was necessary to show the surface of a figure in motion. His findings are recorded in his sketchbooks (pp. 152–153). Now, the study of skeletal and muscle structure is a necessary discipline for all students of art.

APSE The easternmost, semi-circular recess of the choir of a church. It usually contains the high altar. Smaller "apsides" attached to the transept or ambulatory are called radiating chapels. (See GOTHIC PLAN.)

AQUEDUCT Artificial channels used to supply towns and cities with water. The Romans built many such structures, cutting through underground rock and then lifting the channels above ground, when necessary, on high arcades. These arcades influenced Roman building design, such as that of the Colosseum (p. 55).

ARCADE An architectural form consisting of a line of piers or columns carrying curving arches above. An arcade may be part of the structural support of a building, as the interior arcades of Gothic churches or in the courtyards of Renaissance palaces. Arcades may also be used as sheltered passageways along streets. The arcade is essentially a development of Roman architecture

Ambulatory of the Abbey of Mont St. Michel, France.

ARCH A fundamental unit of architecture which describes a curved line rising from the top of one vertical element to the top of another. Arches are usually of stone or brick and may take one of a number of forms, such as semicircular, pointed, or elliptical. The arch stands because each small, wedge-shaped block presses against and helps to support the adjacent pieces. (See also VAULTING.)

ARCHAIC This term generally refers to the very early phase in the development of an art style. In an archaic period, the elements of the fully developed style are apparent, although in simpler forms. Most commonly, the word refers to the art of the ancient Greeks between about 700 and 500 B.C., when artists first began to show the human figure in a more or less natural manner. This early phase of the Greek style may be seen in sculpture (pp. 40–41) and terra cotta vases (p. 38, 40).

ART NOUVEAU A style of art, architecture, decoration, and furniture design that spread across Europe and America in the 1890's in opposition to the imitative conventions of 19th-century art. Under the initial lead of William Morris (p. 290) in England, Art Nouveau attempted to combat the effects of the Machine Age on society. The emphasis was on craftsmanship as a means to save art from the destructive force of commercialism and mass production. Unfortunately, this new style of ornamentation, which was naturalistic in design, was borrowed by manufacturers, who turned it to graceless productions for a mass market.

ASSYRIA The area between the Tigris and Euphrates rivers in upper Mesopotamia, which was, in early times, the home of the Assyrians. Assyrian art (about 1200–600 B.C.) was characterized by massive urban and military architecture as well as delicate stone reliefs of hunting and ceremonial scenes.

AUGUSTUS OF PRIMAPORTA The best-known statue of the first Roman emperor, who reigned from 27 B.C. to 14 A.D. Made of marble, it shows Augustus as a general wearing a richly worked breastplate upon which are depicted the triumphs and benefits of Roman civilization. The head is an idealized portrait (p. 54).

AZTEC A warlike people who established themselves in the valley of Mexico about 1325 and soon dominated that area from coast to coast. The Aztecs did not originate the Toltec tradition, but they did develop many aspects of that culture, such as the pyramid temple and architectural sculpture. Through their superior organization and determination, the Aztecs accomplished much that is impressive in government, military organization, and the arts. Their capital, Tenochtitlán, which was destroyed in 1521, stood on the site of the present Mexico City. Although the Aztecs built pyramid temples in the Toltec tradition, they excelled in making monumental stone structures. The famous disk-shaped calendar stone of the Temple of the Sun weighs an estimated 20 tons. Other huge sculptures are completely covered with religious carvings and bear a resemblance to Asiatic sculpture (pp. 104–106).

BABYLONIA An area in southern Mesopotamia which was occupied from about 3000 to 1500 B.C. by the Babylonians, who were the contemporaries of the Egyptians. They built ziggurats, or artificial hills, for religious purposes, and, on a smaller scale, their metalwork and cylinder seals were of a high quality. Babylonian figure sculpture is sharp and precise and tends toward cylindrical form.

BAMBERG CATHEDRAL Consecrated in 1237, the cathedral in Bamberg, Germany, was built on the old Romanesque plan of square bays. The west towers, however, are copies of the typically Gothic ones built earlier on the cathedral at Laon, France.

BASILICA Originally, a royal hall in ancient Greece, but later, a town hall or public building for the use of magistrates and citizens. Basilicas were rectangular in plan, with two or four sets of columns set along the longer axis to support the roof. The term has been adapted to designate churches of the basilican plan (p. 60) and, more loosely, any Christian church.

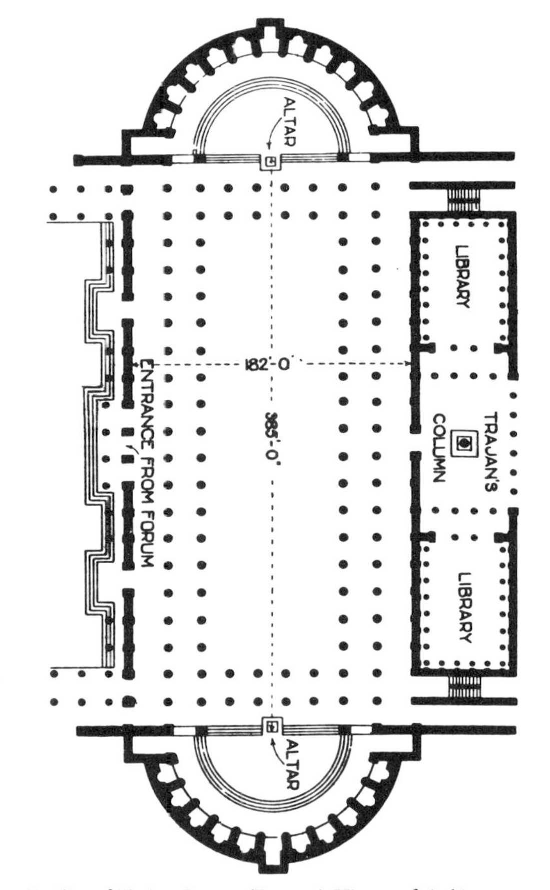

Basilica of Trajan, Rome. (From *A History of Architecture on the Comparative Method*, Banister Fletcher, Charles Scribner's Sons, N.Y., 1948. page 165)

BAS-RELIEF A sculpture whose design is raised only slightly from the background surface. It is also called low relief, as opposed to high relief, in which the design may appear almost detached from the background. The frieze of the Parthenon (p. 46) is one example of bas-relief. Others are the huge stone reliefs, found at Nimrud and Nineveh (pp. 30–31) and Persepolis (pp. 32–33).

BAUHAUS A school of design at Dessau, Germany, founded in 1919 by Walter Gropius. The Bauhaus was interested primarily in housing, urban planning, and high-quality mass production. Though handicrafts were stressed as the natural training for industrial artists, painting formed an essential part of the curriculum. Such painters as Feininger, Kandinsky, and Klee worked at the Bauhaus, and its program has remained the ideal for current design education. Gropius' architectural design for the Bauhaus building itself was an important example of the International Style.

BAY An alcove or opening in a building set off by columns or pillars. Or, bays may be the compartments into which the roof and space of a building are divided. In a church, the nave space is divided into bays by means of pillars, vaulting, etc.

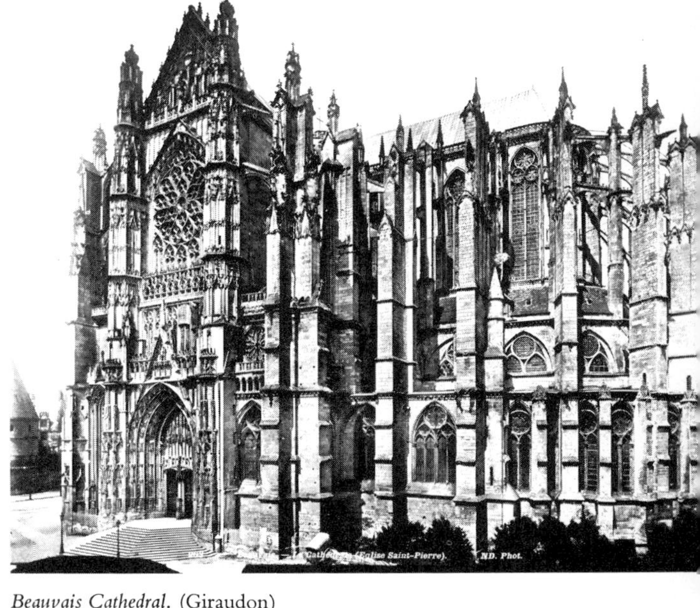

Beauvais Cathedral. (Giraudon)

BEAUVAIS CATHEDRAL High Gothic cathedral in Beauvais, France. Destined to replace a still-existing 10th-century church, the structure was to be the marvel of the Gothic age. The choir with its four aisles was completed in 1272. It consists of a daring skeletal structure whose interior height of over 157 feet was never equalled in the Gothic age. When the vaults over the choir collapsed in 1284, the pillars were doubled and an immense tower was built over the crossing. The tower, also, fell in 1573. The cathedral was never completed, but the high-ceilinged nave realizes the dream of Gothic architects.

BOOK ILLUSTRATION Pictures describing scenes from the text of a book. Roughly speaking, illustration dates from pictures in antique scrolls. Later, these long scrolls were broken up into single pages to form a codex, or book. Medieval books, "illuminated" with initials and pictures in gold and brilliant colors, are preserved by the thousands in today's libraries. It was only after the invention of the printing press and the cheaper production of paper that illustrated books became available to a large number of people. In the 20th century many well-known painters have illustrated books. Among them are Maillol, Derain, Matisse, Picasso, Chagall, and Shahn.

BOOK OF KELLS Early medieval manuscript written and decorated by Irish monks in the 8th century. The major work of Anglo-Irish illumination, the Book of Kells is characterized by interlacing animals and endless linear and spiral patterns (p. 110).

BRICKWORK Oblong blocks of sun-dried or kiln-baked clay used as a building material. Bricks were used by early societies which lacked stone and timber. The sun-dried bricks were used for the body of a building, while the more durable kiln-baked ones served as a decorative facing, as in the lions on the Ishtar Gate (p. 31). Fine decorated brickwork can be seen in some early Christian churches, Georgian mansions, and in the non-structural curtain walls of contemporary buildings.

BRONZE AGE An age which began about 3500 B.C. during which weapons and tools of copper and bronze came into general use in Mesopotamia and Egypt, replacing stone as the chief material for implements. This was a radical change, affecting cultivation, art, building, and civilization in general. By about 2000 B.C. the Bronze Age had spread to Europe.

BRONZE VESSELS Of the many Bronze Age remains, the Chinese bronze vessels stand out as important cultural expressions. These containers for liquid and food were designed, in the Shang and Chou dynasties, to be used in connection with sacrificial rites (p. 87). Of extremely high quality both technically and artistically, these bronzes are rich in sculptural design and are covered with religious motifs of stylized animal forms. Inscriptions in early Chinese writing are found on the vessels.

BUTTRESS A support for a wall which counteracts the outward pressure exerted by a vault or arched roof. Roman and Romanesque architects used wall buttresses—piers supporting the wall on the outside—and buttressing vaults in the form of a quarter-circle along the upper wall. Gothic architects developed the flying buttress when the height of the main vault was increased in relation to the side aisles. It consists of a "flying" arch, which transfers the thrust from the nave wall to the side walls (p. 116).

CALLIGRAPHY A term applied to writing which shows excellence in design or execution. Calligraphy has always been more of an art form in China and Japan than in the West.

CAMPANILE A tower for church bells, rising higher than the church and often a little apart from it. The word comes from *campana*, Italian for "bell." The dainty campanile designed by Giotto in Florence is shown on page 134. A particularly fine Renaissance example stands next to Saint Mark's in Venice.

CANTERBURY CATHEDRAL An outstanding example of the Early English Gothic style. Begun in 1175 by the French architect, William of Sens, Canterbury shows a strong French influence. Especially English, however, are the linear, vertical elements, emphasized through the use of colonettes, or little columns, rising up to the vault, and through the use of towers. Canterbury became a pilgrimage center when Thomas à Becket's relics were placed in a crypt beneath the altar there.

CANTILEVER A projecting part of a building or sculpture that stands unsupported in space. The cantilever principle is the same as that of a board wedged into a crevice of a stone wall: the board stands out free in space because the weight of stone above the fixed end of the board is greater than that of the board. Cantilevering lies behind many remarkable effects in modern architecture: examples are the Guggenheim Museum, New York, and Kaufmann House, Bear Run, Pa.

CAPITAL A carved cap on top of a column or pier. Capitals have many forms taken from geometric, vegetable, animal, or human sources. The three basic types, which originated with the ancient Greeks, are Doric (a round, wafer-shaped plate), Ionic (scrolls at the corners), and Corinthian (with acanthus leaf decoration). The three orders are shown in Figs. 1, 2, and 3 as they are used in three contemporary buildings: the Lincoln Memorial, the National Gallery of Art, and the Supreme Court.

CARICATURE A drawing which over-emphasizes the individual peculiarities of its subject, usually a person, so as to make it appear ridiculous. In antiquity caricatures appeared on Greek vases and in Roman wall paintings. In the Middle Ages, demons in the Last Judgment were caricatures of humanity. Hogarth and Daumier (p. 210) were great caricaturists.

CARTOON A full-scale drawing on paper used as a model for a panel painting, fresco, mural, stained glass design, or tapestry. The famous cartoons made by Leonardo and Michelangelo for murals in the Palazzo Vecchio were eagerly studied by their contemporaries. Some cartoons (such as Mantegna's of *The Triumphs of Caesar*) may have been only stage ornaments. Raphael's cartoons for the Sistine tapestries, unusual in that they were colored, were used in Flanders as a guide for making the tapestries.

CASTING A basic method of shaping metals into statues, reliefs, or other three-dimensional works of art. For casting parts of a statue or relief, the molten metal may be poured directly into an open mold of stone or of sand. The parts thus produced are assembled later. For casting a work of art in one piece, the "cire-perdu," or "lost wax," process is often used. A wax model of the object to be cast is built around a fireproof core; the model is then covered by a mold connected to the core with metal rods. The molten metal poured into the wax melts and replaces it, producing a hollow cast of the object. Casts in other materials—plaster, artificial stone, terra cotta, etc.—may be preliminary models or finished works of art. In ceramics the term describes the process of forming ware with slip-in molds.

Fig. 1.—Doric: *Lincoln Memorial*, Washington, D.C. (Philip Gendreau)

Fig. 2.—Ionic: *National Gallery of Art*, Washington. D.C. (Philip Gendreau)

Fig. 3.—Corinthian: *U. S. Supreme Court Building*, Washington, D.C. (Philip Gendreau)

CATACOMBS Branching tunnels cut through underground rock, in which the early Christians, in Rome and in some other communities, buried their dead. The word "catacomb" comes from the suburban quarries of Rome which were early put to this purpose. The decorations that have been preserved in the catacombs, chiefly painted, were based on Roman precedents. They are the earliest known forms of Christian art (p. 60).

CELADON A European term which indicates a glaze varying from a pale to an olive-green color, found on Chinese ceramics. Celadon refers to a heavy-bodied porcelaneous ware of that greenish color, with or without carved or molded surface decoration. It is usually of the so-called "export" type, a coarser but more durable ware than those ceramics referred to by the same term in domestic Chinese collections. The Chinese have been exporting celadon since the Middle Ages. The best examples are the Sung Dynasty (see DYNASTY, CHINESE) Lung-ch'uan wares from Chekiang province.

CHARTRES CATHEDRAL One of the most famous of religious buildings in Europe. The sculpture and stained glass of this French cathedral are of equal importance in medieval art. The towers, built in the 12th and 16th centuries, guide the pilgrim to the Virgin's shrine. This shrine itself rests upon foundations of pre-Christian, Carolingian, and Ottonian sanctuaries. Most of the church structure was begun in 1195 and was completed around 1230. The façade contains the "Royal Portal" which is flanked by statue columns representing dignitaries of the Old Testament. A *Christ in Majesty* dominates the tympanum above the main portals. There is a huge clerestory, and rose windows (pp. 116–119).

CHIAROSCURO From the Italian "light" and "dark". The term refers to the shadings of tones from white to black in a work or art. Chiaroscuro is used to differentiate one part of a picture from another, to indicate relief, or to show the location of a source of light. Leonardo's chiaroscuro was so subtle that the word *sfumato*, "smoked," was coined for it. Rembrandt used it to achieve dramatic meaning and intensity in his paintings.

CHINOISERIE Literally, "in the Chinese manner." This idea originated in France in the latter part of the 17th century, and became fashionable throughout Europe in the 18th century. Chinoiserie appeared in garden architecture, furniture, and decorative details of the period. The Chinese pagoda by William Chambers, in Kew Gardens near London, is an example of chinoiserie.

CLERESTORY The top row of windows in the elevation of a church above the arcade, tribune gallery and triforium. (See diagram under GOTHIC PLAN.) Because of the heavy walls, the clerestory windows of Romanesque churches were small, admitting very little light. The desire of Gothic architects to enlarge this window zone led to the development of the flying buttress. The light admitted through the clerestory windows in churches, from high above, is believed to produce a contemplative atmosphere.

CLUNY A Benedictine reform congregation founded in 910. Cluny's fame spread throughout Europe in the 11th century but the order's center remained at Cluny. Three churches were built in succession and each influenced Romanesque architecture. Cluny III (1088–1095) was the most splendid Romanesque structure ever built. Its long fore-church leads to an immense nave flanked by four side aisles and interrupted by two transepts. The rich decoration included columns of African marble, capitals representing the musical scale, and fluted pilasters reminiscent of Roman prototypes.

CNOSSOS A city on the north shore of the island of Crete, where a sea-going, Greek-speaking race established their capital during the second millenium before Christ. These people, called Minoans, were well advanced in the arts of painting, architecture, and ivory carving. The palace at Cnossos has the form of the labyrinth described in the legend of Ariadne and Theseus. (See CRETE, p. 268; see also pp. 38–39.)

CODEX A manuscript bound into a volume. The codex (from the Latin, meaning "wood-block") usually designates a parchment book, in contrast to the scroll which was in use throughout antiquity.

COLLAGE (From the French *coller*, "to stick".) A composition combining various materials, such as newsprint, wallpaper, photographs, cloth, or seeds, all stuck onto canvas or board. Introduced by Cubist artists, the technique was widely used by Dadaists and has become a familiar device in abstract art. Some of Matisse's very late work, including designs for the chapel at Vence, were executed in the collage technique.

Collage: *Merz Konstruktion 1921*, by Kurt Schwitters. Painted wood, wire and paper. Philadelphia Museum of Art.

COLOGNE CATHEDRAL Thirteenth century Gothic cathedral in Cologne, Germany. The choir of the cathedral, built in 1248–1322, is patterned after the chevet of Amiens cathedral. The façade was begun in 1350, but was not completed until the 19th century.

COLONNADE A line of columns supporting a horizontal or arched superstructure. (The latter is usually called an arcade.) Colonnades are used along streets, in courtyards, and around temples (see the Parthenon, p. 44).

COLOSSEUM A great oval amphitheatre in Rome, built toward the end of the first century A.D. (see p. 55). Rising rings of seats surround a central stage or floor for spectacles and gladiatorial combats. The building is made of concrete faced with stone, and the cliff-like exterior, some 3,500 feet around, is composed of three tiers of arcades.

The Colonnade, Versailles. (French Cultural Services)

COLOSSUS (*Plural*, Colossi). A huge statue. The ancients were much drawn to the problem of designing and erecting statues of human form on a colossal scale. The most famous of these was the Colossus of Rhodes, a bronze-sheathed figure beside the entrance to the chief harbor of that Greek island. Roman emperors, among them Nero and Constantine, had colossal statues of themselves erected. The Egyptian colossi of Ramses II and Amenhotep III are shown on pages 14 and 21.

COLUMN A round, upright shaft used as a support and made either in one piece or of assembled, drum-shaped sections of stone. The column usually has a base molding and a capital; it may be smooth or have vertical channels (fluting), and it is usually slightly smaller at the top than at the bottom. In contemporary architecture the word is often loosely applied to various kinds of vertical supports. (See Greek columns, pp. 44–45, also *Figs. 1, 2, 3,* p. 266.)

COMPOSITION The arrangement and relationship of the parts of a work of art. A picture of the crucifixion, for example, with the crucified Christ elevated in the center and two figures right and left below has a triangular composition. An infinite number of complex arrangements is possible. Composition is a fundamental aspect of art because it communicates the vision of the artist and the meaning of his work of art to the viewer. Composition is often what we first see and feel in a work of art.

CONSTRUCTIVISM Principally a Russian artistic movement which developed after World War I. The collage technique was developed into constructions of metal, glass and wire. The "Realistic Manifesto" of Constructivism was published in 1920, saying that movement, not volume, was significant in art. By 1921, however, political forces killed the movement but it has continued in Europe and the United States. It is now most commonly seen in the form of stage designs, furniture and sculpture in plastic.

CORNICE A horizontal molding projecting along a wall. Cornices can be used, both on the inside and outside of buildings, to mark the change from wall to ceiling, to divide vertical surfaces into zones, or to frame pediments, windows, and other major architectural parts.

COROMANDEL WORK A term which refers to certain oriental furniture pieces made of dark, hard tropical wood. The Coromandel Coast is the southern part of India's east coast. Coromandel ebony (*Diospyros melanoxylon*) may have given the furniture its generic name. A Coromandel screen, however, refers to a Chinese lacquered folding screen, often with inlaid work and usually of south China origin.

CRACKLE Tiny cracks, sometimes deliberately produced, in the glaze of oriental pottery. The term is also used for cracks in an old paint surface, which extend through to the support. When a painting has been forged, such cracks penetrate little further than the varnish or may even have been painted on.

CRETE A long, narrow island south of the Greek mainland. From about 1800 to about 1400 B.C. the Minoan peoples, maritime traders, flourished there, and Crete has many remains of the Minoan civilization, especially at Cnossos, Phaestos, and Hagia Triada. The island is very important in the study of the art of antiquity because its geographical position in the Mediterranean Sea made it subject to Egyptian, Hittite, and Greek influences.

Cubism: *Portrait of Picasso*, Juan Gris. 1912. The Art Institute of Chicago, Gift of Leigh B. Block.

CUBISM An art style developed by Georges Braque and Pablo Picasso after 1906, and the source of all abstract art in the 20th century. Cubist artists sought an intellectual conception of form. From Cézanne, they derived the idea of the unity of the picture surface and the analysis of different forms in relation to each other. Negro art, as well, had some influence on the free distortions and the interest in planes of Cubism.

DADAISM A nihilistic movement in which all customary beliefs were rejected. The movement began in 1916 and 1917 in Zurich, Barcelona, and New York. Meaningless in name, "Dada" was a product of the hysteria and shock of the war, and was deliberately anti-art and anti-reason. Marcel Duchamp's reproduction of the Mona Lisa, upon which he drew a moustache, the cut-paper collages of Jean Arp, and Francis Picabia's drawings of machines are all characteristic Dadaist works. Dadaism has undergone a revival in certain aspects of Abstract Expressionism.

Dada: *Object 1936—Fur-lined Tea Cup*, by Meret Oppenheim. Museum of Modern Art, New York.

DELPHI A city in ancient Greece. Delphi overlooked the Gulf of Corinth from the lower slopes of Mount Parnassus. It is the site of the oldest and most sacred religious sanctuary of ancient Greece. Just below the main temple to Apollo, the famous oracles were heard. Delphi was studded with many lesser shrines and with the treasuries of the several Greek city-states. It also had a theatre and a stadium.

DIPTYCH A work of art consisting of two hinged panels which can be folded together. It may be carved in ivory, wood, or fashioned from metal. (See the *Wilton Diptych*, p. 126.)

Diptych: *Scenes from the Passion. Scourging of Christ, Christ Bearing the Cross, Crucifixion, Entombment.* 14th century French. Ivory. The Metropolitan Museum of Art, Rogers Fund, 1910.

DOLMEN A tomb or monument to the dead, formed by large, flat stones placed horizontally on vertical stones set on end in the earth. These monuments are found in northern France and in the British Isles. Sometimes the word "cromlech" is used synonymously. Stonehenge, in England, has the best existing examples of dolmens.

DOME A vaulted roof which rises above the central part of a building or bay. Domes are usually, although not necessarily, circular in plan and hemispherical in shape. The dome has traditionally symbolized heaven or the cosmos and is frequently used on religious and public buildings. The Pantheon, Saint Peter's, the Taj Mahal, and the United States Capitol all have domed roofs.

DRY-POINT A kind of engraving in which lines are scratched on a copper plate, with a steel needle or diamond point. On both sides of the incised line a ridge of copper, called the burr, is turned up. When the plate is inked for printing, the furrows are filled, and some ink remains under the burr, producing a soft, velvety effect in the printed picture.

DYNASTY, CHINESE Period when the country is ruled by a certain royal house that has chosen a dynastic name for itself. The important Chinese dynasties are Hsia (protohistorical to about 1523 B.C.), Shang (1523–1028 B.C.), Chou (1027–256 B.C.), Han (206 B.C.–220 A.D.), Six Dynasties (220–589), T'ang (618–906), Sung (960–1279), Yuan (1279–1368), Ming (1368–1644), and Ch'ing (Manchu) (1644–1911).

DYNASTY, EGYPTIAN There are 30 dynasties in Egyptian history, from Menes to Artaxerxes III. All were pre-Christian. Important dynasties, their numbers given in Roman numerals, are grouped by scholars as follows: The Old Kingdom, III–VI (4000–2260), The Middle Kingdom, XI–XIII (2100–1700), The Empire or New Kingdom, XVIII–XX (1580–1085), XXI–XXX (1085–332)—The Late Period, XXVI (663–525), XXVII (525–404) under Persian rule, XXVIII–XXX (404–332). Egypt came under the rule of Alexander the Great in 332. It was followed by the Ptolemaic Period (323–30 B.C.).

EIGHT, THE A group of American painters, formed when the works of George Luks, John Sloan, and William Glackens were rejected by the National Academy in 1907. Aside from Luks, Sloan, and Glackens, the group included Robert Henri, Everett Shinn, Ernest Lawson, Maurice Prendergast, and Arthur B. Davies. Although unlike each other in style, the artists were united by their friendship with each other and by the subject matter they chose to paint: city genre.

ENAMEL The decorative technique in which glass is fused onto metal at high temperatures. Glass paste may be poured into tiny strips of metal welded onto the surface; this is known as "cloisonné" enamel work (p. 65). The popular enamels of the 16th and 17th centuries were not true enamels because the picture was painted on the background rather than being made of tiny cells of colored glass.

ENGRAVING The art of cutting designs or pictures in plates, blocks, etc. An engraving is the print made by such a process. In line engraving a sharp steel rod (burin) is pushed into the copper to cut V-shaped furrows; the shavings at its sides are removed so that a clear line varying in thickness and depth is achieved. This method has been used since 1446 for original works or reproductions.

ENTABLATURE In architecture, a horizontal band of stone supported by columns or arches and consisting of three parallel parts—architrave, frieze, and cornice. (See diagram of a GREEK TEMPLE, page 271.)

EPHESUS One of the great cities of classical antiquity, located on the west coast of Asia Minor (Turkey). Of Athenian and Ionian foundations, it was famous for its magnificent temple to the goddess Artemis, and under Roman rule it became the chief city of the province of Asia. The remains of the city have been excavated, and large numbers of both pagan and Christian buildings and sculpture have been found.

ETCHING A method of print-making in which the lines of a drawing or design are cut into a metal plate by the action of acid. A copper plate is covered with varnish that is impervious to acid. The design is then drawn on the varnished plate with a needle, exposing the copper. The plate is washed with acid which bites into the exposed copper. The varnish is removed, ink is rubbed into the etched lines, and the plate is printed. (See Rembrandt etching, page 197, *Fig. 3*.)

EXPRESSIONISM An artistic movement which has flourished in central Europe since 1915, it is primarily concerned with the formulation of emotions. Space, form, and color are purposely distorted in order to achieve the artist's personal expression of emotional intensity. Stemming from primitive art on the one hand, and from the work of van Gogh, Munch, and the Fauves, on the other, Expressionism denotes a type of art which is neither naturalistic nor impressionistic. It should be understood more as an artistic fashion than as a particular school of artists. Among the many artists connected with this movement are Nolde, Kirchner, Soutine, Klee, and George Grosz.

FAÇADE The front or chief side of a building. The façade accents the entrance and major axis of a building and usually prepares one for the architectural style of the interior.

FAÏENCE Usually applied to all kinds of glazed pottery, although correctly it is the French word for fine glazed and painted earthenware from Faenza, Italy. The term is also used for French pottery of the 15th to 18th centuries, particularly from Rouen.

FAUVES, FAUVISM Fauves, or "wild beasts" in French, was a term of derision applied to a group of young artists including Matisse, Derain, Vlaminck, and Rouault in the first decade of this century. The term referred to the vibrant, flashing hues and vigorous, broad brushwork that they used on their canvases. Inspired by the Post-Impressionism of van Gogh and Gauguin, the Fauves brought back the use of rich areas of flat color and unbroken contour lines into painting. The movement was a reaction against the flat, subdued color effects of artists like Bonnard and Vuillard. The strongest period of Fauvism was before World War I. (See pp. 246–247, 251.)

FLAMBOYANT A style of architecture that became popular in France and England in the late 14th and 15th centuries. Developing from the cold patterns of radiating lines (called Rayonnant) that were typical of Gothic window tracery and decoration, the flamboyant style was dynamic and "flamelike." The flamboyant style was especially popular in England.

FLORENCE CATHEDRAL One of the few outstanding examples of Gothic architecture in Italy. The cathedral of Florence was begun in 1296. It is topped by an immense dome which was completed by the famous Renaissance architect, Brunelleschi, in 1437. The extreme spaciousness and the horizontal accents of the simple elevation give the interior its Italianate character.

FLORENCE, MEDICI PALACE Built for Cosimo de Medici by Michelozzo in 1444–1460, and enlarged in the 17th century. Three stories high, with a rusticated façade, arched Gothic windows, and a Roman cornice, the design of the building is transitional between the architecture of the Middle Ages and that of the Renaissance.

FLORENCE, PAZZI CHAPEL A small, early Renaissance church built for the powerful Pazzi family in about 1430, by Brunelleschi. The portico suggests a Roman triumphal arch, while the interior space is joined together with Corinthian pilasters and roofed by a ribbed dome on pendentives.

Brunelleschi: *Pazzi Chapel*. Cloister of S. Croce, Florence. (Alinari)

FLORENCE, UFFIZI Literally, "offices," a building constructed in 1560–1580 for the administration of the state under Cosimo I. It occupies three sides of an extension of the Piazza Vecchio in Florence, beside the Arno River. The Uffizi now shelters archives and part of the vast art collections bequeathed to the state of Tuscany in the 18th century by the last direct descendants of the Medici family.

FLUTING Vertical, concave grooves in a column or pilaster. The practice of fluting began in early antiquity in order to give richer form and a greater play of light and shade to the surface of architectural members.

FONT A receptacle which holds the water used for baptism in the Christian church. Fonts were often cast in metal and decorated with themes symbolizing rebirth in God. They came into general use after about 1000 A.D., when the practice of baptism by total immersion began to be less popular.

FONTAINEBLEAU PALACE The French royal residence near Paris. Reconstruction of the palace in the Italian style was begun in 1528 by Francis I, under the direction of Rosso, Cellini, and other Italian masters. Fontainebleau became the center for the spread of 16th century Florentine Mannerism throughout northern Europe. (See pp. 158–159.)

FONTAINEBLEAU, SCHOOL OF The art style called Mannerism was imported into France by Francis I when he brought Italians to decorate his palace at Fontainebleau. The style spread among local French and Flemish painters, such as Jean Cousin, Francois Clouet, and others. Characteristic are the small-headed female nudes, narrow-shouldered, broad-hipped, and slim-ankled. Exponents of the movement were Pontormo, Parmagianino, Rosso, and Primaticcio. The school in France survived into the 1590's, after the Italian movement had long since given way to the early Baroque. (See pp. 158–159.)

FORUM The assembly hall or meeting place of the Romans. In Rome, the Forum of the Republic lay in a valley between three of the seven hills. As Roman responsibilities and business became more complex, additional forums, on a majestic scale, were built by the emperors; the Forum of Trajan, built in the 2nd century A.D., included libraries, markets, offices, and a huge basilica. All provincial cities of ancient Rome had forums. The term is now used to denote an assembly for the discussion of current events or public affairs.

FRESCO The technique of painting with water colors on wet plaster. The colors sink into the plaster and are preserved indefinitely if kept dry. Its durability has encouraged the use of fresco despite the difficulty in applying it. Only as much plaster as the artist can paint before it dries can be applied at one time to a wall. A preliminary cartoon must be quickly traced onto the plaster. (Such tracings can easily be seen in photographs of Michelangelo's Sistine ceiling.) Fresco technique permits very little reworking or correction. High contrast and brilliance of color are almost impossible without retouching in less permanent dry pigment; Michelangelo retouched his *Last Judgment* in ultramarine and gold in this manner.

FRIEZE An ornamental band or strip placed horizontally as a wall decoration; or, in architecture, that portion of an entablature above the architrave and below the cornice. (See GREEK TEMPLE, p. 271.)

GABLE The triangular upper end of a building. It is formed by the end lines of the two sloping sides of a roof and a horizontal base line at the level of the eaves. In classical usage, as on a Greek or Roman temple, the gable is called a pediment, and because the triangular space has depth, it is used as a setting for sculpture. Many houses have multiple gables because of the complexity of the roofing, as in the famous "House of Seven Gables" in Salem, Massachusetts.

GARGOYLE A long, stone waterspout, frequently made in the form of a monster, used to drain water on cathedral roofs away from the walls. Originally, gargoyles were intended to ward off evil influences.

GENRE A style of painting that shows scenes from everyday life in a realistic manner. Such painting was at one time considered inferior to styles which dealt with more elevated subjects drawn from religion or mythology. Although there were elements of genre in certain Italian paintings of the 14th and 15th centuries, it did not become popular until the advent of Caravaggio and his followers. Genre achieved its greatest popularity in 17th century Holland, with the work of Ostade, Steen, de Hooch, and Vermeer. Crespi and Longhi in Italy and Chardin and Greuze in France were the most important 18th-century painters in the genre manner.

GESSO A mixture of chalk and glue which is applied as a ground to canvas or a wood panel, and then polished. It gives a smooth surface to the tempera or oil paint applied over it. Some form of gesso has been used in all periods, but it reached the peak of its development in the panel paintings of Italy and Flanders in the 15th century.

GLASS A brittle substance that is formed by melting silicates with soda, or potash, lime, and the oxides of certain metals. The technique has been known since antiquity: the Egyptians practiced glass blowing at least as early as 2000 B.C. Roman blown glass was famous and was sometimes carved in relief, as in the Portland vase in the British Museum. (A Wedgwood copy of this vase is shown on page 212.) The finest glass of the Middle Ages and the Renaissance was Venetian. Tiffany, Orrefors, and Steuben have produced some of the best modern glass.

GLAZE A term used in ceramics to denote a thin coating over earthenware, chemically similar to glass. A glaze is fixed by baking the pottery in a kiln, which renders the surface smooth, shiny, and impervious to water. Probably, the use of glaze began a thousand years or so earlier than the making of glass in Mesopotamia and Egypt, where it was used for architectural ornaments as well as for practical objects such as bowls.

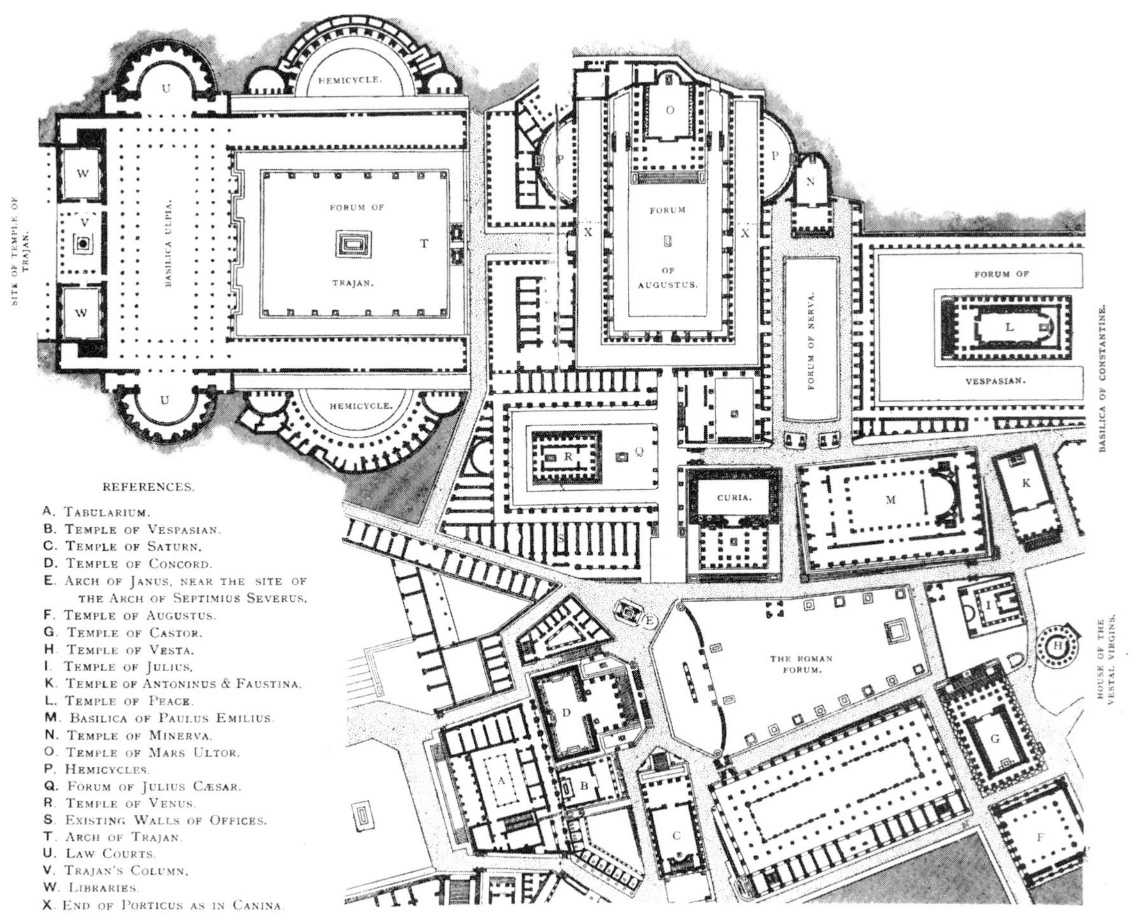

Plan of the Forums at Rome, by A. F. V. Dutert.

GOTHIC PLAN

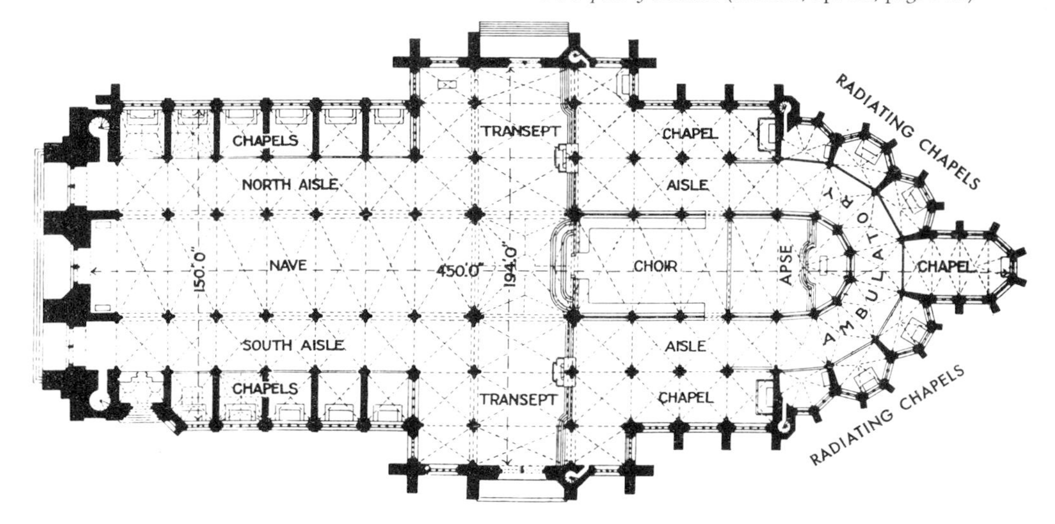

Floor plan of Amiens. (Fletcher, op. cit., page 501.)

GOUACHE An opaque watercolor paint which usually has a pliable adhesive with the binder to retard drying. In gouache, highlights are produced by white pigment, unlike true watercolor, where the bare white paper provides highlights. Gouache is often used for miniature painting.

GREEK TEMPLE

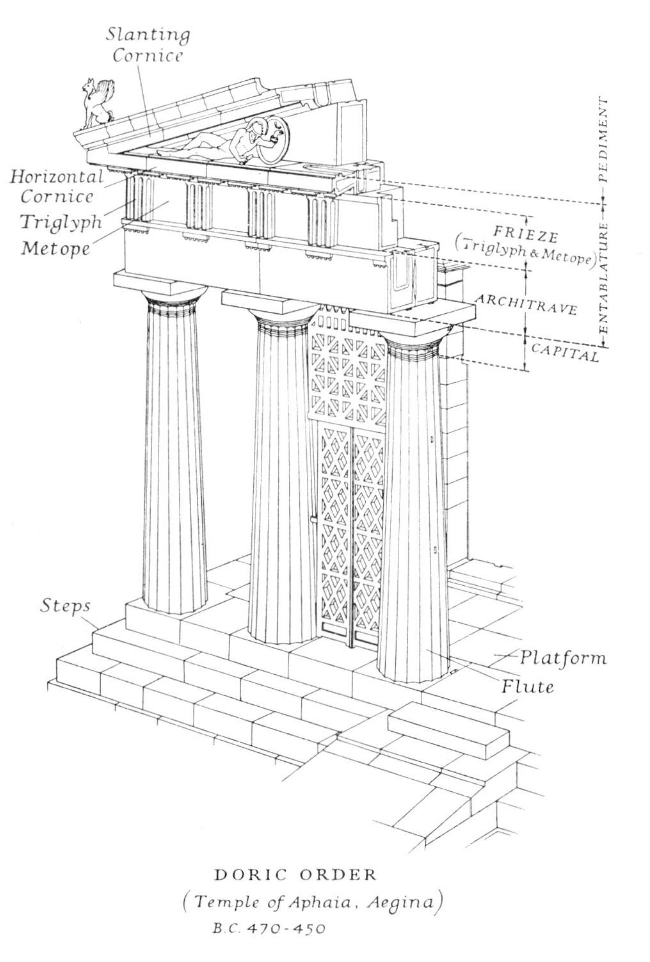

GROUND The surface upon which a work of art is executed, or against which it appears. For example, the ground of a Greek black-figure vase is red but of a red-figure vase it is black. The ground of the Parthenon frieze was blue, so that the figures would be more visible.

GUPTA DYNASTY In India, a period from 320 to 620 A.D. during which the royal house of Gupta ruled the country. The Gupta Dynasty was a period of refinement and great cultural vitality. Buddhism prospered during this period, but toward the end of the Dynasty, India saw a resurgence of Hinduism.

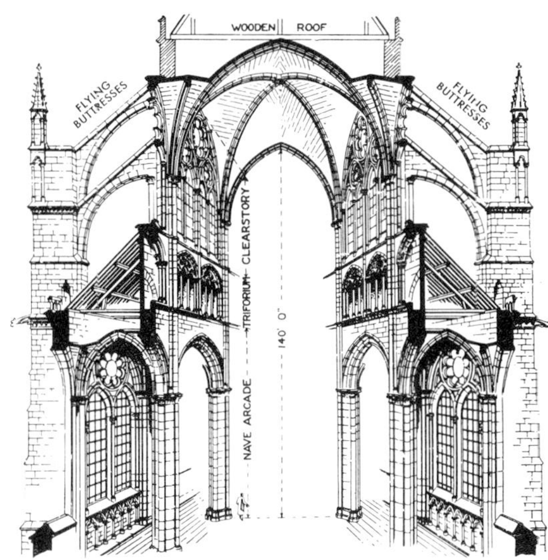

Transverse section of a typical Gothic cathedral (Amiens). (From Fletcher, op. cit., page 327.)

HAGIA SOPHIA A church in Istanbul (Constantinople), considered to be the masterpiece of Byzantine architecture. Commissioned by the Emperor Justinian, the building was erected in 532–537. Rectangular in plan, Hagia Sophia (meaning Holy Wisdom) is crowned by a succession of towering domes. Four huge pillars which are connected by arches, support the pendentives which carry the 184-foot-high dome. The drum of the dome is pierced by 40 windows. (See p. 63.)

The building is an excellent example of Roman methods of construction, using brick to make thin shells that cover huge spaces. The wall surfaces, covered by marble veneer and gold mosaic, reflect the changing light and make the structure appear to be weightless. As in all great architecture, the effect is one of effortless control.

HALLMARK Formerly, the official mark of the Goldsmiths' Company in London stamped on gold or silver objects to attest to their genuineness and purity. The term now generally refers to all makers' marks on objects of silver, gold, pewter, and similar metals.

HUE The term which means color. Blue and red may have the same *value* (relative lightness or darkness) but differ in *hue*. A light and a dark blue will have the same *hue* but will differ in *value*.

ICON Literally translated, an icon is a "picture" or "image." The term applies primarily to Byzantine panel paintings. They are usually painted in vivid egg tempera colors on a gold ground. Religious subjects predominate—saints, the Virgin, the Trinity, the twelve feasts of the year—and every detail of the picture is prescribed by custom. Icon painting centered in Russia and the Balkan countries and continued into the 19th century. The Russian artist Andrei Rublev was the most accomplished master of this difficult technique (see p. 68).

IMPASTO The heavy application of paint on a canvas, causing the pigment to stand out in relief. It also describes the mixture of pigment and medium. A heavy impasto is achieved with more pigment and less medium, a light impasto, the contrary.

INCA A highland tribe of Peru who were ruling the land from Ecuador to Chile when the Spaniards attacked them in 1533. The highly organized, theocratic government did not inspire individualistic art, but was responsible for the magnificent stone works seen in the remains of Machu Picchu and the capital city of Cuzco. Inca craftsmen were also known for their techniques in metalworking and for geometric design in textile. (See p. 107.)

INCUNABULA The term refers to books which were printed just after the invention of movable type (about 1440) until 1500. These early printed books usually looked like a manuscript. Spaces were left for initials and illustrations which were added by hand. The word derives from a Latin term for swaddling clothes and was first employed in the 17th century to refer to the infancy of printing.

JADE A semi-precious stone. Nephrite and jadeite and a few other semi-transparent stones of compact texture are often called jade when used as a material for carving. In the Chinese culture, jade has been associated with many human virtues and was thought to have supernatural powers. For this reason, jade pieces have been carved throughout Chinese history for ritual and decorative purposes, and they exhibit distinctive historical styles.

KEYSTONE The central and highest stone in an arch. It cannot fall because it is wedge-shaped, with the widest part of the wedge at the top. By pressing equally on either side, the keystone holds the arch together. It it were removed, the whole arch would fall.

LACQUER While commonly used to mean a varnish, the term "lacquer" in Oriental art refers to the material which is made from the sap of the lacquer tree, *Rhus vernicifera*. It is indigenous to China and was brought to Japan around the 6th century. Lacquer gives wood a protective finish and has been in use since ancient times. In addition to being a varnish, lacquer is also the material for such techniques as lacquer carving and dry lacquer sculpture.

LANDSCAPE PAINTING Pictures in which nature is the primary interest. Early examples of landscape painting are found in Roman wall paintings, and later examples in the work of Dürer, Altdorfer, and Leonardo. Landscape painting became popular in 17th-century Holland with painters like Van Goyen, Cuyp, and Jacob van Ruisdael. It reached a peak of importance again in the 19th century through Turner and Constable in England, and Corot, the Impressionists, Cézanne, and van Gogh in France.

LAOCOÖN In Greek legend, a prince of Troy who protested against bringing the famous wooden horse within the town walls. Because of this, serpents came and destroyed him and his sons. The legend intrigued and challenged the talents of classical painters and sculptors; one of the most famous sculptures, now in the Vatican Museum, shows the death agonies of Laocoön and his sons, and dates from the 1st century B.C.

LASCAUX A town in south-central France near which prehistoric cave paintings have been discovered. The paintings, dating from approximately 15,000 B.C., are of animals, and were probably conceived as some sort of magic to aid in the hunt for food. Lively and realistic scenes of bison charging, deer swimming, and herds running are depicted in a variety of colors (see pp. 9, 10, and 11).

LITHOGRAPHY A method of printing from a prepared flat stone or metal plate, invented in the late 18th century. A drawing is made on the stone or plate with a greasy crayon and then is washed with water. When ink is applied to the stone, it sticks to the greasy drawing but runs off the watered surface, thus permitting reproduction of the drawing.

LOUVRE An ancient palace in Paris, now a museum containing many of the world's greatest treasures of European art. Begun as a medieval fortress, the Louvre was transformed into a royal palace under Francis I and his successors. The structure became a museum in the late 19th century. Housed in it are the museums of the Louvre and Les Arts Decoratifs.

LUSTERWARE A highly glazed earthenware characterized by a shimmering, translucent luster. Lusterware pottery is first painted, then fired with metallic oxides. From the 7th to the 8th centuries, various ceramic centers in Egypt and the Mesopotamian world produced lusterware. It has enjoyed periodic vogues since then, and is still produced today.

LUXOR A city on the Nile River in upper Egypt. In the 14th century B.C. Luxor was the site of a magnificent temple built by the Pharaoh Amenhotep III and added to by later kings. Here the columned halls, statues, reliefs, and obelisks of the ancient Egyptians, all constructed on a vast scale, are well preserved. Together with Karnak, Luxor occupies the site of the ancient Egyptian city of Thebes.

MANNERISM A style of painting, sculpture, and architecture which is most often associated with the 16th century. Primarily court art, Mannerism is sometimes said to reflect the period of disillusion and anxiety throughout Europe in the few decades between the sack of Rome by German mercenaries in 1527 and the end of the Council of Trent in 1563. The Mannerist artist employed forms reproduced from his mental image rather than from direct observation. This often resulted in unnatural human proportions, as in Parmagianino's *Madonna*. (See pp. 158–159.)

MASK A face covering, used to hide or disguise the identity of the wearer. Found in almost all cultures throughout the ages, masks can either be painted on or worn over the face. Many theatrical masks have their origin in religious ceremonies. Some developed into expressive art forms. African and Oceanic masks, famous for their sculptural quality, are celebrated for the inspiration they have given to modern artists. Equally admired are Japanese and Chinese theatrical masks.

MAUSOLEUM A monumental tomb. The word comes from King Mausolus of Caria (western Turkey), in whose memory his family erected a vast monument in the city of Halicarnassus, in the 4th century B.C. Among the famous mausolea of antiquity were those of the Roman emperors Augustus and Hadrian, in Rome, both huge circular structures on the banks of the Tiber. The latter has survived as Castel Sant'Angelo and served for a time as the fortress of the medieval popes.

MAYA An Indian race of Central America who developed a high culture in the early centuries of the Christian era, in an area from Gautemala to the peninsula of Yucatan. Reaching the height of their civilization around the year 1000, the Mayas excelled in mathematics, astronomy, architecture, and art in general. The Mayan calendar is considered more accurate than the Julian. Mayan temples containing powerful sculptures and elaborate painting compositions are on richly decorated, terraced pyramidal platforms. The Mayan system of hieroglyphic writing has not yet been completely deciphered. After the 13th century, before the Spanish conquest, the Mayan people were subject to repeated Mexican aggressions and absorbed much of the culture of the invaders. (See p. 104.)

MEDIUM The material that is added to a pigment to make it liquid, so that it may be brushed on, or otherwise applied to, a canvas or panel. The medium may be wax, oil, or egg yolk. In a more general sense, the term is used to describe any material or method the artist may employ, for example, metal, wood, or stone, dry point etching, lithography, seriography, or collage.

MESOPOTAMIA This Greek word, which means "between the rivers," refers to the land between the Tigris and Euphrates rivers, running northwest and southeast, and roughly equivalent to modern Iraq. In ancient times the area linked the non-classical East with the Greco-Roman world of the west and was a thoroughfare for armies, ideas, and art forms. Before the rise of the Greeks, Mesopotamia was the home of the Babylonians and the Assyrians.

METOPE In ancient Greek architecture, rectangular blocks of sculptured stone spaced regularly along the entablatures of temples. Often these sculptures told a myth, such as the battle between the centaurs and the lapiths, on the metopes of the Parthenon in Athens. Between the metopes were placed stones with three vertical channels cut in them; these stones were called triglyphs. The spacing of the metopes and triglyphs was determined by the spacing of the columns below them. (See GREEK TEMPLE, p. 271.)

MINARET A slender tower which is an important component in the Islamic architecture of a mosque. It usually reaches great heights, and from its balcony the muezzin, or town crier, calls the faithful to prayer at appointed hours of the day. (See p. 71.)

MINIATURE PAINTING Any small portrait or picture on ivory, paper, or vellum. The term may have arisen in the Middle Ages, when manuscript illuminators used minium (red lead) in preparing the ground for gold leaf. Miniature painting in manuscripts declined in the West with the perfection of printing in the 15th century; but it was continued in Persia and India into the 18th century. Some famous illuminated manuscripts are the Winchester Bible (Romanesque), the Psalter of Saint Louis (Gothic), and the *Tres Riches Heures* (late Gothic), the last of which is shown on page 126.

MOSAIC A picture or design made by inlaying in mortar small bits of colored stone or glass, called tesserae. Used in Egypt and Mesopotamia, mosaic became a major art form in Roman and Byzantine art. The Pompeiian mosaics range from rough, simple designs to imitations of paintings, made of very small stones, like the Alexander mosaic (p. 46). Constantinople, Ravenna, Sicily, and Venice became the centers of Byzantine mosaic workshops. Neither medieval nor modern mosaics ever reached the perfection and glorious liveliness achieved by the Byzantine mosaicists (see pp. 65–67).

MUGHAL PAINTING A 16th century school of miniature painting in India. A secular court art, Mughal (or Mogul) painting was contemporary with the Rajput schools of painting. Using a technique brought from Persia, the Mughal painters portrayed scenes of the rulers of India in colorful and picturesque designs. (See pp. 82–83.)

MUMMY PORTRAITS Ancient Egyptian portraits of the deceased, done in encaustic (colored wax) technique on wooden boards placed over mummy wrappings or on the coffin. Several hundred such portraits have been found in the dry Faiyum region of Egypt in the last century. Ranging in date from the 1st to the 5th century A.D., they are excellent examples of the frontality and abstraction that characterize eastern Christian art. (See p. 27.)

MYCENAE An ancient city south of the Isthmus of Corinth in Greece. Beginning as a Bronze Age settlement, the town was well built up and fortified by the end of the second millennium B.C. "Beehive" tombs, so called because of their shape, exist there in perfect condition. The graves of Mycenaean heroes, with their many pieces of jewelry and carving, have made Mycenae one of the richest of archaeological sites.

NAVE The center aisle or main body of a building, especially a church. The word nave is derived from the Latin *navis*, meaning a ship. Attached to the nave are the side aisles. In Christian churches the nave serves the congregation. It is preceded by an entrance hall and is followed by the choir, ambulatory, and apsides. The term "choir" designates the part reserved to the clergy.

NEFERTITI A queen of Egypt, wife of the Pharaoh Ikhnaton in the 14th century B.C. The art of that age was naturalistic and finely modelled, and from it comes one of the best known portraits of all antiquity, the painted limestone bust of Nefertiti, now in the Berlin Museum. The head, neck, and shoulders are shown, and the Queen wears a cylindrical, gold-banded hat. The work is life-sized, and the eyes are of rock crystal. (See p. 21.)

NEOPLASTICISM An early 20th century school of art that set up the supremacy of mind over visual sensation. Neoplastic art aims at the total abstraction of natural forms by progressive elimination. Thus, as in the paintings of Mondrian, vertical and horizontal lines are used exclusively, and the palette consists of primary colors and "non-colors" (white, black, and grey). An artistic idea that evolved around 1916, Neoplasticism has had a lasting effect on modern design through the architecture of Gropius and Mies van der Rohe.

NINEVEH The ancient capital of Assyria, near modern city of Mosul, on the Tigris River. The ruins of Nineveh, excavated in 1845, yielded the remains of many buildings and much sculpture. The library of Ashurbanipal (7th century B.C.) was here, and the city was profusely decorated with fine reliefs of religious, hunting, and military scenes.

NUMISMATICS The study of coins. Art historians, archaeologists, and other specialists use coins in a variety of ways. When found at a particular level in an archaeological excavation, a coin of known date helps to determine the age of that part of the ruins. Coins are also studied for their design, and for their distribution in the world, as an aid to historical knowledge. Their inscriptions often yield information about the society from which they came.

OBELISKS A square stone pillar, which rises tapering to a pyramidal cap. The Egyptians used obelisks to mark avenues, temple entrances, and the like, and often they were inscribed with hieroglyphs recording the deeds of kings. Many were taken in later ages to Rome and erected in the racecourses for chariots. In late Renaissance and Baroque times (16th and 17th centuries), a number of obelisks were re-erected in various cities to mark the centers of public squares.

OIL PAINTING A general term for the application of pigment, in a medium of linseed or other vegetable oil, to a prepared canvas or panel. The oil dries with a hard film, and the original brilliance of the color is protected. Colors may be worked together on the canvas or they may be applied in a transparent glaze, to provide a depth and translucence impossible in tempera or fresco. Contrary to popular opinion, oil painting was not invented by the brothers van Eyck but was brought by them to a perfection previously unknown. The Venetians were the first Italians to master this technique.

OLYMPIA A sacred shrine in southern Greece. The Olympic games were held there in a huge stadium, and the sanctuary was filled with city treasuries, votive altars, and shrines. The chief temple was dedicated to Zeus, and nearby was a slightly smaller temple to his consort, Hera. The sculpture of the temple of Zeus, still largely preserved, dates from about 460 B.C. and is perhaps the finest example of early classic Greek form known to the modern world.

ORDERS Classical styles of architecture, determined by the type of column used. Ancient and Renaissance writers classified the kinds of columns, capitals, and entablatures used by Greek and Roman architects. Three fundamental kinds of orders were used: the Doric (quite plain, with round, plate-like capitals), the Ionic (slimmer, with scroll-capitals), and Corinthian (elegant and slim, with capitals carrying acanthus leaves). There are many subvarieties of the orders, but for each of the three basic kinds there is a related family of moldings and a standard system of proportions. (See CAPITAL, p. 266.)

ORNAMENT Any element of design in color, relief, or incision added to an otherwise purely structural or functional form, for no other purpose than to please the eye of the observer or user.

OTTONIAN ART German art under the Ottonian emperors, from the late 10th to the early 11th centuries. The two major centers of Ottonian art were Reichenau and Hildesheim, which contain many examples of manuscript painting, bronze casting, and church architecture typical of this period.

PAGODA A multi-storied, tower-like structure associated with a temple or monastery, which is one of the typical architectural expressions of China. Having a wide variety of forms, and built from stone, wood, and even iron, the pagoda may have its origins in both the lookout towers of the Han dynasty in China and the Buddhist stupa of India. Usually associated with a temple in China and Japan, the pagoda became a garden ornament in Europe in the 18th century. (See CHINOISERIE, p. 208, 210.)

PAINTED POTTERY From the early Bronze Age, the societies of the Mediterranean area made and painted pots and vases. These were usually made of clay, shaped upon a potter's wheel, and then baked in a kiln. The earliest vases have geometric and orientalized decoration, but by the year 600 B.C. the painters of Athens had perfected black-figure ware, upon which the lines of the forms were scratched or incised through the black painted glaze. In the late 6th century this gave way to red-figured work with the lines painted on. Later still, other variations of color and technique appeared. A Neolithic vase is shown on page 11 and an early Greek one on page 40.

PALMYRA An ancient city in the desert between Syria and Babylonia. A caravan oasis originally, it became a flourishing city, largely independent of Greek and Roman authority. In the middle of the 3rd century A.D. the Palmyrenes ruled a large part of the eastern Roman dominions. Much of the city remains today: colonnaded streets, temples, a theatre, and tall square tombs with painted interior decoration. The sculpture of Palmyra is geometric and frontal, and is an important landmark in the development of early Christian and Byzantine art.

PANTHEON A huge, domed temple in Rome, built between the years 118 and 125 A.D. by the Emperor Hadrian. The word is from the Greek and means "all the gods." The Pantheon, which stands today in a good state of preservation, has been studied by architects since the time of the early Renaissance and is one of the most influential buildings in western architecture. The great dome, 150 feet across, is of concrete.

PARIS CATHEDRAL (Notre Dame of Paris.) Commissioned in 1163, Notre Dame of Paris was completed around 1250. The imposing façade has three shallow portals, a King's Gallery, a huge rose window, and a vast nave, which, as a sign of early Gothic architecture, still retains tribune galleries. Late 13th century transformations of the transept, with its magnificent rose windows, remain in line with the side-aisle walls, and thus keep the unity of the plan. Much of the sculpture shows liveliness and even treats anecdotes referring to the student life of the famous Paris University.

PARTHENON A temple on the Acropolis in Athens. Usually considered the ultimate masterpiece of ancient architecture, the Parthenon is a Doric-style temple to Athena. Made of white marble, it was built between 447 and 432 B.C., during the reign of Pericles. The Parthenon is rectangular in plan, magnificent in proportions, and originally contained many sculptures by Pheidias, one of the most renowned of the classical Greek sculptors. Fragments of the external sculpture are now in London and Athens, and the frieze under the porch is still fairly complete. The colossal statue of Athena, once housed within the Parthenon, has disappeared. (See p. 44–45.)

PEDIMENT The gable or triangular end of a monumental building. The idea originated in the ancient Greek temples, where the space above the end colonnades was used as a setting for heroic sculptures. These sculptures portrayed a semi-mythical past and referred to the history and traditions of the town that founded the temple. (See diagram of a GREEK TEMPLE, p. 271.)

PERGAMON An ancient city just inland from the seacoast of western Asia Minor (Turkey). Pergamon flourished as a local Greek capital during the last three centuries before Christ. The city was renowned for its magnificence, particularly for its stone carving, and it is proper to speak of a Pergamene school of sculpture. Its chief example is the heroic frieze of the altar to Zeus, where the battle of the gods and giants is shown in a swirling, dramatic style typical of the school.

PERISTYLE A colonnade which surrounds a building. The word comes from the Greek words for "around" and "column" and is most properly applied to the colonnades around ancient Greek temples (see pp. 44–45). The Romans often enclosed their gardens and public places in peristyles.

PERPENDICULAR STYLE A phase of Late Gothic architectural style, in England, in use from 1350 to 1550. The name was derived from the vertical and horizontal (i.e., perpendicular) decorative accents which typified the style. This was combined with a highly ornamental system of vaults with supplementary ribs and cross-ribs and arches, forming an ornamental gridwork.

Perpendicular style: *The Chapel, King's College,* Cambridge. (British Information Services)

PERSPECTIVE The art of creating the illusion of depth on a two-dimensional surface. This effect may be achieved by means of lines approaching an apparent vanishing point, if the object shown is architectural; or by a decrease in the size of objects further from the observer; or by color: distant mountains may appear bluer, or the varying distinctness with which an object is seen, as distant mountains disappear in a haze. Antique perspective employed no single vanishing point but used all the other types, as did the Middle Ages. Modern linear perspective derives from the Renaissance.

PEWTER An alloy of tin and lead with certain other metals added for hardness and color. Known to the Romans, pewter has been extensively used ever since as an inexpensive substitute for silver, but it has esthetic qualities of its own.

PIETÀ A sculpture or painting of the Virgin Mary holding the dead Christ on her lap. This was a well-established form in Christian sacred pictures in the late 13th century. It is also used as a symbol of deep mother-love. To clarify this, Christ's body is often reduced in size as in the *Pietà, Fig.* 4 of Michelangelo. (See p. 155.)

PIGMENT The term applied to any type of coloring matter, animal, vegetable, or mineral, which can be ground into a powder and mixed with a medium such as oil, egg, or water.

PILASTER A type of column that lies flat against a wall and which is not separate from it. Pilasters are used to frame the sides of doorways and niches, or to divide facades into surface units.

POMPEII An ancient city on the Bay of Naples. In the summer of 79 A.D. a violent eruption of Mount Vesuvius covered the city of Pompeii with ash and lava. Since 1748 the remains have gradually been uncovered, bringing to light the streets, houses, public buildings, paintings, and sculpture of an ancient town. Etruscan, Greek, and Roman influences were at work in Pompeii, and its art shows the mixture and synthesis of forms that existed at the end of the 1st century. Of particular interest are the houses with their open courts and peristyles, and the mural paintings which decorated them (pp. 57, 58–59).

PORCELAIN A hard, translucent ware, which can be either pure white or glazed, made from fine clay called kaolin. The Chinese invented porcelain. After it was imported to Europe in the 15th century, many efforts were made to imitate it. Finally, in 1709 the correct process was discovered in Meissen, Germany, and the Meissen factory was pre-eminent in Europe for many years (see figurine on page 205). Factories were founded all over Europe; a very famous one at Sèvres, France, is known even today for the delicacy, taste, and beauty of its products.

PORTRAITURE The representation of a distinct person. This may be completely idealized as in Egyptian portraits or naturalistic as in those of Republican Rome. In the spiritual atmosphere of the Middle Ages there was no place for the image of a mortal, but with the end of the 14th century portraits of kings began to appear. Certain masters such as Titian, Rembrandt, and Gainsborough were particularly gifted portraitists.

Interior of Medici Chapel, Florence, showing pilasters. (Alinari)

POSTER A public announcement to attract attention and to be understood at once. In one way or another poster art has always existed, especially since printing has been known. The modern era of poster art began with the invention of lithography, which provided a direct and cheap printing method. French artists were the leaders of this art; Toulouse-Lautrec is the best-known of poster designers. His poster of Yvette Guilbert is on page 241.

POTTERY A term usually applied to the coarser forms of earthenware fired in a kiln under relatively low heat. Pottery is comparatively soft, and may be unglazed, lustreware, enamelware, or stoneware. In stoneware, the firing has turned the entire substance into a vitreous material similar to, but heavier than, porcelain, and opaque rather than translucent.

PRE-RAPHAELITE BROTHERHOOD Dante Gabriel Rossetti first used the mysterious initials P.R.B. in 1849. A group of 19th century artists emulated the painters who came before Raphael, whom they considered overpraised in academic criticism. Their work, characteristically detailed and bright in color, was based on highly elaborate symbolism. The movement was attacked by Dickens but defended by Ruskin.

Pre-Raphaelites: *The Awakening Conscience*, by William Holman Hunt, 1855. Coll: Sir Colin Anderson, London.

PYRAMID Monumental tombs of the Egyptian Pharaohs, built about 2600 B.C. beside the Nile River. The largest pyramid is 775 feet on a side and was originally 480 feet high, yet the geometry of the huge bulk is almost perfect. The indestructibility of Egyptian civilization is symbolized by these great massive forms. Inside are galleries and small chambers; the rest is solid masonry.

RAJPUT SCHOOL A style of painting from the 16th to the 19th centuries at the courts of the Rajput princes of the Himalaya valleys. The Rajput artists mixed folk art with the classical traditions of Indian painting; at the final phase of development they showed signs of Mughal influence in their work. The Rajput paintings illustrate Indian literature, from the ancient epics to the romantic adventures of the beloved god, Krishna.

REIMS CATHEDRAL A 13th century cathedral, used for the coronation of the French kings. A building of exceptional architectural harmony, Reims introduced window tracery and translucent tympana. Over the west portals a rose window almost forty feet in diameter projects a jet of light into the nave. The interior of the cathedral contains many characteristics of High Gothic architecture. Horizontal cornices check the motion of compound piers, which rise to support slender ribs. Sculpture is abundant throughout the whole building including the inner west wall, roof galleries, and towers. The smiling angels are among the most charming sculptures ever carved. The capital leaves show a new interest in nature.

RELIQUARY A small box, casket, or shrine, made to hold a religious relic. Costly receptacles for relics came into use in the 4th century, and thousands of examples, made later, have been preserved. They may be in the form of medallions, statuettes, or head and arm reliquaries (p. 108). Frequently, they represent houses or churches.

REPOUSSÉ A metal-working technique in which a sheet of metal is hammered out from the back into the desired shape. Examples of repoussé work are shown on pages 35 and 107.

ROCK PAINTINGS Prehistoric men often painted and scratched, upon rock cliffs and particularly in caves, pictures of those animals they sought in their hunt for food. At Lascaux in France and Altamira in Spain there are rock paintings in caves executed in a most lifelike manner. Probably these paintings were intended as magic to insure the success of the hunt. Colors were daubed or painted onto the rock surfaces; often the natural contours of the stone were used to give shape to the paintings. (See pp. 9, 10–11.)

ROSETTE A circular ornament, usually a conventional flower, radially symmetrical with any number of petals. It has been used commonly in all periods, but was particularly favored by the Assyrians and, later, by the Greeks, especially with the Ionic order.

SAINT DENIS A church in Paris, built in the 12th century. The royal abbey of St. Denis had long been the burial place for the French kings when Abbot Suger assembled architects and craftsmen to build a church which would be a memorial to the monarchy and to himself. Influenced by neoplatonic theories, he wanted the structure to be showered in light. In 1140 the west facade was completed and in June of 1144 the choir with its ambulatory was consecrated. Slender marble columns resting on a mosaic floor carry ribs which support a thin stone webbing. The thrust concentrates on four points instead of the whole wall as in Romanesque architecture. From the high altar one would see a crown of windows. These structural innovations and the new interest in light make St. Denis the cradle of Gothic art.

SAINTE CHAPELLE A 13th century Gothic church in Paris. Completed in 1248, and destined to house important relics, the Ste. Chapelle is really an immense reliquary. Narrow buttresses carry the vault. The whole wall consists of a glowing expanse of stained glass. Elegant statuary and colorful patterns heighten the festive effect.

ST. PETER'S, ROME The great basilica over the tomb of Saint Peter, and the seat of the Pope as Bishop of Rome. The structure, founded by Constantine, was replaced in 1506 by a building designed by the Renaissance architect, Bramante. Final design for the basilica, however, was established in 1546 by Michelangelo. The great colonnades, built in about 1660, by Bernini, outline the huge piazza. Bernini also fashioned the *baldacchino*, or canopy, over the altar beneath the dome, and the chair of Saint Peter in the apse. The crypts shelter many important monuments of early Christian as well as pagan art, and the church itself contains many important paintings and sculptures. (See p. 176.)

SAN VITALE A medieval church in Ravenna. The Italian city of Ravenna, long a part of the Eastern Roman Empire, possesses a considerable number of important early Christian and Byzantine monuments. The most outstanding is the octagonal church of San Vitale, built in 530–547 under the patronage of Bishop Maximianus. Its dome, made partly of light amphorae, is supported by galleries and squinches (light corner supports). The apse contains some of the most beautiful mosaics ever made, representing the Emperor Justinian surrounded by courtiers, and the Empress Theodora, his wife.

SARCOPHAGUS A sarcophagus is a coffin, usually of stone, although occasionally made of clay, wood, or metal. In ancient times sarcophagi were often carved with representations of the deceased (Carthaginian, Etruscan) or with some mythological or religious subject (Greek, Roman, and Early Christian). Some of the earliest Christian art is to be seen on sarcophagi, where Old and New Testament scenes, sometimes in elaborate compositions, have been carved.

SCYTHIAN ART The Scythians were nomadic people who appeared in what is now southwest Russia in the 7th century B.C. Subsequently they came in contact with the neighboring Mesopotamian and Greek cultures. They produced fine jewelry and small-scale sculpture. In their tombs have been found a great number of gold ornaments which depict animal and hunting scenes. (See page 69.)

SEPIA A reddish-brown ink made from the secretion of the common squid or cuttlefish. Sepia was known in antiquity but was not much used again until the 18th century, when it was employed for pen and wash drawings.

SILHOUETTE A profile portrait cut out of black paper, or, more generally, a two-dimensional outline of an object. The latter form has been used since paleolithic times; the black-paper portraiture reached its climax in 18th century portrait busts. Its popularity declined after the invention of photography.

SILVER POINT A drawing made with a silver-tipped pencil on paper coated with Chinese white. It leaves very fine lines that are grey in the beginning, later oxidizing into a darker, warmer tone. Silver point was used mainly in the 15th and 16th centuries.

SPHINX A legendary monster with a lion's body and a human head. In several ancient societies the sphinx was reputed to have oracular powers and to ask riddles. Sphinxes appear throughout ancient art, in sculpture as well as in metalwork. The most famous is the colossal stone sphinx beside the great pyramids of Egypt; it is 172 feet long, and a small temple is placed between its forepaws.

STAINED GLASS Colored glass, set in a design or picture, used especially in church windows. Stained glass was used in the 10th century, but the large workshops in cathedral towns developed only at the end of the 12th century. Gothic glaziers mixed glass with metal oxides or fused thin films of colored glass to clear panels. Thirteenth century glass is never flat and shows imperfections (bubbles, etc.), which enhance its brilliance. The glass pieces were cut, assembled over a cartoon, and connected with lead bands. In the late Middle Ages flat glass and silverstaining were frequently used. The skeletal structure of Gothic cathedrals was designed to house as much glass as possible. (See pp. 118–119.)

STAVE CHURCH The Scandinavian church of the 11th to 13th centuries. The stave church derives its style from the Nordic King's Hall and its construction from ship-building techniques. The high churches with steep roofs are decorated with animal motifs.

STILL LIFE A painting of inanimate objects arranged by the artist. Still life was known in Italy during the Renaissance but was limited to designs of inlaid wood known as *intarsia*. Still life flourished mainly in northern Europe in the 17th century. Many early still lifes contained symbolic references to the transience of human life or complex religious symbolism, all of them made through objects of everyday use. Others reflect the bourgeois luxury in the Netherlands and the artist's pleasure in treating rich, colorful materials. With the exception of Chardin in the 18th century, major artists did not again turn to still life until the later 19th century, when subject matter was no longer of primary concern.

STONE AGE The first period of human culture of which we have any considerable record. It is divided into three periods—The Eolithic, The Paleolithic, and The Neolithic. It lasted for thousands of years and ended, roughly, two to three thousand years before Christ, depending upon geography. Early Stone Age man shaped flints and blades of stone; later Stone Age man improved upon the earlier techniques, made pottery, and erected large stones as monuments and markers. The Stone Age was succeeded by the ages of metals, the Bronze Age and the Iron Age.

STUCCO A term which refers to a plastic mixture of lime, sand, marble dust and water, which can be plastered on the surface of a wall or worked into figures and designs before it hardens. In fairly dry climates it may be used as the final surface finish of exterior walls. In ancient and Renaissance times both plain and colored stucco was used to decorate the walls and, particularly, the ceilings of rooms, with figured designs and reliefs.

STUPA A Buddhist relic mound, usually circular in plan with a passageway around it for ceremonial purposes. The stupa originated in India and has developed into various pyramidal and terraced mounds with elaborate surface ornamentations. Similar structures may be found in the architecture of almost all the countries of Asia.

SUMER The name for southern Babylonia, where from very early times, on the banks of the Euphrates, a highly developed culture was located. Sumerian accomplishments included cuneiform (wedge-shaped) writing and precise methods of reckoning time. Under King Gudea (about 2250 B.C.), Sumerian sculpture of imported stone was massive, compact, and yet lifelike (see p. 29).

SURREALISM. An artistic movement of the 20th century, whose aim is to transcend the reality as seen by the eye and to show instead the images of the subconscious. Rejecting the traditional principles of form and perspective, the Surrealists create a new world by the unexpected juxtaposition of unrelated objects and themes. Surrealist art can be representational, establishing a dream world out of deep perspectives and an extremely detailed execution of naturalistic objects (as in Dali and Tanguy). It can also be more abstract, making use of capriciously arranged, unrecognizable forms (as in Miro and Arp).

SYMBOLISM A movement of the 1880's in modern painting whose aim was "to clothe the idea in a form perceptible to the senses." Paralleling a pronounced tendency in literature (Rimbaud and Mallarmé, for example), Symbolist painting attempted to suggest the world of the imagination by symbols arranged in decorative form. The critic Albert Aurier defined Symbolist painting in the *Mercure de France* for March, 1891, as "ideational, symbolic, synthetic, subjective, and decorative." Gauguin was the declared leader of the movement. Among others involved were Sérusier, Denis, and Vuillard. But the Symbolist painter par excellence is perhaps Odilon Redon.

TAPESTRY A handwoven fabric or its machine-made imitation, in which no wefts are carried the full width of the web; the thread is inserted only over the section where the color appears. Early examples are dated in the second millennium B.C. in Egypt. From there, the technique spread over the Orient and Far East. In Europe the oldest examples date from the 12th century. Tapestry-making flourished in the centuries following, particularly the 18th. The art of tapestry design and weaving has been revived in the 20th century by Jean Lurçat and other notable French artists.

TEMPERA PAINTING A form of painting in which the medium used leaves a *matte* or non-reflecting surface. Egg-yolk, fig-milk, honey, and certain gums may be used. Tempera is usually applied to panels over gesso (a plasterlike material) and, since it is opaque, variations in value or color must often be obtained by very fine cross-hatching.

TERRA COTTA Literally, Italian, "cooked earth." Terra cotta is baked clay; brick, pottery, tiles, and sometimes decorative architectural members are made of it. The length and temperature of cooking (firing) in the kiln determine its color, texture, and durability.

TOTEM Animate or inanimate objects considered to have a blood or supernatural relationship to a clan or a race. The American Indians of the Northwest coast are famous for their totem poles. These are covered with carvings of animals and birds, and sometimes may reach a height of eighty feet.

TRACERY Architectural ornaments made of circular forms, traced with a compass. Gothic tracery will fill an entire window arch. Consisting originally of simple geometric forms hewn in stone, tracery later became slender and linear (Rayonnant), then complex, even asymmetrical in the flamboyant ornamention of the 15th century.

TRIPTYCH A sculptured or painted panel with two attached wings. It was the most frequently used altarpiece of the 14th and 15th centuries. (See DIPTYCH, p. 268.)

TROMPE-L'OEIL (Literally "deceive the eye".) A painting which attempts to fool the observer into taking the painted object for a real one. Trompe-l'oeil artists frequently avoid the difficult problem of the illusion of space by picturing flat objects against a flat background, close to the picture surface.

TUDOR STYLE A term applied primarily to architectural forms evolved during the reign of the Tudor family in England (1485–1603), from Henry VII to the first Queen Elizabeth. Renaissance decorative motifs were grafted to architecture whose structure and plan was that of the later Middle Ages. The earlier portions of Hampton Court Palace are typical of this style.

TUTANKHAMEN An Egyptian Pharaoh who lived in the 14th century B.C. When his untouched tomb was opened by archaeologists in 1922, it revealed a magnificent gold coffin, now in the Cairo museum, and a wealth of works of art (pp. 22–23). The tomb was decorated with painted scenes of animal life, and contained gold and silver vessels, blue faïence pottery, and much jewelry.

TYMPANUM A semicircular stone slab bounded by a door lintel and the arch above it. The space it provides is often used in churches for the representation of the Last Judgment. (See Vézelay, Autun, Moissac, Chartres, and Bourges cathedrals.)

VALUE The difference between the lightness and darkness of one or all the colors in a painting. A high value will contain much white, a low value, much black.

VAULTING An arched roof, ceiling, or covering of masonry. (See also DOME.) The earliest stone-covered structures show corbeling vaults with horizontal stones which are gradually pushed toward the center until they meet at the apex. The true stone vault consists of radially arranged stones. A continuous arch will form a barrel vault; two intersecting barrels form a groin vault. Vaulting had the advantages of being fireproof (being made of stone) and of allowing a wider span between walls. Almost unknown in Greece, various techniques of brick and cement vaulting were developed by the Romans for their baths and basilicas (see BATHS OF DIOCLETIAN, page 55). The main diagonal thrust of these huge vaults was checked by heavy wall buttresses. After a long interruption during the early Middle Ages, stone vaults were introduced by Romanesque architects (St. Martin du Canigou, Cluny II). In the 12th century, the rib system was introduced. This made a flexible vault shape possible, and the thrust of the main vaults was counteracted by the flying buttress. The height and boldness of the Gothic vaults has only been surpassed by the steel or ferro-concrete vaults of the last hundred years, which give a maximum of strength and elegance with the least mass of material.

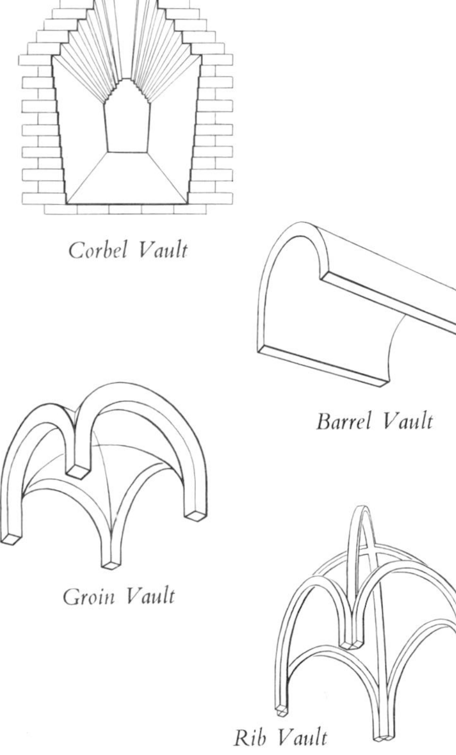
Corbel Vault
Barrel Vault
Groin Vault
Rib Vault

Doge's Palace, Venice. (RG)

VENICE, DOGE'S PALACE Built for the first Doge in 814; the existing structure was completed in the 15th century. The huge façade rests on a colonnade. Impassive and secretive, the crystalline mass it encloses became a symbol of Venetian power.

VENICE, SAN MARCO Saint Mark's Cathedral, dedicated to the patron of Venice, and facing the square named after it. Five domes arranged over a Greek cross plan are a direct import from Constantinople and give the church an oriental flavor. Completed in 1071, the church is lavishly decorated with marble columns, reliquaries, and mosaics.

VENUS OF MEDICI A famous statue of the goddess Venus, made in the Greco-Roman period, of white Parian marble, (p. 43). Venus is shown with her hands held in front of her body, and she is looking toward the left. The statue was found in the villa of the Emperor Hadrian near Rome and was taken to Florence about 1680 A.D. by one of the Medici princes.

VENUS OF MELOS (Also called Venus of Milo.) A statue of Venus (Aphrodite) found on the Greek island of Melos in 1820, and now in the Louvre in Paris. The statue dates from late Greek (Hellenistic) times and shows the goddess in a turning position; the lower half of the body is draped. The arms are missing and their proper restoration is a subject of dispute. It is probably the best-known statue from all classical antiquity.

VENUS OF WILLENDORF A small limestone statuette of a woman, found at Willendorf, Austria. It dates from the Old Stone Age and is a precious survival from that distant period. The figure, perhaps a mother goddess or fertility cult object, has greatly enlarged breasts, abdomen, and hips, and almost certainly represents the early and continuing interest of man in the mystery of generation. (See p. 11.)

VERSAILLES, PALACE OF Begun as a hunting lodge for Louis XIII in 1627, Versailles became, under Louis XIV, the nucleus for a vast residence designed by Mansart and others, decorated by Le Brun, surrounded by formal gardens by Lenotre, all aimed at glorifying the principle of the absolute monarch. The palace remained the principle seat of the French kings until the revolution. It is now a museum.

VÉZELAY A 12th century French church. The façade hides three inner portals. The central tympanum shows Christ, elongated and gigantic, sending out the apostles. A striking vividness of linear technique makes this tympanum one of the most inspired works of Romanesque sculpture. Below, St. John predicts the coming of Christ. In the nave, cross-shaped pillars support groin vaults. A tall clerestory floods the interior with light.

VIENNA GENESIS The Vienna Genesis is a rare Byzantine manuscript of the 6th century. It contains scenes from the Genesis which were transposed from a scroll to a book sequence. They show a transition from late antique to medieval illustration techniques.

WASH A color floated over the surface of a painting, either in a very fluid medium or in one which has been thinned. The term usually refers to watercolor painting but can also be used for a brush drawing.

WOODCUT The main form of relief printing. On a plain woodblock, the drawing which is intended to be reproduced is applied. Then, with special knives the blank parts are cut away, leaving the original drawing standing out in relief. When the block is inked and a print taken, it shows only the blacked high parts, leaving the rest white. Woodcut has been used since about 1400, mainly for book illustrations. Dürer was one of the greatest masters of this art. This technique has had a great revival since about 1900 in both America and Europe.

GLOSSARY OF ARTISTS

ALBERS, JOSEPH (1888–) German non-objective artist who now teaches at Yale University. Albers paints squares within squares and rectangles within rectangles with the purpose of contrasting shades of color. He never mixes colors but uses them in varying shades of intensity, straight from the tube.

ALBERTI, LEONE BATTISTA (1404–1472) Italian architect, scholar and humanist of the Renaissance, who profoundly influenced the art of his century. Beauty, for Alberti, was the harmony of all parts of a structure, where nothing may be added or subtracted without disturbing its balance. He admired the classical proportions of Greek temples, the monumentality of Roman buildings, and the new perspective of Masaccio. The facade of his Rucellai Palace in Florence has three stories of pilasters of the Greek orders, just as in the Colosseum in Rome—Doric at the bottom, Ionic for the second story and Corinthian at the top. His last design, for the church of Sant' Andrea in Mantua, embodies what Alberti considered the ideal form for Christian churches. It is a centrally planned building; its nave is a Roman barrel vault, and the emphasis is on the space at the domed crossing of nave and transept. Alberti's greatest influence was through his writings, especially his *Della Pittura* and *De Re Aedificatoria*, which helped persuade patrons to accept the Renaissance order of art and summarized Renaissance ideals in a guide for later architects and artists.

ALBRIGHT, IVAN LE LORRAINE (1897–) American painter, born in Chicago. Albright paints, with irony and pitiless realism, such subjects as decaying people and their possessions. His subjects are from Chicago and the Middle West. His style stresses tactile illusions through heavy application of paint. Albright has exhibited widely in the United States and abroad.

ANGELICO, FRA (1387–1455) Florentine painter, whose pictures are outstanding for their precision of detail and brilliant color. Fra Angelico's early works are flat, lacking depth, in typical Sienese style, but his later work shows that he had been influenced by the new methods of perspective, just then becoming known. Fra Angelico became a friar of the Dominican order in 1408. He moved around Italy to Fiesole, Florence, Cortona, Orvieto and Rome and painted in monasteries wherever he he was. For Fra Angelico, art was merely the handmaid of religion. He painted only religious subjects, either to record the history of the Church as in his frescoes in the Vatican, or to instruct and guide his fellow monks in meditation as in the beautiful frescoes in the monastery of San Marco, in Florence.

ANTONELLO DA MESSINA (c. 1430–1479) Italian painter born in Messina, Sicily, where he became acquainted with the northern Flemish style of painting. He was later to carry this northern influence throughout Italy and to Venice, particularly, where he introduced oil painting. Thus Messina became responsible for the warmth of color which distinguishes the Venetian painting of Titian and Tintoretto. In his own art, Messina tried to synthesize the ideal geometric forms of the Renaissance with warm, glowing colors. During his lifetime, his fame came from portraits he painted in three-quarter front view, now easily recognizable in many museums.

ARP, JEAN HANS (1887–) Exceptionally versatile Alsatian painter, sculptor, graphic artist and poet who participated in many of the major artistic movements of the early 20th century. Arp was associated with Kandinsky, Marc and Klee in the expressionist Blue Rider group; later, as a founder of European Dadaism, he constructed the irrational "fatagaga" collages with Ernst. Arp first worked with rectangular, geometric forms, but after 1917 he turned to the simple curvilinear shapes now associated with him. The restrictions imposed by a flat canvas first caused Arp to experiment with abstract shapes, then eventually to work in sculpture and three-dimensional works in cut-out wood. After 1924, Arp joined the Surrealist movement. His work includes illustrations, woodcuts, engravings, lithographs, collage, and designs for rugs, embroideries and tapestries. His art makes a humorous, childlike appeal both to one's mind and one's senses.

AUDUBON, JOHN JAMES (1780–1850) American painter, famous for his drawings of birds and other wildlife. Audubon studied drawing in France under David, around 1802. Soon afterward, he returned to the United States and entered into the first of several businesses, with which he had only minimum success. His intense love of the birds of his native country led him to travel extensively, collecting specimens and drawing them with scientific accuracy. Audubon became absorbed in producing what was to be his great work, the illustration of all the birds of North America. In 1826, after his pictures were acclaimed by British scientists and art critics, he found a publisher for his works in London. *The Birds of America* was published in London in 1827–1838, followed by *The Quadrupeds of North America* in 1845–1848. (See also p. 243.)

Angelico: *Noli Me Tangere*. San Marco, Florence. (Alinari)

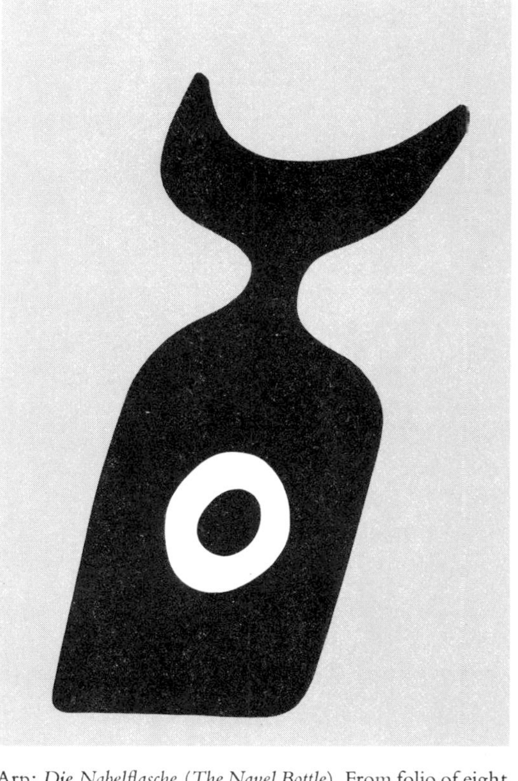

Arp: *Die Nabelflasche* (*The Navel Bottle*). From folio of eight reproductions of drawings. About 1918. Museum of Modern Art, New York.

BASSANO, JACOPO (c. 1510–1592) Italian painter of the Venetian school. Bassano portrayed religious themes in the settings of everyday peasant life. These genre paintings are among the earliest of their kind and were very popular in his day. With his four artist sons Bassano maintained a productive workshop in which it is thought that El Greco may have received his training.

BECKMANN, MAX (1884–1950) One of the leading German Expressionist painters during the 1930's. Beckmann painted numerous triptychs on general social themes, i.e., the struggle between good and evil, and several self portraits. Beckmann was concerned with expressing symbolically "the idea hidden behind reality." In this he differed from most other Expressionists who depicted personal neuroticism or pessimistic social criticism. His paintings are usually made in strong colors with a dull finish. Beckmann came to the United States after World War II and his powerful art has had an influence on many American painters.

BELLINI, GIOVANNI (c. 1429–1516) Italian painter, the son of Jacopo and the brother of Gentile. Giovanni was the foremost Venetian artist of his generation. His early style was influenced by the austere purity of form of Mantegna, his brother-in-law. He later softened this sculptural style with his Venetian love of light and warm colors of nature. These give life and vigor to Bellini's paintings. Profoundly religious, his most frequent subjects were the Madonna and Child and portrayals of Christ. Two of his outstanding paintings are *The Portrait of the Doge Leonardo Loredan* and the *Agony in the Garden*, which now hangs in the National Gallery, London.

BERNINI, GIOVANNI LORENZO (1598–1680) Italian sculptor and architect, the dominating figure of the Italian Baroque in these fields. Bernini was a flamboyant artist, choosing to represent such dramatic scenes as the transfixing of St. Teresa with an arrow, or the very instant that the nymph, Daphne, is changed into a tree. Bernini's statues, busts and buildings are charged with movement; their surface texture and shadings of light and shadow are designed to deceive the eye and entice the senses. In the buildings he designed, too, the architectural elements lead to a climax, as in the grand sweep of the colonnades of the Piazza of St. Peter's which finally brings the spectator's gaze to focus on the façade of the church. Inside St. Peter's, swirling, ornate columns and ornaments lead the eye directly to the immense bronze canopy over the high altar. Bernini's statues, fountains, and buildings can be seen all over Rome today. He truly dominated and epitomized the Baroque period (pp. 176, 179).

BINGHAM, GEORGE CALEB (1811–1879) American genre painter of scenes of the expanding frontier, political subjects, and life in the countryside and small towns of the 19th-century Middle West. Bingham spent most of his life in Missouri. Until 1856, he was chiefly self-trained and these early paintings, in the simple tradition of American primitive painting, are his most popular (p. 244). They contain both humor and pathos. From 1856–1859 Bingham received his formal training in Dusseldorf, Germany.

BLAKE, WILLIAM (1757–1827) English poet, artist and engraver. Blake was first recognized for his poetry, which he published himself and illustrated with hand-colored engravings. Characteristically, his illustrations are swirling, ethereal, twisting forms in pale tinted colors. Blake always thought of his art as secondary in importance to literature. His major works are his watercolor illustrations of Dante's works and the *Book of Job* (1820). Because of his mystical temperament, Blake is usually associated with the Romantic movement, although he was not affiliated with it (p. 217).

BOCCIONI, UMBERTO (1882–1916) The outstanding sculptor of the Italian Futurist movement and possibly the only one whose fame will be lasting. He attempted to represent, in one sculpture, forms in successive stages of movement, thereby adding the element of time to a heretofore static technique. *Unique Forms of Continuity in Space* (1913) shows a striding human figure in forceful forward momentum. The edges of the sculpture project into space and space penetrates the figure, giving the subject a dynamic force (p. 252). Boccioni also executed some paintings and drawings showing figures in motion.

BONNARD, PIERRE (1867–1947) French painter. Bonnard's paintings at first glance appear to be Impressionistic. Unlike the Impressionists, however, Bonnard painted from recollection, not direct observation, and he used dissonant combinations of colors instead of reproducing the colors of nature. Landscapes, bathing nudes and quiet scenes of small rooms are his most frequent subjects. Posters, reflecting Toulouse-Lautrec's influence, and book illustrations in etching and lithography represent his graphic work.

BORROMINI, FRANCESCO (1599–1667) Italian architect of the Roman Baroque. He and Bernini were the two chief architects of this period, but Bernini's tremendous popularity overshadowed Borromini. Borromini's buildings have inventive, often fantastic architectural designs (*i.e., San Carlo alle Quattro Fontane*, p. 177) composed of fluid, swirling lines and decorated with a dazzling profusion of scrolls, sculptures, paintings, pillars, etc. Another of his outstanding works is the façade of Sant' Agnese in the Piazza Navona, Rome.

BOSCH, HIERONYMUS (c. 1450–1516) Flemish artist. Bosch is popularly known for his fantastic landscapes peopled with monsters, hostile animated objects and surrealistic creations. Bosch was a critical cataloguer of the vices, stupidity, and fears of the medieval world and this is reflected in the titles of his paintings (*Ship of Fools, Cure of Folly, Seven Deadly Sins*, etc.). He also painted the traditional religious subjects of his day: *The Temptation of St. Anthony*, emphasizing the fantastic creatures tempting St. Anthony, *The Last Judgement*, showing only the torments of the damned, *Crowning with Thorns* and *Bearing of the Cross*, depicting the brutish venality of Christ's tormentors. Bosch's sarcastic visions were set in landscapes or architectural frames receding to the horizon, in the Flemish tradition. They are painted with sharp, clear details (p. 124–5).

BOTTICELLI, SANDRO (1444–1510) Florentine artist and a pupil of Filippo Lippi. Botticelli placed artistic emphasis on the pattern that flowing contour lines make on the surface of the painting rather than on creating the illusion of reality through form and color. His feeling for line can be seen in his drawings for the *Divine Comedy* (p. 143). In Botticelli's mythological painting, *Primavera* (pp. 144–5), we see the sensuality, artificial patterns of foliage and flowers, the flowing drapery, swaying figures and the "Botticelli face" which represent the familiar aspect of his art. Botticelli's more serious, melancholy side becomes evident in later works. The incisive, cold, and firm figures in *The Nativity* in the National Gallery, London, and *St. Augustine* in Florence, reflect virility and religious belief—an aspect of Botticelli which surprises many. In his later life, his art mirrors his despondency over the dire prophecies of doom predicted by the reforming monk, Savonarola. In despair, Botticelli burned a number of paintings.

BOUCHER, FRANCOIS (1703–1770) Boucher, Fragonard and Watteau were the three major French Rococo artists. Boucher's gay, bright-colored rustic scenes were eagerly sought after by society for wall and ceiling paintings and tapestries. He was court painter in Paris and a protégé of Mme. Pompadour, the King's mistress. Boucher was the most popular and fashionable painter of his day.

BRAMANTE, DONATO (1444–1514) Italian architect, originally trained as a painter in his native Urbino. Moving to Milan, Bramante soon absorbed and developed the classical ideals of the High Renaissance under the influence of the works and writings of Brunelleschi and Alberti. His *Tempietto* in Rome (p. 146) is a perfect, self-contained classical building composed of balanced architectural elements. When Bramante was commissioned by Pope Julius II in 1505 to rebuild St. Peter's, he discarded the traditional basilica plan and designed a magnificent square church on the plan of a Greek cross crowned with a dome. He attempted to create the same harmony of parts and unity of interior and exterior design that he had in the *Tempietto*. St. Peter's was not built in Bramante's lifetime though, and his plan was altered by succeeding architects (p. 154).

BRANCUSI, CONSTANTIN (1876–1957) Roumanian sculptor, who spent most of his life in Paris. He was the most completely abstract sculptor of the modern school. Brancusi's sculpture emphasizes pure form, depending for its effect on simplicity of outline and the highly finished texture of the material, usually stone or metal. Although abstract, each of his works expresses its title (p. 260).

BRAQUE, GEORGES (1882–) French painter and sculptor. Trained in his father's decorating business, Braque was associated with the Fauve group around 1905 and with Cézanne around 1908, but by 1909 he was working closely with Picasso in developing the kind of painting known as Analytical Cubism. One of the early artists to work with collage, Braque constantly experimented with texture and color. In collage he used the texture of the canvas for part of his effect. His cubistic works and characteristic still lifes are done in off-color tones of delicate subtlety—grays, whites and browns (p. 252). Braque's other work includes sculpture, mostly plaster reliefs, and some lithographs and etchings.

BREUGHEL, PIETER THE ELDER (c. 1525–1569) A great Flemish genre painter. Breughel's subjects were the comedy and simplicity of everyday peasant life—merrymaking, feasting, working and resting (p. 174). These scenes are shown in minute, clear detail amidst bright, warm color. Breughel was also an excellent landscape painter. Some of his paintings contain grotesque figures similar to those of Hieronymus Bosch.

BRONZINO, AGNOLO (1503–1572) Florentine Mannerist painter. Bronzino painted compressed space, unnatural proportions and off-shades of color, all characteristics of Mannerism. He is best known for his portraits of elegant, worldly Florentines (*Portrait of a Young Man,* p. 158) in artificial and formal poses. He painted his portraits as dark subjects against a bright background.

BRUNELLESCHI, FILIPPO (1377–1446) Italian architect and sculptor, the architectural pioneer of the Florentine Renaissance. Brunelleschi made the foremost discovery of the Renaissance—the mathematical laws which govern the size of objects as they recede into the background—known as perspective. Artists could now represent the correct relationship between man and nature; they could discard the hierarchical proportions of the Middle Ages. As a sculptor, Brunelleschi lost the competition in 1402 for the design of the Baptistery doors. He then became interested in studying Roman monuments and finally turned to architecture. His designs are based on mathematical proportions. Each embodies the Renaissance spirit, from the height and grandeur of the dome of the Cathedral at Florence (p. 134) to the harmony and intellectual coolness of the Pazzi Chapel (p. 269).

BUFFET, BERNARD (1928–) A French painter. Buffet's particular form of Expressionism has enjoyed a considerable vogue since 1945. Painting in a limited range of colors (at first, only in black and white), he represents impoverished and thin figures, sparse still lifes, and barren land- and cityscapes in characteristic spikey forms. Buffet has done lithographs, stage designs, and book illustrations.

BURCHFIELD, CHARLES (1893–) An American watercolorist. Burchfield took his subject matter from the small towns of his native Middle West. His early work is gently expressionistic with distorted houses and foliage and swirling elements of nature, shown in radiating lines. Burchfield also shows the romance and the suggestion of mystery which exists under the shabby exteriors of rural towns (p. 245). Later, he became more of a realist, painting tawdry subjects with little romanticism. Recently, he has returned to his early style.

CALDER, ALEXANDER (1898–) American sculptor in wire and metal. Calder took a degree in engineering at Stevens Institute, Philadelphia, and this training carried over into the mechanical ingenuity of his sculptures. He experimented first with "stabiles," rigid constructions of metal and wire. These were gradually enlarged into "mobiles"—flat, painted pieces of metal joined by jointed wires, which

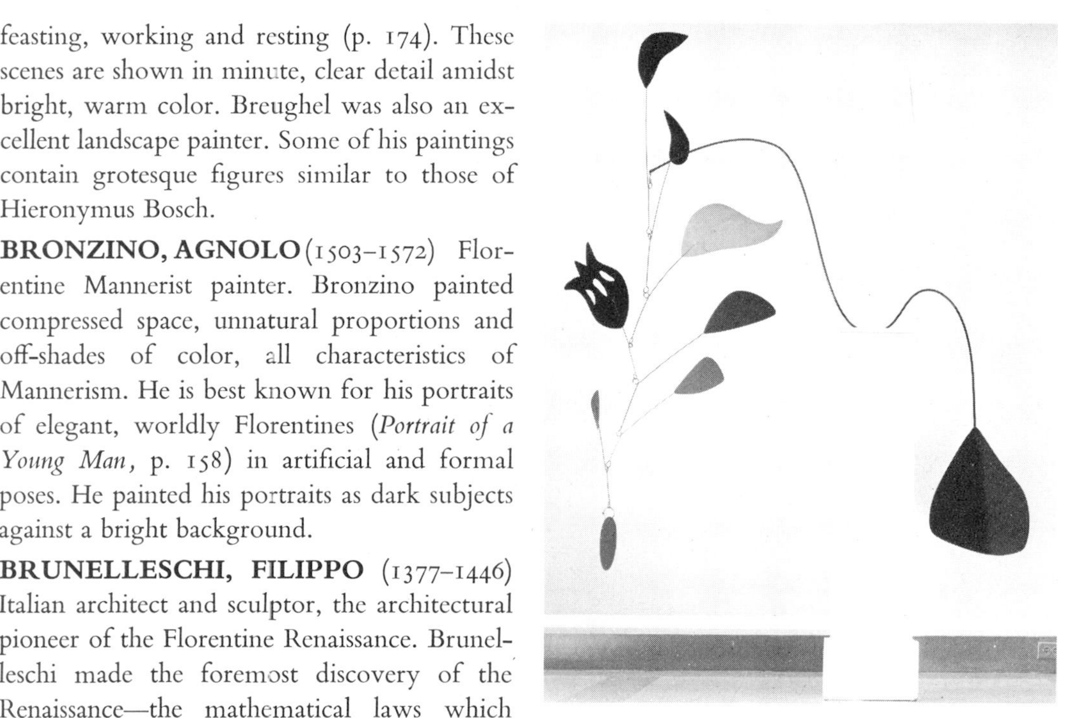

Calder: *Pomegranate.* Mobile—sheet aluminum and steel wire and rods. 1949. Whitney Museum of American Art, New York.

move in space when touched by air currents. Mobiles are designed to hang free in space. Their beauty lies in their fragile appearance and changing patterns.

CANOVA, ANTONIO (1757–1828) Italian sculptor who popularized the Neoclassic style. Canova idealized the human figure, eliminating all spontaneous and natural movement, with the result that his statues are cold and dull. Canova's Neoclassical scupltures were greatly admired and often copied in his day. He executed many commissions for Napoleon.

Canova: *Napoleon.* Gallery of Modern Art, Florence. (Anderson)

CARAVAGGIO, MICHELANGELO MERISI DA (1573–1610) Italian painter, one of the principal originators of the Baroque style. In his highly dramatic compositions, Caravaggio emphasized contrasts of light and shadow by spotlighting his subjects and using highlights to outline forms. Caravaggio painted from direct observation, reproducing with careful detail, the textures of objects and their glowing surfaces (p. 178). His paintings were in opposition to the more idealistic school of the Carracci and at first were rejected. Ultimately, his dynamic style was the more popular and spread throughout Europe, influencing particularly the artists of Spain and the Low Countries.

CARRACCI, ANNIBALE (1560–1609) Italian painter who, with his brother and his cousin, founded an academy in Bologna for the practical training of Baroque artists. The academy taught a conservative version of the Baroque. It encouraged the study of the styles of Michelangelo, Raphael and other masters of the Renaissance, but heightened the drama and pathos of a painting by adding the effect of visual extension into space and heightening the contrasts of light and shade. Carracci's major works are the frescoes in the Farnese Palace, Rome.

CASSATT, MARY (1845–1926) American painter, daughter of a wealthy Pennsylvania family, who went to Paris to study painting. There she became interested in the art of the Impressionists and participated in their exhibitions between 1879 and 1886. Although she was influenced by Degas and Manet, she developed an individual style, sensitive and gentle, with the emphasis on pleasing color rather than form. Her predominant subjects are mothers with children. Mary Cassatt also created prints which are outstanding for their technical excellence. She introduced her American friends to Impressionist art and encouraged them to buy, thus helping many an Impressionist survive during bad times and, ultimately, resulting in a good collection of Impressionism in America. Her own paintings went unappreciated in her day, but she is now regarded as America's most famous woman painter.

CELLINI, BENVENUTO (1500–1571) Florentine goldsmith and sculptor of the Renaissance. Cellini designed medals and statues in bronze. His two remaining works in gold are the saltcellar in Vienna and the Rospigliosi Cup in the Metropolitan Museum, New York (p. 159). His craftsmanship was exceedingly fine and his work has a Mannerist elegance. Cellini wrote his famous autobiography in 1558.

CÉZANNE, PAUL (1839–1906) The most revolutionary figure in the development of modern art. Born in Aix-en-Provence, Cézanne went to Paris to study and joined the Impressionists. He felt, however, that Impressionistic art lacked form and structure and he sought to add dignity to it, to "make of Impressionism something solid and lasting like the art in the museums." Ultimately, Cézanne brought revolutionary changes in spatial organization, form and color. He did not mark out spatial construction before beginning to paint, but built up depth through the interplay of small planes of color and by representing each object in its most characteristic aspect in relation to the objects around it. Thus, different subjects in the same picture are often shown from different perspectives. Cézanne built up form, also, through a series of facetlike planes, each a different color, rather than by the traditional outline of form. He believed that all forms in nature could be expressed as simple, geometric shapes, in large basic volumes. Integral to his theories of form, volume and space were his observations about color. Cézanne observed that warm colors, such as yellow and orange, seem to come forward in paintings and cool colors, such as blue and blue-green, seem to recede. He used this discovery, for instance, to model his fruits. After 1886, Cézanne lived in seclusion in Aix-en-Provence, painting the hot, open countryside of Provence, one familiar scene being Mont Saint-Victoire which he could see from his studio window (p. 227). His primary subjects were still lifes, figure studies and landscapes (pp. 230–231).

CHAGALL, MARC (1887–) Russian-born painter, who has spent most of his life in France. Chagall paints delightful fantasies embodying memories of his childhood—Russian villages, folk life and fairy tales. In these poetic evocations of village life, figures and symbolic creatures are combined in curious juxtaposition. His paintings are brightly colored. Although Chagall experimented with Cubism, he is primarily an Expressionist and a happy, warm and tender one. During the 1940's he was deeply affected by the persecutions of Jews and his tragic pictures of the sufferings of his people from the time of Christ to the Nazis date from this period.

CHARDIN, JEAN-BAPTISTE SIMEON (1699–1779) French painter, whose bourgeois subject matter and soft colors are in striking contrast to the gay, frivolous paintings of his Rococo contemporaries. Chardin's subjects are still lifes, interiors and genre scenes which he painted with loving attention to detail. With simple brush strokes he portrays daily household occurrences (*The Blessing*) and amusing scenes (*Blowing Bubbles*). His colors are soft harmonies with reposed compositions (p. 211).

CHIPPENDALE, THOMAS (1718–1779) English cabinet-maker, whose designs incorporated French Rococo and Chinoiserie forms into his own English style. Much of his furniture was of mahogany and the designs were practical and comfortable. Chippendale's pattern book, *The Gentleman and Cabinet-maker's Director* popularized his style in England and throughout Europe (p. 210).

CIMABUE (1240–1303?) Florentine painter. In his early life, Cimabue painted in the Byzantine style, with figures stiffly posed and symmetrically arranged, and with flat color on a gold background. Later, he became the first artist to attempt to represent figures solidly and naturally, with a material existence in space. Cimabue stands at the beginning of the Florentine tradition, later represented by Giotto, Masaccio and the artists of the Renaissance.

Cimabue: *Virgin and Child.* Uffizi, Florence. (Alinari)

CLOUET, JEAN (c. 1486–1540) French portrait painter of Flemish origin, father of François. Clouet was the outstanding portraitist of his time, and in 1516 Francis I appointed him court painter. A purity of line, attention to detail and rich use of colors, typical of Clouet's Flemish-French style, are evident in the portrait of Francis I in the Louvre (p. 172).

CONSTABLE, JOHN (1776–1837) Major 19th-century English landscape painter. Constable loved the beauty of nature and the unassuming life of the country. He painted spacious, open landscapes with meticulous detail, recreating the exact atmosphere of the scene, be it light and warm, shady, windy or raining (p. 222). His color has a vibrant quality which results from applying blobs of paint with a palette knife. In 1824 Constable scored a success in Paris with the exhibition of his *Hay Wain* and strongly influenced French artists. He gained only limited recognition in England.

COPLEY, JOHN SINGLETON (1737–1815) Along with Gilbert Stuart, one of the two leading portraitists of colonial America. Copley, an untrained painter, developed a style of forceful, candid realism coupled with brilliant use of color which was rarely flattering to his sitters (p. 213). He left Boston in 1774 and settled in London. There he obtained professional training, which is thought to have weakened his style.

COROT, JEAN BAPTISTE (1796–1875) French painter of the 19th century. Born in Paris, Corot did his first mature work in Rome (1825–1827). He painted numerous scenes, notable for their clear definition of landscape and architecture (p. 223). In his mature years, he painted many calm, beautiful portraits of women (p. 220). Corot anticipated Impressionism in his careful arrangement of light and dark areas of color.

CORREGGIO (ANTONIO ALLEGRI) (1489?–1534) Italian painter who lived in the small town of Parma. His real name was Antonio Allegri. Correggio's art was popular for the soft flesh tints and graceful beauty of the figures. His rich color, bold foreshortening and brilliant way of spotlighting his subject in a dark background anticipated Baroque painting of a century later. He was one of the first to use foreshortening in the ceilings of churches to create the impression of space opening into heaven. Most of Correggio's paintings have religious themes, but the mythological series of *Antiope* (Louvre), *Danae* (Rome), *Leda* (Berlin) and *Io* (Vienna) are considered to be his outstanding works.

COURBET, GUSTAVE (1819–1877) French realist painter. Courbet had a vigorous, naturalistic style and painted only subjects and scenes as he had experienced them himself. Many of his subjects reflect Courbet's social conscience which had been aroused by the 19th-century revolutions in Europe. The direct honesty of his paintings shocked his contemporaries. His nudes were nuder, his peasants were unromanticized and his landscapes were lusher than traditional art decreed. Courbet's colors were bold and rich, the edges of the light areas and the dark areas met squarely. The huge paintings, *Burial at Ornans* and *The Studio* (p. 220), are his chief works.

CRANACH, LUCAS THE ELDER (1472–1553) German painter and engraver. Cranach frequently painted idyllic landscapes, mythological subjects and portraits. His work is characterised by a linear style and bright colors.

DALI, SALVADOR (1904–) Contemporary Spanish painter, Catalan by birth. Dali is probably the most controversial painter in the Surrealist method. He achieves bizarre effects either by taking real objects and juxtaposing them in unrelated situations or by distorting a real object until it becomes grotesque (a burning giraffe with open bureau drawers in its neck). These images are meant to have symbolic meaning drawn from Dali's subconscious. In some, such as the *Persistence of Memory* (p. 254), the symbolism is clear to us—it represents time and decay. In others the symbolism is clear only to Dali. Dali paints with the same precise detail as the early miniature painters. He has recently turned to religious themes. His *Last Supper* in the National Gallery, Washington, D.C., and the *Crucifixion* in the Metropolitan, New York, are paintings of much contemporary controversy.

DAUMIER, HONORÉ (1808–1879) French lithographer and painter and one of the outstanding caricaturists of his century. Daumier illustrated for the Parisian reviews, *La Caricature* and *Le Charivari*, producing some 4,000 lithographs of timely political and social satire. In seemingly casual sketches, he caught the whimsy, folly, humor and tragedy in men's lives. His paintings, which were fully appreciated only after his death, show a more sympathetic concern with the patient stoicism of the Parisian lower classes. The solemn and resigned passengers in *Third-Class Carriage* (p. 221) illustrate Daumier's insight into the human situation. His painting style retains the draftsmanship of his lithographs.

Daumier: *"And that they have turned down, the ignorant fools!"* 1859. Lithograph. Bibliothèque Nationale, Paris.

DAVID, JACQUES LOUIS (1748–1825) French painter and arbiter of artistic taste. David began painting in the Rococo style, but abandoned it abruptly for Neoclassicism after a trip to Rome between 1775 and 1781. His *Oath of the Horatii* (p. 215) was the first French Neoclassic painting and represents the manly republican virtues which David found in Antiquity. Considered the most imaginative of the Neoclassicists, his *Death of Marat* is the epitome of classical modeling of a figure bathed by a clear, cold light. During the French Revolution, David became the official painter for the Republic and the dictator of the arts. Later, he was Napoleon's official painter and painted numerous portraits of the Emperor and his court.

DAVIS, STUART (1894–) American painter who studied in New York. Davis painted in several successive styles, (Impressionism, Expressionism, Cubism), before arriving at an abstract posterlike style. Davis' paintings represent scenes from contemporary life, often with large words painted in them because Davis feels that words "are a part of urban subject matter." His jumbled abstract patterns in pure, bright colors give an effect of decorative warmth and gaiety. Davis' subject matter is often witty and has a carnival atmosphere. He painted murals in Radio City Music Hall in New York in 1932, and for the New York World's Fair in 1939.

DEGAS, EDGAR (1834–1917) A great French Impressionist. Degas received his first training in the academic tradition, heeding Ingres' advice to "draw lines." By the late 1860's, he had developed his characteristic manner of composition, deceptively casual and based on unexpected viewpoints. He caught a spontaneous moment in a seemingly accidental composition, often cutting the subject off at the edge of the painting. Nevertheless, Degas' scenes are always complete and every detail has meaning. Compositionally, he was a master at balancing a picture by pairing its weight against its center of interest. In *Rehearsal on the Stage* (p. 240), the mass of figures is at the left, but the lighting and the arms of the dancers point out the main figure, the dancing ballerina alone on the right. Degas' style of painting diverged from Impressionism in several important ways. He preferred to draw indoor scenes of ballet dancers or models bathing or outdoor scenes of places where people congregate, such as the city or the race tracks, whereas the Impressionists were concerned with atmospheric effects over a landscape. He was also the only Impressionist interested in portraying the psychological meaning behind a portrait or scene. Degas experimented with nearly every media, including all the print techniques and sculpture.

DELACROIX, EUGENE (1798–1863) French painter who succeeded Géricault in France as the leader of the Romantic rebellion against the classicism of Ingres and his followers. Delacroix chose exotic subjects from history, mythology and literature (*Massacre of Scio*, *Entrance of the Crusaders into Constantinople*, *Dante and Virgil in Hell*) and painted them in brilliant color and turbulent movement. Twisting arms and bodies are accented by spots of light. Backgrounds stretch hazily to the horizon. A trip to North Africa in 1832 intensified his interest in exotic subjects. Delacroix executed numerous large-scale decorations on official commissions. Some of his paintings are overpowering in size; *Liberty Leading the People* (p. 219), for instance, measures 8½ by 12⅓ feet. Bitterly criticized by the official art world, Delacroix was worshiped by young artists as a symbol of revolution and independence.

DELAUNAY, ROBERT (1885–1941) The principal painter in the style called "orphism" which attempted to free Cubism from the dull browns, grays and blacks of its analytical days and from its dependence on a real subject. Delaunay painted in abstract planes and curves of color, trying to represent movement, again in contrast to the static analytical technique of Cubism. He has a brilliant, free use of color and transposes planes of color to build form. The *Eiffel Tower*, his favorite theme, indicates Delaunay's interest in mechanical forms.

DERAIN, ANDRE (1880–1954) One of the major Fauve artists in the early phase of his career. He painted landscapes and views of London, using short brush strokes and clashing, arbitrary color. This early art was Derain's best for he later became absorbed in a study of the historical traditions and old masters and painted more conservatively. He produced etchings, illustrations for books and theatrical designs.

Derain: *Portrait of the Artist.* The Minneapolis Institute of Arts, Gift of Mrs. Elizabeth Bates Cowles.

DE CHIRICO, GIORGIO (1888–) Italian painter, born in Greece. De Chirico anticipated Surrealism with "metaphysical painting," a way of placing incongruous objects in an unreal space that is both visually unnerving and philosophically puzzling to the viewer. He places classical statues and familiar objects like trains, trees, and geometric shapes in a sur-

Delaunay: *Eiffel Tower.* 1910. Pen and ink on brown cardboard. Museum of Modern Art, New York.

rounding of classical architecture. An arcaded street is a familiar setting. Although De Chirico's pictures seem to have a vista, we are always held within the architectural frame of the picture by the blankness of the scene and a flat, golden light. A mysterious and melancholy mood pervades most of De Chirico's work—a feeling that we are looking at disillusionment in a new fantastic way. In recent years De Chirico has outspokenly rejected his early work and returned to a conventional style (p. 254).

DONATELLO (1386–1466) The first great sculptor of the Florentine Renaissance. He was Ghiberti's assistant and an associate of Brunelleschi, with whom he worked on the Cathedral. Donatello's innovations in sculpture were comparable to Michelangelo's in painting. He scorned the grace and refinement of the International Gothic style and modelled his figures from observation of actual models. The bronze *David*, commissioned by Cosimo de' Medici, has classical proportions plus the Renaissance concern with man's awareness of himself. David with Goliath's head at his feet seems more aware of his strength and manhood than of the mighty deed he has just done. Some of Donatello's works are heavy and monumental, some are light and graceful. They range from statues to sculptured reliefs. His later works, such as the *Magdalen* and the pulpits in the church of Santa Maria Novella are increasingly expressionistic, showing a concern with emotion (p. 136).

DOVE, ARTHUR (1880–1946) Contemporary American painter. Soon after his graduation from Cornell, Dove became a successful commercial illustrator. He joined Stieglitz's Gallery "291" in New York, with which he was associated during the rest of his life. From this time, his art became increasingly abstract, tending toward a limited vocabulary of geometric shapes. Never does he totally abstract his subject, though. We can always identify the subject of the painting. Dove was America's most original experimenter with collage. He was very interested in contrasts of texture—a patch of sand and fragment of sailcloth in marine scenes, or tapestry and pressed leaves on an old book page in his collage, *Grandmother*. Dove's work is often humorous and tender.

DUCCIO DI BUONINSEGNA (1255–1319) Duccio was the most prominent Sienese painter in the Italo-Byzantine tradition of the late 13th century. Duccio tried to breathe new life into Byzantine-Medieval stylized patterns without discarding them for natural forms, as the Florentines were doing under Giotto. He added a feeling of space and drama to his art, although still continuing in the Sienese tradition of glowing color and liberal use of gold. His major work, the "Maesta," a complex altarpiece painted for the cathedral of Siena between 1308 and 1311, has always been famous for its superb craftsmanship and elegance. Duccio's flowing lines and delicate details give these religious scenes an added poignancy (p. 131).

DUCHAMP, MARCEL (1887–) Duchamp was the champion and philosopher of the Dada movement in the United States. He made his name with the famous fractured figure of a *Nude Descending A Staircase*, exhibited in the New York Armory Show (1913). This was America's first introduction to avant-garde art and provoked a storm of outraged criticism. Duchamp also constructed large glass compositions with ridiculous names (*To be looked at with one eye, close to, for almost an hour*). When a glass picture broke on its way to an exhibition, Duchamp insisted that it had broken according to the scheme of the painting and exhibited it. His subject matter was always irrelevant. Duchamp has also worked on abstract films and as a journalist. In the early 1940's he edited the avant-garde magazine *VVV*.

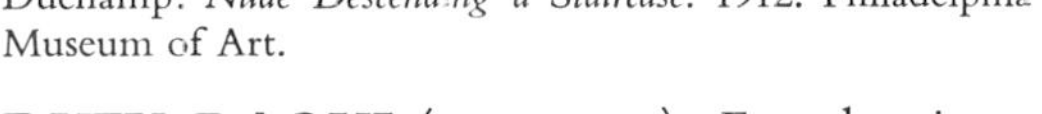

Duchamp: *Nude Descending a Staircase*. 1912. Philadelphia Museum of Art.

DUFY, RAOUL (1877–1953) French painter of gay, social, frivolous scenes. Dufy first tried to paint in a monumental style and then turned to the intense color of Fauvism (1905–1907). Finally, he developed the style which is so familiar today, a pastel wash of color over a skeletal outline of his subjects. In addition to his paintings, Dufy made designs for ceramics, textiles and tapestries. His work reflects a seemingly effortless execution and a gaiety of spirit, which account for his continued popularity.

DÜRER, ALBRECHT (1471–1528) German painter and engraver whose initial work was done in the late Gothic style. On trips to Italy, Dürer became exposed to the High Renaissance theories of proportion and perspective. Henceforth, the soft line of Italian painting humanized the harsh Gothic line of his paintings. Frequent subjects of Dürer's paintings were Biblical stories, sympathetic rendering of nature's beauty, and precise architectural structures. He was an outstanding master of detail and his drawings for woodcuts and watercolors are among his best works (p. 170).

EAKINS, THOMAS (1844–1916) Leading American realistic painter. Eakins observed the world and, supported by a thorough understanding of anatomy, perspective and photography, painted with physical realism and shrewd, honest character interpretation. These perceptive paintings, especially the portraits, were never a popular success. His *Gross Clinic* (1875) shocked his contemporaries with its portrayal of surgery (p. 243); he was later forced to give up his position at the Pennsylvania Academy of Fine Arts because of his insistence on the study of the nude model.

EL GRECO (DOMENIKOS THEOTOCOPOULOS) (1541?–1614) Spanish painter, born on the Greek island of Crete. He acquired the name "El Greco," or "the Greek" from his birthplace. His early training in Crete was in the rigid, formal manner of Byzantine painting. He later came to Venice, where he studied under Titian, and was strongly influenced by Tintoretto's stress on the dramatic element of a scene. After 1577 El Greco lived in Toledo, Spain, where he painted the visionary, religious scenes with elongated, dematerialized figures with which we associate him. He disregarded natural color, manipulating light and shade to create tension in his paintings. The *View of Toledo* and the *Burial of Count Orgaz* (p. 182) are characteristic works.

ENSOR, JAMES (1860–1949) Belgian painter whose art is distinctly recognizable by the mask-like funny faces of the people. Ensor paints in bright, cheerful colors and at first glance his work has a carnival aspect. Upon closer examination, however, it is seen to be an ironic comment on man's falsity and mortality—which Ensor represents by his masked figures and skeletons (p. 254).

EPSTEIN, SIR JACOB (1880–1959) American-born sculptor who settled in England about 1906 and later became a British subject. Epstein's sculptures are realistic though some of his early works inclined toward abstraction. Now, the emphasis is on surface texture which he uses to express personality, and for the aesthetic pleasure of handling the material. Although Epstein is currently known for the portrait busts in bronze which he has done in recent years, his work also includes large-scale architectural sculptures, several of which decorate modern buildings in London.

ERNST, MAX (1891–) German painter, now a Surrealist, who was first associated with Jean Arp in the Dada movement. Together they fashioned a series of nonsense collages called "fatagaga," made up of cut-out pictures combined in unusual positions and supplemented by drawing and lettering. As a painter, Ernst combined real objects and dream images in fantastical scenes. He has also painted frescoes, "rubbings," and decors for the theater.

FEININGER, LYONEL (1871–1956) American-born painter who went to Germany in 1887 to study music, but changed to art. At first, Feininger was a cartoonist and illustrator, becoming in 1906 a cartoonist for the Chicago Sunday Tribune. From 1919 to 1924 Feininger taught at the Bauhaus in Weimar and his art has always been closely associated with this school's aesthetics. He returned to the United States in 1937. Feininger's paintings are patterns of form and color, neat, precise and delicate, imparting a gentle human warmth. Boats, skyscrapers and locomotives are constant motifs.

FOUQUET, JEAN (*c.* 1415–1480) The outstanding French artist of the 15th century. Painter and miniaturist, Fouquet became acquainted with the new Renaissance spirit of Italian art through his travels in Italy between 1445 and 1447. Many of his paintings have architectural settings, modeled on the antique monuments of Rome. Fouquet's style combines precise Flemish rendering of detail with Italian perspective and plasticity with striking effect, especially in his small book illustrations.

FRAGONARD, JEAN HONORÉ (1732–1806) A pupil of Boucher and the most popular painter of the French Rococo. Fragonard's light-hearted, erotic compositions were the delight of society under Louis XV and Louis XVI (p. 214).

FRANCESCA, PIERO DELLA (c. 1410–1492) Italian painter of the Umbrian school, who lived south of Florence in the towns of Arezzo and Urbino. Piero learned the new science of perspective from Paolo Uccello and studied the use of light and color to describe form under Dominico Veneziano, both great teachers. Piero's art surpassed both. His motionless, simple and dignified figures stand in a serenely ordered space, illuminated by glowing light (pp. 146, 148–9). The cycle of frescoes of the *History of the True Cross* at Arezzo is his major work.

GABRIEL, JACQUES-ANGE (1710–1782) French architect who revived the academic classicism of the 17th century as a reaction to fanciful, asymmetry of the Rococo which was favored in the early 18th. The two ministries on the Place de la Concorde in Paris and the Petit Trianon at Versailles are among his works.

GAINSBOROUGH, THOMAS (1727–1788) Portrait painter of English society and the major rival of Sir Joshua Reynolds. Gainsborough was famous for his delicate brushwork and the rich, glistening pastels with which he depicted the shining silks, glittering buckles, fragile lace and starched ruffles of the clothes of his day. One of his best known paintings is *Blue Boy*. Gainsborough was also a landscape painter of great originality.

GAUDI, ANTONIO (1852–1926) Spanish architect whose career began in the Neo-Gothic style. His typical works, however, are associated with Art Nouveau, as in the church of the Sagrada Familia, the Casa Batillo and the Casa Mila in Barcelona. These buildings show an extremely personal style, with their plastic exteriors of stone and the organic ironwork of the parapets and railings. The Casa Mila is often considered the masterpiece of the curvilinear style of the Art Nouveau. The church of the Sagrada Familia has no building behind its façade.

Feininger: *Glorious Victory of the Sloop "Maria."* Courtesy of the City Art Museum, St. Louis.

GAUGUIN, PAUL (1848–1903) French post-Impressionist painter. Gauguin, a vigorous, handsome man, was a successful broker and banker who took up painting as a hobby. Under Pissarro's influence, Gauguin exhibited in Impressionist group shows. Finally he gave up his job and turned to painting as a career. For the rest of his life, Gauguin moved restlessly from Paris to Brittany, to Provence, to Martinique, Tahiti and the Marquesas, in search of exotic subject matter for his paintings. Gauguin broke away from the Impressionists in his use of color and choice of subject. He scorned their minute dabs of color and painted in large areas of pure strong color. As an example, although he accepted the Impressionist belief that shadows were not gray but were a combination of colors, he painted them solid blue, or solid red, however the shadow struck him, rather than trying to show a reflection of the color of the object. The unnatural colors in Gauguin's landscapes are part of an arbitrary approach to nature which reduced it to a decorative scheme. He painted people as flattened and slightly distorted forms, squarish and monumental. Gauguin spent the last years of his life in the South Seas painting the beautiful Tahitian women and the exotic landscape he loved so much (pp. 232–233).

GELLÉE, CLAUDE (called Lorrain) (1600–1682) French landscape painter who studied in Rome and spent most of his life in Italy. The composition of Claude's paintings follows a regular pattern, one large and another smaller mass framing the picture in the foreground (usually trees or buildings), with a view into luminous, golden distance beyond. Figures on a small scale, often representing mythological or religious scenes are usually included (p. 191). Claude tried to capture on canvas the stillness and calm of the Italian landscape.

GÉRICAULT, THÉODORE (1791–1824) A major artist in the French Romantic movement, Géricault greatly influenced Delacroix. He introduced the general public to Romantic painting with his huge *Raft of the Medusa* (1819). This painting depicts 15 survivors of a disastrous shipwreck in which hundreds of French immigrants on their way to North Africa perished, a tragedy blamed on official negligence which was a vital political issue at the time (p. 219). Géricault's choice of this dramatic subject and his realistic portrayal of the survivors were both characteristically Romantic. The turbulent mass of forms, pyramidal design, intensified emotion, and the play of light in *Raft of the Medusa* all illustrate Géricault's break with the balance and calm of David's prevailing Neoclassicism. Géricault made many animal studies from nature and brilliant portraits of lunatics, both subjects breaking with the Neoclassic belief that men, and sane well-behaved men, were the only fit subjects for art.

GHIBERTI, LORENZO (1378–1455) Florentine goldsmith and sculptor in bronze, best known for his doors of the Baptistery in Florence. In 1402 Ghiberti won, over Brunelleschi, a competition for designing the second bronze doors of the Baptistery (p. 134). In 1425 he began the famous third doors, the "Gates of Paradise," for which he used large square panels, releasing the scenes from the confining frames of the earlier doors, and from one-point perspective. He also emphasized the illusion of depth by making the front figures stand out almost in relief while the further ones are flat. Michelangelo later said of these doors, "They are so fine that they might fittingly stand at the Gates of Paradise" (p. 135). Ghiberti used the new Renaissance ideas, but his style never lost the fluid lines of International Gothic style.

GIACOMETTI, ALBERTO (1901–) Swiss-born sculptor who joined the Surrealist movement about 1930. He is known primarily for his extremely elongated human figures shown in motion, singly or in groups (e.g. *City Square*). These anonymous figures are given a vast surrounding of space seeming to symbolize man's feeling of insignificance in the modern world. The scupltures have a rough, eroded surface of bronze or plaster, which gives them a nervous and agitated vitality (p. 255).

GIORGIONE, GIORGIO DA CASTELFRANCO (1476/77–1510) An outstanding Venetian painter of the High Renaissance. Giorgione profoundly influenced Venetian painting (and his pupil Titian in particular), by his use of color instead of the pattern of lines to unify his paintings and give them spatial depth. Warm, rich blues and reds create the mood. Little is known of Giorgione; only five paintings can definitely be attributed to him (p. 163).

GIOTTO DI BONDONE (1266?–1337) Florentine painter and architect. In the *Divine Comedy* Dante immortalized Giotto, his Florentine contemporary, as a genius who had escaped the bondage of the "maniera byzantina" to introduce a new vision of the world. For the first time a vast inner world of feeling was expressed through attitudes of figures, composition of the action and use of light. In Giotto's frescoes, men and women are three-dimensional and bend towards each other in natural attitudes. Their faces express suffering, joy, jealousy. His frescoes are composed so that the action (as in the *Lamentation* in the Arena Chapel in Padua) is directed at a central subject. In *Lamentation*, all faces are sorrowfully directed toward Christ, angels above are mourning Him, a diagonal hill in the background is lighted so that it leads the eye to Christ. This may not seem unusual to us now, but it should be compared to the stiff Byzantine art which preceded it. Giotto expressed the emotional meaning of his scenes, the physical and spiritual reality. He was influenced by his Florentine compatriot Cimabue, and later in Rome, by another artist in the Florentine tradition, Cavallini, but his additional contribution was immense (p. 132). Between 1305 and 1307 he painted the magnificent frescoes for the Arena Chapel which had been built to accommodate a major pictorial cycle. It contains scenes from the life of Christ and the Virgin and a Last Judgment.

GIOVANNI DA BOLOGNA (also called Giambologna) (c. 1524–1608) French sculptor born in Douai and trained in Antwerp, who came to Florence in 1562. Bologna was a Mannerist sculptor. In his well-known *Mercury* (p. 159) we see the elongation of figure and graceful but staged pose which are characteristics of Mannerism. He executed numerous statues under the patronage of the Medici family.

Giotto: *Lamentation*. Fresco. 1305. Arena Chapel, Padua. (Alinari)

GOGH, VINCENT VAN (1853–1890) Dutch-born, Post-Impressionist painter. Van Gogh's first artistic years, from 1880 to 1886, were spent in Holland. In this period his subjects were poor peasants, miners and farmers, and his colors were dull, heavy and depressing browns and blacks. In 1886, van Gogh moved to Paris where he met the Impressionists—Gauguin, Seurat, Degas, Pissarro. Here he developed the vibrant style which burst into maturity in the two years (1888–1890) at Arles in the south of France. In violent contrasts of pure color and turbulent brush strokes, van Gogh painted magnificent canvases which reflected his troubled personality. Sometimes van Gogh painted with short, choppy strokes, at others with sweeping, swirling strokes, adding a tactile counterpart to the visual appreciation of his work. The figures are simple and blocky, important primarily as areas of color, and the paintings have a relief surface. In 1890 van Gogh ended his lonely, troubled life by committing suicide (pp. 236–239).

Gonzales: *Woman Combing Her Hair*. 1936. Wrought iron. *h*. 52″. Museum of Modern Art, New York. Mrs. Simon Guggenheim Fund.

GONZALES, JULIO (1876–1942) Spanish sculptor, who was first trained as a blacksmith in his family's shop. An evening course in painting at Barcelona Art Academy led him into painting. Later he turned to sculpture in wrought iron, usually of female figures handled in an abstract manner. Gonzales was a good friend of Picasso's, whom he instructed in metal techniques (1929–1932).

GOTTLIEB, ADOLPH (1903–) American Abstract Expressionist painter, whose art style is similar to Klee's and Miro's. Gottlieb paints large abstract pictographs. Aside from his oil paintings, he did a mural for the Post Office in Yerrington, Nevada, and huge stained-glass windows for the Park Avenue Synagogue in New York City.

GOYA Y LUCIENTES, FRANCISCO JOSÉ (1746–1828) Spanish painter and portraitist to the court of Charles IV of Spain. Goya's personal life was excitingly chaotic and romantic, but he was also a moralist whose paintings depicted the foolishness, ignorance and cruelty of the turbulent age in which he lived. He painted unflatteringly realistic portraits of the royal family and portraits caricaturing the vicious and corrupt natures of those who were then a part of court life. His criticism seemed to go unnoticed, however, for his paintings remained popular. Goya's prints, *Disasters of War*, catalogue the futility and cruelty of war. In *Caprichos* (a set of 80 aquatints) greed, superstition, and indifference are displayed in devastating vignettes. Toward the end of his life, Goya did a series of superb etchings of the history and technique of bullfighting. His style is realistic, using simple forms not especially articulated, and dramatic contrasts of light and shade (pp. 216–217).

GRAVES, MORRIS (1910–) American painter, often associated with Surrealism. In San Francisco, Graves discovered the art and philosophy of the Orient and from it developed a delicate, linear style of painting. His subjects are animals, birds, rocks, and pines which he uses as personal symbols to create a supernatural and romantic world. Since 1938 most of Graves' painting has been in gouache and watercolors on thin Chinese paper.

GRIS, JUAN (1887–1927) Spanish painter and illustrator. He received his training in Madrid, then moved to Paris where he became interested in Cubism. He was a significant figure in the transition from the analytical Cubism of Picasso and Braque to "synthetic" Cubism. Gris insisted that the subject matter of a painting be recognizable. However, he improvised and enlarged on his central theme to produce variations and combinations of abstract shapes (p. 268). He brought color, lacking in analytical Cubism, back in force. Gris's art was impersonal, almost scientific, and was not particularly successful until late in his career. He also did illustrations for several books and designed decors for Diaghilev's ballets.

GROPIUS, WALTER (1883–) German-American architect, one of the most influential names in modern architecture. In 1919 he organized the Bauhaus School in Weimar, where painting, sculpture and architecture were developed in close association, and where Feininger, Klee and Kandinsky taught. The Bauhaus stressed the integration of design with the industrial world and became a preparatory school for the modern International style. In 1925 Gropius designed the famous glass and steel building in Dessau for the school (p. 260). After the rise of Hitler he came to the United States, and in 1938 was appointed chairman of the Harvard Architectural Department, in which capacity he designed the Harvard Graduate Center. In 1946 he returned to active practice.

GROS, ANTOINE JEAN "BARON" (1771–1835) French painter and pupil of David whom he succeeded as the leader of the Neoclassical school. He tended to paint in a more romantic style than David, dramatizing scenes with action and play of light. He painted many portraits and battle scenes for Napoleon.

GROSZ, GEORGE (1893–) German-born American painter and graphic artist. He first joined the Futurists and the Dadaists and later carried on his bitter, scathing social criticism of fat militarists and greedy bourgeoisie in a group of masterful pen-and-ink drawings. Since Grosz' arrival in the United States in 1932, he has turned his attention toward landscape and the nude.

Grosz: Page from folio *Die Rauber*. Mr. and Mrs. Bernard J. Reis, New York.

GRÜNEWALD, MATTHIAS (1460/70–1528) German painter born in the troubled period of the Reformation. Grünewald's art fully expresses the harshness of 16th-century German art before it was touched by the softening Italian influence of Dürer, Holbein and Cranach. Grünewald's paintings are religiously oriented, providing vivid sermons on canvas. Consequently, the important religious figures are large in scale and lesser figures are correspondingly smaller (p. 123). The major figures are emphasized by bold color and spotlighting.

GUARDI, FRANCESCO (1712–1793) Venetian painter, pupil of Canaletto. In contrast to the almost photographic paintings of his teacher, Guardi has a loose manner and a sketchy brushstroke conveying the natural interplay of light and shadow (p. 209).

HALS, FRANS (c. 1580–1666) Dutch painter, renowned for his portraits of smiling Dutch burghers. Hals painted rapidly, in "shorthand," capturing on canvas the vivacious and happy burghers of his native Holland (p. 200). He painted single portraits and large group portraits of civic associations, arranging his subjects naturally in contrast to the usual stiffly posed portraits. The colors are robust and warm in his early paintings, later becoming limited to gray, brown and black tones. Much of his work remains in the Frans Hals Museum in Haarlem.

HARTLEY, MARSDEN (1877–1943) Modern American painter. Hartley first painted Impressionist landscapes, then went to Europe and turned towards abstract art, exhibiting with the Blue Rider group in Munich (1913). After 1918 he renounced non-objective art for a violent Expressionist style using a bold, flashing palette. Best known of Hartley's paintings are his Maine still lifes of rocks and ropes, shells and dead sea birds.

HECKEL, ERICH (1883–) German painter and graphic artist. He was an original member of the group of German Expressionists calling themselves *Die Brücke* or "The Bridge." Heckel's Expressionism has a poetic, sensitive quality and is less violent in feeling than the art of Nolde and Kirchner, two other members of *Die Brücke*. He uses delicate colors. Heckel's paintings reveal his concern for the unhappy, introspective individual and a sensitive appreciation of nature. Much of his work has the angular appearance of woodblocks, at which he excels.

HOFMANN, HANS (1880–) German-born American painter associated with Abstract Expressionism. Hofmann is very important as a teacher of art, having schools in Munich (1915–1934), New York and Provincetown (since 1934). His painting has become progressively more abstract, his color bolder.

HOGARTH, WILLIAM (1697–1764) English painter and engraver. He is most famous for three series of paintings: *The Harlot's Progress*, *The Rake's Progress*, and *Marriage a la Mode*, in which he criticizes the existing social order. In choosing the subject matter for his paintings, Hogarth followed the trend toward social satire in literature. His paintings had great appeal to the English public, which had hitherto shown little interest in English painters. Hogarth used the bright, cheerful colors of his French Rococo contemporaries and translated them into the typical English idiom. His reputation comes mainly from the engravings he made from his paintings, which were eagerly purchased by the English public (p. 210).

HOLBEIN, HANS THE YOUNGER (1497–1543) German painter and engraver. Holbein's early work was done in Basle (where he became a citizen in 1520), and the Kunst Museum there has a superb collection of his paintings and woodcuts. In 1532 Holbein settled in London, gained wide renown as a portraitist, and became Henry VIII's court painter. Holbein painted his subjects with objective detachment and softened the harsh, often busy, German linear style. He achieved this softness by using layers of flat enamel paint which brought out the richness of the English clothes. Symbolism interested Holbein deeply and he generally placed a symbolic object in his paintings. In the *Ambassadors,* for instance, the long gray shape in the foreground is a death's head (p. 171). His woodcuts are exceptional.

HOMER, WINSLOW (1836–1910) Outstanding American painter of the Maine coast, seascapes and hunting and fishing scenes (p. 244). Homer painted from direct observation and endowed his work with the drama and force found in nature, from the energy of the sea pounding on the shore to the rough texture of a sailor's rainjacket in the driving rain. His early paintings, done while in Paris and London, show an affinity for Impressionism. Later he did more powerful canvases using the large, massive subjects mentioned above. His color areas are large and simple.

HOOCH, PIETER DE (1629–1684?) Dutch genre painter, who lived in Delft. Hooch painted the square neat rooms or courtyards of Dutch homes. His colors are warm and his canvases are usually lighted by a single shaft of light. Hooch reproduces the precise details of the quiet, composed clean room, lingering over the different textures of the tiles, furniture, beamed ceilings and walls. His scenes are warm and comfortable, reflecting Dutch domesticity.

HOPPER, EDWARD (1882–) American painter and etcher. Hopper paints in a style similar to the "Ashcan School" of American social realism. His subjects are the people and buildings of the small towns and the big cities of America, portraying the loneliness and pathos of modern life. Hopper creates his moods by using simple figures and bare buildings, in areas of simple color and clear, sharp light. Typical of his scenes are a few people sitting at a luncheon counter, or an empty, desolate street. This emptiness, this austere form, is what gives Hopper's art its feeling of loneliness (p. 244).

HOUDON, JEAN-ANTOINE (1741–1828) French sculptor of the late Rococo, famous for his many busts of statesmen, scholars, artists and generals of his day (p. 214). Houdon turned from the frivolity of the Rococo to a more classical style. His sculptures were simple in detail, allowing personal characterization of the sitter to dominate the portrait. Houdon executed several busts of Washington and a standing figure, now in Richmond, Virginia. Several of his busts are also at Monticello.

INGRES, JEAN AUGUSTE DOMINIQUE (1780–1867) French painter and leader of the Neoclassic school after the death of David. Ingres' pictures are smoothly painted with carefully outlined contours and stress on sinuous line. The modeling of form is absolutely simple. Some of Ingres' best work is seen in his portraits. He also painted historical, mythological, Oriental and religious subjects (p. 218).

JONES, INIGO (1573–1652) English architect who introduced Palladio's classical forms into English architecture. The Queen's House in Greenwich and the Banqueting Hall at Whitehall (p. 202) were designed while he was architect to James I and Charles I.

KANDINSKY, WASSILY (1866–1944) Russian-born painter, teacher and art theorist. Kandinsky was one of the organizers of the Blue Rider group. This was the non-objective branch of German Expressionism which emphasized line and color in a painting rather than the subject. Kandinsky felt that a mood could be created through lines, shapes and colors without a recognizable subject. His book, *Concerning the Spiritual in Art,* was published in 1912 and is a superb discussion of the principles underlying his work and that of modern painting (p. 256).

KIRCHNER, ERNST LUDWIG (1880–1938) German painter, graphic artist and sculptor. Kirchner was one of the founders of *Die Brücke,* or "The Bridge," an objective offshoot of Expressionism that emphasized the seamier side of life, as opposed to the principles of the more cheerful, non-objective Blue Rider group (p. 250).

KLEE, PAUL (1879–1940) Swiss-German painter and draughtsman. Klee's art is based on personal fantasy, on the symbolism in the art of children and primitive minds. His personal style was developed after experimentation with the styles of Cézanne, van Gogh, Ensor, the Blue Rider group, Dadaism and Surrealism. Klee's purpose was "to make memories abstract" and to this end he used a subtle language of signs, expressing essential sensations and meanings. This hieroglyphic expression, coupled with a mastery of delicate line and color and texture variations, makes Klee's paintings naively attractive, yet highly communicative (p. 254).

KOKOSCHKA, OSKAR (1886–) Austrian painter who shocked Vienna in the early decades of this century with his "morbid" Expressionist paintings. Kokoschka's paintings are vital with swirling lines, bright colors. The harsh, distorted images of his portraits attempt to reflect the inner personality of the sitter. Portraits and landscapes are the primary subjects of his paintings.

KOLLWITZ, KATHE (1867–1945) German graphic artist and sculptor, outstanding for her etchings, woodcuts and lithographs. Each is a protest against the suffering, hunger and sorrow in the lives of the poor and against the separations and privations caused by the two World Wars. Kollwitz lived in Berlin. She was in great disfavor under Kaiser Wilhelm II because of her criticism of social conditions in Germany, and prohibited under Hitler from working and showing her work because of her affiliation with the Socialist Party. Her prints include illustrations for Gerhardt Hauptmann's *The Weavers,* for Zola's *Germinal* and the Peasant War Series which were done between 1902–1908.

KOONING, WILLEM DE (1904–) Dutch-born painter and one of the leading Abstract Expressionists in America. De Kooning came to the United States in 1926 and turned from house painting to painting in an abstract manner about 1934. His work is more controlled than much other Abstract Expressionism. Recently he has turned toward representation of the human form (p. 258).

KUNIYOSHI, YASUO (1893–1953) American painter born in Japan. He came to the United States in 1906 and received his artistic training here. Kuniyoshi's early style was a mixture of Japan and the West, but later he became absorbed in the stream of American art. His art remained consciously naive, humorous, and full of fantasy; a famous motif is the triangular cow. His lines are sharp and precise and his colors luminous. In the late 1920's, his style changed noticeably, and he started painting in the subtle nuances of gray for which he became famous.

LE BRUN, CHARLES (1619–1690) French painter and director of the French Academy under Louis XIV. He was responsible for much of the decoration of the Palace of Versailles, including the frescoes of the Hall of Mirrors, tapestry cartoons, and designs for decorative sculpture. His type of decoration is referred to as "Louis Quatorze" (pp. 194–195).

LÉGER, FERNAND (1881–1955) Celebrated French painter and designer. Léger has a personal brand of cubism interrelated with the idea of "machine art." He painted modern urban life, gray, robot-like men, and large blocky structures. All the forms in his paintings are large and mechanical; their simple bold effect is reinforced by his use of areas of strong primary colors, red, yellow and blue. His composition is controlled with precision. Léger's portrayal of the machine age was not critical; rather, it reflected an optimism about the

Kollwitz: *Seeds For Sowing Must Not Be Milled.* Lithograph. 1942. Courtesy: Galerie St. Etienne, New York.

future of society. On his travels in the United States, for instance, Léger was greatly impressed by the vigor and architecture of New York. One of his later paintings, *Pleasures, Homage to Louis David* (p. 252), represents a return to a more classical portrayal of the human figure, warmer, although not very realistic. Léger's work includes décors for ballets, mosaics, ceramic work and a film (*Ballet Mechanique*).

LEHMBRUCK, WILHELM (1881–1919) German sculptor, whose distinctive personal style developed from trips to Italy and Paris. Lehmbruck fashioned slender elongated figures in stone, many with heads bent, suggesting tragedy. These sinuous silhouettes, brooding and introspective, were violently attacked by critics during his short lifetime. Best known among them are *The Kneeling Woman* (1911) and *The Fallen* (1915–1916). He also produced etchings and lithographs which include illustrations for the Bible and for Shakespeare.

LEONARDO DA VINCI (1452–1519) Italian genius of the Renaissance, a painter, musician, scientist, engineer and inventor. Leonardo speculated upon, wrote about and sketched every phenomenon of life—a child's growth in the womb, the laws of waves and currents, the solar system, weapons, fortifications, etc. (pp. 152–3). He was searching for underlying principles so that he could accurately paint outward appearances. Often Leonardo's interest faded after discovering these principles; consequently, few of his paintings are finished. As a painter, Leonardo was a genius at portraying real people such as the thoughtful and alert *Lady with Ermine* (p. 152). He often grouped figures to express the spiritual meaning of his subject as in the *Last Supper*, where one sees the individual reactions of the disciples at the moment Jesus says, "One of you shall betray me." Leonardo invented a delicate atmospheric shading called *sfumato* which he used to blend outlines of figures and to create an enigmatic shadow at the corners of his subject's eyes and mouth. This contributed largely to the psychological impact of his art. Leonardo's writings, which were unpublished for centuries, show him to be one of the most profound thinkers of his age on art.

LEVINE, JACK (1915–) American realistic painter concerned with themes of social satire. Using the profuse color and emotional intensity of the Expressionists, Levine paints social allegories meant as bitter commentaries on contemporary man's meanness, self-satisfaction and injustice. One of his most famous paintings is *The Feast of Pure Reason* (1937), which is now hung in the Museum of Modern Art in New York.

LIPCHITZ, JACQUES (1891–) Lithuanian-born sculptor who translated Cubism into the sculptural medium. As his style developed, Lipchitz turned to softer forms with greater emphasis on modeling. *Mother and Child* (p. 255) is from this later phase. Since 1941, Lipchitz has been living in America and has been working on large sculptures for buildings, such as *Prometheus and the Eagle* for the Ministry of Education in Rio de Janeiro.

LIPPI, FRA FILIPPO (c. 1406–1469) Florentine painter. Lippi's most frequent subjects were women and religious scenes, often of the Virgin. Although he painted realistically, Lippi imparted a gentle, human touch to his subjects. He popularized Masaccio's style.

LYSIPPUS (c. 400–350 B.C.) Greek sculptor. His *Apoxyomenos*, or "athlete scraping himself after the bath," illustrates the new elements Lysippus introduced into Greek sculpture. It has new slender proportions, represents a momentary action rather than a formal pose and reaches out into space in a natural gesture. Lysippus was official sculptor to Alexander the Great.

Lysippus: *Apoxyomenos*. Vatican Museum, Rome. (Alinari)

MACKE, AUGUST (1887–1914) German painter associated with the Blue Rider group. Macke's art derives essentially from Cézanne. He was later influenced by Delaunay. Except for a few abstract compositions in 1913–14, Macke's painting remained representational. His subjects were women and children gently portrayed in graceful and luminous colors.

MAILLOL, ARISTIDE (1861–1944) French sculptor who was originally (in the 1880's) a painter and designer. His painting style was at first impressionistic. Later, he used flat color planes and broad designs in the manner of Gauguin. Maillol became a sculptor at the age of 40. His sculptures are primarily female nudes, modeled with massive solid volumes. They have full peasant forms, de-individualized in order to express the symbolism of their titles (i.e., *Mediterranean*, *Leda*, etc.). Maillol restored the serenity, balance and stability of classical Greek sculpture to modern sculpture (p. 227).

MANET, EDOUARD (1832–1883) One of the leading French Impressionists. Manet was first revealed as an artistic innovator with the *Absinthe Drinker* (1859). In this painting, his characteristic technique was already apparent; the subject matter was a scene from contemporary life which fixed one moment of action; the color showed an absence of half-tone transitions between light and shade, and a limited palette based on a Spanish use of color. Throughout the 1860's Manet's technical innovations aroused violent critical attack (especially the frank treatment of the nudes in *Olympia* and *Le Dejeuner sur l'Herbe*) and he was importantly represented in the Salon des Refuses of 1863 by three paintings. *Mlle. Victorine in the Costume of an Espada* (p. 221) was one of them. Eventually Manet's flat objectivity was superseded by Impressionist techniques and sentimental subjects closer to the style of Monet.

MANSART, FRANCOIS (1598–1666) French architect after whom the "mansard" roof is named. Mansart added classical dignity to French architecture of his time, contrasting with the free, fanciful architecture of the Italian Baroque. Maisons-Lafitte, near Paris, was one of his first buildings in the style which became known as "Louis Quatorze."

MANTEGNA, ANDREA (1431–1506) Northern Italian painter. Mantegna's art is outstanding for a brilliant mastery of the new discoveries of foreshortening and diminishing perspective enriched by the warm colors of northern Italian art. Mantegna studied classical antiquity and the Roman ruins thoroughly. His *St. James on the Way to His Execution* is placed in a receding setting of Roman arches and buildings. The *Ceiling of the Gonzaga Bridal Chamber*, in Mantua (p. 161) again creates an illusion of receding space and diminishing figures. Most of his work was done in Padua and Mantua.

MARC, FRANZ (1880–1916) German Expressionist painter and, with Kandinsky, one of the founders of the Blue Rider group. Marc used color symbolically, regardless of the natural color of his subject, and most frequently his themes were animals (*Tower of Blue Horses*, *Red Horses*, *Fate of Animals*). In 1912 under Delaunay's influence, Marc's painting progressed toward a pattern of intersecting planes of color fusing foreground and background.

MARIN, JOHN (1870–1953) American painter best known for his watercolor landscapes in an expressionist style. In Paris from 1905 to 1911 Marin was exposed to Impressionism, Fauvism, Cubism and Expressionism, which transformed his realistic style. On his return, he painted numerous pictures of the vitality of New York and then settled in Maine, where he painted its landscape, shores and sea (p. 253). These paintings are generally panoramic views, seen as if through a window. Marin reduced his subject to a shorthand of brief, basic strokes. His colors are cheerful, somewhat Fauvist in nature.

MARINI, MARINO (1901–) Italian sculptor who began as a painter. His sculptured works are often small with rough textured surfaces. In one period (1930–1940) he worked primarily on representations of acrobats. Another favorite theme is "the horse and rider" (p. 255).

MARSH, REGINALD (1898–1954) American painter, cartoonist, and illustrator. Marsh's usual subject matter was city life, primarily that of New York City, its tumultuous crowds, its streets, bars and slums. He painted critically, representing the seamy or hypocritical, aspects of humanity.

MARTINI, SIMONE (1284–1344) Italian painter born in Siena who, after Giotto, was the most important Italian painter of his time. Like Giotto, Martini began to represent space, peopled by realistically proportioned figures having some emotional relationship to each other. Unlike Giotto, however, this emotionalism is not arresting. The famous *Annunciation* in the Uffizi is typical of the delicate forms, with a lyric quality of line, which Martini gracefully fits into the pattern of the frame. In 1340, Martini joined the court of the exiled popes at Avignon, in southern France. Here his fragile, elegant style made him a pioneer of the Gothic International style in Italy.

MASACCIO, TOMMASO DI SER GIOVANNI DI SIMONE GUIDI (1401–1428) Florentine painter. Masaccio was the first to apply Brunelleschi's discovery of perspective to painting, and in his short 27 years, he revolutionized painting. For the first time, we see simple and solid figures moving in a deep, atmospheric space. In his *Tribute Money*, three episodes take place, in the foreground, middleground, and distance, in groups separated by light and air. His *Expulsion* also in the Brancacci Chapel, employs the whole human body to express emotion. Painters for generations after Masaccio visited the Brancacci Chapel to study these frescoes. Another painting, the *Trinity*, in Santa Maria Novella, expresses mathematically the new principles of perspective. Christ is shown on the cross before a barrel vault which recedes into the wall as an extension of the spectator's space (pp. 133, 138).

MASTER OF NAUMBURG (active 1235–1260) A medieval sculptor whose work can be recognized in the cathedrals of Amiens, Metz, Mainz, but whose outstanding sculptures are the donors in the west choir of Naumburg Cathedral. These were innovations because of their dramatic content and individual characterization.

MATISSE, HENRI (1869–1954) French painter, sculptor and graphic artist. Through participation in the Fauve movement, Matisse learned to love color as a method of expressing joy and beauty. He was a genius at combining colors into patterns and decorative areas. Frequently he juxtaposed several different, highly colored patterned materials, such as striped material against a background of flowered wallpaper (p. 246). Matisse's favorite subjects were women, flowers and fruit. His forms often seem distorted because they eliminate details, but actually they are intended to express the essence of a body, a fruit, etc., rather than its exact outlines. After 1930 Matisse's style became flatter and he concentrated on large, simple line drawings and abstract shapes (p. 247). In 1949 he designed the stained glass and the decorations for a small Dominican chapel in Vence, France (p. 251). This chapel epitomizes the guiding principles of all his art—simplicity, serenity and joy.

Marsh: *Twenty Cent Movie*. 1936. Egg tempera on composition board. Whitney Museum of American Art, New York.

MICHELANGELO BUONARROTI (1475–1564) Italian sculptor, painter and architect, the most famous Florentine artist of the Renaissance. Michelangelo considered himself primarily a sculptor, although his fame rests largely on the magnificent paintings in the Sistine Chapel. These paintings, however, are compositions of statuesque bodies in painted form. Michelangelo studied anatomy until he was able to show the human body in every imaginable position. His large, muscular statues have an incredible firmness, strength and reality, yet their outlines are simple and clear. Another element of Michelangelo's art was the Renaissance stress on balanced and unified composition. Behind much of his work lay symbolic or religious meaning. The detail from the Sistine Ceiling showing Adam and God (*Creation of Man*, p. 154) contains many of the elements that make Michelangelo great: the modeling of the two bodies, the compositional balance of the two sides and the unity within each side, and the way God's encircling arm brings the two angels into the scene. We see God's power in his extended arm and man's helplessness in the languor of Adam who, in the next electric second, will be infused with life by God's touch. The touch is the center and the focus of the picture. Its suspense is magnificent. Among Michelangelo's other works are the *Pietà* in St. Peter's, the figures on the Medici tombs, and the design for St. Peter's and for the Laurentian Library (pp. 154–6, 275).

MIËS VAN DER ROHE, LUDWIG (1886–) German-American architect who shares honors with Gropius and Le Corbusier for the creation of the modern concept of building with free-flowing space instead of dividing interiors into box-like rooms. He was associated with the Bauhaus School until 1938 when he emigrated to Chicago. Miës' buildings are characteristically of glass and steel construction, symmetrically designed, with the emphasis on vertical and horizontal lines. Miës first won international fame with his German pavilion at the Barcelona Exhibition (1929) and again a year later with the Tugendhat House in Brno, Czechoslovakia (p. 260). In the United States, he first designed the skeletal steel-and-glass buildings for the campus of the Illinois Institute of Technology (where he headed the Department of Architecture), later, the famed Lakeshore Drive apartments in Chicago, and most recently, the striking bronze Seagram's Building in New York City.

MILLET, JEAN FRANÇOIS (1814–1875) Born of peasant stock in Normandy, Millet revealed talent at an early age and in 1938 went to Paris to study. He painted scenes of rural life, peasants at work, family groups and landscapes. Millet gave the peasant dignity; his subjects usually are standing or working quietly. Today Millet's paintings (*The Angelus, The Gleaners*) are considered by many to be overly sentimental.

MIRÓ, JOAN (1893–) Spanish artist associated with the Abstract Surrealism movement. Miró's surrealism lies midway between total abstraction and representational art. He uses bright primary colors, simple curved lines and amoeba-like forms. Some figures are recognizable, but often Miró's paintings have no meaning at all but are a spontaneous expression of a whimsical, charming dream world full of gaiety. At other times we sense an uneasy loneliness in the space surrounding the figures.

MODIGLIANI, AMADEO (1884–1920) Italian-born painter and sculptor, Modigliani moved to Paris at 22 and lived a restless and tragic life in Montmartre, finally dying of tuberculosis. His sculpture, powerful and primitive, was strongly influenced by Brancusi and by Negro art. Modigliani's portraits and nudes show a mastery of pure line, close in feeling to Botticelli. His languorous women with elongated faces and swan-like necks are among the best-known of all modern paintings.

MONDRIAN, PIET (1872–1944) Dutch painter of abstract geometric compositions. Mondrian's early paintings were landscapes and still lifes; later, in Paris (1910–1914) he turned to Cubism. After 1914, back in Holland, Mondrian developed his personal style of art which came to be called Neo-plasticism. He outlined his theories in *le Neo-plasticisme*: (1) all painting consists of line and color, therefore reduce them to the bare essentials; (2) universality of expression requires simplified forms; (3) the purer the color, the more universal it will be. Mondrian used only the primary colors, red, yellow and blue. His paintings are patterns of straight, black lines binding rectangles of white and the primary colors. Through his arrangement of lines and color areas he tried to achieve a dynamic balance and rhythm in his painting, not a static pattern (p. 257). This emphasis on balance of proportions had a strong influence on the Bauhaus and on modern architecture.

Modigliani: *Madam Pompadour.* 1915. The Art Institute of Chicago, The Joseph Winterbotham Collection.

MONET, CLAUDE (1840–1926) Leading French painter of the Impressionist movement. His *Impression-Sunrise*, exhibited in 1874, gave the movement its name. Monet painted outdoors only, at different times of day and in differing atmospheric conditions, in order to capture the color values of light. He (and the Impressionists) saw color not as a flat mass but as a result of reflections from neighboring objects. Shadows for instance, were not gray or black but were shades reflecting the color of the objects that cast the shadow. Monet did not outline the forms in his pictures but painted in many short strokes of color. Seen close up, his subjects are difficult to visualize, but they are perfectly clear when viewed from a distance. He painted many series of the same subject (*Water Lilies, Waterloo Bridge, Rouen Cathedral, Haystacks*) capturing the blue of dawn, the yellow-white glare of noon, the red of sunset and the gray of dusk (pp. 223–225).

MOORE, HENRY (1898–) British sculptor and painter, known best for his monumental figures in stone, wood and bronze which lie midway between realism and abstraction. He tried in these sculptures to build up an interplay of solid and void; thus he pierced his sculptures with great holes which, he says, "can have as much shape-meaning as solid mass." His works show connections with the great archaic traditions of Pre-Columbian and Egyptian art (p. 253).

MORRIS, WILLIAM (1834–1896) English poet, artist and social reformer. Morris was an opponent of the ugliness of industrialization and was distressed at the growing tendency to divorce art from utility. In 1861, he founded the firm of Morris and Company to produce furniture, wallpaper, tapestries and stained-glass windows in a fresh style, one more attractive than that of the current Victorian decoration. Morris revived the art of handprinting in his Kelmscott Press and through this press he was important in improving book design.

MOSES, "GRANDMA," ANNA MARY ROBERTSON (1860–) American painter who started painting at 76 and was "discovered" in 1938. Her subjects are genre scenes of American life, as for example, *The Harvest, Christmas at Home*, etc. Her unsophisticated folk art depends on rhythmical, flat design and fresh, clear coloring. Her paintings are widely reproduced on Christmas cards, ceramics, and fabrics.

MUNCH, EDVARD (1863–1944) Norwegian painter and graphic artist whose art gave strong impetus to later German Expressionism. With long, heavy lines and sharp contrasts of flat color, Munch created a very subjective art. A high-strung, tense person himself, he portrayed strongly emotional pictures of fear, loneliness and despair. His woodcuts are perhaps his most original and powerful works (p. 250).

MYRON (mid-5th century B.C.) Greek sculptor. Myron sought new effects in the relatively untried art of bronze-casting. In this technique he was able to increase the variety of poses and compositions available to the sculptor. His works were much admired and copied in antiquity, and one of them, the *Discobolus*, or discus thrower, is among the best known pieces of ancient sculpture (p. 42).

NASH, PAUL (1889–1946) British painter, graphic artist, and designer. He was official artist for both World Wars. Between wars he devoted his time to industrial arts. In 1933 Nash helped to form Unit One, a group devoted to the modern movement. His landscapes show Fauve and Cubist influences.

NEUMANN, BALTHASAR (1687–1753) German architect of some of the finest Baroque buildings. German Baroque was an adaptation of French Rococo, adding an airy atmosphere flooded with light and color. Among Neumann's masterpieces are the Wurzburg Residenz with its famous staircase and the pilgrimage church of Vierzehnheiligen ("Fourteen Saints") (p. 208).

NOGUCHI, ISAMU (1904–) Japanese-American sculptor, designer and writer. He studied with Brancusi in Paris in 1927–28 and was also influenced by Calder and Giacometti. He is known for his large reliefs, in which the rise and fall of the ground gives a vitality of form to his abstract compositions. Many of Noguchi's designs are practical—furniture that is adaptable and attractive from all sides (p. 261), gracefully shaped lamps making soft pools of light, murals, large interlocking stone sculptures for gardens, etc. He has also done a variety of works on commission ranging from dance sets to the ten-ton stainless steel relief at the entrance of the Associated Press building in New York.

NOLDE, EMIL (1867–1956) German Expressionist painter and graphic artist. After a start in the Impressionist idiom, his colors became bolder and more violent, depicting large grotesque forms. A deeply religious man, Nolde treated themes from the life of Christ with a savage cruelty that is awe-inspiring.

O'KEEFFE, GEORGIA (1887–) Contemporary American painter who began painting in an abstract manner, but in the 1920's turned to an abstract form of realism. Unlike other Cubist-Realists, however, she has not shown an interest in industrial motifs. Her art has a very feminine character. She paints such subjects as giant-sized flowers, landscapes and austere still lifes of bones and shells. The lines of her paintings are sharp and clear. O'Keeffe creates poetry from loneliness, silence and inner contemplation.

OROZCO, JOSE CLEMENTE (1883–1949) Mexican muralist and graphic artist, largely responsible for the artistic renaissance in Mexico. Orozco's paintings contain a message, either political or humanistic; he saw mankind both as the oppressed and the oppressors. His art is impressive because of its bold lighting of large, squarish figures or machines, for the dynamism of the lines and for its amazing technical virtuosity. A macabre element is always present, reminding one of the savage religious practices of Mexico's Aztec past. Orozco painted several huge murals in the United States: at Dartmouth College, the New School in New York City and Pomona College, California.

PALLADIO, ANDREA DE PIETRO (1508–1580) The most important Italian architect of the Late Renaissance. Palladio began as a stonemason in Vicenza and went on to become the leading North Italian master of the 16th century. His works include the Vicenza Basilica, the Villa Rotonda (p. 169) and the church of the Redentore in Venice. In 1554 he published a book on the antiquities of Rome and in 1570, his famous *Four Books of Architecture*. In the latter, which were very influential in 17th-century France and 18th-century England and America, Palladio set down architectural rules for the proportions of the orders. Formality, restraint and proportion were characteristic of Palladio's buildings and of those of his followers such as Inigo Jones in England and Thomas Jefferson in America.

PARMIGIANINO, FRANCESCO MAZZOLA (1503–1540) Italian Mannerist artist, from Parma. Parmigianino was an excellent portraitist and used the brilliant, glittering colors so loved by Mannerists. His *Madonna With the Long Neck*, in the Pitti Palace in Florence, shows how he elongated his figures, curving them into the picture in an attempt to create beauty in a different way from the classical harmony of the Renaissance.

PEALE, CHARLES WILLSON (1741–1827) American portrait painter, inventor, and founder of a private museum of natural history. His sons, Raphael and Rembrandt, were also painters, Peale is most famous for his extremely realistic portraits of George Washington, John Adams, James Madison and other well-known men of his day.

PHEIDIAS (c. 490–c. 415) Greek sculptor of the Classic age. Pheidias was an Athenian who was commissioned by Pericles to design the sculptures of the Parthenon on the Acropolis. He made the models from which the sculptors worked and supervised the whole extensive program. He made a colossal statue of Athena in bronze, his favorite material, and also one of ivory and gold for the sanctuary of the Parthenon. Pheidias' dynamic style marked the height of the Classic age. None of his original works have survived to the present day.

PICASSO, PABLO (1881–) Spanish-born painter and sculptor who is the most famous and probably the most influential artist of this century. Picasso was an artistic prodigy who, at the time he came to Paris in 1900, had mastered traditional art techniques. His tremendous ability and imagination resulted in many "styles" or "periods." The first was his Blue Period (1901–1905) of moody, sad scenes with elongated, emaciated figures; this was followed by pictures of harlequins and circus scenes, and his Rose Period (1905–1906) in which the subjects were more tender and sentimental. By 1909 he and Braque had invented Cubism, a movement of tremendous significance in modern art. In Cubism, a form is broken into planes and volumes and portrayed as if seen from several angles simultaneously. *Les Demoiselles d'Avignon* was one of the first paintings in the Cubist manner (p. 252). From 1920–1925, Picasso was in his Classical period of portraying Grecian women with straight noses and ponderous forms. Around the 1930's he inclined toward Surrealism in paintings such as *Guernica*, an allegorical account of Spain's plight during its Civil War. At present he paints in no one style, but lets each subject develop itself. His active imagination creates unceasingly in almost every medium (graphics, sculpture, ceramics, etc.), although each bears an unmistakable personal stamp (pp. 248–252).

PIRANESI, GIOVANNI BATTISTA (1720–1778) Italian engraver and etcher, well known for his series of views of Roman antiquities in which the archaeological detail is balanced by a strong sense of the picturesque. His fame rests on the *Carceri*, or prison, etchings (c. 1745), a series of fantastic compositions which foreshadow the Romanticism of the late 18th and 19th centuries.

PISSARRO, CAMILLE (1830–1903) An early French Impressionist, whose style developed under the influence of Corot. Pissarro never abandoned the order and discipline of early Impressionism for decomposition of subject as later Impressionists did. In fact, for a time late in his life, he painted in the orderly, unified "pointillism" of Seurat. Pissarro's main subjects were landscapes and city scenes. As a person, Pissarro was the most beloved of the Impressionist group. He was the oldest and in many ways a father to the other painters, moderating their squabbles and giving vital encouragement to younger artists, particularly Degas, Cézanne, Gauguin, and van Gogh. He watched over them, giving suggestions for improving their styles, boarded them at his home and helped them financially. The range of Pissarro's production was great and included etching and lithography.

POLLAIUOLO, ANTONIO (c. 1432–1498) Italian painter, engraver, and sculptor whose major interest was the study of the human body in motion. His *Hercules and Antaeus* (p. 137) shows his mastery of anatomy in a moment of dramatic, energetic action. A later engraving, *Battle of the Naked Men*, shows Pollaiuolo to be a precursor of Michelangelo in the vigorous and expressive use of the nude figure in action.

POLLOCK, JACKSON (1912–1956) American painter and leading figure in the movement of Abstract Expressionism. His early painting was inspired by his teacher, Thomas Hart Benton, and by Albert Ryder. By 1942, however, he had arrived at a forceful abstract style which derived its power from curving, mazelike lines. His manner of dripping paint on canvas became famous. For Pollock, the physical act of painting was self-expression. As is characteristic of the modern school, many of his canvases are very large (p. 258).

POLYKLEITOS (5th century B.C.) Famous Greek sculptor. Polykleitos was a younger contemporary of Pheidias and, like Pheidias, had a great reputation during his lifetime. Unfortunately, none of his originals is left to us. The best known copy, a Roman one, is of his *Doryphoros*, or "spear holder."

POUSSIN, NICOLAS (1594–1665) French painter who lived most of his life in Italy. Poussin was much attracted to classical Antiquity and to the calm compositions of Raphael. He painted mythological, historical and religious scenes in quiet, well-ordered landscapes. His style opposed the current vogue of Italian Baroque led by his contemporary, Rubens. It was typically French in its restraint, precision and its cool colors (p. 190).

PRAXITELES (4th century B.C.) Athenian sculptor. His best known work is that of the god Hermes holding the infant Dionysus; it is of marble and is in the museum at Olympia in Greece (p. 43). Praxiteles' works were extremely popular in ancient times and many copies have survived, particularly his sculptures of Aphrodite.

PUCELLE, JEAN (active 1327–1347) French miniaturist. Pucelle was one of a group of late medieval painters who gathered at the courts of Burgundy and Paris to paint miniatures for aristocratic patrons. His manuscript illuminations, often of a secular nature, were distinguished by the use of sharp enamel-like colors and an interest in explicit detail.

RAPHAEL, SANZIO (1483–1520) Italian painter of the High Renaissance. Raphael studied in Perugino's workshop in his native town of Urbino. From Perugino he learned the symmetrical composition of space and serene beauty of figure which can be seen in his early work, *The Marriage of the Virgin* (p. 147). Raphael moved to Florence around 1504 and there, influenced by the work of Leonardo and Michelangelo, his figures became muscular and more realistic, his colors stronger and his composition less artificial. Raphael later moved to Rome and became immensely successful. He was commissioned to decorate the Pope's library in fresco, decorated other rooms in the Vatican in fresco and drew cartoons for Vatican tapestries, (pp. 150–151).

REDON, ODILON (1840–1916) French Symbolist painter and graphic artist. Redon's art explored the world of dream and mystery. He painted vases of flowers, dreamy faces, and scenes with religious overtones, using soft, dematerialized forms and luminous colors.

REMBRANDT, HARMANSZ VAN RIJN (1606–1669) Outstanding Dutch painter who, early in his career, was a popular portraitist of well-to-do families in Amsterdam. Rembrandt's portraits are instantly recognizable by the rich texture of costume and by his use of chiaroscuro to highlight the sitter's face and hands against a dark background. Like Frans Hals, Rembrandt painted several group portraits, such as *The Sampling Officials of the Drapers' Guild* (p. 196). In 1642, his career took a turn for the worse. A large group portrait, the *Night Watch*, was considered a failure, and his beloved wife Saskia died. After this, Rembrandt painted an increasing number of religious subjects in which he aimed to convey the spiritual meaning behind the scene. In the religious scenes and portraits of this later period, Rembrandt developed his mastery of chiaroscuro. He became increasingly expert at depicting personality. Velvety shadows at the corners of the eyes and mouth create the introspective mood of these later portraits and self-portraits. Their psychological insight has never been equaled. Rembrandt's etchings are unequaled in simplicity and excellence (pp. 196–199).

RENOIR, PIERRE AUGUSTE (1841–1919) Famous French painter and sculptor. Working with Monet, Renoir developed an Impressionist style, dissolving forms in light. His colors were vibrant and glowing, with special emphasis on brilliant shades of red. This early work, of dance hall scenes and riverside landscapes, appeared in several of the Impressionist exhibitions. Later in life, Renoir returned to more solid forms and greater compositional unity. Women, their sensuality, their gaiety and their affectionate natures, are one of Renoir's most frequent subjects. He loved life and usually painted gay scenes with carefree people enjoying life (pp. 228–229).

REYNOLDS, SIR JOSHUA (1723–1792) English portrait painter, very popular with society in the 18th century. Reynolds' portraits continued the tradition of van Dyck, representing aristocratic persons, richly dressed. In 1768, he became the first president of the Royal Academy in London. Failing eyesight ended his career in 1786 (p. 212).

RIBERA, JOSÉ (1591–1652) Spanish painter who worked in Naples, where he learned and adopted the extreme chiaroscuro technique of Caravaggio. Ribera was very popular with his Spanish patrons. His compositions, nearly all religious, are emotional and intense and in later years, even brutally realistic.

RICHARDSON, HENRY H. (1838–1886) American architect and pioneer in the development of modern architecture. He is best known for a simple, severe style of structure based on the Romanesque. The Allegheny County Jail in Pittsburgh is a masterful example of this style, but the building most influential in its effect on modern architecture is the Marshall Field Warehouse in Chicago (p. 245), constructed of an iron skeleton covered with great ashlar blocks.

RIVERA, DIEGO (1886–1957) One of the foremost Mexican painters, who has concentrated primarily on large murals and frescoes. Despite a long stay in Europe, Rivera did not identify himself with artistic movements there, but returned to Mexico and created a bold national style. He was an important force in Mexico's artistic renaissance and helped contribute to a revival of fresco painting in Mexico and the United States. Rivera's subjects are drawn from the history of Mexico and Mayan civilization, concentrating on revolutions and events with social and political significance. His art has a direct popular appeal. In the early 1930's Rivera painted frescoes in San Francisco, Detroit and New York.

ROBBIA, LUCA DELLA (1399–1482) Florentine sculptor. Luca is famous for his marble *cantoria* in the Cathedral at Florence, but is even better known as the head of his family's workshop which produced reliefs in glazed and colored terra cotta. These were very popular and can be found today in countless churches and private houses throughout Tuscany.

RODIN, AUGUSTE (1840–1917) Great French sculptor of the 19th century whose work ranges from the superb to the sentimental. In the former category, *The Burghers of Calais* (p. 226) is a study of six individuals. The way light and shadow play over these figures in order to create a mood of despair is Impressionism in sculpture. In the second, sentimental, category are his popular and mystical sculptures, *The Kiss* and *The Hand of God*. The characteristic materials of Rodin's work are craggy bronzes and smooth marbles, partially released from their rough marble matrix. Nearly all of Rodin's major commissions were poorly received by the public. His simpler works were very popular, however, and often he made several casts from a mold; consequently copies of *The Thinker* can be seen in several museums today. The *Gate of Hell*, a monumental door meant to be a formal and iconographical summary of his work, was unfinished at his death.

ROSSO, FIORENTINO IL (1494–1540) Florentine painter. Under Michelangelo's influence, Rosso developed a dramatic Mannerist style, shown in his *Moses Defending Jethro's Daughters*, where muscular figures in violent action are crowded into a too confined space. He was called to France in 1530 by Francis I where he helped decorate Fountainebleau. His frescoes there exercised a major influence on French painting.

ROSZAK, THEODORE (1907–) Polish-born American sculptor and painter. His early sculpture was in the manner of the Constructivists. After 1945, however, his style changed radically: the abstract geometric order of his early constructions was replaced by dynamic forms in welded and brazed metal. These forms are meant "to be blunt reminders of primordial strife and struggle" (p. 259).

Rivera: *Liberation of the Peon.* Fresco. Philadelphia Museum of Art.

ROUAULT, GEORGES (1871–1958) French painter and graphic artist. As a child, Rouault was apprenticed to a maker of stained-glass and here he acquired his subsequent characteristic style, luminous colors surrounded by thick black lines like the lead in medieval windows. Rouault was an original member of the Fauve group, but later he moved into the passionate idiom of German Expressionism. His most frequent subjects are religious, or of characters drawn from the lower ranks of society. They are always treated with sympathy and sorrow (p. 251).

ROUSSEAU, HENRI (1844–1910) French primitive painter, nicknamed "le Douanier" (the customs officer) because of his former profession. Rousseau began painting at the age of forty. He painted two-dimensionally in bold, simple designs which are nevertheless minutely detailed. Among his subjects are remarkable, exotic scenes of patternlike, tropical jungles with wild animals peering out, which have a childlike combination of magic and reality. Rousseau also painted portraits, patriotic scenes, landscapes, family groups and allegories.

Rousseau: *The Dream*. 1910. Museum of Modern Art, New York. Gift of Nelson Rockefeller.

RUBENS, PETER PAUL (1577–1640) Greatest of Flemish painters, trained in Antwerp. Rubens spent his early years, until 1608, in Mantua where he was strongly influenced by the works of Titian and other Venetian masters. His art was the artistic epitome of the Baroque, huge canvasses with swirling composition and filled with active figures. He used rich colors, gaily combined; later in life he strove for even greater color effects, especially with tones of red. Rubens' subjects were battle pictures, mythological scenes, bacchanals, nudes and portraits (pp. 186–187). A huge shop of trained assistants helped Rubens with details on many of his largest works. His most important assistant and pupil was van Dyck.

RUISDAEL, JACOB VAN (1628–1682) Dutch landscape painter, trained by his father and uncle. The moods of Ruisdael's paintings range from melancholy, romantic scenes of marshes and woods to calm, warm pictures in golden light such as his *Wheat Fields* (p. 200).

RYDER, ALBERT PINKHAM (1847–1917) American painter. With Homer and Eakins, Ryder was one of the great independent artists of the post-Civil War period. Ryder is best known for his marines in which dark sailboats move across moonlit seas. Firmly defined shapes and somber colors thickly applied emphasize the symbolic content of his work. His imagination was nourished by occasional sea voyages and solitary walks around New York harbor. He had only modest success until late in his career when he had become a recluse and was reluctant to part with his works (p. 242).

SAARINEN, EERO (1910–) Finnish-born American architect whose building designs are among the most imaginative of the present day. Saarinen attempts to express the purpose of his building: sweeping curved lines bending up at the edge for such buildings as the hockey rink at Yale, which should give the onlooker a light and happy feeling; a simple cylindrical stone building surrounded by a moat and lighted inside only by a skylight for the contemplative atmosphere of the chapel at Massachusetts Institute of Technology. Saarinen is foremost among architects who insist on the landscaping (fountains, trees, pools, lawn) of a building as of utmost importance. He studied sculpture in Paris and architecture at Yale University and then worked with his architect father, Eliel Saarinen, on various projects. Among his outstanding independent designs are the chapel and shell-domed auditorium at Massachusetts Institute of Technology, the General Motors Technical Institute at Warren, Michigan, and the Trans-World Airlines terminal at Idlewild Airport in New York (p. 262).

SAINT-GAUDENS, AUGUSTUS (1848–1907) Most successful American sculptor of the 19th century. Saint-Gaudens studied at Cooper Union and the National Academy of Design in New York, then spent six years studying in Paris and Rome. After his return to America in 1873, he made numerous portraits and many public monuments. The *Adams Memorial* in Rock Creek Cemetery, Washington, D. C., *Lincoln*, in Grant Park, Chicago, *Admiral Farragut*, in Madison Park, New York City, and *The Puritan* in Springfield, Massachusetts, are among his more important works. Saint-Gaudens brought a free pictorial modeling and sensitive treatment of bronze surfaces to his works, using techniques much freer than the older classical styles which had lingered on in American sculpture. He was able to create the mood of the subject without being unrealistic or overly dramatic.

Saint-Gaudens: *The Puritan*.

SARGENT, JOHN SINGER (1856–1925) American portrait painter, who was born in Florence, studied in Paris, and spent most of his life abroad. Sargent was immensely successful as a fashionable portraitist on both sides of the Atlantic, probably because he portrayed his sitters as elegant, charming people. His paintings are noteworthy for the virtuosity of his brushwork and their brilliant surface quality. Less successful than Sargent's portraits were his mural decorations (Museum of Fine Arts and the Public Library, Boston).

SARTO, ANDREA DEL (1486–1531) Italian painter of the Florentine School. In 1518–19 he painted at the court of Francis I. His earlier works, such as the *Madonna of the Harpies*, have the subtle modeling and transparent glazes of Leonardo. Later, under Michelangelo's influence, his forms became more ample and complex, as in the *Madonna del Sacco*, at the Annunziata, Florence.

SASSETTA (Stefano di Giovanni) (c. 1392–1451) Sienese painter. Sassetta's subjects were religious and, in the Sienese tradition, were dominated by effects of line and color. We can see, however, the influence of the contemporary Renaissance discoveries of Massaccio in Sassetta's attempt to portray plastic figures, depth and perspective (p. 130).

SCHONGAUER, MARTIN (died 1491) German painter and engraver. In his paintings and graphic work, this South German artist merged Gothic linearity with a new sense of realism. His most famous painting is the *Virgin in the Rose Arbor* (1473) in St. Martin's, Colmar.

SCOPAS (4th century B.C.) Greek sculptor. Only fragments of Scopas' work have come down to us but those, and literary descriptions from antiquity, show that he specialized in sculptures showing emotional intensity and violent movement. He cut deep, shadowed eye sockets as one way of acheiving these effects. Scopas' work greatly influenced Hellenistic (late Greek) sculpture, such as that at Pergamon.

SEURAT, GEORGES (1859–1891) One of the primary Post-Impressionist painters who created a new style from Impressionism. Influenced by the new scientific literature on optics and color, Seurat evolved "Divisionism" (often called "Pointillism") in which complementary pure colors are applied in small round dots and mixed only by juxtaposition of areas. Unlike the fleeting effects sought by the Impressionists, Seurat produced a mathematically ordered composition. His most famous work, *Sunday Afternoon on the Grande Jatte*, has numerous figures in profile which, with the trees, provide strong vertical accents. These are counteracted by horizontal accents in the shadows. In this painting, Seurat has created an illusion of great depth (pp. 234–5).

SHAHN, BEN (1898–) American painter and graphic artist, born in Lithuania. Shahn developed a style with flat colors and a sharp line. In the Depression years he gave himself to themes of social criticism (*The Passion of Sacco and Vanzetti*). Tremendously versatile, he has worked on murals, advertising commissions, magazine illustrations, ballet sets, and posters. Shahn's early experience as a lithographer's apprentice and as a documentary photographer greatly affected the content, the draughtmanship and the color massing of the works on social themes for which he is best known. Since the late 1940's Shahn has turned from themes of an unfulfilled humanity to a private mythology of phoenixes, rooftop antennas and lost letters of the Hebrew alphabet. We can still recognize however the sureness of his line and the stark juxtaposition of warm blues and reds.

Shahn: *Troubled Man*. 1958. Drawing. Courtesy: The Downtown Gallery, N.Y.

SHEELER, CHARLES (1883–) American painter. Sheeler was influenced by Post-Impressionism and Cubism and his art style went through both of these phases. In 1912 he returned to New York and became a photographer. Eventually he turned to an objective art style based on careful, almost photographic, observation. A series of paintings of the River Rouge plant of the Ford Motor Company (1927–1930) awakened his generation to the clean, severe beauty of functional design.

SIGNORELLI, LUCA (c. 1450–1523) Italian painter of the Umbrian school, who probably studied with Piero della Francesca. Signorelli's outstanding works are the frescoes of *The End of the World* in Orvieto Cathedral (1499–1504). His nude figures indicate an interest in anatomy and expressive movement prefiguring Michelangelo, who borrowed from them for his own *Last Judgment* in the Sistine Chapel. Signorelli also painted one of the wall scenes in the Sistine Chapel (p. 139).

SISLEY, ALFRED (1839–1899) French Impressionist artist of English descent, Sisley painted landscapes almost exclusively. In 1862 at the École des Beaux Arts, he met Monet, Renoir and Bazille, and thereafter he remained within the Impressionist circle. Sisley tried to achieve the color effects of Impressionism without going so far as to dissolve his subject. Therefore, his quiet little pictures retained the realism of early Impressionism.

Sluter: *Well of Moses*, Abbey, Dijon. (Giraudon)

SLUTER, CLAUS (active 1375–1406) Flemish sculptor who came to the court of Burgundy in 1385 to work for Philip the Bold. One of his main works is the *Well of Moses* in the monastery at Champmol. Here, Sluter frees sculpture, which in Gothic times had been only a subsidiary of architecture. He shows four prophets whose faces are individualized and treated with such exceptional naturalism that one even wears glasses. Their swirling draperies and bent attitudes further illustrate the new realism. Some other works are portraits of Philip the Bold and his wife on their tomb and the portal of the Chartreuse at Champmol.

STEEN, JAN (1626–1679) Dutch genre painter and chronicler of middle-class life, who painted his surroundings in witty scenes from Delft, where he leased a brewery, and from Leyden, where he kept a tavern. He never seems to be serious nor are his colorful pictures free from misdrawing, and yet most of the 700 known paintings are enjoyable.

STUART, GILBERT (1755–1828) American portrait painter who was trained in London. He returned in 1793 to America where his loose style, catching the personalities of his sitters, made him extremely popular. Stuart is famous today for painting numerous portraits of George Washington (p. 213).

SUTHERLAND, GRAHAM (1903–) Contemporary British painter whose style is Surrealistic in nature. Sutherland paints landscapes composed of disquieting, ominous forms, often thorns or thorn bushes. He is also known for his expressionistic portraits of celebrated personalities, such as Sir Winston Churchill and Somerset Maugham (p. 253).

TANGUY, YVES (1900–1955) French-born painter who emigrated to the United States in 1939. Tanguy joined the ranks of the Surrealists in 1925. His paintings are subjective in feeling and are filled with amoebic forms executed with great precision. Because of these forms and their cold, diaphanous colors, his compositions recall undersea scenes.

TIEPOLO, GIOVANNI BATTISTA (1696–1770) Venetian painter, the last master of wall and ceiling fresco in the Baroque tradition. Turbulent movement, rich color and light atmosphere make Tiepolo's frescoes an elegant décor. His brushwork was facile and his forms quickly sketched. Most of Tiepolo's work decorates Venetian churches and palaces but his greatest frescoes are in the hall and over the staircase of the Wurzburg Residenz (p. 208). To be fully appreciated, Tiepolo's frescoes should be seen in their settings where figures reach up from the walls into the airy space of the ceiling (p. 209).

TINTORETTO, JACOPO ROBUSTI (1518–1594) One of the leading painters of 16th-century Venice. Tintoretto was strongly influenced by the colors used by Titian, which he attempted to combine with the drawing of Michelangelo. In such paintings as *Saint Mark Rescuing a Slave*, intense drama is created not only by the choice of subject—the miracle of St. Mark rescuing a Christian slave from execution—but also by the eager crowd surging forward around the scene. The composition is so arranged that observers of the painting peer over the shoulders of the crowd, becoming a part of it, and sharing their excitement. In later paintings, such as those in the Scuola di San Rocco, Tintoretto began to use light and space to focus attention on the center of interest, and in *The Last Supper*, painted in 1592, the strong diagonal composition is a herald of the Baroque style that was to follow (p. 165). Geometric composition, exuberance and drama, and robustness of color and line are all typical of this master of the High Renaissance.

TITIAN, TIZIANO VECELLI (1477–1576) Italian painter, the greatest of the Venetian school. Creating an immense number of paintings, Titian is most famous perhaps for the glowing colors he was able to achieve, especially the golden tones which pervade his compositions. The *Assumption of the Virgin* is his most famous work. Titian's subjects included both many scenes from mythology, such as *Bacchus and Ariadne* (p. 160), and portraits, too. His later paintings show an interest in the uses of light foreshadowing the Baroque, as in the *Rape of Europa* (p. 164).

TOBEY, MARK (1890–) Self-taught American painter, active mainly on the West Coast. He developed a calligraphic, highly intricate form of abstraction by the early 1940's. His graceful, almost lyrical patterns are designed to convey emotion; the brushstrokes, in Tobey's words, are "the symbol of the spirit."

TOULOUSE-LAUTREC, HENRI DE (1864–1901) French painter, graphic artist and master draughtsman of the 19th century, who brought the art of the poster to a high degree of development. With fluent, sinuous lines, Toulouse-Lautrec captured the essential traits of his subject matter: cabaret performers, dancers, brothel scenes, and the like. He was not a follower of any special school of painting, nor did he have pupils or disciples. His posters for the various Montmartre cabarets he frequented and his illustrations for satirical journals brought him an enduring reputation (p. 241).

TURNER, JOSEPH MALLORD WILLIAM (1775–1851) English painter, born in London. Turner was a precocious young artist who first exhibited in the Royal Academy when he was only 16 years old. He began working as a watercolorist but by the 1800's he was imitating the grand landscapes of Claude Gellée, whose work he greatly admired. Turner's large oil paintings, such as *Crossing the Brook*, were attacked by critics as being unfinished. Various trips to Italy increased his interest in the effects of light, and of dramatic effects created by the use of swirling colors. His later works present magical visions of forms dissolved in colored atmosphere (p. 222).

UCCELLO, PAOLO (c. 1396–1477) Italian painter of the Florentine school. Uccello became fascinated with the use of linear perspective to indicate depth in his paintings. In the *Battle of San Romano* he explored the techniques of foreshortening and angular placement of the battle figures as an exercise in the complex laws of perspective. His work in the uses of perspective influenced many later artists, especially Piero della Francesca, who based their perspective studies on Uccello's paintings (pp. 138, 140).

UTRILLO, MAURICE (1883–1955) French painter of Paris streets and buildings. As a youth Utrillo was an alcoholic. He started painting under the inspiration of his mother, Suzanne Valadon, herself a notable artist. His early canvases of Paris scenes, in delicate hues of greens and grays, are perhaps his best works. Utrillo belongs to no particular school of modern painting. He carried on the tradition of realism in a personal style based on linear structure and a fine mastery of color.

VAN DYCK, SIR ANTHONY (1599–1641) Flemish painter of the 17th century. Van Dyck was chief assistant to the great Baroque painter, Peter Paul Rubens, before beginning his own career which culminated in England as court painter to Charles I. His portraits were less forceful than Rubens' but were more sensitive to the sitter's character, although they usually tended to show the court ladies at their most elegant best. His paintings established the tradition of aristocratic British portraiture that was continued in the 18th century by Reynolds and Gainsborough (p. 202).

VASARI, GIORGIO (1511–1574) Italian painter and architect of the Florentine school, and art historian. After studying under Michelangelo and del Sarto, Vasari was appointed court artist to the Medici princess, in which capacity he designed the Uffizi courtyard and produced the frescoes in the Palazzo Vecchio. He was an able architect but an indifferent painter. His book, *Lives of the Most Eminent Painters, Sculptors and Architects,* published in 1550, is an invaluable source of information about his own and earlier centuries.

VELASQUEZ, DIEGO RODRIGUEZ DE SILVA Y (1599–1660) Spanish painter who was appointed court artist to Philip IV at Madrid in 1623. His early work, such as *Los Borochos*, or the *Water-seller of Seville*, recalls the intensity and naturalism of Caravaggio. In his mature period Velasquez mastered the depiction of forms in light, as seen in *Las Meñinas* (The Maids in Waiting), without, however, equaling the boundless space of Rembrandt or Rubens. With a few touches of his brush, Velasquez was able to convey a feeling of softness or strength, or the sensuous effects of rich fabrics. The influence of his style upon Manet and his contemporaries was profound, and even the Impressionists owe part of their inspiration to his example (p. 188).

VELDE, HENRY VAN DE (1863–1957) Belgian architect, decorator and educator. Beginning in the idiom of the Art Nouveau, van de Velde moved in the 1900's toward a massive and plastic type of architecture in the school he built at Weimar, where heavy mansards are used together with plain white stucco walls His masterwork is, perhaps, the theater for the Werkbund Exhibition at Cologne with its curved walls and roof.

VERMEER, JAN (1632–1675) Dutch painter and resident of Delft. Although only forty known paintings survive, they establish his reputation as the greatest colorist among the Dutch painters of his century. His cool, glowing domestic interiors, although simply composed, often present complicated moral allegories, (i.e., *Fame*, in Vienna). The miraculous precision with which he showed forms and colors bring to life the simple, controlled genre paintings of this great master (p. 201).

VERONESE, PAOLO CAGLIARI (1528–1588) Italian painter of the Venetian school. He studied under his uncle in Verona, worked in Mantua, and finally in Venice where he attempted to surpass Titian and Tintoretto with his studied elegance and sensuous textures. His frescoes at Saint Sebastian, in Venice, and his *Feast in the House of Levi* (p. 168) are typical of his decorative style which sacrificed religious expressiveness and historical accuracy to artistic ends.

VERROCCHIO, ANDREA DEL (1435–1488) Italian sculptor and painter of the Florentine school who began as a goldsmith and student of Donatello. His painting, *The Baptism of Christ*, and bronze sculptures of *David* and *Doubting Thomas* have an intensity of expression and a violent energy, as does the equally vigorous *Colleoni* equestrian monument in Venice (p. 137).

VILLON, JACQUES (1875–) French painter and graphic artist; brother of the sculptor Duchamp-Villon and the painter Marcel Duchamp. For a time, he concentrated on making posters and newspaper cartoons. In painting he first experimented with the violent Fauve colors, and then in 1911 he adopted Cubism and helped form a group called the Section d'Or. Villon's Cubism has a lyrical quality with a soft, tasteful color scheme and an unforced, limpid structure.

Villon: *Baudelaire with Pedestal.* Etching. Museum of Modern Art, New York. Gift of Victor S. Riesenfeld.

VLAMINCK, MAURICE DE (1876–1958) French painter and novelist. He was an original member of the Fauve or "wild beast" group of 1905, and his early canvases were painted in a robust, enthusiastic style of clashing colors and violent brushstrokes (p. 251). After 1907 Vlaminck came under Cézanne's influence. He began painting balanced and well-constructed compositions. His palette grew darker. The somber landscapes of his late years are a far cry from the Fauve exuberance of his youth.

VUILLARD, EDOUARD (1868–1940) French painter, identified with the Nabi group of the 1890's. Taking his themes from everyday incidents and intimate scenes of family life, he painted two-dimensionally in exquisitely fine shades of color. His canvases are intimate, enchantingly imprecise, and essentially Impressionist in spirit, yet they never lack a solid architectural structure. In his late years he devoted himself more and more to portraiture.

WATTEAU, ANTOINE (1684–1721) French artist of Flemish origin. Watteau developed a shimmering, light-filled style suited to the intimate and delicate world of the Rococo, as opposed to the more robust Baroque. His canvases are filled with graceful, imaginary scenes of lovely parks, peopled with beautiful ladies and gallant gentlemen. His diploma at the Academy was won for the *Embarkation for Cythera* (p. 204) and his last work was the famous shop sign for the art dealer, Gersaint.

WEBER, MAX (1881–) Russian-born American painter and graphic artist. In 1905 he went to Paris and worked with Matisse. From predominantly Fauve beginnings, Weber turned to semi-abstract compositions in the Cubist idiom from 1912 onward. After an interlude in which he returned to representational art, Weber's style became, once more, abstract and Expressionistic in color.

WEST, BENJAMIN (1738–1820) American-born painter who studied in Rome, then settled in London, where he succeeded Sir Joshua Reynolds as president of the Royal Academy. His historical, mythological, and religious subjects in the "grand manner" presaged the styles of both David and Delacroix.

WEYDEN, ROGIER VAN DER (c. 1399–1464) Flemish painter whose agitated, emotional style contrasts with the restraint of his contemporary, Jan van Eyck. Interested in depicting movement rather than space, most of his compositions are like relief sculpture, as is the *Descent from the Cross*, and the Beaune altarpiece of the *Last Judgement*. Despite an Italian sojourn his work shows little Renaissance influence (p. 129).

WHISTLER, JAMES ABBOTT MCNEILL (1834–1903) American-born painter who studied in Paris. Influenced by Courbet, Degas, and the then current interest in Japanese prints, Whistler stressed purely aesthetic values in his work, often entitling his paintings merely "arrangements," "symphonies," or "nocturnes." Unlike his contemporaries,

Wood: *American Gothic.* 1930. Friends of American Art, The Art Institute of Chicago.

Whistler was not so much interested in the Impressionistic effects of light and color, but was concerned with patterns. In 1877 he was the subject of a sensational trial with the art critic, John Ruskin. Ruskin had publicly insulted Whistler and his work, and the artist sued, successfully, for damages. Whistler also made many etchings, some of the finest of which were executed in Venice (p. 240).

WOOD, GRANT (1892–1942) American painter of local themes from his native Iowa. Like John Curry and Thomas Hart Benton, he is known as a painter of the American scene. His hard, harsh realism is very effective in portraits, like the famous *American Gothic*. His landscape painting, however, is replete with rather weak stylizations.

WREN, SIR CHRISTOPHER (1632–1723) English architect, also a professor of astronomy and a celebrated mathematician. His style, although based on that of Inigo Jones, was modified by a sojourn in France. After the great fire of 1666, Wren rebuilt most of London's churches—over fifty between 1670 and 1714. Small parish churches like St. Mary-le-Bow (p. 202) were topped by intricate slender spires. His masterpiece, St. Paul's Cathedral, with its massive dome, combines Jones' Palladian Classicism with more sculptural Baroque forms.

WRIGHT, FRANK LLOYD (1869–1959) The most famous American architect and one of the century's greatest imaginative minds. Wright rejected traditional lines and building materials, stressing the adaptation of a structure to its environment. The use of concrete as a building material, the opening up and fusing of interior and exterior space, and the relating of a building to its setting are all typical of Wright's work. Masterful logic of form and construction are enriched by an ecstatic nature worship. Such buildings as Taliesin West, in Arizona, Falling Waters (a house cantilevered over a swift-running brook) in Pennsylvania, and the Guggenheim Museum in New York indicate the vast range and power of Wright's imagination (p. 261).

ZORACH, WILLIAM (1887–) Lithuanian-born American sculptor. Zorach started out as a painter, and was strongly influenced by Matisse, and later, by Cubism. After 1922 he devoted himself entirely to sculpture. The basic debt of his sculpture is to the primitive art of the past—African, archaic Greek, and Egyptian.

COMPARATIVE CHRONOLOGY OF PERIODS OF ART

DATES	EUROPE	EGYPT	MIDDLE EAST	CHINA	JAPAN	INDIA-INDONESIA
20,000 B.C. 4000	Cave paintings Lascaux and Altamira c. 15,000 B.C.		Mesopotamian,			
3000		Archaic Period	Iranian pottery			Neolithic period Neolithic pottery
2000		Djoser's pyramid Old Kingdom	Sumerian culture Akkad dynasty Neo-Sumerian	Neolithic period		
1000	Cretan culture Mycenaean civilization Stonehenge (c. 1500 B.C.) Greek culture emerges	Middle Kingdom New Kingdom Ikhnaton (1370–1352) Tutankhamen (1358–1350) Rameses II (1292–1225)	Old Babylonian (Middle Assyrian) Assyrian art	1726—Shang-yin 1122—Chou dynasty	Jomon pottery	
500	Geometric art Orientalizing period Etruscan Archaic period Early Kouri	Late Period	Scythian animal art 550—Achaemenid (Persian) art			
1 A.D.	Age of Pericles (460–429) Parthenon (442–437) Praxiteles Lysippus Hellenistic period 27 B.C. Roman period	323—Alexander's conquest Ptolemaic period (Greek rule) Roman rule 30 B.C.	Alexander's conquest—Hellenic influence spreads Parthian era	206—Han dynasty	Ya Yoi pottery	Alexander conquers northern India. Greek influence on Buddhist art in Gandara Ajanta Cave paintings (200 B.C.–500 A.D.)
500	Colosseum (A.D. 70–82) Pantheon (27 B.C.–120 A.D.?) Christian art emerges Byzantium established 476—Rome falls	395 A.D.	Sassanian (Persian) period	Tatar invasions Wei dynasty	Culture of burial mounds Haniwas	Gupta dynasty
1000	Medieval art Byzantine era (in Near East) Carolingian revival (750–887) Iconoclastic controversy (768–814)		7th century Islamic art	589—Sui dynasty 618—T'ang dynasty 960—Sung dynasty	552—Suiko period 646—Hakuho period 710—Tempyo period 794—Jogan period 897—Fujiwara period	Hindu revival Angkor Thom Medieval period
RENAISSANCE 1500	Romanesque Early Gothic High Gothic Late North Gothic Florence (Giotto) Siena (Duccio) 1453—Byzantium falls		Islamic art (Late)	1279—Mongol rule (Yüan dynasty) 1368—Ming dynasty	1185—Kamakura period 1392—Ashikaga period	Angkor Wat Moslem domination Konarak
				1644—Manchu dynasty (1912)	1568—Momoyama period 1615—Tokugawa period	Mogul and Rajput painting (1857)

COMPARATIVE CHRONOLOGY

DATES		ITALY	FRANCE	SPAIN
1300 1350 1400	GOTHIC	Duccio (1255–1319) Giotto (1266–1336) Simone Martini (1284–1344) The Plague Brunelleschi (1377–1446) Ghiberti (1378–1455)	The Plague Sluter (?–1406)	Alcazár (1181–1220) The Plague Alhambra (completed 1354)
1450 1500		Donatello (1386–1466) Fra Angelico (1387–1455) Masaccio (1401–1428) Alberti (1404–1472) P. della Francesca (1410?–1492) Leonardo da Vinci (1452–1519) Pollaiuolo (1432–1498) Botticelli (1444–1510) Bramante (1444–1514) Raphael (1483–1520)	Brothers Limbourg (c. 1400–1455) Fouquet (1415?–1480?)	
1550 1600	RENAISSANCE	Titian (1477–1576) Michelangelo (1475–1564) Correggio (1494–1534) Palladio (1508–1580) Mannerism Fiorentino il Rosso (1494–1540) Tintoretto (1518–1594) Veronese (1528–1588)	Clouet (1486?–1540) Court art of Francis I (1515–1547) Chateau Chambord (begun 1519) School of Fontainebleau Wars of Religion 2nd half of 16th century	Escorial Palace (1563) El Greco (1541–1614)
1650 1700	BAROQUE	The Carracci (1555–1619) Caravaggio (1573–1610) Maderno (1566–1629) Bernini (1598–1680) Borromini (1599–1667)	Louis XIV (1638–1715) Poussin (1594–1665) Lorrain (1600–1682) Le Brun (1619–1690) Versailles Palace (1624–1710) Louvre Palace	Zurbaran (1598–1664) Velasquez (1599–1660) Murillo (1618–1682)
1750	ROCOCO	Tiepolo (1696–1770) Canaletto (1697–1768) Guardi (1712–1793)	Watteau (1684–1721) Chardin (1699–1779) Boucher (1703–1770)	
1800	NEO-CLASSICISM		Fragonard (1732–1806) 1789—French Revolution David (1748–1825)	Goya (1746–1828)
1850 1900	ROMANTICISM IMPRESSIONISM POST-IMPRESSIONISM	Boccioni (1882–1916) Severini (1883–)	Corot (1796–1875) Daumier (1808–1879) Géricault (1791–1824) Ingres (1780–1867) Delacroix (1798–1863) Manet (1832–1883) Rodin (1840–1917) Degas (1834–1917) Gauguin (1848–1903) Monet (1840–1926)	
1950	ABSTRACTION		Cézanne (1839–1906) Seurat (1859–1891) Matisse (1869–1954) Braque (1882–) Léger (1881–1955) Duchamp (1887–)	Picasso (1881–) Miro (1893–) Dali (1904–)

OF PERIODS OF ART

ENGLAND	GERMANY	LOW COUNTRIES	AMERICA
The Plague	The Plague	The Plague	Mayan culture Inca culture Aztec culture
Kings College, Cambridge (1446–1515)	Witz (c. 1398–1447) Dürer (1471–1528)	Jan van Eyck (1382?–1440) Van der Weyden (1399–1464) Van der Goes (1435–1482) Bosch (1450?–1516)	
Chapel of Henry VII Westminster Abbey (1519)	Holbein (1497–1543)	Brueghel (1525–1569)	Machu Picchu 1520—Spanish Conquest Cathedral of Mexico City (1521–1811)
Inigo Jones (1573–1652) Wren (1632–1732) St. Paul's, London (1666–1716)		Rubens (1577–1640) Frans Hals (1580–1666) Van Dyck (1599–1641) Rembrandt (1606–1669) Van Ruisdael (1628–1682) Vermeer (1632–1675)	
Hogarth (1697–1764) Gainsborough (1714–1782) Walpole (1717–1797) Chippendale (1718–1779) Reynolds (1723–1792) Adam (1728–1792) Blake (1757–1827)	Von Hildebrandt (1686–1745) Neumann (1687–1753)		Copley (1737–1815) Peale (1741–1827) Jefferson (1743–1826) Audubon (1780–1850)
Constable (1776–1837) Turner (1775–1851)	Marc (1880–1916) Barlach (1870–1938)	Van Gogh (1853–1890)	Bingham (1811–1879) Richardson (1838–1886) Bierstadt (1830–1902) Whistler (1834–1903) Homer (1836–1910) Eakins (1844–1916) Sullivan (1856–1924) Sargent (1856–1925)
Henry Moore (1898–)	Klee (1879–1940) Kandinsky (1866–1944) Gropius (1883–)	Ensor (1860–1949) Mondrian (1872–1944) Albers (1888–)	Bellows (1882–1925) Wright (1869–1959) Shahn (1898–) Pollock (1912–1956) De Kooning (1904–) Van der Rohe (1886–) Davis (1894–) Epstein (1880–1959)

INDEX